Lip Service

Lip Service

THE TRUTH ABOUT WOMEN'S DARKER SIDE IN LOVE, SEX, AND FRIENDSHIP

KATE FILLION

HarperCollins*Publishers*

HarperCollins books may be purchased for educational, business, or sales promotional use. For information please write: Special Markets Department, HarperCollins Publishers, Inc., 10 East 53rd Street, New York, NY 10022.

FIRST EDITION

ISBN 0-06-017290-8

96 97 98 99 00 ❖ HC 10 9 8 7 6 5 4 3 2 1

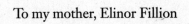

To my mother, Elinor Fillion

Contents

Introduction

Women love, men lust. Women are nurturing, men are aggressive. Women care most about relationships, but men care most about looking out for number one. These old stereotypes are continually repackaged, recycled, and reinforced in bestsellers, box office hits, and everyday conversation. Most of us are so accustomed to thinking of men and women as psychological opposites that we don't even notice that our actual experiences contradict our beliefs.

In real life, men and women step out of their assigned roles all the time, and behave, think, and feel in ways that are supposedly characteristic of the "opposite" sex. Yet, even though we're not following them, many of us continue to pay lip service to oppositional gender roles. For women in particular, this causes untold confusion and unnecessary complications. We think of ourselves as intimacy experts, but we can't seem to get the kinds of relationships we want. We view men as our adversaries, and wind up creating a new set of sexual double standards. We think of other women as our allies, but thereby cause or exacerbate serious problems in our personal and professional relationships with one another.

In short, we pay lip service to myths about ourselves that *sound* flattering — women are better at caring and sharing; women are morally superior — but that actually ends up hurting us. So long as women cannot give themselves permission to behave in "masculine" ways, we have two choices: deny the reality of our own experience, or suffer guilt and shame.

The other alternative is not entirely painless, because it requires us to abandon some cherished notions about who women are: forever loving, cooperative, kind, and more spiritual than sexual. But we may as well disabuse ourselves of these ideas because they don't square with reality. According to an extensive body of research on love, sex, and friendship, men and women do not behave as differently as we tend to think; women are not mythic creatures of sweetness and light, but flesh-and-blood mortals who are capable of all the negative feelings and behavior we currently associate with masculinity. And according to women's and men's own accounts of their experiences, many of the difficulties in our relationships with members of the "same" and the "opposite" sex are directly related to our mistaken beliefs about gender differences.

Lip Service is based on both extensive academic research and in-depth interviews with 108 North American women and men. Six of the interviews were conducted by phone; the remainder were held in person, and ranged in length from 55 minutes to 9¾ hours. There is nothing scientific about my sample of interview subjects, who are predominantly white middle class, and heterosexual, but it does include people from a number of different geographic areas; in all cases, I have changed their names and some identifying details to protect their privacy.

Their stories and the academic research point to the same conclusion: female moral superiority is a myth that keeps women strangers to themselves, judges of other women, and contemptuous of or fearful toward men. Women are, in fact, capable of the full range of human emotions and actions, from the boardroom to the bedroom and every place in between. When we pretend otherwise, we become our own worst enemies — and we create double standards that trip us up just when we are within striking distance of real equality.

Lip Service

Best of Friends

They met at one of those professional gatherings where the women smile too much and the men rock back and forth on their heels, making pronouncements. Anna's opening line was, "I keep expecting the blonde over there to whip out some pom-poms and lead us in a cheer." Julie said, "Thank God. I thought I was the only one here who didn't do perky."

It was as if they'd exchanged a coded signal. Without another word, they retreated to the sidelines of the party, where female friendships so frequently begin, for the exploratory survey of their common ground. Superficially, there didn't seem to be much. Anna is tall, athletic, and square-jawed, with olive skin, a slick black bob, and the air of a woman who expects to be photographed. Julie has the faintly apologetic bearing of a wallflower. She is, in fact, attractive, but more quietly so: short and pale, with a wide startled face, an eruption of brown curls, and the rounded shoulders of a woman who developed early and has been at pains to disguise her shape ever since.

But women who are predisposed to like each other tend to try to compensate for such obvious differences almost reflexively, first through self-deprecation and then through exaggeration of the significance of any similarities they share, a complicated form of courtship that requires the seamless resolution of competing claims:

You are so much better, We are practically the same. So Julie admired Anna's suit, adding that of course, she herself would never be thin enough to wear it; Anna protested that Julie was hardly overweight, and at any rate had the better hair. They made much of the fact that both of them were single, in their early thirties, and had similar marketing jobs in the same industry. They had attended the same university, an unexceptional enough coincidence that attained the status of a mystical bond when it came out that they had also both briefly dated the same charismatic law student, who had recently made headlines when he was charged with securities fraud.

"That was no surprise," Julie said. "Both times we went out, he went through this panic-stricken shtick when the bill came. You know, reaching into his pocket —"

"And saying, 'Oh God, I lost my wallet!'" Anna crowed. "He did the same thing to me, and of course I paid, patting myself on the back for being such a good feminist."

Julie supplied the punch line: "When the truth is, the guy was so good-looking, you felt lucky he was exploiting you." *Exactly!*

They had not been talking more than half an hour, but already had tossed aside several protective layers of privacy. This too is a form of seduction, characterized by urgent understanding — *I know just what you mean!* — and a complete lack of wariness. When sex is not at issue, women rarely bother with coyness or play hard to get. "Here's my number," Anna said. "Call me. Really."

Julie did, the very next day, and they arranged to meet after work at a restaurant Anna suggested. Julie got there first, having taken a taxi so she wouldn't be late, and immediately wished she wasn't wearing a pinstriped suit. It was one of those see-and-be-seen places with self-absorbed waiters and a clientele of chic rubberneckers, and Julie started to worry that she wasn't hip enough to have anything to say to Anna. Then, after half an hour of feigning deep interest in the menu, she began to worry that she was being stood up.

But when Anna finally arrived, she was breathless with can-you-ever-forgive-me apologies and so charming that after the first minute, Julie was no longer annoyed that she'd apparently been kept waiting so that Anna could go home to change into a black catsuit.

Before the wine had even arrived at the table, they'd picked up their conversation of the previous evening as though they'd never left off. Secrets are the currency of female friendship, and soon they were swapping moth-eaten childhood traumas and fresher intrigues like baseball cards, interrupting each other constantly to post bulletins of recognition. *The same thing happened to me!* By the time they left the restaurant, they'd already made plans for the weekend.

Meeting new women is so effortless, Julie thought, such a blessed relief from the awkward, fumbling silences with men. With a man, you had to weigh the consequences of saying anything really personal. He might, for one thing, think less of you as a result. Or worse, he might listen mutely and volunteer no confidences of his own, leaving you feeling cheated and dangerously exposed. But she could say anything to Anna, right from the beginning, and the only consequence was a feeling of greater closeness. "We were completely comfortable with each other," Julie says. "Nothing was taboo."

It was the same kind of effortless rapport that she'd once had with her college friends. But then they got married and, in Julie's opinion, left their personalities at the altar. These days, spending time with them made her feel oddly lonely. It was as though all the points of connection had vanished: women who had once thrived on boisterous late-night discussions about their lovers' annoying bedroom technique and commitment phobia now spoke in the same rueful tones about mortgages and the trials of toilet training. "That's one foreign language I don't want to learn," she confided one evening, and Anna understood completely.

"Think of dating as comparison shopping — there's so much out there to sample," Anna advised. "We have the rest of our lives to change diapers and talk about drapes."

Julie nodded. "Exactly! I couldn't agree more." This was not, however, what she'd thought just a few months earlier, when yet another close friend announced that she was engaged. Then, Julie had been wondering if perhaps she'd made the wrong choices. Maybe she had spent too long trying out men and trying on attitudes. She was, after all, thirty-two — was she going to be a perpetual fifth wheel at her friends' dinner parties? She felt a flutter of panic: Why had everyone else already found a partner, but she had not? Maybe there was something wrong with her.

But there was nothing wrong with Anna, who made being single seem both normal and exciting, more like a madcap adventure than an endless succession of dates from hell. Within a few months, Julie was seeing less and less of her old friends and more and more of Anna. They talked on the phone nearly every day, went out for dinner or drinks almost every week, and developed the sort of in-jokes that never sound funny when you try to explain them to other people.

Anna was a grown-up, sophisticated version of the popular girls from high school, and Julie was flattered to be chosen as her friend. Before, she had seen herself as socially marginal and awkward; at parties, she had the feeling that she was forever blurting out something at the top of her lungs just at the moment when the music stopped and the room fell silent. But Anna was spontaneous, up for anything, and her careless confidence was contagious. She frequented cutting-edge bars and clubs that had slightly intimidated Julie in the past, but now, she looked forward to their evenings together and dressed carefully for them, or perhaps it would be more accurate to say that she dressed for Anna, who paid her the compliment of noticing. "What a great skirt," she'd say, or, "That's the perfect haircut for you."

Julie felt a secret, bursting pride to be seen with Anna, whose looks and charm rarely failed to attract notice. "People gravitate toward her," Julie explains. "Anna's a crowd-pleaser, but she's not saccharine or phony or so nice that she doesn't have a personality. In fact, she has a really sharp tongue and her edge is part of her whole appeal."

Anna seemed to think the two of them were uncannily alike, and perhaps, Julie began to think once she'd acquired a new wardrobe, they really *were*. For one thing, they shared a conversational shorthand about their work, and for another, their career paths were almost mirror images of each other. Yes, Julie's title was more senior, but Anna worked for a larger company; Julie was a better strategist, but Anna had a gift for networking. Moreover, they had the same sense of humor and streak of independence, the same caustic take on the big names in their industry, and the same guilty passion for tabloid television.

Julie was infatuated not just with Anna but with the reflection she provided, which gave her another way of looking at herself: attractive, witty, capable. Anna noticed and appreciated the qualities that Julie had always liked best about herself — generosity, perceptiveness, and a talent for sly one-liners — and Anna, always a little scatterbrained, relied on her. "What would I do without you?" she'd say after Julie had helped her plan a dinner party or reminded her for the tenth time to file her tax return.

They entertained and sustained each other, sharing even the most mundane details of their lives — especially their love lives — and remembering to ask how each other's big meetings had gone. Both were successful, but disaster was the staple of their conversations: men who said they would phone but never did, mothers who turned every phone call into an inquisition about their marriage prospects, male colleagues who got the promotions that would have been theirs if they too had been given the opportunity to bond with the boss on the golf course. The anecdote of failure became something of an art form between them; the narrator usually depicted herself as a hapless naif, bumbling through crises with gallows humor. But there was always a feel-good ending: the more they confessed, the closer they felt.

These heart-baring discussions have a predictable rhythm that women seem to know instinctively: a confession of failure cues revelations of one's own similar troubles and ends with raucous commiseration. Even in the midst of some new mortification — a dressing-down by a senior manager, a date with a man who spent the entire evening talking about how beautiful his old girlfriend was — Julie would find herself thinking what a good story it was going to make and how, when they finished laughing, Anna would proffer the healing balm: *Don't feel bad, it's not your fault. Why, something even worse happened to me...*

One night, by way of concluding a baroque tale about an unreliable ex-boyfriend, Anna sighed and said, "I think I've given up on men. Too bad you're a woman, we'd make the perfect couple." Of all the possible subtexts to her remark, Julie thought the most important one was this: men come and go, but women friends last forever. Monogamy was not the label she attached to her expectations, but it fit. The best friend is, after all, singular by definition.

Intimacy appears to be so easy for many female friends. We let down our guard and free associate about our innermost feelings with other women, and the response we expect is unconditional acceptance. We lavish time and attention on our friends, analyzing one another's experiences blow by blow and cataloguing all the conceivable reactions and strategies, along with their possible ramifications. Together, we comb through our pasts and rehearse for our futures: *What do you think it meant when he said X? Can you believe she thought Y? Should I do Z?*

If only we could have these same sorts of relationships with men, women sometimes sigh, then launch into hilarious and sad stories about their failed campaigns to turn the men in their lives into girlfriends. These tales usually end the same way: *The problem is, he just doesn't know how to* talk.

Gender-based differences in conversational styles are presumed to be so great that virtual Berlitz guides, such as Deborah Tannen's *You Just Don't Understand*, are required for communication between the sexes. Tannen, a linguist, contends that women relish "rapport-talk," which centers on emotions and displays of empathy, while men prefer "report-talk," which imparts information and advice. Although she is careful to stress that she's describing differences rather than making qualitative judgments, women, not men, made her book a bestseller and frequently cite it as proof of their intimacy expertise.

The truth of the matter is that most women believe "rapport-talk" is synonymous with intimacy, which explains why so many display a certain arrogance about their say-anything brand of friendships. To many women, intimacy means excavating one another's inner lives, and they speak of man-to-man talks with a sniff of disdain: exchanging monosyllables at sporting events is hardly evidence of intimacy. *He's your best friend, and he doesn't know that your sister is getting a divorce? What on earth do you two talk about?* "Male bonding" has become the ultimate ironic put-down, since it is assumed that the bonds themselves are so superficial as to be virtually meaningless.

Yet men don't seem too upset about their failure to meet women's standards. They aren't the ones who buy books about loving too much, loving the wrong people, and loving themselves too little — women are. And it is women, suffering in men's silences, who so frequently turn up on Oprah's and Montel's and Ricki's stages, emoting plaintively: "I ask him what he's feeling, and he says, 'Nothing.' He just won't *talk*." An expert with a Ph.D. and a book to hawk then delivers an on-the-spot diagnosis: the man in question has a classic case of fear of intimacy.

Most psychologists and researchers seem to agree. They say "mutual self-disclosure" — sharing one's innermost emotions and deepest secrets — is the hallmark of mature intimacy. A willingness to talk openly about personal topics — feelings, relationships — and reveal one's weaknesses is now considered a strength. The man who does not verbalize what's going on in his heart, rather than the woman who is trying to ferret out the information, is increasingly the one who's considered insecure. Those who resist "rapport-talk" are routinely charged with fear of intimacy, or indicted for "denial" and emotional "repression."

It was not always so. Forty years ago, the stiff-upper-lip ethic prevailed: Silence was associated with strength and self-control. Revealing private thoughts and feelings, even to close friends, was considered overly emotional; inviting others to inspect the skeletons in one's closet was indiscreet. Autonomy, self-sufficiency, and independence — all stereotypically masculine qualities — were thought to be signs of maturity. Stereotypically feminine qualities — sensitivity to the nuances of others' behavior, a tendency to "feel for" other people so deeply that their emotions almost seem to be one's own — were deemed signs of weakness, neurosis, and dependence.

Between men and women, sex, not mutual self-disclosure, was considered by experts the primary "medium to express, sustain and enhance love," writes Steven Seidman in *Romantic Longings*, a history of the changing meanings of love in American culture. "Accordingly, sex was imbued with great personal and social significance as it now carried the burden of being responsible for personal and marital happiness."[1] Before the sixties, marriage manuals did not focus on helping husbands and wives achieve intimacy through talking, but rather on helping them "improve" their sex lives (often by instructing women to concentrate on pleasing men and to ignore their own main source of sexual pleasure: the clitoris).

The successful, uncomplaining performance of obligations, which differed by gender, made for a good marriage. Even if the husband spent most of his time behind the newspaper, emerging only to scold his wife for gossiping about the neighbors, they might still be considered close. Couples were expected to demonstrate their feelings not through conversation but through action: he showed how much he cared by being a good financial provider; she showed how much she cared by cooking, cleaning, and looking after the family. In short, intimacy was defined in "masculine" instrumental terms — doing — rather than "feminine" expressive terms.

The current notion that talking about feelings and airing secrets is healthy and mature is due in part to the profound impact of popular psychology on North American culture. In the sixties and seventies, the imperatives of pop psychologists — "get in touch with yourself" and "let it all hang out" — dovetailed with the younger generation's rejection of Establishment roles and values. Traditions were being challenged, old rules were breaking down, and the human potential movement provided a new roadmap for negotiating a changing world: look within and "find yourself."

Conforming to society's expectations was no longer the ticket to personal fulfilment. Rather, "self-actualization," which required an arduous inward journey of emotional self-discovery, was the route to happiness. Self-expression — not just doing your own thing, but talking about it with friends and family, and in encounter sessions and group therapy — was a critically important part of the quest. Those who could casually discuss their hang-ups had clearly made progress. In certain circles, it became an elitist declaration of personal liberation to announce, "I've enrolled in primal scream therapy to get in touch with my anger."

Today, the therapeutic culture is still growing, but the focus has shifted from self-discovery to purging oneself of "dysfunctions." Self-help books are wildly popular, as are support groups designed to exorcise demons ranging from toxic parents to drug addiction. Talking is a large part of the treatment, but it delivers no permanent cure. Talk is purgative yet never quite gets rid of all the toxins; the sufferer is perpetually "in recovery," and maintenance requires on-going attendance at twelve-step meetings and the continual therapy of disclosure.

The belief that we can heal ourselves by disclosing what ails us is ascendant, not least because those who talk about their problems can be used to turn a profit. Movie stars, politicians, and captains of industry go public with the details of their addictions, divorces, and childhood traumas, and their revelations sell newspapers, magazines, and books, and are turned into movies-of-the-week. The actor who is caught having sex with a hooker goes on television to confess his sins and receive absolution from a cheering studio audience; his candor is applauded, his name-recognition soars, and his new film sets records at the box office. The not-so-rich-and-famous broadcast even more personal confessions on daytime talk shows: I'm a transsexual co-dependent married to a porn addict, My mother is sleeping with my boyfriend, I hate my dysfunctional family. From both instant-opinion therapists on the stage and amateur psychologists in the studio audience, these confessions elicit the same advice: keep talking about it, talking is the way to work through emotions and resolve problems.

The connection between self-help and self-disclosure is relatively new, as is the definition of intimacy in terms of mutual self-disclosure. But the idea that women are intimacy experts has been around for centuries. According to the traditional argument, women's gift for nurturing is a function of biology: nature equips women for the tasks of giving birth and raising children by programming them to be caring, giving, and gentle.

As sociologist Francesca Cancian points out in her landmark study *Love in America*, the notion that women's supposedly unique talent for love renders them morally superior emerged at the end of the eighteenth century, and is connected to the transition to an industrial economy. Before, in an agrarian economy, men's and women's activities overlapped. Although men owned property and women raised children, the "integration of activities in the family produced a certain integration of instrumental and expressive traits in the personalities of men and women," Cancian explains. "Husbands and wives were involved in similar economic activities, and shared the task of caring for household members."[2]

This changed with the advent of industrialization. In the cities, there was a sharp divide between work and home, and each came to represent opposing values: "As public life became more impersonal, immoral, and uncertain, the female world of the family was becoming more intensely personal, pure, and circumscribed."[3] The ideology of separate spheres developed, promoting different ideals for each gender. The masculine ideal stressed independence and achievement in the public sphere; the feminine ideal stressed purity and nurturing in the private sphere of the home.

Men were workers in the harsh, material world, but women's labor — cooking, cleaning, child rearing — was not viewed as labor at all. Rather, women's activities were subsumed under one catch-all label: "love." As gender roles became increasingly polarized, "love became a feminine quality," Cancian writes. Consequently, "the cultural images of love shifted towards emphasizing tenderness, expression of emotion, and weakness."[4]

Clearly, the ideology of separate spheres promotes and justifies inequality. If women are essentially loving, they should be in charge of raising children; if men are essentially achievers, they should be in control of money, power, and resources. For women, Cancian points out, this amounted to a double whammy: "Men's attachments and dependency were obscured," and women's work was viewed as a mere labor of love, essentially unproductive and devoid of economic value.[5]

In the late sixties and early seventies, the modern women's movement emerged to protest just such injustices. Liberal feminists, who aimed to create equality of opportunity primarily through legislative means, argued that most gender differences are caused not by nature but by differential socialization and unequal access to power and resources. Women weren't raising children because they were hardwired to be more loving, but because they were shut out of higher education and discriminated against in the paid labor force. If social roles were not so sharply divided, they believed, many gender differences would fade away.

In the early days, however, many feminists of all stripes argued that legal changes weren't enough. Psychological change was also necessary: women needed to learn to be more independent, more autonomous — more like men. Radical feminists, in particular, viewed love as a serious obstacle to self-reliance and equality. So long as women took their measure through relationships, they would be dependent on others; so long as women believed that romance was what made life worth living, they would focus on trying to catch men and would do just about anything to keep them. "We must destroy love," instructs one early radical feminist tract. "Love promotes vulnerability, dependence, possessiveness, susceptibility to pain, and prevents the full development of woman by directing all her energies outwards in the interests of others."[6]

By the seventies, though, some feminists were arguing that women really are intimacy experts, and a talent for loving is a source of strength, not weakness. They pointed out that women seemed like lesser beings — weaker, more dependent, overly sensitive — only because they had always been measured with a masculine yardstick that overvalued personal autonomy and public achievement. All the things women did to make it possible for men to achieve, like providing emotional sustenance and keeping the home fires burning, were undervalued or dismissed outright as unimportant.

Alternatively called cultural feminists or difference feminists, they began to champion women's traditional role as the construction workers of emotional connection, and wound up arguing that relationships should remain the organizing principle of women's lives. Apparently, the centrality of relationships in women's lives has a positive effect on everything from moral reasoning to conversational style: women are more compassionate, more empathic, and have richer, more meaningful lives because they are so good at caring and sharing. Cultural feminists believe that women's ways of knowing, feeling, and living are better: more life-affirming, more environmentally friendly, more highly evolved.

They invert the meanings of traditional stereotypes and valorize the feminine role: men aren't independent, they're emotionally impaired; women aren't overly emotional, they're in touch with their own and others' feelings. Men, apparently, suffer a deficit of emotional bonds: they're aggressive instead of expressive, they fear intimacy, and they have difficulty forming substantive relationships. Men, cultural feminists advise, should try to be more like women.

Some believe that female moral superiority is linked to reproductive capacity, but most of the theories they cite argue the opposite: namely, that women's intimacy expertise is the result of nurture, not nature. Nancy Chodorow, arguably the most influential feminist theorist in the area of psychological gender differences, believes that women's near-universal responsibility for child care creates oppositional gender identities. She theorizes that when children experience attachment and identification only with female caregivers, girls and boys develop quite differently. Shared parenting, she argued, would erase many of these differences.

For a girl, Chodorow contends, the process of acquiring a sense of herself as female is merged with the experience of attachment to her mother, who in turn identifies with her daughter and views her as being the same as herself. Girls' gender identity is thus fused with feeling emotionally connected. As a result, their ego boundaries are fluid and permeable, and they grow up "with a basis for 'empathy' built into their primary definition of self in a way that boys do not."[7] Being feminine means feeling connected to others.

A boy, however, develops a sense of himself as masculine by relinquishing his attachment to and identification with his mother, who recognizes him from the start as being different from herself. Boys' gender identity is therefore created by emotional separation; they construct strong ego boundaries to repress and deny their feelings of loss, pain, and anger. But their sense of their own masculinity is shaky if their fathers are largely absent, emotionally or physically, so they try to shore it up by renouncing all things feminine. "The very fact of being mothered by a woman generates in men conflicts over masculinity, a psychology of male dominance, and a need to be superior to women," Chodorow writes.[8]

As adults, apparently, men fear closeness, while women fear being alone. Carol Gilligan, another leader in feminist psychology, elaborates, "Since masculinity is defined through separation while femininity is defined through attachment, male gender identity is threatened by intimacy while female gender identity is threatened by separation."[9] She goes on to argue that women therefore speak in a different voice; men's moral code is based on abstract principles of justice, but women's stresses compassion. Men are concerned with being impartial and fair, while women are concerned with empathizing and showing they care.

Like Deborah Tannen, Gilligan says she is describing existing differences rather than making judgments about which style is better or worse, but many critics have pointed out that she clearly favors women's "ethic of care." For instance, she writes that men's abstract moral values "provide scanty illumination of a life spent in intimate and generative relationships" while "women's experience provides a key to understanding central truths of adult life."[10] More seriously, her methodology has been attacked, and many researchers dispute her conclusion that men and women have different moral codes.[11]

Nevertheless, her conceptual framework remains wildly popular, both in academia and the mass media. And in a classic case of broken telephone, Gilligan's ideas, along with Chodorow's and Tannen's, have filtered into the mainstream not as evidence that socialization creates psychological gender differences but as proof that men and women are and will forever remain psychological opposites.

Whatever their own intentions and whatever others' interpretations, there is no disputing that these theorists have implicitly endorsed a binary view of the world: women versus men, connection versus autonomy. They have not challenged age-old assumptions: women are nurturing, men are aggressive; women are loving, men are achieving.

Therein lies the problem. An us/them approach helps to preserve gender stereotypes that are at best inaccurate generalizations and at worst downright harmful — to both women and men. "Framing the question in terms of polarities, regardless of which pole is the valued one, immediately sets up false choices for women and men," Carol Tavris argues in *The Mismeasure of Woman*. "It continues to divide the world into *men* and *women* as if these categories were unified opposites. It obscures the fact that the opposing qualities associated with masculinity and femininity are caricatures to begin with."[12]

Tavris cites a mountain of scientific data to prove that many of the presumed differences between men and women are either nonexistent, wildly exaggerated, or a function not of nature but of the social roles allotted to each gender. The truth of the matter is that differences between individual members of one gender are far greater than group differences between the genders. Although it's possible to make some generalizations about the differences between men as a group and women as a group, Tavris cautions that they tend to be "differences in style and expression [and] must not be confused with differences in male and female nature, or capacity, or personality traits."[13]

Even labeling a single individual "aggressive" can be extremely misleading; he may be highly aggressive at work and on the tennis court, but invariably passive when he's behind the wheel of a car or in bed with his wife. Calling him "aggressive" averages out these trends, but obscures his true pattern of behavior. In reality, most human beings demonstrate a wide range of behavior in the course of a single day: hesitant with the boss, assertive with the real estate agent, supportive with the troubled relative, short-tempered with the whiny child. Surely, if even individuals do not behave, think, or feel the same ways at all times, it is absurd to argue that "all men have this characteristic" and "all women have that trait" without reference to context or any allowances for individual variation.

Yet the notion that women speak in unison in a "different voice" has captured the popular imagination. It is a new spin on an age-old idea: men and women are yin and yang, practically different species. The belief that men and women are and forever will be polar opposites is particularly appealing in times of social upheaval, when gender roles are changing, and many people yearn for continuity and certainty. We seize on new proofs of essential differences because they're reassuring: at least *some* things are still the same. Women are flattered by evidence of their moral superiority; men are not displeased to hear that they're more independent and aggressive, because it reassures them of their power.

Academic researchers, too, are captivated by the notion of fundamental gender differences in communication. In the 1970s, surveys of the then relatively unexplored territory of gender and communication began to chart women's versus men's ways of connecting. Clearly, feminism influenced this research, but so did popular psychology, with its emphasis on self-expression and self-disclosure. Anxiety about rising divorce rates also fueled these studies: was the problem that men and women simply couldn't communicate, because they spoke in different voices? Researchers set out to answer that question by focusing on same-sex communication, in which the particular register, inflection, and tone of each gender's voice should, presumably, be clearest.

Study after study confirmed the common wisdom: women are intimacy experts, men are emotionally challenged. "Research indicates female friendships are both more exclusive and more emotionally committed than male friendships," reads a typical 1991 academic text, which faults the "'weak ties' that typify male friendship." Male friendships are deemed "less intimate and less demanding" because they "do not call for high levels of self-disclosure, nor its reciprocal — trust."[14]

Here, we can see all kinds of biases and *a priori* assumptions at work. The idea that self-disclosure requires trust does not explain the parade of misery on daytime talk shows, where average people discuss their personal problems and brawl with their loved ones while the cameras roll. In less spectacular fashion, many people have on occasion found themselves telling their life stories to complete strangers — or listening to strangers' most intimate secrets — in bars and on planes; it's sometimes easier to reveal yourself to someone you'll never see again. Anonymity, not trust, can prompt full disclosure. ✳

In everyday life, too, self-disclosure often precedes trust. Frequently, it's an opening gambit designed to create intimacy; within minutes of meeting, Julie and Anna were swapping secrets as a way of getting to know each other. Increasingly, because self-expression and emotional openness are valued in our culture, self-disclosure is becoming a form of cocktail chatter: "Hi, I'm Mary. Gee, that goat cheese sure looks great, but no thanks. See, I'm bulimic, and have to be careful not to binge." Whether this is evidence of intimacy expertise or merely undignified blurting is an open question.

Nevertheless, women's friendships are routinely described in scholarly journals, college textbooks, and the mainstream media as deeper, more mature, and far more intimate than men's, precisely because they revolve around self-disclosure. According to researchers, male friends tend to share activities and conversations about "impersonal" issues — work, politics, sports — but female friends tend to share feelings about themselves and their relationships, and therefore, they are closer.

There is, however, an unmistakable bias in this research: it designates "self-disclosure as *the* defining feature of intimacy...measuring closeness primarily or exclusively by how much personal disclosure transpired between people," according to an exhaustive 1993 research review by Julia Wood and Christopher Inman, speech communication experts at the University of North Carolina. "Men were judged less adept at intimacy, because they failed to emphasize the personally disclosive talk characteristic of women's relationships. Not only were women dubbed intimacy experts, but men were alternately pitied and chided for their alleged shortcomings."[15]

Men who say they demonstrate affection by doing things for others typically get low ratings on intimacy scales; women who say they demonstrate affection by telling others about their feelings get high ratings. Men tell researchers that they do feel close to their friends, and show it through "mutual give-and-take," "helping each other out," "being there for each other," and sharing activities.[16] Not good enough, many experts say: only mutual self-disclosure counts as *real* closeness.

Some studies suggest not just that women are better at communicating in ways that create intimacy, but that women actually care more and love more than men do. Again, the methodology of this research is biased. "Part of the reason that men seem so much less loving than women is that men's behavior is measured with a feminine ruler," Francesca Cancian observes. "Most research considers only the kinds of loving behavior that are associated with the feminine role, such as talking about personal troubles...When less biased measures are used, the behavior of men and women is often quite similar."[17]

She cites numerous studies that suggest men define intimacy in terms of "practical help, shared physical activities, spending time together, and sex."[18] When they care about someone, many men apparently prefer to show it rather than talk about it: going to the ballgame with a friend, driving a relative to the airport, washing the wife's car rather than explicitly saying, "I love you."

Nevertheless, some communication experts point out, even these results may be skewed. "The problem with most investigations of intimacy is that researchers use their own understandings of that construct," notes Michael Monsour of the University of Colorado. But participants in studies have their own definitions of intimacy, and may "operationalize" the concept very differently than researchers do. Therefore, Monsour argues, "to capture the subjective reality of relationships," researchers need to take account of the ways the rest of us define intimacy.[19]

He did so by returning to first principles. Instead of asking whether their friendships had certain features and then labeling some of these features "intimate" and others "not intimate," he asked college students what *they* meant when they used the word "intimacy" to refer to their same-sex and cross-sex friendships. Surprise: "self-disclosure was by far the most frequently listed meaning of intimacy" by both women and men.[20] And there was another surprise: more men than women listed "emotional expressiveness." Where did shared activities rank? Right at the bottom of the list, cited by only 9 percent of the men as a meaning of intimacy in their friendships with other men.[21]

Now, more women than men listed self-disclosure as a meaning of intimacy in their same-sex friendships — 87 percent as opposed to 56 percent — but the fact remains that contrary to popular opinion, self-disclosure and emotional expressiveness were at the top of men's lists. Monsour drew two conclusions. First, there are more similarities than differences in how women and men define intimacy, and second, intimacy means different things to different people. Most think it is multidimensional, and has more than one component.[22]

None of this means that men and women don't have distinct styles of communication; what it does mean is that qualitative judgments about intimacy should not be based on these style differences. At any rate, some men's communication style is "feminine," and some women's is "masculine." Above all, it is crucial to recognize that while it is possible to make some generalizations based on gender, there will always be substantial, within-gender variations between individuals.

Having studied all the research, Dr. Julia Wood concludes that claims about women's intimacy expertise cannot be substantiated. "There is no convincing evidence that women exceed men in the degree to which they care or love, nor is there persuasive support for the more moderate claim that women exceed men in the extent to which they express care," she writes. "Existing data demonstrate only that there are gender-linked distinctions in how care is expressed. This hardly grounds inferences either that women care more or that women express caring more than men."[23]

Those inferences are, however, still being drawn. As with love, there has been a feminization of intimacy, which is now defined in terms of *the ways that women are* supposed *to relate to other women*. The feminine norm — mutual self-disclosure — has become the societal norm for intimacy, and the verbal, emotional, and empathic style of women's friendships is widely touted as "the model for intimacy."[24]

Understandably, then, many women want to replicate it with the men in their lives. This is, however, nearly impossible, but the problem isn't that men lack the gene for "rapport-talk." Rather, one of the main reasons women can't talk to men the same way they talk to their girlfriends is that the researchers' heartwarming description of female friendship omits a significant detail: many of these friendships are rooted in a fundamentally adversarial attitude toward men. Women's sharing and caring frequently involves swapping stories about what jerks men are and diminishing men to shore each other up. Making fun of men is a quick and easy way to establish common ground and bond with other women. *They're all just little boys masquerading in suits. They're scared of strong, intelligent women. They'll do anything to get sex. They don't care about anyone except themselves.*

Men are dissected in the laboratory of women's friendships, often with a rigorous attention to detail that would be wholly unacceptable in any locker room. We huddle around the microscope to examine an individual man's motives and puzzling actions, pooling our information in order to arrive at a better understanding of the species.

This is particularly true for those who were raised on the tell-all injunctions of pop psychologists and talk show hosts. Things a young woman is likely to know about a close female friend's man: his sexual attributes, appetite, and performance, his spending patterns and worldly assets, his professional setbacks and achievements, his romantic history and style of conflict management, his vices, deep-seated anxieties, and the details of any therapy he has sought. The mordant flavor of these exchanges is neatly captured by a greeting card currently making the rounds, which depicts a woman introducing two grinning girlfriends to her husband, with the caption, "Bob, these are my friends from work. They know more about our sex life than you do."

Of course, women friends also talk about their own hopes, dreads, jobs, families, feelings, and opinions on all manner of things. But one of the aspects of our friendships that we value most is the comfort they provide when we are in trouble of some sort, which more often than not has something to do with men, either a specific man or male privilege in general. Only another woman can provide validation in some situations, because only another woman knows what it feels like to worry because a period is six days late, or to scurry down a street pursued by the catcalls of construction workers.

Is it any wonder that men make such poor girlfriends? They cannot take our side if they are, ultimately, the problem. Girlfriends are supposed to commiserate, become vicariously outraged, and close ranks in the gender war. *We're in this together. Men are such jerks.* The source of ✳ women's intense sense of connection is not just a unique talent for empathy, but the sense of being comrades on the moral high ground, pitted against a common adversary who dwells in the shadowy depths far below.

It is pleasant, as a woman, to believe that women are the best of friends and that our claim to the moral high ground is assured; it is enjoyable to ratify that claim by joining arms and denouncing men's depravity. It feels good, this solidarity, but it also makes it difficult and painful to acknowledge what many women know in their hearts: men are not always the problem. Frequently, relationships with other women are the source of our deepest frustration, anger, pain, and guilt.

All the gauzy rhetoric in the world cannot change the truth: we are not as good to our friends, nor are our friendships as good for us, as we would like to believe. In real life, mutual self-disclosure is not a recipe for perfect intimacy. In fact, the "feminine" style of intimacy *creates* some serious problems for many women friends. Before we try to turn men into girlfriends, we need to ask ourselves whether we really want this particular kind of intimacy with men, when, in fact, it often doesn't work so very well with other women.

Yes, we are close — sometimes too close for comfort and much too close for our own good. Just as the attachment between mothers and daughters is frequently fraught with tension and conflict, so is the attachment between close female friends. But because we believe that women are intimacy experts, we struggle with guilt when we have "unfeminine" feelings: anger, envy, competitiveness, a desire to be separate. We try to deny these feelings, and tend to express them only covertly, with stealth.

Paradoxically, at the heart of women's say-anything intimacy there is a rich vein of dishonesty: we can talk about everything except the problems between us.

"Tell me honestly, what do you think?" Anna asked, the night before the annual conference where she and Julie had first met two years before. She was standing in her living room, holding the notes for the speech she would give the next day, turning this way and that in a new black dress. She saw it in a magazine and ran right out to get it — two weeks' salary, she'd told Julie on the phone, but worth every penny. Now, however, she seemed uncertain. "Is it too tight?"

"You're too thin for anything to look too tight," Julie declared, then volunteered the gold necklace she was wearing. "Perfect. Now practice the speech." She made a few minor suggestions about phrasing, but said, "It's great, really. Stop worrying! Everything will be fine." They spent the rest of the evening contemplating Anna's imminent triumph and all its possible implications, and by the time Julie got up to leave, they had redecorated the corner office and imagined Anna's first week as CEO.

The next day, however, the speech was received with applause too scattered even to be described as polite. During the question-and-answer period, one person after another took the microphone to say the same thing: You got the facts wrong. Organization had never been Anna's strong point, and she began frantically riffling through her notes, saying, "Just a minute, I have it here somewhere," and then repeating the contested lines of her speech, as though saying them again would correct the mistakes. Her flustered uncertainty seemed only to intensify the attacks. "That outfit explains why *she's* up there," snorted the imperious, silver-haired woman sitting behind Julie. "Window dressing."

Julie's overriding feeling, watching this fiasco unfold, was not anger or vicarious embarrassment. It was guilt. She had known that the speech contained some serious factual errors and that a skimpy dress would further undermine Anna's credibility. Yet she said nothing. In fact, she told the lies that women friends often confuse with support, ✱ which range from "Don't worry, everything will be fine" to "But it wasn't your fault." She had been so careful to be nice that she had "supported" Anna right into a stammering, lectern-gripping ordeal.

Women friends who believe they can talk about anything invariably ✱ discover that there are many things they cannot say. Julie found it difficult to admit, even to herself, how much it bothered her that Anna had been asked to give a speech. Julie doesn't want to sound bitchy, but she has to say it: Anna *did* seem to be breezing through on charm and good looks. It just wasn't fair. Julie put in longer hours and worked more weekends, and she was the one who'd introduced Anna to the conference organizers — she was always doing little favors like that, giving her a hand professionally. She had, after all, been senior to Anna when they first met, and she was — although she doesn't want to seem conceited and, God knows, never held it over Anna's head — more talented. Why, Anna herself knew it: wasn't she always coming to Julie for advice, wanting to talk through every little decision? Surely, Julie ✱ thought, if one of us is going to give a speech, it ought to be *me*.

Perhaps it would not have bothered her so much had she not had the impression that the more successful Anna became, the less their ✱ friendship mattered to her. In the beginning, Julie had concentrated on their similarities, but now she began to focus on what she saw as major differences: *I make an effort, but she's self-absorbed. I'm always helping her, but she's ungrateful.* Things Julie was once prepared to forgive — a certain absence of tact when Anna discussed her rapid career progression, chronic lateness, negligence about returning phone calls — had recently begun to seem less excusable and more like proof of a lack of reciprocity. Granted, they had both acquired serious boyfriends, so they now had less free time to spend with one another. But hadn't they always agreed that it was tantamount to a crime when a woman dumped her friends the minute a man showed up on the horizon? Hadn't they always told each other that men come and go, but women friends last forever? Hadn't they more or less decided that their friendship took precedence over relationships with men, who had, after all, so much less to offer?

They went out a few times as a foursome, but it was stilted: the women couldn't talk about their favorite topic — their love lives — and the men didn't exactly hit it off. Oh well, Julie figured, there was no need to do everything as couples, and certainly no reason to give up her tradition of long, boozy dinners with her best friend. Anna, however, couldn't even seem to make the time to talk on the phone very often. When she did, "she went on and on about how busy she was," Julie remembers, "as though she were the only one of us who had demands on her time."

Julie did not like feeling that she was the junior partner, both in professional and personal terms, but she didn't air her grievances. How could she? A ledger of who phoned whom how many times would sound absurdly petty, and not being happy for Anna's professional success would seem small-minded and selfish.

But how could Julie not be upset? The premise of the friendship was their sameness: same industry, same prospects, same values, same feelings. The more Anna achieved, the less similar they seemed. Julie could not help comparing herself, and found herself wanting, yet also felt herself to be superior — as she had, in some ways, all along. *I deserve what Anna has*, she thought. And then, *I would handle it better, I'd be more sensitive to her feelings.*

Anna's success felt like Julie's own failure, and induced a keen

sense of loneliness. *She's moving on, and I'm stuck in the same place.*
Julie's resentment and hurt had been building for several months by
the time Anna asked, twirling around in her expensive new dress,
"Tell me honestly, what do you think?" The honest answer was that
Julie felt envious, threatened, and underappreciated, but saying so *
would put her in the awkward position of a supplicant. Instead, she
said what a girlfriend is supposed to say: You look great, you'll do
fine, don't worry.

She'd almost called Anna when she got home that night, almost
warned her, but it was late and Anna was already nervous. It would
do no good to shake her confidence further, or at least that's what
Julie told herself. Certainly it was true that she genuinely didn't want
to hurt Anna, who was, despite everything, still her best friend. A
year before, however, Julie would have picked up the phone and
found a tactful way to tell her the dress was a mistake; she would
have offered to stay up all night if necessary — it was a crisis, after all
— to help rewrite the speech.

But things had changed between them, at least in Julie's view, because Anna appeared to have more: invitations to give speeches, hundreds of dollars to spend on a new outfit, and apparently, less need
for her best friend. Julie was so aware of these differences that she as- *
sumed Anna must be, too.

So one of the reasons Julie didn't call to say, "Look, the speech
needs a rewrite," was that she feared Anna would think she was just
jealous. Which, of course, Julie was, but constructive criticism would
have been motivated by compassion, not envy, and her aim would
have been to help, not hurt. Ironically, envy seems to be a partial explanation for her silence: why should she help Anna shine in the
spotlight that should rightfully have been hers?

"It just wasn't my responsibility," she says now, still defensive and
guilty although more than a year has passed. "It's not my job to write
her speech and choose her wardrobe. She's a big girl."

She did not want Anna to fail exactly, but she did not want Anna
to surpass her. Anna's failure would restore the equality of the friendship, and some part of Julie, a part she can still barely acknowledge,
did not want to prevent it. After the speech, comforting Anna with

the offer of Visine and assurances that it wasn't the end of the world, her guilt was shorted by a sudden surge of confidence: *we're back on the same familiar track.*

Julie felt expansive, generous, protective. "It wasn't your fault," she found herself saying, and made caustic remarks about the audience reaction until Anna stopped dabbing at her eyes and attempted a smile. "What would I do without you?" Anna finally said when she'd steeled herself to rejoin the conference, just the way she always used to when Julie helped her with something.

Julie's complicated emotions of the past few months subsided in a ✳ rush of relief. *We're equals again. We're in this together.*

"There is an ethos within women's relationships...that requires staying in the same place together or moving forward together at the ✳ same time," observe Luise Eichenbaum and Susie Orbach in *Between Women*. "In other words, difference cannot be allowed and it is experienced as dangerous and threatening, and invokes feelings of abandonment. To put it very bluntly, the unspoken bargain between women is that we must all stay the same. If we act on a want, if we differentiate, if we dare to be psychologically separate, we break ranks."[25]

The idea that women must all stay the same can be traced back to the habit of binary thought. Women who view men as the "opposite" sex will, understandably, think of other women not in terms of dif-✳ ference but similarity. If a man is "the other," another woman must be the same as oneself. Many women, then, approach other women expecting likeness and anticipating gender solidarity. Already, they seem to have common ground: they are both women, and they are both doing battle with men. *We're the same*, they rejoice, as Julie and Anna did. *Men are the problem.*

From this perspective, change does appear threatening. "We're supposed to be allies who see eye to eye on everything," Julie thought. "But Anna's different from me now. Does that mean we're not really that close? Does it mean we're not on the same side any more?" When differences emerge, they become problems precisely because, right from the start, female friends tend to exaggerate similarities and huddle together under an us-against-the-world banner, which often has a sub-title: girls against boys. Furthermore, differences seem doubly danger-ous when women are afraid to address them directly, as Julie was. *Women are supposed to empathize, nurture, and be understanding — I shouldn't be feeling this way. Better keep it a secret. If she ever found out, she wouldn't like me any more.* ✳

The expectation that women never have negative feelings toward each other arises from an oppositional worldview: men are emotion- ✳ ally challenged but women are intimacy experts. What sets women apart from — and above — men is that they are supposedly more caring, more cooperative, and more loving. Naturally, women who believe they should be intimacy experts take their measure through their relationships; as a consequence, they live in terror of being dis-liked or abandoned. A failed friendship seems to be evidence that they, personally, are failures. So when differences arise, as they in-evitably do between two individuals, many female friends try to con-duct themselves as they think intimacy experts should: *I'll bite my tongue, seethe in silence, and hope the problem goes away.*

Many women believe they are supposed to be so good at relation-ships, particularly with other women, that they should not feel, much less express, anger, envy, or resentment. They get these ideas about who women are and how they ought to behave from many dif-ferent places: the media, the entertainment industry, teachers, par-ents, advertisers, and, as we have seen, from cultural feminists, pop psychologists, and Ivory Tower academics.

Of course, there are also images of tough women who don't give a damn, women who talk back and wield power with little concern for others' feelings: Margaret Thatcher, Roseanne, Madonna, and per-haps a dozen more. But the list is short, and the women on it are con-troversial figures, often reviled for their "aggressive" manners and lack ✳ of "femininity." They stand out precisely because they appear to be ex-ceptions who prove the rule: women are above "masculine" feelings and behavior. Women are supposed to be morally superior — that's what makes us different from men. Female moral superiority is an item of faith with anti-feminists and feminists alike, and with the secu-lar Left, which deduces it from evidence of men's aggression and

women's victimization, as well as the Religious Right, which invokes it
to argue for a return to separate spheres.

 Female moral superiority is the main plot device of the *sexual script*,
which fleshes out gender stereotypes by describing how women and
men should act, feel, and think in the boardroom, the bedroom, and
every place in between. Of course, there is no actual written set of instructions, and no secret cabal gathers to hammer out a consensus on
societal expectations of women and men. But thinking about the cultural messages we receive in terms of a dramatic script is useful, because the metaphor emphasizes that we learn to *perform* socially
assigned gender *roles,* and we learn how to play our own parts and
pick up on others' cues in many different situations.

A sexual script provides stage directions, complex choreography,
and detailed instructions on what is to be done with whom, at what
time and in what place, and which responses and emotions are appropriate to the event. We learn to anticipate certain kinds of behavior from men and other kinds from women, as well as specific
sequences of events, so that we are prepared for situations long before we actually encounter them.

According to the prevailing script, women cooperate with one another in the workplace, run businesses that exploit no one, mount
high-minded campaigns for political office and never stoop to dirty
tactics, and help one another get ahead in the world. There are many
heartwarming scenes of female friendship, all of which share the
same theme: girlfriends are always there for each other. When things
go wrong, women rally round with support and empathy; a girlfriend
really feels for you — she's been there herself.

In real life, many women try to follow this script by employing, quite
unconsciously, a range of strategies to deny and downplay differences.
We "know" what a good female friend is supposed to do — understand,
commiserate, provide emotional backup — and we try to observe the
protocol at all times. We want to show our friends that we validate their
emotions and choices, and back them one hundred percent — even
when we don't. So we pick a friend up and dust her off when she has
failed, but sometimes pack her off to fail again, shouting encouragement: "You're absolutely right! It wasn't your fault! Everything will be

fine!" We commiserate until she's out of sight, then rush to the phone to call another friend, whispering, "You're not going to believe this, but she's doing it again."

The cues for commiseration are engraved on our hearts, so deeply that sometimes we find ourselves trying to make our friends feel better by matching their horror stories, even when it entails significant historical revisionism of our own. Thus does the happily married woman try to console the friend who argues constantly with her boyfriend by casting about for an example that will show her friend she's not alone; she winds up embellishing on a few mild marital disagreements about household finances, and declares, "I know just how you feel, we have screaming matches about money all the time."

For many of us, commiseration is almost an automatic reflex. When a woman tells us something bad has happened to her, our heads start nodding and our mouths open to say, "The same thing happened to me." We trot out anecdotes to reassure our friends that we are no different; we have felt everything they are feeling. Anything less seems unfriendly and unsupportive.

"Commiseration and the allied phenomena of distorting one's own experience ever so slightly to fit in with that of a friend's, occurs so habitually...that even in apparently trivial exchanges, it can be very difficult to not do so," note Eichenbaum and Orbach.[26] Paradoxically, women are supposed to be the experts at mutual self-disclosure, yet we are rarely entirely honest and forthright with one another. We are too busy denying that there are differences between us and that we don't see eye to eye on everything.

"In that lies can be interpersonally distancing and destructive, it might seem that the only way women can manage to be so supportive and so intimate is by resolutely telling nothing but the truth. But this is not what they do," write the authors of a comprehensive 1993 review of studies measuring gender differences in lying. "By their own admission, they tell just as many lies as do men, and sometimes they even shade the truth more than men do. The differences between men and women, then, are in the ways that they lie. Women's lies seem to contribute to their supportiveness. They lie warmly and protectively. A less compassionate way to put this is that women seem to achieve some of their supportive qualities by way of deceit. Men are less supportive in those ways, but also more truthful."[27]

Many women's friendships actually seem to *require* supportive lies and counterfeit commiseration, for reasons that may not be readily apparent. Although mutual self-disclosure has come to be seen as intimacy itself, few researchers have described what it tends to consist of on a day-to-day basis: sharing minutiae. Most friends run out of major revelations fairly quickly; it's not as though there's a new emo- ✳ tional crisis or earth-shattering epiphany to report every day. On a quotidian level, then, mutual self-disclosure means sharing the details of each other's lives, which can be and often is wonderful; there's the feeling of being known, cared for, and not alone in the world.

But these kinds of relationships can also become verbal diaries whose main entries consist of complaints, which seems inevitable when personal feelings are the focus. Most people have more to talk about when things are going badly; "I'm really happy" can kill a conversation — what more is there to say? — whereas "Something horrible happened" can kick-start a discussion that lasts for hours. Furthermore, when a friendship is predicated on the notion that friends are exactly equal and should only move forward in lockstep, it can be very difficult to discuss triumphs because it seems like one is boasting and emphasizing differences. Thus there is the temptation to focus on the one aspect of life that's bothersome: the ongoing dispute with the bank manager, the snub by a co-worker, the fact that your husband consistently fails to put clean clothes away even though you leave them sitting on the dryer for a week just waiting for him to get the hint.

This temptation is particularly compelling when the telephone is the main medium for communication, as it so often is for female friends. If they rarely share any activities or encounters with the outside world, friends' sense of connection depends entirely on disembodied conversation. The cycle of complaint and commiseration keeps them talking and feeling close; they can still feel that they are sharing each other's emotional lives even though they are physically separate.

There can be real pleasure for both parties in hashing over each other's problems, big and small, and mining all the associated negative emotions. Often the exchange of complaints is a comic riff between friends, as it was for Julie and Anna, and many women enjoy my-life-is-so-pathetic humor.

But there is usually a serious subtext: reassurance is being sought. The woman who says, "I just went to buy a pair of jeans and had a frightening encounter with a three-way mirror — God, I'm getting so fat!" doesn't say it because she wants to hear, "Yeah, I noticed you'd put on a few." That kind of validation she most assuredly does *not* want. The response she wants is, "Nonsense, you haven't gained an ounce," or, "Don't you hate the societal pressure on women to be thin? You're *not* overweight." Or, at the very least, "I know just how you feel. I hate my thighs, too."

A certain amount of supportive dishonesty seems to be mandatory in female friendships that revolve around talking about feelings and emotions, because friends reveal weaknesses and vulnerabilities to each other and because women are expected to reassure, nurture, and agree with one another. Sometimes we tell harmless lies to spare friends' feelings. But we also are guilty of serious lies of omission, nodding sympathetically when we want to scream, "Stop complaining about your boyfriend/family/weight/job/life! *Do* something about it!"

It's difficult to tell a female friend when we've heard enough, or when we think it's time for action, or when we think she's making a terrible mistake, because these sound like the kinds of things a man would say. *Women are too good at intimacy to get impatient, judgmental,* ✳ *or just plain fed up with each other.* And since one friend has heard the other talk about her pain so freely, she is loath to inflict yet more injuries. *Criticism would hurt her too much. Friends validate each other.*

So we often try to support our friends by damping down our real opinions and lying supportively. "I know how you feel," we say, when in fact we have no idea, or actually believe that their emotions and behavior are inappropriate. "It's not your fault!" we exclaim, as Julie did to Anna, although she knew perfectly well that Anna was the author of her own fate at the conference. This may make the friend feel better in the short term, but it doesn't help her to extricate herself from a bad situation or break a chronic pattern. Nor does it help her to see a problem in a more objective light or to recognize that she may very well have played a part in creating it or allowing it to continue.

As Carol Tavris warns, "Women's expressive style carries a price tag. It leads many women to rehearse their problems and constantly brood about them, rather than learning to distract themselves or take action to solve them. Some women come to believe that talking *is* doing something about the problem, and that talking is enough."[28] Women friends sometimes help steer each other right into this rut by offering false empathy and insincere reassurances.

However negative this may be for the friend who is being consoled into inaction, it can be even worse for the friend who is doing the consoling. Women often feel frustrated even while they're providing counterfeit commiseration and supportive lies. For one thing, weaving this web of well-intentioned deceit is stressful: women feel worse than men do — before, during, and after — when they lie, particularly when they are lying to close friends.[29] For another, most women feel deeply uncomfortable when they are silencing themselves, which can cause ongoing tension, both internally and in the friendship. The woman who feels compelled to voice support for a friend's decision that she does not in fact support — having an extramarital affair, for instance, or undergoing radical cosmetic surgery — then is trapped into listening to details she would rather not hear.

Over time, self-censorship can create intense anger and resentment that may at first appear disproportionate to the cause: *She drives me crazy, the way she's always going on about how broke she is, but then she takes cabs everywhere and eats out three times a week. I can't stand it any more!* When the boundaries between close friends become blurred by self-disclosure, one may view the other's choices as a personal affront; they are supposed to be the same, so she feels a sense of ownership over her friend's life and can hardly believe that she's making such a bad decision. Yet, she also believes she must continue to listen, agree, and provide support. Differences that are relatively minor can begin to seem monumental, and the pressure to agree, although self-imposed, may come to seem intolerable.

Although women pride themselves on an ability to recognize and articulate their feelings, many have great difficulty directly addressing these kinds of problems with friends. We are supposed to be as one, and thus it seems we are not allowed to disagree. Yet our strategies for denying differences and avoiding disagreements can actually cause even more serious problems: animosity, envy, and rivalry, to name just three. As between Julie and Anna, silence can have the effect not just of magnifying differences, but of creating altogether new difficulties.

We have come to an odd impasse when, in the name of intimacy, we cannot speak our minds and tell each other the truth. This is not a dilemma that most women face with men, because we believe men can handle criticism; they are, after all, emotionally challenged if not downright insensitive. Many women also feel entitled to tell men unpleasant truths because failing to do so might seem to increase male power. We want our voices to be heard by men, and so we speak up: *I am angry, Your behavior was appalling, The tie looks terrible, The memo is poorly written.* Not saying these things would require surrendering our self-respect and turning the clock back thirty years or so.

But while most women understand that disagreements and arguments are inevitable and occasionally necessary in romantic relationships, we expect our friendships to be free of conflict, as though they exist on a higher plane because sex — which usually involves those morally inferior men — is not involved. Ironically, many women talk about the unconditional love they get from their friends, yet conduct themselves as though it could be yanked away in an instant, at the first sign of open conflict.

Partly, we are ashamed to admit just how negative some of our feelings and just how harsh some of our judgments actually are, because they seem so unwomanly and so unfriendly. Yet denial only drives them underground, where they can do us — and our friends — far more harm. We seethe internally, or we vent in passive-aggressive bursts, as Julie did by remaining silent when she had an opportunity to prevent Anna's failure, and only wind up feeling guilty.

But also, we are afraid of what our friends would do if we told them the truth. Women friends defend each other, often by taking shots at each other's enemies with bullets of irony. Women know that other women can be both staunch allies and formidable adversaries; we recognize one another's power not only to defend but to wound, and when conflict arises in the friendship itself, we will do almost anything to avoid having this power turned against us. Usually, we withdraw behind a shield of silence.

So we don't just tell supportive lies. We also lie — not just to our friends, but to ourselves — by remaining silent about the essential truths: I'm angry, I'm envious, I'm hurt.

After the conference, Julie fully expected that her friendship with Anna would improve. Six months on, however, they seemed to be further apart than ever before. Julie did not want to sound like a jealous lover, but that is exactly how she felt. A thoughtless remark, a piece of gossip unshared, a secret untold — what might have seemed like oversights on the part of a boyfriend appeared to be betrayals by the best friend. And although Julie would surely have confronted a man, she said nothing to Anna. *She's my best friend, she should have known.*

The problem as Julie saw it was that Anna had a new friend, a woman who worked in her own company. Julie was prepared to accept, albeit grudgingly, the presence of a serious boyfriend in Anna's life; the boyfriend might monopolize Anna's time, but he could never take Julie's place. Another woman, however, was another matter altogether. She was a rival who could supplant Julie, and that appeared to be exactly what was happening.

Anna's new friend was glamorous, received invitations to the kinds of parties that are written up in gossip columns, and generally made Julie feel as though she had a piece of spinach lodged permanently between her front teeth. They went out a few times as a threesome, but Julie could not get a foothold in the conversation. The other two seemed to chatter endlessly about the byzantine nature of their office politics and the tennis camp they had attended together one summer weekend — a particularly sore point with Julie, who was offended (although she'd never played tennis in her life) that Anna hadn't asked her to go.

The other woman made Julie feel at once socially inadequate and morally superior, and she felt threatened because Anna seemed so dazzled by her. Julie could not compete in terms of connections and party invitations, and could hardly believe that her best friend valued these fripperies over her company. What Julie offered was *real*.

If Anna had been male, Julie would not have hesitated to express anger and hurt, and she would have expected a nice dinner or at least some flowers by way of apology. But they are women — how could it sound anything other than ridiculous, this accusation that Anna was promiscuous with her affections? Of course, Julie said nothing.

Really, there was so much she hadn't said that it seemed impossible to start talking at this point. It would necessitate reading out a long list of complaints that included items like, "I've been waiting for three months to be paid back the fifty dollars you borrowed that night we went out for dinner. You've never even mentioned it and I didn't want to bring it up because it seemed cheap, but it's bothered me every time I've seen you." Julie was not prepared to do that. She believed that Anna should know, instinctively, that she was upset and why. *She's not much of a best friend if she's completely insensitive to my feelings, is she?*

Instead of tearful scenes and tortured conversations about The Relationship, Julie initiated a policy of chilly evasion. She stopped phoning Anna, and then, when Anna phoned her, was slightly formal and distant. She was waiting for Anna to figure out what the matter was and to make amends, but it didn't happen. They simply drifted apart.

It did not occur to her that perhaps she had misread the situation, or that Anna very likely had complaints of her own about their friendship and might resent Julie's possessiveness. Quite possibly, Anna really didn't know what to make of Julie's coldness, and she finally stopped calling because she was hurt by it. Nor did it occur to Julie that perhaps her own insecurity caused her to exaggerate the extent to which Anna's new friend really did pose a threat to their friendship. Certainly, she did not question her own need to be paramount in Anna's life, and thus never entertained the notion that the friendship could survive, albeit in a less claustrophobic form.

Ultimately, despite their supposed closeness, they were ill-equipped to deal with such conflicts. Their friendship had such a strong us-against-the-world flavor that any dissension in the ranks threatened the very foundation of their unity, and that is exactly why Julie had denied and minimized differences between them all along.

Sameness seemed to provide security; difference seemed to imperil their solidarity. When the differences became undeniable, neither Julie nor Anna could address them directly.

In the end, the main distinctions between their relationship and those Julie had with men were ones of degree: her expectations were much higher, her standards were less flexible, and consequently, when the honeymoon was over, she was more bitterly disappointed.

It is no great surprise when men fail to deliver, as the friends who rally round with condolences invariably point out. But women are supposed to be different from men, so there are no mourning rituals when a friendship ends. Breaking up is not supposed to be one of the scenes in the drama of female friendship, which is why there is so rarely a sense of closure and why the pain is always such a sharp, sour surprise.

There is a sharp dichotomy between the script for women's lives that is promoted in the public arena — the media, academia, politics — and what women themselves privately think about their own experiences. According to the sexual script, women are intimacy experts and their relationships with other women are endlessly loving, supportive, and blissful. Real life, however, is a different story.

Every woman I interviewed had at least one anecdote and usually several about being terribly hurt by another woman, and they told these stories with more anger, grief, and bitterness than any they told about men. There were enough neglectful or critical mothers, spiteful or attention-hogging sisters, and malicious or insufficiently loving friends to fill several volumes. Treacherous colleagues were stock characters in these narratives, as were beloved mentors who resented their underlings' success, and ungrateful understudies who connived to supplant their benefactors.

Many women spoke about their difficulties with other women in the present tense. *She puts me down in subtle ways, like always bringing up the fact that I didn't go to college. She puts me on a pedestal but I don't want to be worshipped. It's always about her, her problems, her life — I'm just an audience for her psychodramas. She never makes the effort, I'm the one who has to do all the work to keep the friendship going. Sometimes it seems like all we do is complain at each other. I have to entertain her, she expects me to be witty and clever the whole time. I'm married, she's single, but she expects me to drop everything when she calls — if I don't, she makes me feel like a bad friend. I tell her something and she swears she won't tell her husband, but then next time I see him, he'll let it slip that he knows. She asks for my advice but she doesn't take it, so we wind up having the same conversation a thousand times. She's always telling me how to run my life.*

Usually, complaints were accompanied by a weary, resigned conclusion: *I can't tell her how I really feel, because she'd get upset and the friendship might end.* Women, such renowned talkers and mediators, are frequently struck into silence when they most need to air their differences.

Ironically, many of women's real-life problems with intimacy stem from the notion that women *should* be experts at creating it and *should* be morally superior. This is, among other things, a surefire recipe for low self-esteem. So long as women believe they aren't entitled to express the full range of human emotions and behavior, they'll continue to have unrealistic expectations of themselves — and other women. Every twinge of envy, anger, and impatience will be a source of guilt; silencing themselves to maintain an uneasy peace will make women feel frustrated, overburdened, and put-upon.

Women who believe they should be intimacy experts live in fear of being disliked and being left behind. Frequently, then, they tiptoe around other women's feelings, deny their own rights as individuals, and don't say the things that would actually improve their relationships: "I'm angry," or, "I care about you but I can't honestly support your decision," or, "I'm feeling smothered," or, "I can't listen to another hour of complaints about your job — start checking the want ads, then we'll talk." Such friendships don't make women feel strong, confident, and supported, but weak, dependent, and afraid to tell the truth.

Many women speak of not feeling challenged by their friendships, but they themselves are afraid to challenge their friends. "A lot of the time, you sit around with your girlfriends drinking your own bathwater" is how Stacy, a twenty-six-year-old waitress, puts it. "You're not talking about nuclear physics, you're talking about whether that guy will call. You're validating each other all over the place, it's like mutual therapy. But eventually, you run out of bathwater, you switch to vodka, and you wind up hating your friends. It's a relief to talk to guys in a way, because you don't fall into that trap and you don't feel you have to validate everything they say."

On a practical level, the truth is that some of our friendships could use a few more "masculine" elements. Women friends who go to the theater or run the marathon together know there's a special closeness that comes from having a common history based on something concrete and physical; sharing activities also helps prevent the cycle of complaint and commiseration that creates anger, frustration, and boredom. Friends who talk not just about their inner lives but about "impersonal" ideas — like philosophy, or the economy, or current events — know that a shared intellectual interest creates a powerful bond; challenging each other intellectually and learning to view disagreement as something other than a personal betrayal is good for any friendship. It's unfair to men — and unhelpful to women — when researchers dismiss the masculine style of friendship as so shallow and superficial that women should refrain from incorporating any of its features into their own friendships.

On a more general level, thinking of women as intimacy experts means continuing to think in oppositional terms. We view men as our opposites, when it would be more helpful to acknowledge our similarities. And we continue to believe that other women are the same, when it would be better for all of us to recognize and learn to cope with our differences.

Oppositional thinking is a psychological dead end for women, because it requires us to pretend that we are plaster saints instead of human beings, and encourages us to have contempt for and fear of men, who are seen as unfeeling dimwits or depraved demons. But there's nothing in women's genes that makes us morally superior. Just like men, we can be aggressive, competitive, cruel, exploitative, and domineering. And just like women, men can be nurturing, cooperative, loving, giving, and submissive.

We should be very wary of the concept of female superiority, which has always been used to keep women in their place: at home, where they could embroider pious samplers and remain unsullied by the rough-and-tumble immorality of the business world and free of the deleterious effects of access to money and power. Today, the myth of female moral superiority is still being used to deny women power: the power to insist that we are not and should not have to be more-than-equal to men; the power to improve our relationships so that they serve *our* needs better; the power to choose a new kind of future for ourselves in which we are more than martyrs and less than saints.

This myth is a burden for individual women, but it is also a trap that prevents us, as a group, from acknowledging who we really are: individuals, who are capable of vice as well as virtue. Denying this doesn't make us feel good about ourselves. Rather, it creates false feelings of powerlessness and very real feelings of unhappiness; we're too busy trying to be blameless to feel that we're in control of our own lives. We stagger around under the weight of other people's emotional baggage, congratulating one another on our goodness and wondering what awful things men will do to us next. And we're blindsided, again and again, when other women reveal that they're not quite as morally superior as we are.

We deny, at our own peril, what every schoolgirl knows: we're not always the fair sex, and we're certainly no angels. Little girls are well-acquainted with exclusionary politics by first grade, when two friends frequently prove how much they like each other by shunning a third. Any woman who was ever chosen last for the team, or suddenly found herself the odd one out in a threesome, or sat alone at the lunch table because of some obscure offence she was not even aware of committing, knows that little girls are capable of calculated cruelty.

The passive-aggressive tactics of older girls are both subtler and more brutal. The game of Truth or Dare, for instance, makes boxing seem a gentle sport. If one chooses "truth," the instruction tends to be something like, "Say what you honestly think about all the other girls in the room," which inevitably leads to a flurry of recriminations, tears, and counter-charges.

Girls' aggression tends to be less direct than boys'; girls are less likely to punch one another, but more likely to engage in psychological warfare. By the time they reach puberty, most have learned to cloak aggression with concern: "Poor Sheila. She's got this huge crush on Jeremy, and she thinks it's a big secret, but she's being so obvious, hanging around his locker all the time. I'm worried sick about her — when she likes a guy, she'll let him go as far as he wants and then she just gets hurt. That's what happened with Sean. They went all the way, then he dumped her. Promise you won't tell anyone?"

Adolescent girls police the borders of sexual correctness, deciding which of the others are sluts, a judgment that's frequently based less on their actual behavior with boys than on how assiduously they court the good opinion of other girls. Although boys are typically depicted as the upholders of the sexual double standard, the key role that popular girls play in determining the high school pecking order is largely ignored. Popular girls are tastemakers, and they will forgive and even vigorously defend a girl who sleeps around but is also careful to pay homage to them. A sexually active girl who ignores socially powerful girls, however, will very likely find herself the target of vicious gossip.

The same fate may also befall the pretty girl, whether or not she is sexually active. "They said that I stole boyfriends, that I was a man-eater, that I'd done it with two guys at once. The weirdest thing of all was that I'd never even had a boyfriend when these rumors started. I was fifteen — I'd never *kissed* a boy! And yet, all the girls who were gossiping about me *did* have boyfriends," says Elizabeth. She's thirty-one now, but the injustice still makes her visibly angry.

She had three problems in high school. The first was her beauty: she's tall and very slim, with a face that looks like a cross between Audrey Hepburn's and Grace Kelly's and compares favorably to both. The second was her brain: she was an honors student, and today has an advanced degree in biochemistry. But her real sin was that most of her friends were boys and, as she puts it, "I didn't suck up to the in-group of girls. I was nice to them, but I didn't actively set out to ingratiate myself. I didn't know that was what they expected, and by the time I figured it out, it was too late. They enjoyed hating me too much."

She switched high schools in her senior year. "I just couldn't take it any more. The group of girls who ran the school made my life a complete misery," she remembers. "Constant gossip, whispering and laughing in the halls, saying horrible things to my face. And they turned a lot of the guys against me, too. Boys at that age are pretty weak, I think, and they just weren't prepared to continue being friends with me if they were going to get hassled for it. At my new school, I was careful to be very sweet to the girls in the in-crowd and pretend I was dumb. Not to get guys — guys never had a problem with the fact that I got good grades. I did it to neutralize the other girls. It's all right to be good-looking so long as you're stupid — that became my golden rule for dealing with other girls."

In fact, many teenage girls seem to care far more about their relationships with one another than about their relationships with boys. Girls frequently develop wild crushes of a nonsexual nature on each other; the keenest memories of social triumph in adolescence tend to center not on boys but on winning a trophy friend or being chosen as the confidante of an idol. And the most painful memories — the treachery of close friends who repeated one's secrets, the random acts of cruelty by other girls — often have little to do with boys. Sometimes, of course, the conflict between two girls is over a boy, but he is usually the pawn in a larger struggle; the pain of these episodes has little to do with losing him and everything to do with feeling betrayed by a friend or feeling that another girl is somehow better than oneself.

Particularly in the early teen years, the need to be accepted and the desire to be popular are so strong that any association with a girl who does not meet the prevailing standards of coolness is undertaken at the risk of one's own exclusion. Girls are only too aware of how unpleasant and lonely the existence of a social pariah is, and how conditional their own acceptance is.

At my own high school, two girls were forever orbiting the other cliques, looking for a way in. The rest of us adopted a policy of benign neglect, pretending not to notice their attempts to win our friendship. Individually, probably all of us were secretly kind to them on isolated occasions when we were sure no one else was looking. But none of us risked being closely associated with them in public, for fear of joining them outside the circle of acceptance, looking in hungrily. So occasionally when we were bored, we'd patronize them extravagantly to amuse one another, then subside into giggling derision and call them nicknames behind their backs.

Women's oft-noted kindness and cooperativeness cannot be wholly explained by women's allegedly greater capacity for connection or by a patriarchal conspiracy to brainwash us into being nice and sweet for the convenience of men. Rather, these qualities seem absolutely necessary for same-sex interactions from childhood on. As Elizabeth discovered, girls — and women — have the power to make one's life a misery, and their most deadly weapon is moral authoritarianism: She's a slut, She's selfish, She's *not nice*.

Since the sexual script tells us that we are supposed to be morally superior, slights to our honor wound us to the core. We don't care so much what men think, because everyone knows that men are morally inferior. But women are the ultimate arbiters of virtue, and most of us cannot bear it when other women think badly of us. Even when it's unjust, even when it's petty, even when we know it simply isn't true, criticism from other women brings us to our knees. We learn to be nice and sweet so that other women won't say nasty things about us; we figure out early that the best way to avoid being ostracized is to curry favor and swear fervent assent.

Although it is gratifying, as a woman, to find scholarly confirmation of our peerless skills in the realm of relationships, most women do not need to be convinced that we are one another's best friends. We already know that. What remain to be addressed are the ways in which the feminine style of intimacy makes other women our most formidable adversaries — and makes us our own worst enemies.

Chapter Two

Lies of Sisterhood

"**W**endy knows me like no one else does," says Nadine. "We've been best friends since first grade." They're twenty-nine now, and lead very different lives: Wendy is a stay-at-home mother who still lives in the same affluent suburb where they grew up; Nadine is single, works for a glossy magazine, and lives in New York. "We see less of each other now because of the distance, but Wendy is a constant in my life," Nadine explains. "We keep in touch by phone, and when we do see each other, it's as though no time has passed at all."

She opens a photo album, stuffed with proofs of their closeness, to a picture of two seven-year-olds in a manicured backyard. Nadine is the short one in a pink bathing suit who's sticking her tongue out; Wendy is the scrawny one who's posing like a movie star, thrusting out her nonexistent chest and blowing a kiss to the camera. A few years later at a birthday party, Wendy is wearing bell bottoms and a for-company smile, and Nadine has scraped knees and the wounded dignity of a tomboy whose mother has forced her to wear a dress. She flips through more photographic memories: her riding lessons, Wendy's ballet recital, the camping trip when they tried to spook Nadine's little brother and ended up setting a tent on fire.

What Nadine sees in these photos is how little their friendship appears to have changed over the past two decades: "Wendy's always been super-confident. Very poised, very good with people. I'm the joker, the sporty one who's always in a jam." She prizes this continuity, because it's "an anchor. I feel very sure of who I am when I'm with her. Wendy's my personal historian. I'll tell her something that's going on with a boyfriend, and she'll say, 'That's like that time in ninth grade, when you had a crush on so-and-so.' She remembers things about me that I've forgotten."

In even the most superficial conversations, Nadine explains, there are layers of unspoken meaning and shared experience beneath the actual words: "We can tell each other things without having to go into long, involved explanations. For instance, if I have a fight with my mother, Wendy already knows the whole background, firsthand, so we can dive right into a conversation without a lot of preliminaries."

Nadine is turning the pages of the album more quickly now, rushing past the embarrassing adolescent experiments with purple lipstick and the disco-inspired clothes of the late seventies. In these pictures, there are suddenly not just two girls but three: camera-shy Nadine, fearless Wendy, and a full-lipped girl with streaky blonde hair and enormous blue eyes. "That's Heather," Nadine explains. "We met her in junior high."

Heather got the lead in all the plays, captained the volleyball team, sketched and painted, danced as expertly as a backup singer in a rock video, but wasn't the least bit stuck-up. Heather had "a perfect sitcom life," according to Nadine. Her father was a big-shot doctor, her mother was pretty and sweet, and, although "everyone else looked hideous during puberty, Heather looked like Barbie." Even adults seemed slightly star-struck by her. The first time Nadine brought Heather home, she thought she saw something like accusation in her mother's eyes: Why can't you be more like *her*?

But, Nadine adds, "Heather was really Wendy's friend in high school, not mine." Back then, she was not happy about having to share her best friend, particularly with a girl who seemed to eclipse her in so many ways. Wendy seemed to spend an inordinate amount of time immured in Heather's glamorous bedroom, which had a white ruffled bedspread and a much-coveted vanity table, having long, private talks about — well, Nadine wasn't exactly sure what those talks were about, which made her a little nervous. Were they talking about her? Wendy knew all her secrets — surely she wouldn't tell Heather?

It got so that Nadine actually felt happy whenever the other two had a falling-out, because for a brief spell it would be like old times: she'd have Wendy all to herself. But they always made up, and although Nadine would continue to try to carve out private time with Wendy, her attempts were usually unsuccessful. "Great idea," Wendy would say when Nadine suggested going to the movies or the mall. "Let's see if Heather can come, too."

Nadine recalls being "quite upset and hurt," not just initially, but off and on throughout junior high and high school, that her best friend seemed to prefer to spend time with her only as part of a threesome. A few times, she said something to Wendy, whose response was, "But if we don't ask Heather to come, she'll feel left out." The result, however, was that Nadine herself felt peripheral: "I always felt like I was tagging along."

The problem, in her view, was that the other two had more in common: Heather was the It-girl and Wendy was the life of the party. Nadine saw herself as the reliable but unexciting one, the goody-goody who took advanced classes and didn't drink or do drugs or have boyfriends. Left to her own devices, Nadine figures, she would have been a misfit. Wendy, however, refused to let her sink to the lower castes of their high school, and made a point of saving a seat for her at the in-crowd's lunch table and ensuring that she was invited to their parties.

Nadine, reeling in the aftermath of her parents' divorce, was and still is profoundly grateful. "Wendy was really good to me at a point when my life was godawful. I was thirteen when my parents separated, but it was a very ugly, drawn-out breakup and I was devastated for years. My mother fought for custody of me and my brother to punish my dad — she didn't really want us, and I missed my father desperately," she says. "One of the reasons I love Wendy as much as I do is that she stuck by me through all of that and my mother's remarriage."

Although Nadine readily acknowledges Wendy's "incredible loyalty" — after all, she could have dumped Nadine, who was by her own account not exactly a status symbol — she also believes that her motives were not entirely disinterested. "She's a bit of a snob," Nadine says. "She wouldn't have *let* me be anything but popular." Wendy pulled her into her own social orbit partly because she's "a controller," in Nadine's view.

While Nadine could not reciprocate the social favors, she did have something to offer in return, precisely because she "wasn't a real player in the popularity game, so Wendy could let down her guard and bare her heart to me without worrying that I'd use it against her." In times of crisis — her own or Wendy's — Nadine could count on Wendy's undivided attention. On a day-to-day basis, however, "Wendy was closer to Heather. I remember being afraid that she might leave me behind because she was so cool and I was a nonentity. I never really fit in with the popular kids. They only accepted me because Wendy had clout."

Nadine may see this social imbalance reflected in the pictures, but an objective observer sees a different kind of inequity. Though not unattractive, Wendy is thoroughly ordinary-looking: baby-fine hair of an indeterminate brown color, slightly squashed facial features, pear-shaped body. Nadine, however, is now and always has been extremely pretty: long, curly chestnut-color hair, oval-shaped face with high cheekbones, the kind of lean-yet-lush figure that is more commonly the result of cosmetic surgery than nature.

It's hard to believe, given the photographic evidence, that she was really the gawky outcast she claims to have been. But, Nadine protests, the camera didn't capture Wendy's true appeal: "She has a way of making everyone feel like her special friend. Even as a little kid she had charisma. Girls loved to be around her and guys just adored her. I didn't blossom until I got to university and developed a whole new identity."

That this new identity — social butterfly with an activist streak — emerged only when she and Wendy were attending different schools strikes Nadine as "pure coincidence." She does, however, concede that it was surprisingly easy to reinvent herself: "It wasn't quite so dramatic, but it was like waking up one day in a different world. The same things that were liabilities in high school were suddenly advantages — being smart was valued, my kind of looks were valued." There was also no one around to remind her that Wendy was supposed to be the social one, Heather the pretty one, and Nadine their mascot. What she calls a new identity actually sounds more like coming into her own.

Her success was exhilarating, but for the first time in her life, she felt she "had to conceal things from Wendy": her good grades, her triumphs at the campus newspaper, and her adventures with a series of tall, dark, and stubble-chinned men. "It would have seemed like bragging," Nadine says at first. Normally, she conducts a conversation from the edge of her chair, as though she's so engaged that she has to throw herself into it physically. Now, however, she's folded in on herself like an accordion, studiously avoiding eye contact. "Wendy didn't get into my university, and I felt bad that I did," she finally says. "She was genuinely happy for me, I knew that, but I still felt like I had to reassure her that she wasn't missing out on anything. Plus she was miserable at her own school, so I didn't want to make her feel worse by telling her what a great time I was having."

So she downplayed her own triumphs — *no big deal* — or neglected to mention them altogether. Instead, she regaled Wendy with long, amusing tales about her own mishaps and mistakes. "I always looked up to her when we were growing up, so telling her how well I was doing would have been like knocking her off a pedestal," Nadine says. Being the social mover and shaker was, after all, Wendy's role, and Nadine didn't want her friend to get the idea that she was trying to usurp it. "I didn't want her to think that I was doing better than she was," she explains. "I didn't want her to see me as a threat."

Nadine had never looked at her best friend as a mirror image of herself, as Julie did in the previous chapter, nor had she exaggerated their similarities. Rather, she had exaggerated their differences, and had come to feel that the strength of the friendship depended on her own relative weakness. But both Nadine and Julie believed that change threatened their friendships and neither felt comfortable directly addressing the differences that emerged over time. So while Julie's version of mutual self-disclosure did not include telling Anna how upset she was when Anna surpassed her professionally or seemed to slight her personally, Nadine's version omitted anything that might threaten Wendy or highlight the ways in which her own relative position in the world had changed for the better.

Ironically, once she started getting ahead in life, she still had the same old fear: being left behind. Nadine viewed her own success as a destructive force, an invasion of Wendy's territory and a threat to the equilibrium of their friendship, so she denied it, minimized it, and mastered the pre-emptive strike of self-deprecation.

She didn't want her success to come between them, and the easiest way to maintain the closeness of their connection seemed to be to continue to play to type: socially inept and deeply insecure, with a knack for converting these failings into funny stories. It did not occur to Nadine that these habits she was developing with Wendy — denying her own success, making believe that their relative positions in the world had not changed — might not be good for her, good for Wendy, or good for their friendship. And it never crossed her mind that these habits might actually wind up causing her harm in relationships with women who had less reason to be kindly disposed toward her than Wendy did — namely, her colleagues.

She was playing perfectly the role cast for women in the sexual script: women are supposed to be exquisitely sensitive to each other's feelings, and to disclaim any responsibility for their own triumphs, or better still, declare them inadmissible. *No big deal, it was just luck*. That way, at least in theory, no one gets hurt.

Of course, Nadine didn't think of what she was doing in terms of mechanically following a script, nor did she consciously choose to maintain the cycle of complaint and commiseration, even when she had little to complain about, as an appeasement strategy. All she knew was that when good things happened in her own life, a warning flare went off in her head each time she picked up the phone to call Wendy: *careful, think about how this might make her feel*.

Making her own life sound bad to make another woman feel good simply seemed tactful and considerate, particularly after Nadine became a member of the glitterati: "The first time I met a big-name actor at a press party, I called Wendy up and started babbling away, but after a while I realized she wasn't saying anything, there was just dead silence on the other end of the phone. So I trailed off, really

guilty, and asked her what was going on with her. She made some remark like, 'Not much, compared to you. Who would ever have
thought you'd wind up leading such a glamorous life?' The implication being, 'Given what a loser you were in high school.' I know she
was proud of me in a way, but she was also threatened."

Nadine immediately began backpedaling: she'd made a fool of
herself by spilling a drink when she was talking to the actor, she
earned a pittance, her apartment was a hellhole, it was impossible to
meet nice men in New York. The cycle of complaint and commiseration was so familiar that Nadine slipped back into it without even
questioning why she felt the need to do so.

Today, she avoids having to backtrack by editing her professional
success out of their conversations altogether. "I almost never tell her
about my job, unless something terrible happens. Mostly we just try
to make each other laugh, and talk about relationships, which is one
area where I do tell her everything. I can pour out my heart to her
and tell her my deepest feelings about my boyfriend. I absolutely
trust her. She's really sympathetic and gives good advice." Not coincidentally, these conversations also serve to reassure Wendy that her
own life is good and that Nadine still needs her: Wendy is happily
married, and Nadine's "deepest feelings" about her relationships
with men are rarely entirely positive.

When Nadine wants to share good news about work, the person
she phones is Heather. "Heather and I have become really close in
the past five years, independent of Wendy. She's a graphic designer,
so she knows what it's like to work in a creative field and what it's like
to have to work for a living, period," she says. "We have more to talk
about in the present."

One of their favorite topics is Wendy: her galling materialism, her
annoying need to be the center of attention, her obvious fear that
her friends will have more than she does. Up to this point, Nadine
has been portraying Wendy as the perfect friend. Now, however, she
clarifies: "She's a great friend but she drives me crazy, too, in ways
that only Heather can understand."

For instance, Wendy has one habit in particular that infuriates
them: she doles out barbed remarks in a maternal tone. "I'm really

worried about you!" Wendy exclaims each time she sees Nadine. "You look practically anorexic." Nadine knows that Wendy says this because she's worried about her own weight, yet still it bothers her: it's untrue, it implies that she's unhealthy, and it's "kind of mean."

But Wendy's habit is almost impossible to challenge head-on, as Heather learned four years ago when she got engaged to a man she'd known for three months. Wendy, who was still waiting impatiently for her own longtime boyfriend to propose, ran around declaring, "It'll never work, they barely know each other," and, "He's not good enough for Heather." Then, she skipped the engagement party, offering a last-minute excuse that was less than convincing. Heather, who'd been complaining about these and other slights all along to Nadine, finally exploded: "You're really hurting me! Why are you so jealous? Why can't you be happy for me?"

Wendy burst into tears, hotly denying that she wasn't thrilled for Heather. "I can't believe you think I'm jealous!" she cried. "I want the best for you, that's all." Heather wound up apologizing profusely for causing offense, although later, of course, she complained bitterly to Nadine about the way Wendy had turned the tables on her.

Wendy, for her part, has never quite forgiven what she saw as a slight to her honor. "There's still fallout," Nadine says. "They've never talked about it with each other again, but separately, each of them still mentions it to me. And they spend more time together because they live closer to each other, but Wendy finds ways to put me above Heather, like asking me to be the godmother of her kids and coming to me first in a crisis. Sometimes it's a little uncomfortable when I go back to see them, because Wendy tries to monopolize my time and then I feel bad that Heather is excluded."

One of the ways she attempts to make it up to Heather is by comparing notes on Wendy. "We feel sorry for her that she's seen so little of the world and has a fixation with money and status," Nadine says. "She drives us insane by always talking about what she has, her possessions. She feels entitled to money and doesn't think she has to do anything to get it, she just expects her husband to provide."

While they're occurring, she enjoys these conversations with Heather, which create a delicious bond of secrecy and superiority.

Afterwards, however, Nadine sometimes feels guilty: Wendy is supposed to be her best friend. So she tries to compensate for criticizing Wendy's values behind her back by seeming to endorse them to her face. "I focus on not having money and not having a serious boyfriend because I know it pleases her," Nadine says.

It also allows Nadine to cling to her old role, pretending that she's still the same person she always was and still idolizes her best friend. "It's comforting to slip back into being the person I was," she concedes. "It's a bit of an escape from the way my life really is. And it makes me feel grounded, like everything could go wrong but I'd still have this friendship."

Nadine's routine of self-deprecation makes her feel secure, makes Wendy feel better about herself, and means that Nadine doesn't have to confront what she sees as her friend's deficiencies, like "how empty Wendy's life is." But playing her old role of the bumbler who's always in a scrape also creates real tension between them. It bothers Nadine that Wendy seems to see her life as sad and squalid: "She thinks my profession is a hobby and I really should be married by now." Nadine minimizes her own accomplishments — then gets upset that Wendy doesn't see her clearly. She pretends not to have changed since she was thirteen — yet is annoyed when Wendy treats her like she's still in need of guidance.

Nadine tries to protect Wendy — from her own negative judgments, her own success, and her own feelings of superiority — just as Wendy used to protect her socially. But Nadine is also trying to protect herself: "If we redefined our roles so that they reflected reality, the friendship would probably suffer and we wouldn't be as close. It's easier just to revert back to the person I used to be, nice and nonthreatening.

"I don't want Wendy to feel she has to compete with me," Nadine concludes. Clearly, she believes that she would win any contest between them over success, but equally clearly, she believes that she would lose the friendship if she allowed such a contest to occur. In Nadine's view, then, she has to shield both of them from Wendy's competitive instincts. "Competition would drive us apart," she says, intending no irony. It seems never to have occurred to her that they have, in fact, been competing all along.

In the world of business, "competitive" is a compliment. When we say a particular company is competitive, we mean it's successful relative to others in the same field. Competition is the engine of a free-market economy, and it's supposed to be a force for good: companies compete to devise better products at cheaper prices, and consumers reap the benefits. Likewise, competition among colleagues is, at least in theory, beneficial: it spurs creativity and productivity, and challenges individuals to do their best.

In the realm of female friendship, however, competition tends to be viewed as a force for harm. The competitive woman appears to be trying to break away from other women and assert that she is different — better, in fact. She seeks recognition for herself alone, and plays to win without seeming to mind that her own victory may entail someone else's defeat. Thus, between women, "she's so *competitive*" is a criticism that implies serious transgressions: wanting too much for oneself, and caring too little about others.

It is, above all, a moral judgment. In the sexual script, men jockey for position and look out for number one, but women look out for everyone and make sure that nobody gets hurt — our moral superiority depends on it. So the competitive woman appears to commit the ultimate sin: she acts like a man.

Women are expected to be above wanting anything for themselves alone, too cooperative to compete and too charitable to covet. So when a woman winds up with more — more money, or recognition, or happiness, or physical charms, or whatever it is that her friends value — than others, she is supposed to pretend that she doesn't really *want* it. The cues in the sexual script are clear: "It just fell from the sky," "I don't really deserve it," and "Here — take half." Women who will not apologize for their success and who will not pretend that they don't want it come in for harsh criticism: how immodest, how insensitive, how *competitive* to strut one's success!

"She drives us insane by always talking about what she has, her possessions," as Nadine says of Wendy, who does not conceal the truth about her privileged life or her enjoyment of it. While her friends might be able to forgive Wendy for having more, the fact that she makes no secret of her desire for money and delight in having it strikes both Nadine and Heather as highly insensitive: *Can't she see that we have less? Why is she trying to make us jealous?* They blame Wendy for "provoking" their jealousy, as though wanting more for themselves were so shameful that they cannot even own the desire. It's really Wendy's fault.

The woman who talks openly about what she wants and what she has in the way of worldly success tends to be viewed as a self-promoter rather than a self-discloser, insufferably arrogant rather than candid. She's "striving," not to do her best but to get ahead of other women, she's "competitive," and she's "careless" of others' feelings.

Most women are well aware that failing to downplay their own success may arouse hostility and personal criticism, and may cost them friends. Furthermore, many who are more successful than their friends — or are successful in different ways — feel guilty about the disparity, as though they are showing them up. Thus, women have good reasons to succeed in silence: not merely to protect other women from feeling bad or feeling jealous, but to protect *themselves* from other women's negative reactions. Many women simply don't talk with their friends about their own triumphs, or if they do, they maximize their failures in order to minimize their successes.

For instance, Nadine attempts to ward off Wendy's envy and prevent competition between them by exaggerating her own weaknesses: *I'm penniless and lovelorn.* Tactically, this is a brilliant defensive strategy, because it pacifies Wendy with flattery — *You have it all! You're rich and happily married* — and disarms her with self-deprecation: *I'm weak and defenseless.* Nadine is announcing that competition is unnecessary. She's already declared Wendy the winner.

But self-deprecating appeasement doesn't really forestall competition. Rather, it reverses the usual direction; Nadine competes to lose, not win. Between women, this form of downward competition is as habitual as the cycle of complaint and commiseration from which it takes its form. "I'm getting fat," frets the willowy woman. "No one seems to like me any more," the gregarious one sighs. The listener may be frustrated because she knows the complaint is artificial and perhaps feels insecure about her *own* body or popularity, so she tries to provide consolation and commiseration while also asserting her own claim to relative disadvantage: *That's terrible, but I feel even worse.*

This can become a perpetual contest, as friends swap credentials of victimization in pursuit of a dubious prize: the title of most hard-done-by. Anyone who has listened to two rail-thin women trying to prove to each other that they see themselves as morbidly obese knows that the diplomacy of one-downmanship can be a cheap form of entertainment. But it also carries the serious danger of creating a sense of solidarity grounded on weakness and insecurity, so that feeling bad is fused with feeling connected.

When the differences between two women are undeniable, the one who appears to be in the better position may still compete downward in an effort to compensate the other for having less. She tries to apologize for her own success by equalizing the imbalance it causes: "I may seem to have more, but what I have really isn't worth winning, so the differences between us even out in the end."

Having more does not mean that a woman needs other women any less or has a lower emotional investment in her friendships. In fact, precisely because many women are so uncomfortable about "sticking out" and having "too much," successful women may well prize their friendships even more highly. They want to be known, valued, and seen for who they really are, but fear that what they have may create hostility or blind other women to their need for connection. The "Don't hate me because I'm beautiful" ad campaign perfectly captured this fear; "rich," "powerful," "happily married," or "popular" could all be the operative adjectives and the sentiment would still apply.

Just as some women attempt to deny differences with strategies like counterfeit commiseration, others quite unconsciously employ a range of compensatory strategies to prevent open competition and strengthen connections with their friends. These strategies can and frequently do backfire spectacularly, however, and may even wind up heightening competition.

Some women try to make up the difference with friends by constantly seeking their advice and reassurance, which is designed to send the message: *I'm just as bewildered as you are that I've wound up in a better position, and I still need your help with every little thing.* This seems to be what Anna was trying to communicate when she tried on her new dress and practiced her speech for Julie, but rather than feeling included in her friend's success, Julie was reminded once again of her own relative failures. To her, it seemed that Anna was flaunting her good fortune, not apologizing for it or asking for guidance. Instead of staving off competition, Anna appeared to be inviting it.

Other compensatory strategies carry similar risks of backfiring and intensifying competition. Some women try to share what they have by performing favors and attempting to pull their friends along with them into the land of plenty, as Wendy did in high school, but may wind up incurring resentment instead of gratitude. *She's patronizing me, treating me like a failure,* complains the friend who's never allowed to pick up the check or who's constantly being offered rides on another woman's coattails. *She shoves her success down my throat and just assumes that I want it!*

Interestingly, the most obviously risky strategy — highlighting the downside of success — is also the most popular, particularly in friendships that are propelled by the cycle of complaint and commiseration. Understandably, the friend who's earning minimum wage and praying that her poems will some day be published tends to have a low-tolerance threshold for hearing about the private pain of being a highly paid executive. *She's so self-absorbed and negative, constantly whining. Can't she see that her problems are nothing compared to mine?*

Even the seemingly most foolproof gambit, deflecting attention from the imbalance altogether by focusing with laserlike intensity on the other woman's accomplishments, can backfire. The friend who receives lavish praise and thousands of questions about her own life, but whose own enquiries are greeted with evasion or silence, may wind up feeling frustrated and hurt: *She doesn't think I can handle her success — she just won't* talk to me any more.

Women who openly discuss their success, seem to want it, and clearly enjoy it tend to be perceived as competitive, but so may women who try desperately to avoid open competition for success. Likewise, the woman who tries to avoid competition for failure, and

will not engage in the cycle of complaint and commiseration or practice the diplomacy of one-downmanship. By focusing on what is positive in her own life, she can seem to be communicating either a
conviction that she is superior or an unwillingness to open up and
really *talk*. If she responds to revelations of one's own weaknesses
with "Maybe you should consider counseling," instead of "I know
just what you mean, I'm so depressed that I feel like slitting my
wrists all the time, too," she may be thought of as cold, judgmental,
and competitive. *She's saying she's better, she's putting me down.*

"Judge not" is an unwritten commandment of female friendship,
and as we have seen, many women perform complicated maneuvers
to deny differences of opinion. It just doesn't seem friendly and supportive to contest another woman's views, decisions, or behavior, and
open conflict seems to raise the specter of separation. But although
we scramble to find common ground, we may wind up competing to
be right and competing to be different in indirect, covert ways.

The truth is that we *do* pass judgment on our friends, all the time.
We would hardly be human if we listened to all the intimate details
of their lives, blandly agreed with everything they said, did, and
thought, and never formed opinions of our own. But we tend to
avoid pronouncing our verdicts directly. Instead, all the opinions
that cannot be shared in one friendship — disapproval of the way
she's raising her children, dislike of her boyfriend, discomfort with
some of her political views — are siphoned into another, which acts
as a sort of safety valve for the first. We delicately refrain from men-
tioning anything to the friend with whom we disagree, but run
around courting public opinion and appointing third parties as arbiters of an undeclared competition: Who is right, me or my friend?

These complicated backchannels of communication also allow
women to express negative emotions of anger, hurt, and envy. "I'm
so mad at Wendy. She has no respect for my time, just turned up at
my house an hour late, as usual," Heather calls Nadine to confide,
who phones back a week later to say, "Wendy just announced that
she wouldn't consider driving anything but a BMW. The woman is
obsessed with status."

Sometimes, of course, third-party venting is simply a healthy way of blowing off steam. Other times, though, it's a way of conducting a competition for the title of most wronged or most long-suffering. "Can you believe she said that to me?" women ask each other. "Do you think I did anything to deserve this treatment from her?" Usually, the third party will attempt long-distance psychoanalysis of the perpetrator — "She probably didn't mean to hurt you, she's just so wrapped up in her own problems that she's being thoughtless" — but validate the victim's feelings, too: "Still, it was insensitive, and you have every reason to feel hurt."

Occasionally, however, third-party venting can turn into a competition for affection, particularly if all three women are friends. Clearly, one of the ways that Heather and Nadine solidify their own friendship is by trashing Wendy; more than likely, Heather and Wendy have a few choice comments and favorite complaints about Nadine, as well. At the very least, this habit of draining all the frustrations with the first woman into the friendship with the second can create byzantine misunderstandings of the she-said-that-you-said-that-I-said variety.

It can also lead to more serious ruptures, especially if one woman repeats another's secrets. Repeating secrets can be a particularly devastating form of competition in which the tattler may be seeking confirmation — *Don't you think what she's doing is terrible?* — but also trying to prove to a third party that the other woman feels closer to her and tells her more: *I know something that you don't.* Usually, this last motive is not readily apparent, since the woman who is betraying a confidence also appears to be honoring the third party: *I'm really close to you, and will prove it by telling you something I swore not to repeat, after which we can dissect the other woman's behavior.* Telling our own secrets is a way that we bond; repeating someone else's is a way of double-crossing one friend to connect with another, while competing for the affection of both at the same time. It's a high-risk maneuver that can cause trouble all the way around — *But I told you not to tell her!* — and lingering distrust: *Can I trust this one not to tell the other one? What are they saying about me?*

We need to ask ourselves why, when a friend hurts us or angers us or otherwise comes into conflict with us, we have to seek validation from third parties. If maintaining the peace in one friendship requires denial and repression, and if that in turn can create competition that is twice as destructive because it involves third parties and simmering resentments, wouldn't it be better simply to agree to disagree?

Most women, however, are so afraid that any direct expression of disagreement will result in abandonment, and so terrified of their own negative feelings of envy and fear of being surpassed, that they would prefer to suffer in silence when they differ with a friend. There seems to be only one acceptable way to express these fears: in tones of concern.

Of course, it should be said at the outset that women's concern for each other is often genuine, and that many friends vigilantly guard one another's interests. In fact, we care so deeply about our close friends' well-being that serious threats to them can arouse a protective response that's even fiercer than it would be if we were in danger ourselves. Consequently, we may find it far more difficult than our friends do to forgive someone who hurts them, as any woman who has ever consoled a friend through a nasty breakup can attest. We are so outraged on the wounded woman's behalf, and want so much to protect her from the person who has caused her pain, that even if she gets back together with the man, we may very well continue to view him as our own mortal enemy.

It is also true, however, that concern is an effective cover for feelings that have nothing to do with altruism or protection and everything to do with envy and fear of abandonment. A friend's success raises the possibility of separation — *maybe she won't need me any more* — and also raises the specter of our own relative failure, yet we're supposed to respond with pure enthusiasm. *I'm so happy for you!* A woman who is dissatisfied with her own life may find it impossible to deny her own feelings — jealousy, pain, fear of abandonment — and become a cheerleader for the friend who appears to have it all, but it's equally impossible and even more undesirable to withdraw from the friendship altogether. Just as counterfeit commiseration seems to provide a safe solution to the dilemma of difference and change, false concern seems like a safe way to express envy and to compete without risk of detection.

Concern can mask "selfish" desires and "unfriendly" longings to have what our friends have — or to have even more — while protecting our own individual reputations as the best of friends. The woman who sounds concerned about a friend's welfare also sounds admirably caring and protective; she can safely express less altruistic feelings while appearing blameless and forestalling retaliation. Although it is impermissible to begrudge another woman her success, not least because it implies an unfeminine desire to have it for oneself, it is permissible and even sounds admirably compassionate to say, "I'm really worried about you. You're so stressed out all the time, and you look *exhausted*. Are you getting enough sleep?"

This is a clever trick: the worrier maintains the illusion that she's not on the attack, yet puts the other woman on the defensive. "I feel fine!" the latter protests, then rushes out to invest a small fortune in under-eye concealer and spends the next few days wondering if everyone thinks she's dangerously close to a nervous breakdown. Her friend's "worries," which camouflage a more complicated agenda, may become her own very real concerns.

In its most extreme form, concern can be wielded as a weapon, to cut a friend down to size. Women who would not dream of openly disagreeing with a friend may feel free to channel all of their pent-up frustrations into remarks that drip with sympathy yet are actively intended to wound. The woman who is most likely to use concern to cause damage is the one whose friend started out in similar circumstances (think of Julie and Anna, with their mirror-image careers and personal lives) but accelerated faster and accumulated greater rewards. If one friend is accustomed to looking at the other and seeing a reflection of herself, she may try to redress an imbalance in their relative positions in the world by chipping away at her friend's confidence with the concealed weapon of concern.

This can become a form of guerrilla warfare, so insidious that the target has no idea what her friend's real purpose is. The woman who competes to prove how much better she is through displays of concern does so because she feels inadequate, a fact that may not be readily apparent since she's adopting a lean-on-me stance and appearing to offer protection. "How *are* you?" she asks in a hushed, soothing voice, as though speaking to an invalid. "I'm so worried about you!" she will say, wringing her hands, because "you look so pale and drawn" or "your children are so difficult" or "it must be impossible to meet men who are secure enough to cope with your six-figure salary."

Since her goal is to whittle away at her friends so that she feels like a bigger person herself, she will always be able to spy dark, ominous clouds on the horizon, even when everything seems to be going well. She purses her lips and sounds alarms about everything from your new job — "I'm worried about how you'll handle all that pressure" — to your new house: "Lovely, yes, but I worry about you rattling around in it all alone."

This is the same friend who runs to us to repeat everything that anyone else says about us, taking care to present their comments in a sinister light. She will announce theatrically that we must brace for the worst, and then recount every remark, slight, and snub, always with the same disclaimers: *It's for your own good, I thought you should know, I'm so worried that people are saying such awful things behind your back*. And of course, we will reel right into her arms for comfort, until the day we notice that *everything* about us is a source of concern to her: the way we do our jobs, conduct our relationships, stock our refrigerators, and brush our hair. The better off we are, the worse she tries to make us feel.

It's easy to portray these passive-aggressive saboteurs as harmless figures of fun, but anyone who has actually had a close friendship with one of them knows how dangerous they can be. They are control freaks who want to keep us weak and dependent, and they know exactly how to push our buttons, trip our panic switches, and make us slavishly grateful for their "helpful" attentions. As a rule, they are deeply angry women who believe they must repress their anger, and the close friend who has what they want can become a symbolic target for all the rage they feel about everything that is wrong with their own lives. But it can take years to recognize that they are not the blameless martyrs they seem, because they have the perfect disguise: they try to act like our mothers, and pretend that they love us just as much.

Fortunately, they do have one recognizable calling card: a roster of former best friends who, for reasons that at first seem inexplicable, no longer speak to them. And, thankfully, this strategy of using concern to slash away at a friend's self-esteem is relatively rare.

More commonly, a friend sounds a false alarm of concern to elicit reassurance about the strength of the friendship. "Living in New York must be so exciting," Wendy tells Nadine, "but you sound so lonely these days." The subtext is clear to both of them: *you still need me, right?*

Other times, a friend adopts the posture of concern merely to vent some of her own negative emotions and try to make herself feel better. Thus does Wendy seek to console herself about gaining weight by pronouncing Nadine "practically anorexic." Amazingly, given women's reputation for sensitivity to others' feelings, many women do not seem to realize that their friends are hurt by these casual verbal jabs. Nadine, for instance, is insulted by what she sees as a slur on her physical and mental health. And Wendy's sucker punches are doubly frustrating because the etiquette that governs undeclared competition prevents Nadine from responding with a knockout: "Stop picking on me because you're getting fat. Try laying off the potato chips for a change!"

Even in the closest and most loving friendships — and Wendy and Nadine's does belong in this category — each woman tends to have a small hoard of unforgotten, needling remarks. Without a doubt, Wendy too has been on the receiving end of some "worried" jabs about her provincialism or lack of a career. At the time, the object of concern takes the hit and rationalizes it away as evidence of the other woman's insecurity. Later, however, during one of those rare blowups when friends actually do talk about what's been bothering them for the past decade, she may reveal that she's still smarting from an ancient put-down: *It really hurt me that time five years ago when you said you were worried that I was too much of a perfectionist to enjoy having kids.*

Individually, these little jabs seem minor, but when added to a mass of other unspoken resentments and denied differences, they can begin to seem like major grievances. Ultimately, the woman who is forever turning the other cheek may resent most of all the requirement that she protect her friend by tactfully ignoring her envy, when in fact the friend is the one who is causing offense, however inadvertently.

So often, outsiders cannot understand why a female friendship ends or is irreparably damaged by what seems to be a "petty," isolated incident. *She didn't come to my engagement party, She blew off my wedding, She never once came to visit me in the hospital*. But the friend who takes offense is not heartbroken that the other woman failed to be there on one occasion; rather, she sees it as proof of a pattern that she felt she could not complain about before. This one event is, for her, symbolic of all the ways that she has been let down over the years. At last, she feels she has permission to get angry. Now that it's too late, she can finally say something.

The last straw in many friendships is one woman's failure to honor a special moment in another's life. *It was my big day, she should have been there*. What's really at issue here is difference; the woman who is disappointed wanted her friend to recognize her separate achievement. But all too frequently, she did not conduct herself in the friendship as an individual who was entitled to have different opinions, feelings, and needs. She hid behind a shield of silence, didn't speak up when she disagreed, and believed that her friend should know, intuitively, when she was upset and why. Women are intimacy experts, after all. So she should not be terribly surprised that her friend didn't turn up on the big day to applaud her difference — she herself denied their differences all along, and has a long list of unaired grievances to prove it.

Furthermore, she should recognize that the friend who "forgets" to turn up for the big day or who cancels at the last minute is frequently all too aware of the importance of the event. This may be her passive-aggressive way of making a point: she too has complaints about the friendship, or perhaps she simply can't cope with her own feelings of envy and fear of abandonment. She may have grievances of her own, and may also feel she doesn't have permission to air them. For her, too, the event is symbolic: by not being there for her friend, she is asserting her difference.

Many of us say nothing when we're upset with a friend, particularly if we feel envious or competitive. We believe we're not entitled to these feelings; we believe women should be morally superior. Sometimes, we are literally afraid to tell a friend what's bothering us; we rehearse it in our heads, but lose our courage when the moment arises. *It sounds so trivial. I don't want to make her mad. I don't want her to think I'm not a nice person.* We shy away from standing up for ourselves and discussing our differences, and wind up feeling hurt, resentful, and put-upon.

The mantle of virtue is, in reality, a straitjacket that prevents us from expressing our true feelings, some of which are not very virtuous or positive. Trying to wish them away, however, seems to have the curious effect of doubling their destructive power. They fester inside us and, when they surface, are expressed in subtle, indirect ways that may be more harmful to our friends because they are so insidious.

Yet we cling to our strategies of appeasement and covert competition to avoid openly acknowledging differences and to preserve our image of ourselves as intimacy experts: supportive, caring, other-directed. Female friendship is supposed to provide a refuge from the cut-throat world of competition, and many of us are prepared to do just about anything to maintain the illusion that our closeness is entirely unproblematic.

We find it easy to yell "Go, girl!" when a friend is striving for something that doesn't threaten our relationship with her or our own sense of ourselves as individuals. But we find it more difficult to call out encouragement if it seems that she is moving away from us, passing us by, or getting something that we desperately want for ourselves. There's nothing wrong with these feelings — if anything, they indicate just how deep our sense of connection and identification with each other is — but we feel we have to pretend that we are above envy, anger, "selfish" desires, and "unfriendly" longings. And this requires that we also damp down qualities that women possess in abundance, like ambition and a desire to be separate enough that we can do our personal best without feeling compelled to apologize and without worrying that someone else's feelings may be hurt.

Our ways of coping with competition not only complicate our friendships; they also fail, utterly, to prepare us for situations where we *need* to compete with other women in order to survive — namely, at work. It is in our working relationships with other women that we can see most clearly just how dangerous and self-defeating our attempts to conceal competition really are.

Nadine's first real job was at a television station in a city not far from the suburb where she grew up. By the time she was twenty-six, she'd worked her way up from a position as a glorified gofer to that of a producer on the nightly newscast. The station was small enough that she had a lot of independence and as much responsibility as she cared to take on. It was the perfect job for an eager, ambitious person who wanted to learn the ropes quickly, and for the first year she loved it. "Then our star reporter, who was a really solid journalist and great to work with, got a job at a bigger station. We hired someone from out of state to fill his slot: Sharon," Nadine says with a grimace. "To this day, just saying her name makes me feel queasy."

At first, Nadine viewed Sharon as a welcome addition to the newsroom. She had an impressive résumé, and had at one point worked in New York City, which was Nadine's own dream. She hoped she could learn something from Sharon, but quite apart from that, she was glad there was going to be another woman around the place. Sometimes Nadine had the impression that her boss and the managers of the station didn't really listen to her the way they did to her male co-workers. There was nothing specific she could cite as evidence of discrimination; it was just a feeling she got sometimes, like she had to yell at the top of her lungs to be heard. Sharon was a no-nonsense forty-year-old with a crisp manner and an air of vigilance; she was the kind of woman who made it clear from the outset that she wouldn't take crap from any man. Nadine was looking forward to working with her, and entertained visions of the two of them going out after hours for drinks and shop talk.

As it happened, Sharon was ambitious and had a taste for the same kinds of stories that Nadine herself was drawn to, so they worked closely together almost from the start. Nadine's job was to oversee and edit Sharon's segments on the newscast; although she wasn't Sharon's boss, and although technically they were working in tandem, Nadine still saw herself as the one who was, ultimately, in charge.

Within a few weeks, she had reached a disappointing conclusion: Sharon needed more help than all the other reporters combined.

"To be fair, she was very good at spot reporting. She was great at covering fires, for instance, because she was fearless and kept her head in an emergency. She also had a ton of energy and no real life outside of work, so she'd work long hours," Nadine says. "But it was all quantity, no quality when it came to the kinds of in-depth, complicated stories that she really wanted to do. She made mistakes constantly — confusing local and federal politicians, getting the facts of a story dead wrong — huge ones that could've got both of us fired if I hadn't caught them."

But Sharon was a seasoned veteran. How could Nadine, a twenty-six-year-old in her first real job, give her a talking to? She couldn't, she decided, and tried to correct the mistakes with oh-by-the-way breeziness, as though they were minor errors that anyone could make. "No big deal," became her stock phrase with Sharon, just as it was with her best friend back home. And, as she did with Wendy, Nadine felt she had to apologize to Sharon for her own talent. "You're from out of state, you couldn't be expected to know," Nadine would say after rescuing her from another blunder. "The only reason I know that is because I grew up around here."

Even though she wasn't overly impressed with Sharon's work, she wanted Sharon to like her. She certainly didn't want Sharon to think that she was hyper-critical or bitchy. So Nadine tried to administer her corrections gently and apologetically, and threw in plenty of self-deprecation for good measure. Nevertheless, it was clear that Sharon viewed her help as an unwanted intrusion. It was also clear that she was less than pleased to be taking instruction from a considerably younger producer, and didn't view Nadine as her equal.

Nadine figured this was really her problem. She'd deferred to Sharon because she was older, and hadn't worked hard enough to win her respect. "I thought if we could deal with each other on a strictly professional basis, the age difference would cease to be an issue," she says. "If she respected me, we could work on her weaknesses and I wouldn't have to double-check her work all the time."

So Nadine began casually dropping references to her credentials and her experience into conversations with Sharon, and tried to match her crisp, all-business manner while remaining friendly. She clipped articles that would help bring Sharon up to speed on local affairs, leaving them on her desk with little notes: "Thought you might be interested in this," or simply, "FYI." But Sharon merely pushed the clippings to one side, and never gave any indication that she'd actually read them.

In fact, Nadine's attempts to impress her with her own professionalism seemed to amuse Sharon, who responded with patronizing little swipes, often in front of colleagues. Once, when Nadine made a passing reference to President Kennedy, Sharon interrupted theatrically, "Wait — you know who he is? But you weren't even born yet." It sounded like a joke, and it got a laugh from the others, but Nadine felt as though she'd been slapped. Another time, when Nadine walked into a meeting wearing a new suit, Sharon cooed, "Nice suit. You could pass for nineteen today."

"The irony was that Sharon was supposedly this big feminist, and if a man had made the same remarks she would've been screaming 'Harassment!'" Nadine says. "When a man treats you like a twelve-year-old and is totally disrespectful, it's called sexism and you know what to do about it. But women aren't supposed to act like that, so I didn't know how to respond."

She dismissed the idea of telling her boss about the problems she was having with Sharon: "He was very old-school and wouldn't have been sympathetic." He was also of Sharon's vintage and might, Nadine worried, take Sharon's side automatically. Anyway, Sharon had made her self-conscious enough about her age that she didn't want to do anything that could be construed as immature or incompetent. "I thought if I said something, people would think that I was the one who had the problem, not her," Nadine remembers.

There were other reporters, and two other producers for that matter, but Nadine and Sharon seemed to wind up working together — or at cross-purposes — too frequently for either of their tastes. "She was a thorn in my side, but it was bearable," says Nadine.

She forgot all about her mounting irritation and anxiety, however, when she finally got the go-ahead to do a project she'd been lobbying for almost since her first day as a producer: a series on the region's health care system. It was a meaty topic, politically important in an election year, and a chance for her to make her mark. She saw it as a stepping-stone to New York, the kind of thing she could proudly show potential employers, and she'd long since decided which reporter she wanted to work with — Jack, who was both smart and methodical, but lacked initiative and preferred to let someone else be in charge. He was a perennially single man in his thirties, the kind of guy who lacked confidence with women and was only too happy to let a pretty young producer tell him what to do.

Nadine was completely unprepared for her boss to veto her choice. "Sharon's going to do it. She really wants it," he said. Nadine mumbled something about thinking that Jack was better qualified to handle the story, but her boss cut her off with an impatient wave of his hand.

"Sharon's been here four months. She's proved herself, she's hungry, and she's the one I want," he barked. Nadine found herself obediently scurrying out of his office without saying a word about the fact that she'd been covering up for Sharon or that Sharon refused to accept authority, least of all from her. Telling her boss that she couldn't work with Sharon might make him question her own skills. Besides, she didn't want to appear to be tattling or whining, and she certainly didn't want to seem like the kind of woman who has problems getting along with other women.

After work, one stiff drink later, she silently listed all the pluses she could think of: she'd been researching health care for months and knew just what she wanted to do, Sharon would be grateful for the opportunity to sink her teeth into a big story and would quickly realize that she needed all the help she could get, this could be the perfect opportunity to improve their working relationship. "All right," Nadine said to herself, attempting pluckiness. "I'll look at this as a challenge. I'm just going to have to set the tone right from the start, be firm but fair, show her I'm in charge."

She initiated this new policy the next morning by suggesting that Sharon watch a series that the station had aired the previous year. "And why would I want to do that?" Sharon bristled. Nadine tried to stand her ground, replying that the series had been good, viewers had liked it, and it might give them some ideas. She was particularly proud of the way she'd phrased the last part — "it might give us some ideas" — since she'd really wanted to say, "Look, Sharon, you're in way over your head. Thank God I have enough ideas for both of us." Nadine was still congratulating herself on her restraint and tact when Sharon snapped, "I've been in this business almost twenty years — much longer than you. I know what I'm doing."

But she didn't, according to Nadine. "We'd hammer out what she was supposed to do, and then she just wouldn't do it. She'd go out to talk to a hospital CEO but come back with a sappy segment on candy stripers," she remembers. "And she couldn't write. This was supposed to be investigative journalism, but her style was like something out of a romance novel."

Nadine would try to find something to praise, then would attempt to steer Sharon back to first principles: this was intended to be a hard-hitting, hard news series. Sharon would seem vaguely interested, would nod her head, and would not change a word. "It turned into a turf war," says Nadine. "But she didn't have a clear idea of what she wanted to do, and even if she had, she wouldn't have been able to do it without me cleaning up after her."

Nadine was developing a permanent knot in her stomach. This was supposed to be *her* series, her big chance. They missed one deadline and then two, and she became increasingly frantic. Her own reputation was on the line.

But she literally could not talk to Sharon about their professional relationship. Nadine would start conversations feeling confident and self-righteous, but somehow Sharon managed to intimidate her out of standing her ground. Sharon would raise an eyebrow or deliver an arch put-down, and Nadine would retreat, feeling furious but also feeling that she shouldn't hit back.

Nadine felt that she was constantly under attack, defending herself against Sharon's animosity. She had less respect than ever for Sharon, and was in fact coming to the conclusion that Sharon was a thoroughly unpleasant human being, but Nadine was trying harder than ever to win her favor. It really bothered her that Sharon didn't like her, so much so that she found herself courting Sharon's pity just as she sometimes did with Wendy. "I had the worst fight with my boyfriend last night," Nadine said once, to cover for the fact that she was so anxious her hands were shaking. Another time, she invoked an external enemy in an attempt to create a closer connection, which was a tactic that had always worked with Heather. "If only everyone else would leave us alone," Nadine said to Sharon, "I just know we could get through this. These deadlines are so unfair!"

Sharon was unmoved, and if anything, seemed to resent these attempts to win her sympathy. But Nadine hid her mounting panic about the series and kept trying to be nice, until, one desperate evening, she finally sat down and rewrote all the scripts herself. She couldn't even muster the courage to tell Sharon what she'd done, just left the scripts on her desk and came into the newsroom the next morning, her heart pounding wildly, expecting to face a massive explosion.

Something worse happened: Sharon gave her the silent treatment. She simply wouldn't speak, not even when Nadine was directly addressing her. "It was ludicrous, because we were supposed to be working together but we couldn't even have a conversation," Nadine recalls.

At the time, however, she was embarrassed and humiliated, and worried that others would read Sharon's silence as an indication that she herself had done something unspeakable. Even though she felt something not unlike hatred for Sharon, she couldn't bear the thought that Sharon might feel the same way about her. It seemed so unjust to Nadine. *I really am a nice person, and I've tried very hard — why doesn't she like me?* Nadine was mortified by Sharon's silence, and tried to make it up to her by using some of the least awful segments of footage that Sharon had seemed particularly proud of, and in return, she got a few grudging words out of her. This encouraged her to include even more of Sharon's work, but rather than feeling manipulated, Nadine felt all the more guilty about her own behavior.

"Why am I being so territorial?" she asked herself. "This should be collaborative, I *should* be using some of her ideas." Sharon was competitive, just like Wendy, and Nadine should have recognized it sooner and tried to avoid competition. Now, she had to soothe Sharon's wounded feelings; it never occurred to Nadine that she herself had been competing. Nor did it occur to her that now, she was competing downward, selling out her series and her own ambition in order to lay claim to the title of "nicer person." The more ground she yielded, the more amicable Sharon became, and when they finally wrapped up the series, they were on speaking terms again. Yes, it was still tense, but they'd found a compromise.

The night the first segment aired, however, Nadine watched it with growing horror. Somehow, she had deluded herself in the editing suite that it would look better, be less of a hopeless mishmash, when it was actually broadcast. She'd been wrong. "Compared to what I wanted it to be and what it could have been, it was a disaster," she says. It certainly wasn't anything she could use to line up a new job in New York. If anything, it seemed to make her hold on her current job somewhat less certain. "That was one time when I called Wendy and told her everything. She was great, totally outraged on my behalf. We psychoanalyzed Sharon for hours that night, but I already knew what the problem was: she couldn't stand the fact that I was younger, more talented, and in a position where I had some authority over her."

As far as Nadine was concerned, the problem between them was entirely personal, not professional. Sharon had a vendetta against her. Sharon was competitive — just look at the way she reacted to Nadine's popularity with men. "She'd make cracks about men phoning me — 'I'm surprised you have time to do any work' — and insinuate that I got my job because of my looks," Nadine says. "It was weird, because she was the on-camera person, so her physical appearance *was* a criterion when she was hired. Producers can look like trolls and it doesn't matter."

On one level, however, she understood perfectly well why Sharon was "frantic about aging": television news is a hostile environment for women over thirty-five, unless they're at the very top of the career ladder. Sharon had good reason to worry that her age was a liability, and she had good reason to be obsessed about her own looks.

"But I didn't want her job and tried to make it clear that we were both on the same side, fighting the same fight," Nadine protests. "She got mad that I presumed to be her equal when I was younger and had things easier than she did. She gave me a lecture about how her generation had opened the door for women, like I personally owed her one and should be down on my hands and knees thanking her for my job. Meanwhile, I was bailing her out all the time."

Nadine was irritated by Sharon's "lack of generosity." In her view, Sharon should have been glad that other women were coming up through the ranks and didn't have to fight so hard, and should have been happy that there were finally some female producers. "But she didn't want me to have it easier," Nadine says, still amazed. "She wanted me to suffer like she had."

They were both women — shouldn't they be sticking together? "For a long time I just rationalized her behavior and excused it, on the grounds that she felt threatened, she was worried about her age, TV is unfair to women, et cetera," says Nadine. "Talking to my boss or the station manager seemed like crossing into the enemy camp."

Sharon, however, was not burdened with a similar sense of gender solidarity, as Nadine discovered when she had a severe asthma attack. They were in the state capitol covering a gubernatorial campaign, and even as Nadine was fighting for breath, Sharon's main reaction was that this was a personal inconvenience, not to mention highly unprofessional. "While I was in the emergency room thinking, 'This is it, I'm going to die,' she was on the phone with my boss, saying that I couldn't handle stress and was so handicapped that I shouldn't be allowed to work on breaking stories," Nadine says. "She actually hinted that I should be fired because I had an asthma attack!"

It was the last straw. "It had got so bad that I felt sick to my stomach on Sunday nights when I thought about having to face her the next morning," she recalls. She'd reached the point of thinking, Who needs this? And more generally, Who needs the aggravation of working in a collaborative medium? She started looking for a job in print journalism.

Before the 1960s, it was well known that women viewed each other with a certain amount of suspicion and hostility, because they were vying for the same prize: a man, who was the only route to economic security and social position. The feminist fiat — sisterhood is powerful — changed the focus; the real enemy was not another woman but the patriarchy. Feminism provided a brand-new perspective on competition: it is a patriarchal, divide-and-conquer strategy designed to keep women weak and isolated from one another. Competition pits women against each other in a struggle to please men (an arrangement whose only real beneficiaries are male) and thus prevents women from uniting to demand control of power, resources, and their own lives. The main tenet of sisterhood is that women must look to each other for salvation, not competition.

The rhetoric of sisterhood bears the stamp of the particular historical moment during which it developed, when women were shut out of the citadels of power and the commonality of their interests was easy to perceive. There was so much ground to be gained — in terms of reproductive rights, equal pay, equal opportunities, and equal protections under the law — and so much evident discrimination that it did not seem overly simplistic to say that whatever the differences between individual women, they were, as a class, all in the same disadvantaged position.

The betrayed wife and the Other Woman, the bored suburban matron and the impoverished welfare mother, the harassed secretary and the adored actress — all were manacled in the prison of second-class citizenship, dependent on the same fickle master. The notion that one woman's new dinette set was another's grievance was part of the whole incredible scam the patriarchy had devised to keep women anxious to please men, who had all the resources, rewards, and power. *Don't you see?* feminists prodded, and many women who were accustomed to viewing other women as rivals suddenly *did* see: they had been fighting the wrong enemy.

The feminist movement was envisaged as a sort of demilitarized zone in the war against oppression, a place where women could lay down their weapons for a while and embrace one another as fellow freedom fighters. Feminist psychology held out the promise that women, with their talent for empathy and nurturing, would not jockey for position or hoard the spoils as men were wont to do. Competition was deemed a "masculine" behavior, and condemned as aggressive; inequity and the hierarchical organization of power were remnants of the patriarchy. When women ruled, they would do so collectively. Women were going to abolish the cut-throat ethic of capitalist competition; sisterhood demanded nothing less than a wholesale revolution.

Feminism provided the rationale and language for female bonding, and consciousness-raising groups encouraged women to strengthen their bonds by talking freely about what had previously been considered isolated, private difficulties. "I'm not alone, it's not just me," women were elated to discover, as they uncovered a pattern of sexual politics that revealed their oppression not just as individuals, but as a group. Women could see how much they had in common with one another, and how many of their problems were caused by individual men or by a male-dominated society. The personal was political in more ways than one: not only did individual difficulties point to larger social inequalities, but women's personal connections could be used to effect political change. Men were the problem, and other women were the solution.

Most feminists did not, however, anticipate serious political disagreement among women, and when it appeared, tended to cast it in terms of disloyalty. *You're either for us or against us.* Today, when prominent feminists disagree on key points, they frequently dismiss one another's views as anti-feminist. Women of color accuse white women of selling out the cause and vice versa, and anti-porn feminists dismiss anti-censorship feminists as "collaborators in oppression," who retaliate by calling them small-minded prudes. Christina Hoff Sommers, author of *Who Stole Feminism?*, accuses "ideologues" like Susan Faludi of promulgating a "divisive and resentful philosophy [that] adds to the woes of our society and hurts legitimate feminism."[1] Faludi, author of *Backlash*, lashes back with charges that Sommers and others of her ilk are "faux feminists" and "pseudofeminists" who "favor advances not for other women but for themselves."[2]

These debates are really about ideas — the mandate of feminism, the future of the movement — but often take the form of personal attacks or are interpreted by the participants as such. Disputes over goals and strategies frequently have a strong flavor of moral intimidation.

Agree with me — or you're not a real sister. Won't take my side? Obviously you don't care about other women as much as I do. Faludi's charges are instructive in this respect; the reason "faux feminists" contradict her is not that they have their own opinions, but that they are not as selfless, caring, or morally superior as she is. They want things not for other women, but for themselves.

Such criticisms can be and often are deeply wounding, because one is being accused not merely of political betrayal — false consciousness — but of personal failure to perform the duties prescribed for women by the sexual script: care, share, empathize, cooperate. In feminist circles, the term "anti-feminist" is a powerful insult, whether hurled from the left, right, or center of the movement, because it suggests not just political transgressions but personal and moral ones. One has committed the unforgivable crime of daring to differ. "Selling out the sisterhood" can mean only one thing: siding with those morally inferior men.

Although feminism forged the tools for fighting with individual men and for protesting systemic discrimination, it has constructed no armor to deflect the blows of women who aren't feeling too sisterly. Sisterhood is about solidarity, and very few feminists foresaw that having more important things than men to compete for — like ideas, power, resources, and the mantle of leadership — would create less rather than more cooperation, or that the persistent denial that competition exists has the curious effect of doubling its potential for destruction. Competitive feelings can be driven underground, but there they simply build up, and either eat away at us or erupt in passive-aggressive explosions that we try to mask with concern.

Today, the yawning gap between rhetoric and reality is most visible in the workplace, where women talk about sisterhood yet frequently practice sibling rivalry. Feminism has taught us to see one another only in terms of selfless friendship, so we are blindsided, again and again, when it turns out that in fact we are colleagues first and comrades second. Direct competition, which is inevitable when people are working together and their performance will be compared, takes on the character of an epic struggle when not only relative merits but the moral obligations of sisterhood appear to be at stake. This is why it hurts most to lose to another woman: the competition seems personal as well as professional.

"Behavior that, in a more neutral 'other,' might be understood and forgiven as ordinary self-protection, perhaps even healthy competition, is recast as unforgivable hostility," write Evelyn Fox Keller and Helene Moglen in a 1987 essay on competition among women academics. "The dream of harmonious sisterhood has not vanished, but neither has it softened the edge of sisterly rivalry when conflict and competition do erupt. Indeed, in some ways, it seems to make it worse. Competition denied in principle, but unavoidable in practice, surfaces in forms that may be far more wounding, and perhaps even fiercer and more destructive, than competition that is ideologically sanctioned."[3]

And the winner — even when the fight has been fair and, at least on the surface, friendly — cannot help but fear that there will be a price to pay: the disruption of female bonding, the ultimate punishment of being treated like a man.

This fear is justified, because when a woman does get real power, she is often studied suspiciously: Does she fight for other women? Would she loan you her blazer if, say, you had a job interview and you really, really needed it? If she fails these tests — think of Margaret Thatcher or Leona Helmsley — it is often said that she has sold out to the masculine power structure, which implies that if only the structure could be changed, she would behave less like a man and more like a woman. What is more likely, however, is that if the playing field between the sexes were completely level, there would be more rather than fewer Thatchers and Helmsleys.

The playing field will not be level so long as we continue to live in a society in which a man's willingness to change a diaper once in a while is hailed as heroism. But the position of women *has* changed, radically, and what has become evident is that the nurturant empathy women are said to possess is less a function of gender than of circumstance. Numerous studies show that when women are assigned the role of "boss" or "leader" in experiments, they conform to masculine stereotypes: "express[ing] more direct hostility toward the low-power group, less covert, indirect hostility, and less anxiety than low-power groups of either sex."[4] Even women's body language and voices change: more direct eye contact, more authoritative orders, fewer questions, and fewer supportive and affirming comments.[5]

People who have power do not have to, and often cannot afford to, concern themselves with currying favor, and people who negotiate from a position of strength need not worry so much about being nice. Women who make it to the corner office don't get there because they took a wrong turn somewhere, or because they waited for rewards to drop from the sky, drawing no attention to themselves and being unfailingly nice to the little people. A certain degree of single-minded aggression is necessary to get ahead in most professions — and to succeed academically, to be heard in a discussion, to compete in a sport, and to raise children.

Yet maintaining the myth of sisterhood requires that women continue to denigrate competition, continue to believe that they are morally superior to men, and continue to locate their sense of solidarity in oppression, with its diplomacy of one-downmanship. Clearly, this was a recipe for self-sabotage for Nadine, who made the crucial error of thinking that if she could only make Sharon like her, Sharon would stop competing with her. Nadine was prepared to do anything to placate Sharon, short of confronting the issues between them head-on and openly competing herself. Ultimately, she was more concerned about being liked than about doing her job well, and she had learned the lessons of sisterhood so well that she refused to shore up her own position by appealing to her boss, largely because he was male. She behaved like a sister, and wound up with one wrecked series, the beginnings of an ulcer, and the feeling that she had to quit her job.

Sharon was the co-worker from hell, but it is also true that for every time she undercut Nadine, Nadine undercut herself. Conflict between women of different ages is a common theme in the office, where frequently two or three generations of women, each with its own set of expectations and unique claims to oppression, must work together. Sharon clearly felt that she'd had it much harder than Nadine and wasn't about to do her any favors, particularly not when she viewed younger women as a threat to her own livelihood. Nadine, for her part, felt that Sharon should act as her mentor, providing tips on job-hunting in New York and applauding vigorously as she ran up a ladder that had taken Sharon many years to climb.

The oldest generation of women in the workplace fought in the front lines for employment equity; having fought so hard and so long, some of them may quite naturally feel that they are under no obligation to bend over backwards to help women who have had it much easier. The youngest generation of women in the workplace are victims of demographic misfortune; more doors are open to them as women, but many cannot find work because the economy has changed and baby boomers appear to have a stranglehold on all the good jobs. The middle generation of women have their own problems; many of them put off having children in order to focus on their careers, and now find that it's still extremely difficult to combine family and work. They look ahead and see older women who were "lucky" enough to have kids first and then enter the workforce; they look back and see hungry young women who appear to have it all and are ready to take what they have, too, given half a chance.

Each generation has its own particular anxieties, and they can erupt into full-fledged hostility in the office, particularly when the combatants are women who have never learned how to compete openly for success. The most common reaction still seems to be the one we learn in our friendships: scramble for common ground, and affirm our solidarity by turning all our negative feelings outward, toward men. This can become "an oppression derby"[6] that no woman can truly win.

It is odd that we do not question why vying for the title of most oppressed reinforces our sense of solidarity, but competing to succeed threatens our feeling of collectivity. The problem is not simply scarcity of resources, although the world could certainly use a few more good men and good jobs. Nor is the problem a fear of success; the strong undertow of envy in many women's friendships is clear evidence of the size of our ambitions and the strength of our desires. The real issue is that we fear that if we achieve more or have more than other women, we will lose our connections with them, because the contract of female solidarity is an implicit pledge to remain equal and to remain the same.

The rhetoric of sisterhood exhorts us to stick together, and the feminization of intimacy tells us that our way of connecting is not just the right way, but the only way. We're the best of friends, and we should view our female colleagues as our girlfriends.

A lack of power has been confused with a sense of connection. You can call men's conversational style "report-talk," as Deborah Tannen does, and argue that it creates an appalling deficit of emotional bonds, as Carol Gilligan does. Or you can call it the "language of the powerful," as linguist Robin Lakoff does. In *Talking Power* she argues, "Women's language developed as a way of surviving and even flourishing without control over economic, physical, or social reality. Then it is necessary to listen more than speak, agree more than confront, be delicate, be indirect."[7]

It is, in short, the language of appeasement and inaction. It's understandable, given women's history of oppression, that this mode of communication developed. What is incomprehensible, particularly since feminism instructs us to adopt a confrontational tone with men, is that we are told that this is the right way to talk to each other. Politically, competition is portrayed as inimical to the ideals of sisterhood; personally, it is understood as inimical to female moral superiority. This is why even the most competitive women are loath to own competition and express it in positive terms of trying to do their best, or trying to challenge other women. More commonly, we view ourselves as innocent of competition, as though it were a criminal act, and blame other women for it. *She's the one who's competitive — the problem lies entirely with her.*

The cult of connection imposes a separate and unequal moral standard for women's behavior that seriously hinders us both in professional situations and in personal relationships. Insisting that women are different — better — than men requires us to prove it not by encouraging each other to be independent but by clinging to one another and insisting that we are the same. Real autonomy means being tough enough to take criticism and to give it, confident enough to speak up and disagree, friendly enough to compete openly, and compassionate enough to forgive in each other the things we so readily forgive in men.

If we can take on men, but we cannot challenge one another, it is hard to see how this makes us stronger. In fact, all the support and agreement we get in our friendships seems to make us weaker in one important respect: we have enormous difficulty coping with criticism from other women, particularly on the job. It feels like a personal attack. "Why doesn't she like me?" we ask, cut to the quick. "Why is she so *competitive?*"

Ultimately, women's allegedly greater capacity for connection is no cause for celebration if it renders us incapable of viewing competition as a challenge to do our best, and disables us when we most need to compete. We find it extremely difficult to separate our professional and personal identities, which can mean we wind up as office martyrs — or wind up not knowing where to draw the line for ourselves when it comes to our other co-workers: men.

Chapter Three

Potent Pleasures

Elaine has corporate-cut sandy hair, startlingly green eyes, and a preference for flowing wide-legged pants that create the illusion of height and are forgiving to the figure. She looks like the wise-cracking best friend of the heroine in a Hollywood movie, the sensible one with the good personality.

She is sitting on the sofa, legs tucked beneath her, studying the curve of Bill's back as he hunches over a stack of papers. He is poised like a parenthesis waiting to be filled in, not turning a page or writing anything either, so Elaine asks, "Should I make some coffee?" Her voice is soft and her tone is the lilting one that women use to soothe babies and placate husbands, but Bill jolts, his trademark shake of irritation, and snaps, "Yes. Coffee." No "please," no "darling," no "I-know-you've-had-a-hard-day-too."

Snapping back, however, is not Elaine's way. Like many couples, she and Bill have long since divided up roles in a wordless agreement: you be hot-tempered and I'll be calm, you be sentimental and I'll be down to earth. You snap, and I'll be the one who holds her tongue but whacks the spoon down on the counter and slams the refrigerator door so emphatically that the rattle of bottles echoes down the hall. Bill hears this, of course, knows very well what it means, and is already penitent by the time she returns with the coffee. He pulls her close, muffling his face into her pink blouse, and she stares out through the window into the darkness. She is wishing it were Friday night, instead of only Wednesday, in which case they could make love right here, right now, and afterwards she could sink into a hot bath and doze until the skin on her fingertips contracted into raised, white ridges.

Too soon Bill breaks the mood, pulling away to announce, "The client is going to walk." The self-importance of his despair annoys Elaine, who is ready to say, "Forget the client. What about me?" But she looks at his face and sees fear there, so she swallows her irritation, rubs his shoulders, and asks if there is anything she can do.

Bill shakes his head. There's nothing anyone can do. Tomorrow morning he is going to walk into the boardroom and present a strategy for the launch of his biggest client's newest product, and then he is going to be fired. "It's not a strategy — it's a suicide plan," he says.

He cannot believe that he let himself get caught up stamping out fires all over the office and trusted that cretin Jim to do a credible job. Not that Bill had had much choice, given the endless subterfuge and jockeying for position with the other vice-presidents. Still, it was his ass on the line, and he should have been paying more attention as the strategy was being developed, should've been more than half listening when Jim droned on in the planning meetings. But Bill had been so impatient to get back to finding out what the hell was going on behind the closed doors in the president's suite that he'd said, "Fine, fine, go ahead, sounds like we're on the right track" — and really, he had to give himself this much credit, everything *had* seemed fine. How could he have known that the day before he was going to present to the client — his most important client, he might add, his millions-in-annual-billings client — another goddamn advertising agency would steal their market niche right out from under them?

He soliloquizes, blaming and then absolving himself, while Elaine nods and makes sympathetic noises and thinks very hard. She purses her lips and cocks her head to one side when she's concentrating, which makes her look a little like an owl, or so Bill said a few weeks ago. That's his new pet name for her: Owl. Elaine likes it a lot better than some of the others — sweetie, baby, honeybunch — partly because it's not generic, but mostly because it connotes wisdom. She does not tell Bill that she saw a nature show on owls once that portrayed them as vicious, slightly stupid creatures.

"Tell me the strategy," she says now, and Bill reels off the focus group numbers, the consumer research, and the marketing data. (If I named the product, you would recognize it and Bill's peers might recognize him; let's say it's fruit juice, which is not far from the truth.) Then he explains the whole sorry reasoning behind the decision to target the teen market with an advertising strategy based on the premise that all-natural fruit juice can lead to unnatural and downright sexy good times. Actually, it wasn't a bad idea until the new ads for a competitor's fruit-flavored soda were launched today, with an identical theme.

What Bill does not say, does not have to say, is that his last marketing strategy for this particular client had been less than a rousing success. Elaine could hardly forget how proud he'd been of his plan for repositioning one of their established-but-unexciting product lines, or how he'd flailed around in disbelief when the new campaign was launched and sales of these same products actually started to decline slightly, at which point the new ads were hastily yanked. One evening while this disaster was unfolding, she was in the midst of delivering a stand-by-your-man pep talk — *I'm sure it's not as bad as you think* — when Bill cut her short, saying, "Honey, I shrunk the sales." He is a compulsive phrase-maker and pundit, and Elaine loves this about him but it bothers her, too. Bill has a half cornball, half apocalyptic way of dramatizing every situation.

But he isn't doing that now, so she knows just how serious his predicament must be. No amount of hand-holding and stroking from the president of the agency will mollify the client if Bill delivers another dud; the client won't put up with it, not when other ad agencies are coming courting, and neither will Bill's boss.

So Elaine stands there in her stocking feet, massaging his shoulders and thinking hard about fruit juice, who drinks fruit juice, who could be made to drink the stuff. Marketing data, focus groups, fancy research — all that is just hocus-pocus make-work as far as she's concerned. You don't need to be a rocket scientist to figure out how to sell a citrus beverage, she thinks, you just need some common sense. Elaine is the pragmatist.

Bill is the idealist. His great gift is his ability to rise above the products, to see beyond the detergent and potato chips to the higher purpose: creating demand. He can make people want things, want them so much they rush to the supermarket singing his jingles and repeating his promises as though they are statements of fact. He can take an everyday thing like shampoo and invest it with the hint of salvation, so that a housewife in Des Moines pulls it from the shelf believing her whole life is about to change. His unseen hand stretches out from Madison Avenue to every home in America, holding out sodas and deodorants and toothpastes, inciting desire. This is, at any rate, the way Bill talks about himself when he has a few whiskeys in him. But he is not a cynic. He genuinely believes he is creating the best of all possible worlds, a world where people find hope at the mall. Elaine loves this about him — at least now she does, although she will come to suspect that it is a character flaw and a trick. But that is later.

Now, she is pulling up a chair beside Bill and talking off the top of her head, free-associating about teenagers, how they want to rebel and conform at the same time, how fruit juice could be a metaphor for that paradox. She is saying anything that crosses her mind, however silly, because she has no illusions about advertising or higher purposes. When there's work to be done, Elaine rolls up her sleeves and gets on with it. She is the person you would want around if your house was a mess and guests were headed up the front walk. She would not complain, get flustered, or ask what to do next; she would start pushing things under the couch and throwing together a cheese plate. And Bill loves this about her, her cheerful, no-nonsense efficiency, although he will come to resent her practicality and see it as a form of heartlessness. But that is all in the future.

Now, Bill has nothing left to lose, not when the only other option is presenting a strategy tomorrow morning that will seem like a lame copy of the competitor's brand-new campaign. So, although he said that no one could possibly help at this late stage, he does listen to Elaine and he does start bouncing ideas back and forth with her, halfheartedly at first but then with more urgency. He is hopped up on caffeine and last-minute desperation when it comes to him like a revelation: a strategy for positioning the product that is so deceptively simple, it has to be the right one. It's a thing of beauty, this idea, so surefire that even without fancy graphics and laminated charts, he could weave a spell that would send the client reeling from the boardroom the next morning.

Bill barks out "Yes!" and flops down over the table like a runner throwing his body across the finish line. But then he's up again, talking a blue streak, grabbing Elaine and kissing her so hard she forgets for a moment that she didn't make it to the dry cleaner and God only knows if she has anything clean to wear tomorrow.

"Are you going to work much longer?" she asks when he stops scribbling notes, which can be read as a straight question or as something more suggestive, because there is a definite invitation in her voice. But Bill chooses door number one. He is going to stay up and hammer out a report that he can give to Jim in the morning, and he plans to enjoy watching that puppy scamper around, setting the document in color type and groveling for forgiveness. Jim's naked ambition has cost Bill some sleep lately; this will show that upstart who's the boss. And then at ten a.m., the copies will be passed around the boardroom, shimmering and still warm.

"Revenge," Bill says, "is a dish best served hot off the presses." Well, it's easy to love him when he's punch drunk, and there may still be time for a quick bath. "I'll let you get on with it, then," Elaine says, kissing the top of his head and leaving the faintest smudge of coral lipstick on his shiny, balding crown. He is already at his computer, tapping away and straining forward in his chair, too absorbed to say anything more than a distracted good night.

But she feels the exaltation of having been present at the creation and the secret, swelling pride of having rescued him — the vice-president, the group account director — from certain disaster. It is quite a feat for a thirty-year-old junior employee to pull her forty-nine-year-old boss from the flames, and Elaine's heart is so full she practically floats out of his office and down to the street to hail a taxi. She feels good enough that she doesn't think even once about later that night, when Bill will take off his glasses and fumble blindly into bed, the endearing, mole-like way he always does, and his wife will turn to him, opening her arms to receive him into sleep.

When we think about sex in the office in the 1990s, we tend to think of men who demand blow jobs in return for real jobs, men who proposition women colleagues and grab at them and talk dirty. In the public discourse there is an explicit assumption: sex would cease to be an issue in the workplace if only men would get the message. Men, those perennial frat boys who never quite grow up, are the problem.

Lamentably, there is some truth to this. Some men do not seem to get it: chronic sexual innuendo creates an atmosphere that is at best uncomfortable for women and at worst extremely intimidating; offers of rewards in return for sexual services are an unconscionable violation of workplace ethics and women's rights. Sexual harassment is demeaning, it can be threatening, and it almost always interferes with a woman's ability to do her best at her job. For far too many years, men got away with treating women like sexual playthings instead of as respected colleagues and employees — and some men are *still* getting away with it.

The women most at risk for harassment are, not coincidentally, those least able to counter it: illegal immigrants, nannies and housecleaners, unskilled single mothers who are the sole support for their families, and women in low-paying jobs that require little education or training. It is absurd to argue, as some conservative commentators do, that a woman with few marketable skills and no other employment options can, without risking her job, issue a cease-and-desist order to a higher-ranked man who talks a blue streak or paws at her body. Equally absurd is the notion that her male supervisors live in terror of being slapped with a lawsuit if they make an off-color joke; she is in no position to muster serious legal firepower even when hands-on harassment has occurred.

Critics who pooh-pooh the seriousness of sexual harassment betray their ignorance of the world that many women inhabit, where land-lords in low-rent buildings grope tenants, where managers in fast-food restaurants manhandle female employees, and where protesting either offense may result in a one-way trip to the homeless shelter. Class and, to a lesser extent, ethnicity and race are crucial determi-nants of a woman's ability to counter sexual harassment effectively — and increasingly, these factors also influence the likelihood that she will experience sexual harassment in the first place.

Middle-class, white-collar women are in the best position to bring sexual harassment charges, but even so, some risk ostracism within their professions, along with staggering legal bills and a good chance of losing in court. A legal triumph can be something of a Pyrrhic vic-tory; the woman may find herself branded a troublemaker and viewed as unpromotable, or even unemployable. Those women brave enough to seek legal redress for sexual harassment have, however, done the rest of us a tremendous service: employers are beginning to realize that harassment is bad for business, creates negative publicity, and can cost millions in legal fees and reparations. Some, particularly blue-chip, white-collar employers, are beginning to implement their own in-house policies and to dismiss offenders without having to be court-ordered or embarrassed into doing so.

As serious an offense as sexual harassment is, however, cases of un-wanted touching and no-sex-no-job threats are much rarer than in-stances of plain old sexism. For every woman who is hit on by the boss there are a hundred who feel they are ignored by the boss altogether: their suggestions and contributions in meetings go unrecognized, and they are passed over when it's time to hire, promote, and hand out raises. The woman on the street is far more concerned, and rightly so, about gender discrimination in the workplace. But, partly because other groups — blacks, gays, disabled people, visible minorities — also encounter employment discrimination, the public discourse on barri-ers to women's equality in the workplace has tended, particularly in the past ten years, to focus on sexual harassment, where women can make a unique claim.

This focus is at once too narrow and too broad. Sexual harass-ment is *not* the primary problem faced by women in the workplace;

discriminatory hiring practices, the absence of flexible policies for working parents, and the absurdly low pay in female-dominated job categories such as child care rank much higher on the list of most women's concerns. Furthermore, sexual harassment has been so broadly defined that it has become one of those catch-all, trigger phrases whose meaning is open to wildly different interpretations. Women in the military have invoked it to protest the predations of serial fondlers who seem to think that sexual assault is a prank; women in universities have invoked it to protest both the public display of artwork in which women are not fully clothed and the mention of certain words — "belly dancing," for example, or simply "sex" — in undergraduate lectures; one political candidate recently invoked it to protest a privately circulated cartoon in which a photo of her head was superimposed on a picture of a nude male body.[1]

When sexual harassment is defined as anything that creates "a hostile climate," its meaning becomes highly subjective. A comment that fifty people consider innocuous may strike one person with a highly developed sense of indignation as deeply offensive, and who can dispute her claim that she now feels her work environment is hostile? When harassment is loosely defined, the stage is set for high-minded censors to confuse sexuality with sexism and to conflate off-the-cuff remarks and outright threats. Sex, not harassment, can become the issue, and this is precisely what has happened in certain high-profile cases at the upper end of the socioeconomic scale, especially in universities.[2]

Quite rightly, this has raised serious concerns: Who should decide if a remark or a visual image is harmless or objectionable? What about free speech — how can we protect it if words result in lawsuits and if people become afraid to state their own opinions for fear of being charged with sexual harassment? And what about the rights of the accused to due process?

These questions are pressing and important, but they have also been overstated by many conservatives and certain prominent women commentators, who dismiss sexual harassment charges as the last refuge of thumb-sucking whiners. Pitched battles make good copy, and thus, in the media, the debate about sexual harassment gets more play than other gender issues in employment precisely because it tends to explode into highly quotable and telegenic shouting matches between extreme protectionists of women's delicate sensibilities and tough-talking skeptics who say that women are big girls now and need no protections at all.

In these debates, competing claims are made about women: women are fragile victims; women are strong enough to laugh it off when some bozo cracks a smutty joke or gets a little too friendly. These appear to be diametrically opposed positions, but underlying the overheated rhetoric of both sides is an unspoken, shared supposition: women are not sexual actors, but mere reactors. The issue is *male* sexuality in the workplace and how women should *react*: hire a lawyer, or take it in stride? Apparently, women automatically check their sexuality at the threshold of the workplace, as though it were an item of clothing that could be taken off and put back on again at will.

This notion that women do not have sexual agency, in either the boardroom or the bedroom, comes straight from the prevailing sexual script. The first kiss, the first date, the first time — men are the leaders in all these scenes in the sexual script, the ones who seize the moment, deliver the lines, make the moves, and push the limits. Their role is entirely active: pursuing, initiating, and conquering, all the while maintaining a constant lookout for new sexual opportunities. Women, on the other hand, are cast in a reactive role, as gatekeepers who restrict sexual opportunities and display little erotic desire. Female sexuality is, in this script, primarily defensive: women are the ones who set limits, beg off claiming headaches, and just say no — which isn't that difficult because what women really want, apparently, is love, not sex.

In the sexual script, women and men are at best complementary opposites and at worst outright antagonists, with different patterns of behavior, different sexual drives, desires, and agendas. Accordingly, the "happy ending" is really more like a negotiated truce: men give love to get sex, and women give sex to get love.

Men are from one planet, women from another. Men are aggressive, women are nurturing; men are competitive, women are cooperative. We have already seen how these descriptions of women's "nature" do not even begin to tell the whole story about who individual women (and, as we shall see, individual men) really are. In fact, women and men step out of their socially assigned gender roles all the time, and think, feel, and behave in ways that are supposedly characteristic of the "opposite" sex. Judging from women's relationships with one another, women can be every bit as competitive, insensitive, and aggressive as men, but tend to express "masculine" feelings and behavior in distinctly "feminine" ways. These gender differences in terms of style and expression occur at least in part because both women and men attempt, often quite unconsciously, to conform to the social expectations outlined in the sexual script: aggressive women, for instance, try to seem nurturing, just as nurturing men try to appear aggressive.

In many respects, the descriptions of gender roles in the sexual script are not really descriptive at all, but *prescriptive*. Partly because so many people are trying so hard to follow these prescriptions, and partly because as a society we are intolerant of ambiguity and prefer thinking in oppositional, good/bad and us/them terms, the sexual script blinds us to what is really going on between women and men today. We learn to look at situations a certain way, and often fail to perceive evidence that confounds our expectations.

Even if we detect that something unexpected is occurring — a woman is competing with others, say, or a powerful man is sleeping with a secretary who is trying to exploit their relationship for her own gains — we literally lack the language to discuss what is happening. Often, we try to reinterpret the situation to fit the script we've learned: the woman isn't competing, she's merely concerned; and the boss isn't being exploited, he's actually abusing his position of power.

We have particular difficulty seeing beyond the script when it comes to sex; gender differences — men lust, women love — appear to be so instinctive and natural that the notion that there is a script at all may seem absurd. Most people think of sex as something elemental that we are programmed to know how to do, just as we are programmed to know how to breathe, eat, and sleep. We talk about hormonal drives and biological urges, losing control and getting carried away, as if sex were a pure force of nature. Men want sex, women want relationships — that, we tend to think, is just the way men and women *are*, always have been, and always will be.

Men initiate, women react; men lust, women love — these assumptions inform the sexual harassment debate, as do feminist assumptions that a man with worldly power and greater resources will
inevitably have the upper hand in a sexual relationship. There is very
little public acknowledgment that women as well as men sometimes
blur the line between professional and sexual behavior — or that it
matters at all when they do.

Again, there is a sharp divide between the public discourse and private experience. As most women know perfectly well, men are not the
only ones who mix business with pleasure — and men are certainly not
the only ones who have something to gain from sex in the office.

Elaine does not own a sheer blouse, a push-up bra, or stiletto
heels. She looks like the woman standing behind you in the
checkout line, the one with the big leather tote and the friendly
smile that says, "I'll be happy to hold your place if you forgot to get
milk." Her equanimity and real-ness would make you think: the
motherly type. You would not think: mistress.

She seemed such a paradox that I interviewed her once in New
York, shortly after she had helped Bill rescue the fruit juice account,
and then kept on interviewing her, over the phone and in person, for
more than a year. At first I was looking for some concealed tragedy
and reading her life as a parable of pathetic victimization; later, I was
sniffing around for clues to explain what I perceived as her wilful
self-destruction and lack of self-esteem. Elaine was remarkably candid and endlessly patient, submitting to hours of questioning. Finally, I realized that the sexual script could not help me understand
her relationship with Bill, that in fact its explanations and interpretations were downright misleading, and I listened to what she had
been saying all along: *it's not like that, it's not what you think.*

For Elaine, there was no question of the order of her priorities
when she graduated from university: career first, marriage and children second. She wanted a family, there was no doubt in her mind

about that, but some time in the not yet foreseeable future. She had seen close up what a bad bargain it could be for a bright, ambitious woman to forsake a career in favor of raising a family. Her mother is a reluctant housewife who, judging from her managerial impulses and talent for domination, should have been a CEO. Elaine did not want to spend the rest of her life feeling frustrated and wondering, What if?

Like all her women friends who came from traditional Dad-works-Mom-keeps-house families, she had a horror of turning into her mother. Although feminist psychology tends to emphasize the positive aspects of the mother-daughter bond — indeed, the entire theory of women's intimacy expertise is founded on the closeness of the connection between mothers and daughters — most women share Elaine's fear: *I don't want to become my mother*. The emotional intensity of the relationship and the lack of psychological separation create this fear, but it seems to be strongest among women who not only want a little more distance from their mothers but also reject their values and choices.

As only daughters can, Elaine and her friends extravagantly patronized their homemaking mothers. They delivered pious lectures about equality, and instructed them to stop saying "Just a housewife" and start announcing proudly "I work in the home." And then, without missing a beat, they'd drift out of the kitchen with one last instruction: "Call me when dinner's ready."

They were passionate about getting degrees and getting ahead, not just ahead in the world but ahead of their mothers. For all their eloquent speeches about the value of housework and child care, these enlightened daughters pitied their mothers and believed they had wasted their lives. Some of their mothers seemed to agree, telling them, "Don't rush to get married. Follow your dreams and explore the world — once you have a family, you won't have the chance." Elaine's mother was even more explicit, commanding, "Make something of yourself!"

Elaine and her friends viewed work in terms of liberation, and a career in terms of adventure. Settling down meant selling yourself short, and they were determined to have it all. Their heads were full of big plans but they were short on details and practicalities, because they had very few female role models. "I think Mary Tyler Moore has a lot to answer for," Elaine says with a laugh. "I thought, 'That's what it's going to be like — great apartment, lots of dates, an exciting job. Life will be so fabulous that I'll run down the street tossing my hat in the air.'"

After a few years as a single career woman she had lost some of her naivety, but work had lost none of its allure; she still firmly believed that a career would make her life meaningful, and she still measured success in terms of employment. When she joined the ad agency she was twenty-seven, eager and earnest, thrilled to be living in New York. It was her second job, a shot at the big leagues after working for a small midwestern manufacturing company, and she envisioned a ladder stretching ahead of her, beckoning her to climb.

Up was the only way to go: her title was account executive, which, roughly translated, meant peon. At first, she was assigned to focus on only one product at a time, usually something glamorous like toilet paper, and her duties consisted of doing the grunt work that more senior people did not want to do themselves: making up graphs and complicated spreadsheets, and reading stupendously dull studies on the relative softness of various kinds of toilet paper. Elaine, however, understood the concept of paying one's dues, and wasn't afraid of hard work. She threw herself into the job, expecting that rewards would inevitably follow.

But if marriage had been romanticized for her mother's generation, so had the office been romanticized for Elaine's. Feminists had focused primarily on the benefits of independence and the joys of having a career. There was a notion that men were having a grand time at the office; their complaints — the anxiety, the drudgery, the cog-in-a-machine aspects of paid employment — were dismissed as typical male whining or as disingenuous attempts to dissuade women from seeking work outside the home. When Elaine was growing up, men's labor was often depicted as self-serving; men weren't working because they had to support their families but because they wanted to, enjoyed it immensely, and got huge rewards for doing it.

More generally, especially in the eighties, work was glamorized as a kind of constant party — money! power! great suits! — and a life in itself. A career was the true path to self-fulfilment, and the measure of happiness and success was loving work above all else. Having leisure time and eight hours of sleep a night were sure signs of failure; the reward for good work was more work.

No one had told Elaine she'd wind up working nights and weekends not out of passion but because it was expected as a matter of course in most white-collar jobs. No one warned her she'd spend hours hunched over a computer, staring at rows of numbers that seemed to have nothing to do with anything that anyone might possibly care about. She hadn't counted on credit-grabbing and backstabbing and the stomach-churning envy that comes from observing the seemingly effortless ascent of undeserving colleagues.

On the surface, everyone in the office was friendly, but in a wary, distant way. Unlike her role model, Mary Tyler Moore, Elaine was by no means the only woman in the office, but even among the women, the atmosphere was less than convivial. They were all competing for the same high-profile accounts and the same promotions, and alliances shifted, subtly, and seemingly without warning. Elaine felt constantly surprised and off balance.

By the middle of her second year at the agency, she was working on three products, but that seemed less like a promotion than a punishment: three times the grunt work. She was starting to feel like she was treading water in a cesspool. *This is my life's work, hawking toilet paper and coming up with new euphemisms for tampons?* She was slightly disgusted with advertising and more than a little disappointed in herself. Was this her fate, to spend the rest of her days scurrying around laying the groundwork for other people's ascent?

The boss gave her little reason to hope. In fact, he paid her about as much attention as he would a coat rack. He'd brush by in the hall, hot on the trail of a big new client, seeming not to register her presence. The only time he really seemed to notice her was when she did something wrong, and then his attention had a laserlike intensity. She thought of him as a tornado, blowing past her cubicle to wreak destruction and then whirling off to clinch a deal or mastermind an ad campaign.

On good days, when she was absorbed in her work, she told herself,

It's nothing personal, he's just like that. On bad days, when she had the feeling that she could do nothing right, she thought, He sees through me, knows I'm an impostor.

"You're twenty-eight, you have the world at your feet!" her mother said, dismissing Elaine's complaints. Her father was more empathetic. "Keep at it," he said, then added quietly, "It's no better anywhere else."

After these visits with her parents, Elaine headed back to New York determined to count her blessings. She had a good job at a major agency, she was living in the most exciting city in the world, and by the second year she could actually scrape together enough cash to buy a few of those up-to-the-minute outfits that women's magazines call "statements." On paper, her life looked great, but...

It wasn't the life described in those magazines, where women needed accessories to transform power suits into sexy evening wear (the social whirl was such that they never had time to go home and change), and required the input of several advice columnists to sort out the delightful complications of juggling numerous suitors. There was no advice on what to do at the end of another twelve-hour day, when your suit looked as though it had been wadded up at the bottom of a suitcase for several weeks and you felt so drained that you had to steel yourself for the effort of exchanging a few words with the doorman.

Elaine's social life consisted primarily of dinners with several women friends, gatherings that were difficult to arrange given that they all regularly worked late. "I thought living to work went out with the eighties," her friend Cathy sighed one evening. "Who's living?" said Elaine. They got to talking about the eighties, which had acquired a rosy glow in retrospect, partly because they had still been in school and weren't yet paying off onerous student loans. But also, there had been limitless opportunities to meet men, even when you were in the library cramming for finals, even when you were immersed in a tragic relationship with a brooding, tortured film major. All of them regretted not having had the good sense to enjoy it while it lasted. At university, they had talked about getting out into The Real World, never imagining it might be a place where you had no time to meet men or even any idea how to go about it, and instead would sit around in restaurants praying that your credit card would not be declined and debating whether, in some respects, your mother's life had in fact been better, easier, happier.

Twice, impelled more by boredom and loneliness than genuine interest, Elaine had halfhearted flings with men she had known for years. "Reheating leftovers" is how she thought of it. "Perhaps I overlooked some sterling qualities," she told herself at the beginning and then, at the end, "Maybe my standards are too high."

"Finding a man was not my mission in life, not by any means," says Elaine, looking back. "But it's nice to have some reason to leave the office before the cleaning crews arrive. If you're used to having relationships, it's a shock to the system if suddenly your entire existence revolves around the one dimension of work, especially if work isn't as fun and fulfilling as you thought it would be."

But eighteen months into the job, things started looking up: she finally got the nod to go on an out-of-town sales call. The rest of the team traveled frequently enough to complain about the inconvenience, but Elaine took one look around the hotel room — the little bottles of shampoo in the bathroom, the fluffy white robe — and felt she'd finally arrived where she wanted to be. They worked hard, of course, and it was exhausting, but she felt like a force to be reckoned with, not least because she could order from room service without worrying about the cost. The second night, celebrating in the hotel bar because they had pulled off the deal against all odds, was one of the first times that she actually felt a sense of belonging with her colleagues. They had chosen her to be on their team; finally, she had a place at the table.

But everyone else decamped, all at the same time, and she was left chatting easily with the boss before it struck her that this was in fact what they were doing. It all seemed hypothetical: having a normal conversation with him and then, instead of paying the bill, having another drink. She found herself telling him about her idea for marketing a new product, an idea she had not been planning to mention until she'd given it quite a bit more thought. But here she was, leaning forward and talking fast, and the boss was looking at her as though he'd just now noticed that she could speak. "Very interesting," he said when she finished, and then he leaned across and kissed her.

She could have reared back and felt a number of things, all unpleasant, but she did not. Mostly what she felt was surprise, but the circumstances — the excitement of closing the deal, the way he'd been belting back drinks, the sheer strangeness of being away from home — seemed to explain everything. She was proud of how quickly she reacted, pulling away and saying, No thanks, but no hard feelings. "Don't worry about it," she said. "We're both adults and we'll just forget it ever happened."

"Thank you," he said. "Thanks for being understanding."

Actually, Elaine found plenty to feel good about back in her hotel room: he had noticed her, been impressed with her idea, seen her as an adult woman instead of as that little account executive who was always screwing up. And his momentary desire, however mitigating the circumstances, seemed to indicate that the balance between them had shifted in her favor. She had his attention now.

Back in New York, he was more receptive. "What do you think, Elaine?" he began asking at meetings, and once, in front of everyone, "The report was excellent. Good work." He was completely businesslike but sometimes in those meetings the memory of his mouth on hers would rise up, unbidden, and she would wonder what he saw when he looked at her, whether he was struggling to mask a more than strictly professional interest when he asked, "What do you think, Elaine?"

Her friends were appalled when she told them about the kiss. "What a pathetic lech!" Cathy screeched, which annoyed Elaine. She had an exciting piece of gossip to report, for a change, had expected them to be just a little bit impressed a vice-president had found her irresistible, and did not appreciate the implication that he was an undiscriminating boor. No, Elaine huffed, it wasn't like *that*. It was just, you know, one of those things. Bill — she'd started thinking of him as Bill, instead of The Boss — wasn't crass. He wasn't some leering jerk who groped women on the subway. Actually, he was really smart, and kind of interesting. He wasn't a half-bad kisser, either.

"He's also married," Cathy said, in a tone of such high melodrama that Elaine had to laugh. *God!* He was balding and had a paunch — he

must be about fifty years old! You wouldn't look at him twice on the
street. She didn't *like* him, not that way, and wished she'd never even
brought it up. Could they change the topic? Please?

Still, she watched him sometimes, speculatively. The kiss had
added some intrigue to her life; it had been a while since a man had
expressed interest, and it made her think. "When someone finds you
attractive, you can't help but consider the possibility," Elaine says.
"It's human nature, and it really doesn't matter whether he's an em-
ployer or some guy at a party. Look, it's hard to meet men after
you've finished school and you're working really long hours. If you
don't have the chance to meet guys outside of work, it's only a matter
of time until you start thinking about the ones you see every day."

Bill assigned her to a particularly difficult new project, and then
while he was looking over her work, started talking about a vacation
he'd taken in Greece. His wife never quite figured out the currency,
she'd just held out a handful of bills and coins and let the shop people
pick the ones they wanted. "That's what's going on here," he said, turning back to Elaine's spreadsheets. "You can't just hold these out and
hope that someone will be honest enough to take the right amount."

It was the kind of criticism she could take, both constructive and
encouraging, and she didn't leave his office smarting and wondering
if perhaps she was in the wrong job the way she had in the past.
When she returned with a solution, somehow it came up that he had
attended boarding school, one of those East Coast institutions for
the scions of wealthy families.

"You don't seem like the type," she said. He was hectic, rumpled,
anything but buttoned down. There was a moment of silence, enough
time for her to worry that she'd offended him, but then he laughed: "I
was expelled my first year."

It sounds meaningless, repeating exactly who said what, as though
the words give any indication of the chemistry between them. It was
just there, as sudden as it was unmistakable. Elaine found herself
dressing more carefully for work, and being aware of the way her hips
moved as she strode past Bill's office to the fax machine. She got a little
charge when she sat beside him in meetings; she was conscious of his
presence across the room as she sat in her cubicle, working away. The

interest was mutual. She could sense him watching her sometimes, and there was something distinctly flirtatious about the way he talked to her, even though the topics were strictly business. Elaine started channeling this current between them into a kind of mock antagonism, by making arch remarks when he blew out of his office yelling about something or other. "I think you should cut back on the caffeine," she said the first time, and he stopped mid-tirade and laughed.

Maybe she'd read him all wrong. Maybe he wanted to be challenged, wanted her to show some backbone instead of cowering and only silently reproaching the grandstanders who took credit for her ideas. How could he respect her if she didn't stand up for herself? Her growing conviction that he saw her as an object of desire didn't make her nervous. It gave her the confidence to assert herself.

She started trying to figure Bill out instead of merely reacting to him. He'd been expelled from school, he'd been to Greece, he wasn't just some desk-bound adman. She noticed that he had the ability to laugh at himself, a quality that had been notably lacking in the brooding film major, a quality she liked in a man. She started to look forward to going to work in the morning.

Six weeks after her first trip, Bill announced it was time for her to meet the client on the new project. It was clearly a compliment and an acknowledgment that she had something valuable to contribute, but she didn't let that go to her head. The best policy was to stay quiet in the meetings, keep her mouth shut unless she was asked a direct question, watch the boss and follow his lead. A whole other side of him came out with clients: he exercised leadership by way of charm, generally creating the impression that there was nothing he would rather do than sit in their stuffy boardroom. It was a masterful performance, and one Elaine could fully appreciate because she was aware of the extent to which he was improvising, plucking the right answers instinctively from a jumble of numbers that had seemed to her, the night before, to have no pattern at all.

Afterward, she can't remember why, the rest of the team did not join them at the bar. It was just Elaine and Bill, talking about the day's meetings and then other things and some time after the third Scotch, she suggested going outside to get some air. "I don't know how you do it, just winging it like that," she said, relaxed enough now not to rehearse every sentence in her head before opening her mouth. It was nice being out for a stroll with the boss, who was letting his guard down and even getting a little goofy, throwing his arm around her shoulder and saying, "It's all show business, all smoke and mirrors." His arm felt intentionally ambiguous, an offer that could be shrugged off as a friendly gesture and that he could deny having made.

"I must be drunk," was her first thought when she kissed him, a sloppy kiss in which their mouths didn't fit together quite right because she had lunged up at him a little too eagerly. But she didn't have any second thoughts, not even when she was putting her clothes back on and preparing to sneak back from his room to her own, beyond thinking that she had to be very quiet so her colleagues wouldn't hear her in the hall.

She didn't think about what it meant that he was married or that he was her boss. She thought only that here was this bright, powerful man who had made her cry out, startled by pleasure, in a large bed in a strange city.

There's nothing new about sleeping with the boss; what *is* new is the power dynamic in many of these affairs. This most traditional of relationships — powerful man, subordinate woman — is, surprisingly, a good gauge of the ways in which women's position in society has changed over the past three decades.

Before the 1970s, there was a power imbalance in virtually every office romance: even co-workers of the opposite sex were not equals, because his opportunities for advancement were so much greater than hers and he was already likely to be making more money for doing the same job. Even if they were performing identical tasks, his had a different social value. Whereas he was expected to work, expected to support a family, and instructed to take his measure in terms of employment, her job was seen as a hobby, a source of pin money, or a temporary occupation to fill her days until she got a permanent posting as a wife and mother.

Although many women had no choice but to work and many spent their whole lives in the labor force, the societal ideal remained the same: women were not supposed to *want* to work outside the home for their entire lives, and those who did were viewed as unfeminine personally, and as less than equal to men professionally. Middle-class women were expected to find a husband at college and then stay home raising a family, which legitimated gender discrimination both in postgraduate education and in the workplace. "Women just get pregnant and quit" was the excuse when women were turned away from Ph.D. programs and turned down for training programs, raises, and promotions in the workplace.

But someone had to take letters and pour coffee, so many women were able to find jobs. Romantic relationships were tacitly accepted if not outright condoned in most offices, not least because no matter how much women actually did, they were seen primarily as decorative hostesses and housekeepers who kept the workplace in order so the men could get on with the real business. They were women first, workers second; it wasn't unprofessional to pester a secretary for a date, because she herself was not a professional, and she certainly was not an equal. She was working *for* men, not with them, and there was every expectation that she must be frantic to meet an eligible bachelor.

The office was considered a prime hunting ground to find a mate, particularly for those who had not attended university. If anything, women were viewed as the predators, the ones who set their sights on men who looked like good providers, laid traps, and finally ensnared them at the altar. The boss was the biggest catch of all, and the woman who landed him wound up with a diamond ring, a house with a white picket fence, and early retirement from the steno pool. Even if he was married, he wasn't necessarily off-limits, not to a woman who was prepared to use her feminine wiles and risk scandal. If she was trapped in the pink-collar ghetto, the boss represented an escape route, even if the escape was only temporary and came in the form of a studio apartment and a new title: kept woman.

But men were by no means helpless victims of marriage-minded schemers in the office. Many viewed the women they worked with as fair game sexually, and some certainly did make abundant use of the casting couch. But it was impossible for a woman to sleep her way to the top professionally: the top was a males-only club. Rather, she might sleep her way right out of the labor force; "the top," for women, meant a marriage license and a house in the suburbs.

Today, women's expectations and opportunities have changed so dramatically that we sometimes forget just how different things were just three decades ago. Now, it is women who choose *not* to work outside the home who feel they must justify their choice to others. "I'm just a mother," they sometimes confess sheepishly, plainly expecting criticism. Others, anxious to prove they haven't lost their drive, crisply announce, "I'm taking a few years off to stay home with the kids, but of course, I'll be going right back to work once they're in nursery school." Some appear to believe that the best defense is a good offense: "Those career women who talk about 'quality time' and dump their kids in day care are just selfish. It's a question of priorities, and I think it's more important to raise my children than to have enough money to take holidays in Hawaii."

This middle-class defensiveness is understandable, because as employment barriers have crumbled and as work has been depicted as a form of feminist liberation and more generally as the highest social good, women's traditional role — never highly valued — has in some respects been further devalued. Thirty years ago, women really were second-class citizens in society, but they were not made to feel there was something *personally* shameful about being "just" a mother — that was what women were supposed to be. Today, however, women who choose to be homemakers report that they are occasionally treated like evolutionary throwbacks, particularly at social gatherings where the first question is, "And what do you do?" The announcement "I'm a full-time mother" frequently gets the same response as would the declaration, "I have no ideas, no opinions, and nothing to say that would interest you. Ask me one polite question about my children, then feel free to patronize me or ignore me altogether."

Housework and child care are still grossly undervalued — and almost entirely unappreciated — in our society, and although feminists pointed out the injustice of this situation, they also tended to portray women's traditional role as a straitjacket from which all women should be released. Thus, full-time homemakers sometimes feel not only that their labor is accorded little social or economic value, but that they are perceived by other women as violating a feminist decree that any self-respecting, intelligent, independent woman *should* want to work outside the home.

Of course, the connection between self-worth and paid work goes far beyond feminism; for centuries now, men have been told that their value as human beings depends on their achievement in the public sphere. The notion that the same holds true for women is less than thirty years old but already widely accepted, apparently even by arch-conservatives, who frame their argument against social assistance in terms of self-respect: "welfare queens" should be kicked off the dole and frogmarched into the labor force, where they can earn an honest living, develop some pride, and make a "worthwhile" contribution to society. Apparently, raising children does not count, not even with those who campaign on a family values platform.

Some of them even believe that women on welfare continue to have children solely to get bigger government checks; this idea that welfare mothers breed and eat bonbons while the rest of us work to support them is increasingly popular, particularly among people who have never seen the inside of a public housing project and who believe that a father's responsibility ends at the moment of conception. The truth of the matter is that many single mothers wind up on welfare because they receive no child support and cannot earn enough to cover the costs of paying someone else to look after their children while they are at work.

Regardless of the low social value accorded to full-time homemaking, however, for most young women it is simply not an option. They have no choice but to seek paid employment: they are single and need to earn money in order to support themselves, or they are married and need a second income in order to survive. Today, most young women simply assume that they will spend the majority of their adult lives in the labor force.

Furthermore, middle-class women expect that they will have careers rather than a series of mere jobs, and they also expect full equality in the office, not just in terms of opportunities, but in terms of actual results. They assume that hard work will be rewarded and, unlike their mothers, tend to assume that gender will be no obstacle to success. In a sense, they are similar to first-generation immigrants in terms of their high expectations and sense of mission; in a very real way, they see the office as the route to the American dream, and they are aware that they have options their mothers did not and are determined to make the most of them. For Elaine, Julie, Anna, and Nadine, work is what bright, aspiring, middle-class young women do as a matter of course, and those who are sensible and independent don't consider getting married until they have proved that they can support themselves and are reasonably well-established in their chosen fields.

These assumptions and calculations are old hat for men, but they are brand-new for women, and they have altered the landscape of the workplace. Two demographic curves have converged: women's labor force participation rate is steadily increasing, and the age of first marriage for women is also rising. Women with university degrees, in particular, are delaying marriage or forgoing it altogether. So there are not just more women in the office — there are more single, well-educated, ambitious, young women. Largely because of feminism, they now have a real shot at reaching the top of the professional ladder. Women are no longer just working for men, but with them; women are not just taking letters and pouring coffee, but are also in — or are within striking distance of — positions of real power.

The working world has changed in other important ways, as the line between work life and social life becomes increasingly blurred. Going out for drinks is not just sociable, it's a networking opportunity; the company picnic is not just recreation, but a chance to prove that one is a team player. Computers, modems, and fax machines make it possible to work just about anywhere, including at home. Conversely, the office is no longer just a place where people toil from nine to five; it's also becoming a second home for many people. Particularly in the professions and on the fast track, employees spend most of their waking hours together.

"I average sixty hours a week, and that's nothing in this industry," says Margaret, a thirty-three-year-old management consultant in Los Angeles. "My first year I worked ninety, ninety-five hours a week, and the office was still full of people when I left at night. It's the same at my husband's law firm. People literally *live* in the office. We've both cut back on our hours or else we'd never see each other, but there's the fear that you'll pay for it, professionally. It's absolutely expected that you'll work insane hours and if you're not willing to do it, they'll just find someone else to take your place. I can understand why people start having relationships at work — they have no life outside the office."

An intense, high-adrenaline environment doesn't just create expectations that employees will work around the clock; this kind of atmosphere can also heighten sexual attractions. As Elaine says, the "pumped-up energy from meeting deadlines and getting through crises" can sometimes "spill over into sexual feelings." There's the excitement, euphoria, and relief of pulling off a victory; naturally, there's also a feeling of closeness to the other people who are sharing this surge of strong feeling. "You're on an emotional roller coaster and you're wired from the tension. All your senses are on red-alert," she says. "Most people connect those kinds of feelings with sex. I certainly do." There are also more mundane factors that make the office a prime place to find romantic partners: propinquity, opportunity, common ground, and shared interests and experiences.

Along with the dramatic changes in the landscape of the workplace, there has also been a paradigm shift in terms of romantic relationships, and it too affects the power balance in office affairs. Equal partnerships, in which the man and the woman are roughly equivalent in terms of education, aspirations, and achievement, are now the societal ideal. Thirty years ago, Bill would have had an affair with a woman in the typing pool; today, however, he wanted a relationship with a woman who was his professional peer, shared his interests, and shared his goals.

Women aren't the only ones who want equality in their relationships, and they aren't the only ones who assess a potential partner at least partly on the basis of social status and earning power. "If one of my colleagues got involved with a temp who hadn't gone past high school, he'd be made to feel embarrassed," says Neil, a thirty-five-year-old Miami lawyer. "It would be seen as going downmarket, which sounds classist, but it's true. If she were gorgeous, it would look even worse. He'd just seem that much more shallow and pathetic.

Most of the men I know want to be with women who are their intellectual and professional equals. Anything less reflects badly on you, and the relationship isn't going to be interesting or challenging. And for purely economic reasons, you want to be with a woman who can pull her own weight financially — in this economy, you need two incomes to survive. You sure as hell don't want to be in a position where you're supporting someone else financially and you can't even have a conversation with her."

The professional performance ethic — work harder, aim higher — has carried over to the realm of romantic relationships, where men and women call themselves partners rather than lovers, and where each basks in the reflected glow of the other's status. Even high-profile conservatives who seem hell-bent on turning the clock back to the 1950s are not shacking up with bimbos or ladies who lunch but with high-achieving women; the power couple is no longer a phenomenon but a fact of life.

Oddly, despite these significant changes in terms of cultural ideals, women's position in society, and the office environment itself, the public discourse on sex in the office lags thirty years behind. Although women have made huge gains in terms of professional power and although they now have legal recourse when employers cross the line sexually, in the public discourse, it is as though conditions have not changed and women have made no progress at all. In fact, sometimes women are depicted as being worse off today; while the stereotype of the gold-digging secretary has all but vanished, the stereotype of the skirt-chasing boss is stronger than ever.

The presumption of women's innocence — women are, after all, morally superior — combined with the presumption that men's collective socioeconomic power translates directly into individual sexual power, means that women like Elaine, when they are discussed at all, are reflexively labeled victims. Many feminists and liberals would see Elaine as vulnerable, an easy target for a Machiavellian boss who exploited her low self-esteem and relative powerlessness. Some would view her as a perfect example of the way that women are brainwashed to believe their only value is sexual, and thus are conditioned to accept subjugation. Many moralists and conservatives would also heap blame

on Bill, but more because he betrayed his long-suffering, Christian
wife than because he went to bed with an employee. Some of them
would add that if Elaine had only stayed where she belonged — at
home, trotting dutifully between kitchen and nursery — she never
would have wound up in such a compromising, unladylike position.

All would agree, however, that Bill was the more powerful one in
the relationship; Elaine was, after all, female, his subordinate, and
only one of two women in his life. Elaine herself, however, flatly rejects the notion that he had the upper hand or that he was responsible for initiating their affair. "It was entirely mutual," she says. "And
in a way I was in a stronger position because Bill had a lot more to
lose. When people look at it from the outside, they see his professional power but ignore the fact that I was holding the trump card:
the threat of exposure. No matter how loving and real the relationship is, that threat is always there in the background, always. You
have the ability to damage that man's marriage, his reputation, and
his career. It's a really negative type of power, but that doesn't mean
it's not real or men are immune to it."

In fact, some men find it a turn-on. "Danger is a large part of why
men get into affairs in the first place. They're attracted by it, just the
same way that some men get off on driving like maniacs," Elaine
says. "And the danger is huge when they're fooling around with
someone in the office, because they're exposed on two fronts, at
home and at work. Bill was risking everything."

Of course, in the meantime he was gaining the opportunity to
have sex with an attractive young woman whose admiration made
him feel like a superhero. But Elaine, as it turns out, wasn't just risking less than he was. She also had more to gain.

Elaine was not, however, thinking in terms of costs and benefits on
the plane heading home from their first tryst. Bill stared out the
window and didn't say much, though he was clearly a man with a
great deal on his mind. The only thing on hers was when they would
see each other again, to which the obvious answer was that they

would see each other in the office, next week. But Bill knew what she meant, and knew what she was asking when she summoned all her courage and invited him, in what she hoped was a casual tone, to drop by her place on Monday night. For a drink. He hesitated, said he didn't know what his schedule was, and spent the weekend with the family whose photos were on his desk. She spent the weekend replaying their night together, remembering it in little dazing flashes that left her unable to concentrate on anything except what might happen next.

He was out of the office all day Monday; she was so distracted by the suspense — would he or wouldn't he? — that she read the same page of a report over and over without registering a word. She went home early to shower and make up a tray of hors d'oeuvres, then paced back and forth checking her watch and compulsively re-applying her lipstick. When he knocked on the door at a few minutes past seven her heart started pounding so crazily that she couldn't say anything for a minute, just stood there blocking the entrance until he asked if he could come in, and then they both laughed, but it was a startled whinny of nervousness that only underscored the awkwardness of the situation. He was holding a bottle of red wine (expensive, but she didn't know about wine yet) and a fistful of flowers (roses — she pressed them).

It was a thrilling sensation, this breathless certainty that whatever else happened, she would remember this moment for the rest of her life. They had a glass of wine and a few minutes of exquisitely stilted conversation about one of the framed posters on her wall, and then they didn't need words because they were sliding between the clean sheets she'd raced home to put on the bed. Two hours later he staggered up to get dressed, looking shell-shocked and leaving no doubt: he would be back. The fact of Bill in her apartment, *risking everything for a few hours with me*, was not conducive to making Elaine ask herself what she was getting into.

"At first it was just a big adventure, an escapade," she recalls. The uneventful narrative of her life had suddenly acquired an intriguing plot twist: she had become a femme fatale. She felt like a character in a movie, and in fact, a fair degree of acting ability was required in order to behave normally in the office. Initially, Elaine got a rush from the details of deceit: pretending to ignore Bill in meetings, talking to him in code about when they'd see each other again. But she was so self-conscious about covering her tracks that she overcompensated, pulling aside co-workers she barely knew and telling them elaborate fictions about places she'd gone and things she'd done the night before. After the first couple of weeks, however, she calmed down enough to begin practicing the discipline of discretion. She discovered that it was easi-est to hide her feelings when she was immersed in work, so she flung herself into her job with renewed vigor. Partly, too, she wanted to show off for Bill, to prove to him how smart and capable she was.

The usual all-consuming intensity and excitement of a sexual be-ginning was heightened not just by the secrecy but by Bill's status. "This powerful, successful man was totally besotted with me," she explains. "It's a big ego boost when a real player wants you, because it makes you feel like a player too. It was very, very heady."

With little effort, she had brought a vice-president of the agency to his knees, helpless with desire. Bill came to her apartment several times a week; she never sat by the phone wondering if he would call, because she knew he would, every night from the extension in his basement, to whisper longingly about how much he wished he could be with her. He was full of compliments and jokes and insights into ad-vertising; he made her think and he made her laugh. She made him yearn. Elaine began to view her body as a source of wonder, because that is how he viewed it. She stopped fretting about her thighs and quit dieting altogether. "I could just lie here looking at you for hours," Bill said one evening while he was dressing to go home, with such pure regret that she actually felt sorry for him, sorry that he had to leave.

His body did not hold the same fascination for her — he was decades older than any man she had ever slept with — but she did feel a certain sympathetic tenderness toward him precisely because bits of him sagged and others were too fleshy. His imperfections, the overhang of his belly and the deep, pleated wrinkles on his forehead, made her own body seem more perfect by comparison. Who cared, in the end, if he didn't look like he'd stepped from the pages of *GQ*?

It was easy to be generous because he made her feel so good about herself. "It was the convergence of feeling both smart and beautiful,"

Elaine explains. "My self-esteem went through the roof. A big part of it was being treated as his intellectual equal, because aside from everything else that was happening between us, he saw me as someone bright and interesting who was an asset to the agency. He was endorsing and creating a lot of the things I wanted to be — a woman, not a little girl, and a big person professionally."

Naturally, Bill and Elaine began traveling together a great deal after she was promoted. She deserved the promotion, had deserved it for some time, and didn't care that it had only materialized after she'd been having sex with the boss for four months. "I'd earned it and should've got it much earlier than I did. And I proved that I was competent in the role," she says. "I was a lot more comfortable around Bill, so I had the confidence to contribute in meetings."

She started trusting her instincts rather than relying so heavily on the market research; she still number-crunched and read the reports, but increasingly she followed her own common sense. Dispensing with the notion that advertising was a science seemed to unstop a creative dam in her head, and she began to develop a reputation as a bright young thing, a comer in the agency. Bill applauded her professional development wholeheartedly; she was sure of his affection, which freed her to focus on her career, and every success just seemed to make him love her more.

Six months into the relationship, she was happy, noticeably so. She'd been promoted, a powerful, charismatic man was wildly in love with her, and she was being showered with lavish floral arrangements, so many that she actually had to go out and buy vases. People at work commented on her glow, so she quickly invented a fictional boyfriend and redoubled her efforts to act completely professionally at all times around Bill. That got easier and easier, because his mood had improved markedly. He wasn't wheeling around the office yelling at people any more, and he was so respectful toward her in meetings that she started to grow into the role of a person who is mindful of her own authority.

Mostly what they did when they were alone in her apartment was talk for hours, drink wine, and make love. Bill confided that he was terribly unhappy in his marriage and had been for years. He'd married too young, to a woman who didn't understand any of the things Elaine understood so well, like the roiling anxiety and exhilaration of a high-powered career. "He painted it as a very traditional marriage, where the wife lived for him and the kids and took a lie-back-and-think-of-England approach to sex," Elaine says. "She wasn't a challenge to him and I was, or at least that's how he presented it."

Bill told Elaine that he felt as though he'd been sleepwalking until he met her, and announced that he wasn't going to pass up what might be his last chance for true happiness. His kids were teenagers, nearly all grown up, certainly old enough to understand that he had to start living for himself and looking out for number one for a change.

They talked about work — everything from the nitty-gritty details of marketing plans to all the weird personalities in their office — but their favorite topic was their own relationship. He enjoyed dissecting it as much as she did, and was even more likely to ask, "Why do you love me?" He wasn't like the other men she had known, who were so ambivalent that she felt she had to downplay her own feelings just to save face. Bill was always saying how lucky he was to be with her, and he needed abundant reassurances that she really did care for him, especially when the topic was their future and what would happen after he got a divorce.

Elaine treasured the no-holds-barred intimacy of these stolen hours, but still, it was something of a relief to be out on the road where, with some careful planning, they could have dinner together and act like a normal couple. He treated her so well, pulling out her chair and helping her with her coat, fascinated by every little thing she said. "There's a lot to be said for men who can tie a tie, are on time for meetings, and know how to order wine in a restaurant," she contends. "I felt like a real woman for the first time."

On these trips, too, they could sleep in the same bed until daybreak, when she'd tiptoe back to her own hotel room and rumple the sheets so it would look as though she'd been there all night. She was superstitious: if she took extra precautions, she would not get caught. Beneath that was an even deeper hope: if she didn't get caught, she hadn't done anything wrong. They always slept in his room when they were traveling because she didn't quite trust him to be careful enough to avoid detection in the morning. Bill got so carried away by his emotions. Sometimes it seemed like he almost wanted to get caught, wanted people to know how in love he was — or perhaps, she thought much later, wanted them to know he was getting away with something.

By the end of the first year of their affair, their lives were completely intertwined: they spent most of their waking hours together, in the office or on the road. "Bill started to rely on my judgment, especially about people," Elaine says. "It was the kind of partnership that probably only comes along once or twice in your professional life, where there's creative synergy and the total is more than the sum of its parts. We sparked off each other and pushed each other, and we did some ground-breaking stuff. There was the excitement of being allies who were building something together."

He inspired her, and he was her best friend. Her girlfriends thought she'd lost her mind. "You're destroying your career," they said, and, "He'll never leave his wife. You know that, don't you?" Her father was too uncomfortable even to discuss the relationship, but her mother made no secret of her opposition; after years of telling Elaine to make something of herself, she was now making pointed comments about how all her friends' daughters were already married and having children. This lack of understanding did not make Elaine feel inclined to spend a whole lot of time with anyone but Bill. She was spending so much time in the office that she was on first-name terms with the after-hours security guards.

At work, she felt confident and sure of herself. "I had the inside track on what was going on in the agency, and business is all about who knows what, particularly in my industry. I couldn't assume power on my own, but I could broker the information I got from Bill, which gave me a real advantage over everyone else at my level," Elaine says. She was also getting the benefit of his considerable expertise: "It was like a crash course in business — I got the kind of knowledge from him that you can usually only get from direct experience."

It paid off with a second promotion, which made her his right-hand woman in name as well as fact. "Account supervisor" — she loved typing her title on memos to clients. She had three people working under her, three very respectful people who had not failed to

notice that her word carried weight with the boss, and was responsible for all the household products manufactured by a major international brand. A year after that first heady night with Bill, she was in
love, she had established her own power base, and her career was finally starting to live up to all her early expectations. As soon as Bill
got a divorce, which he assured her was imminent, she really would
have it all.

By the end of their second year together, however, Elaine was less
enthusiastic about her situation, and she was agitating for Bill to stop
talking about leaving his wife and just do it. After two years of rapid
professional progress, her life seemed to have stalled, emotionally. It
had begun to bother her that she was living a lie in the office, acting all
the time; it made her feel bad personally, and she worried that it would
wind up discrediting her professionally. At the beginning of the affair,
she had felt like a sexual dynamo, but now she sometimes felt tainted
and dirty after sex. She loved Bill, more than anything, and she knew
she was a nice person and a hard worker, but she also knew that none
of this would matter to anyone looking at the situation from the outside. She wanted Bill to make an honest woman of her.

Frankly, she was a tiny bit bored of their hothouse intimacy. It was
tiring to talk about the relationship constantly instead of just living it,
and she wanted to be able to go out with other couples and have a social life just like everyone else. She'd run out of things to say when Bill
asked, "Why do you love me?" and had become a little brusque with
her reply: "You *know* why." She was starting to resent loving him so
much when she couldn't have him all to herself, and starting to resent
having to reassure him when she was the one who sat at home alone
on her birthday because he had to attend a dinner party with his wife.

She was thirty-one, most of her friends were married, and she had
started to want children so much that she felt a physical ache when she
saw mothers pushing strollers in the park. In professional terms she
was still young, but in reproductive terms she was beginning to feel
old. As soon as Bill got his divorce, they could start a family. They'd
also talked about starting up their own advertising agency, just something small at first, where they could be their own bosses — they
would be on completely equal footing, which appealed to her. Mostly,

though, what she wanted was a baby, and she was not prepared to wait much longer.

Bill was always just about to leave his wife, but then something came up: a mortgage renewal, a death in the family, his daughter's graduation from high school. There never seemed to be a good time. "You're first in my heart," he told Elaine, and, "I can't live without you." He was still sneaking down to his basement every evening to whisper good night into the phone, and if she was out with friends or at the laundromat or wherever, he kept calling until he got her. But this no longer seemed so sweet and wonderful; in fact, it alarmed her, the way this man she'd thought was so strong was leaning on her so heavily and full of need. She didn't want flowers and maudlin whispers in the phone line any more; she wanted a man who didn't need to be mothered and bossed, a man who was capable of making a plan and then executing it.

One of the most striking aspects of Elaine's affair with Bill is that it sounds uncannily similar to the glowing academic description of female friendships: the relationship revolved around sharing secrets and talking about feelings. These are common features of romances between single women and married men, whether or not they work together, according to Laurel Richardson's sociological study of extramarital affairs. "In contrast to dating couples, whose time together is mostly social, being with other people and going out to movies and parties, single woman–married man time is mostly intimate," she reports in *The New Other Woman*. "Concealment means that most of the activities that sustain the relationship take place in private. What there is to talk about is themselves and their relationship, rather than the movie, the party, the other people."[3]

The situation is designed to induce mutual self-disclosure, which is, according to most psychologists and communications researchers, the hallmark of true intimacy. If that's true, then affairs between single women and married men must be some of the most intimate heterosexual relationships in our society. Certainly, Other Women often single out mutual self-disclosure as the most rewarding aspect of their affairs.

"There are no secrets between you, because you're sharing this thing that you have to keep secret from everybody else," says Kara, a thirty-four-year-old civil servant in Chicago who recently ended her eighteen-month affair with a married man. "I told him things that I've never told another soul, and I know it was the same for him. The sex was fine, but the real attraction was the closeness, knowing another person that intimately."

Susan, a thirty-one-year-old public relations executive in Toronto, offers a similar reading of her ongoing affair with a powerful man in her industry. "At first you're thinking, 'This just is a fling,' only more exciting because it's illicit. I went into it thinking, 'Two months, max.' I never thought I'd still be with him two and a half years later. But the thing is, I got to know him in a way that no one else does. To everyone else, he's just this big, successful guy, but I see another side of him because he can let down his guard and be vulnerable with me. That's why I fell in love with him and why I can't see breaking up, even though he says he won't leave his marriage when his kids are still young. Sex is really the least of it now — I wouldn't stay just for sex. I could get that with anyone and there wouldn't be so many hassles. I stay because it's the deepest relationship I've ever had with a man. We can really talk, and I don't have to pry stuff out of him. We're totally open with each other."

Quite apart from the logistical difficulties caused by the fact that the man is married, the focus on mutual self-disclosure can cause serious problems, just as it does in women's friendships. At first, Elaine was amazed by her good fortune: she had finally found a man who talked like a girlfriend. Bill was happy to spend hours dissecting their relationship and baring his soul. After a while, however, Elaine did not view this quite so positively. In fact, her response was quintessentially "masculine": *Why do we have to talk about the relationship all the time? Why can't we just live it?* For her, the lack of shared social activities and contact with the world outside their love nest became a major irritant. She wanted Bill to behave a little less like a girlfriend and to do what researchers excoriate men for doing: stop talking, and start demonstrating his feelings through actions — in this case, by leaving his wife.

The cyclé of complaint and commiseration in Elaine and Bill's relationship initially strengthened their connection but wound up propelling them into a rut, where Elaine had to silence herself and nod understandingly when Bill presented excuse after excuse for not leaving his marriage just yet. Carrying the burden of intimacy expertise meant she had to pump up his ego and empathize with his problems. Just as she would with her women friends, she pursued a policy of supportive dishonesty that ran contrary to her own needs, desires, and feelings: *I'm not angry, I'm not hurt, I'm not upset. Of course I understand that you can't leave your wife today because you have a hangnail — I'll support you through this trauma, don't worry.*

As is frequently the case in female friendships, Elaine was terrified of open conflict. Like Julie and Anna, who shared a myth of sameness and united under a men-are-the-problem banner, Bill and Elaine saw themselves as soulmates whose only problems were created by external forces: other people in the office, friends who just didn't understand, and, most significantly, his wife. They were as one, struggling uphill with an us-against-the-world attitude, and they could not afford any dissension in the ranks. So Elaine denied the importance of their differences and disagreements, and seethed in silence — her resentment compounded, naturally, by the fact that she now felt isolated from everyone but Bill. Any kind of open confrontation might sever their bond, in which case she would lose not just her only ally and best friend, but also her dream of a family.

For his part, Bill viewed her impatience with the tell-me-why-you-love-me conversation as a form of emotional withholding. Like Nadine in the previous chapter, he deployed a strategy of self-deprecating disarmament to avoid conflict and keep Elaine in a position where she would dole out lavish helpings of empathy: *You're big and strong, I'm weak and helpless, don't hurt me or add to my woes.* He disarmed Elaine into a position where she supposedly had the emotional upper hand, and therefore had to swallow her own shock and hurt when it came out that he was still having sex with his wife occasionally, "to keep up appearances, because otherwise she'd suspect that something was going on."

"It's so hard for Bill," Elaine sighed the first time we met. "He's in real pain about leaving his marriage and about having to be apart from me. The whole situation is very difficult for him, much more difficult than it is for me. And he's been unhappy for such a long time."

Most people can grasp quite readily that in these kinds of extramarital affairs, the prescriptions of the sexual script — be supportive, be caring, be nurturing — serve the interests not of the single woman but of the married man. We protest this because the beneficiary is male, and married, to boot. But in key respects, the psychological dynamic of Elaine and Bill's relationships was not dissimilar to that of many female friendships. Elaine couldn't assert her individual rights — no, she was an ever-patient, ever-understanding intimacy expert. In practice, so-called intimacy expertise is often a recipe for self-sabotage not just in sexual relationships with married men, but in friendships with other women. It creates serious problems that are only exacerbated by the coping strategies used to deny them.

Why, given the high price she was paying, did Elaine cling so stubbornly to the sexual script? The answer, paradoxically, is that while following it exacted an enormous emotional toll, it also allowed her to ignore her complicity in the injury of another woman: Bill's wife.

"At first I really didn't think about her — she was just an abstraction. I didn't know her personally, and Bill was saying all the usual things about being unhappy and misunderstood," Elaine says. "But regardless of what he said or didn't say, I felt no obligation to her. I wasn't the one who was married to her. My attitude was, 'All's fair in love and war.' In fact, her existence sounded so grim that I started thinking it would be good for her to get a life, and in a way, divorce would be the best thing for her. She might really come into her own and develop some independence."

This kind of stunning conceit on the part of the Other Woman is by no means uncommon, not least because women who believe they are intimacy experts tend to believe they know what's best for everyone else's relationships. Every unmarried Other Woman I interviewed was at least ten years younger than her lover, and most expressed thinly veiled scorn or open pity and concern for his wife, because she was "traditional" or "lacked career goals." Interestingly, many said the same kinds of things about their own mothers.

"I feel really sorry for her," says Susan, the public relations executive, of her lover's wife. "She's the perfect housewife, but that isn't enough any more. It's like she's living in the last century and he's living in this one, and he wants to be with a woman who's his equal, someone who can keep up. I'm sure she knows about us — how could she not know? He says he's staying late at the office every single night. But she turns a blind eye because if she loses him, she'll have nothing left."

This idea that the wife already knows and is colluding in her own victimization is a popular one among Other Women, not least because it allows them to believe that the affair has her good housekeeping seal of approval. Like Elaine, some see themselves, at least initially, as the liberator of a benighted woman and may entertain the fantasy that the wife will be grateful to them one day. As Laurel Richardson observes, feminist consciousness hasn't prevented single women from having affairs with married men, but it has created a new way for the Other Woman to ease her own conscience: "She can do feminist social work among the married."[4]

Elaine did not believe she was competing with Bill's wife — she did not even see her as a worthy rival. Sometimes it was easy to pretend that Bill's wife didn't really exist and that she was his true mate. After all, she spent more time with him, they had more in common, and they were practically living together in the office. From Elaine's point of view, she was conforming to the sexual script: she was nurturing an unhappy man who desperately needed her, and applying her intimacy expertise to sorting out his wife's problems, too. She wasn't battling Bill's wife, she was liberating her; she wasn't hurting another woman, she was repairing a broken man.

Of course, as Richardson points out, the single woman who is constantly being compared to the unsatisfactory wife at home is, in fact, engaged in a private duel in which "the husband chooses the weapons: beauty, intelligence, health, business acumen, sexuality, and empathy. He makes the rules, he picks the contestants, and he judges the tourney... The competition with his wife, a competition which the single woman perceives herself as winning, derails her jealousy and raises her self-esteem. And it also binds her closer to her married lover, for she can take sides with him against his wife. She can be his ally in *blaming* his wife. Without demeaning herself, she can express her hostility toward his wife."[5]

The Other Woman has to believe that the wife is at fault and the marriage is disastrous; otherwise, she could not believe in the blameless goodness of the married man, and she would feel constantly guilty. By taking refuge in the caring, maternal role of the sexual script, women can avoid guilt and avoid acknowledging that they are in fact engaged in a winner-take-all competition, while retaining their claim to moral superiority. The Other Woman is morally superior to the awful wife who has made the married man's life a misery (and she is morally superior to him — at least she isn't betraying any wedding vows). Clearly, she is a peerless intimacy expert: she is providing a superior relationship, sharing more with the man, and taking better care of him.

It's understandable that Elaine was able to view herself as a nurturing helpmate rather than a destructive sexual rival, because Bill was weaker, needier, and in many respects more dependent on her than she was on him. But he was the only person who was benefiting from her attempts to follow the sexual script. Elaine herself was becoming increasingly frustrated and feeling increasingly put upon; she also was not getting what she wanted — a man she could have all to herself.

Psychologically, then, the power dynamic was much as it has always been between single women and married men; the husband was having his cake and eating it too, the wife was getting a raw deal, and the mistress was desperately trying to rationalize her behavior so that she could live with herself. Professionally, however, the power dynamic in no way resembled the imbalance between a senior man and a junior woman in, say, the sixties. Neither Bill nor Elaine thought that she was working for him; rather, they were working together. Both of them believed she had reasonable hopes of getting to the corner office under her own steam. Elaine has read Gloria Steinem, has marched for abortion rights, and fervently believes in equal pay for equal work; she didn't want to be treated like a little girl but like a player.

Elaine was not, however, comfortable behaving like one. Before she started sleeping with Bill, she was deeply uncomfortable with the competitive atmosphere in her office. She was distressed by her own envy of more successful colleagues, she didn't like "having to be aggressive to get ahead," and she felt "defeminized" by her job.

Once her affair began, all these conflicts seemed to be resolved. "There was no separation any more between my personal life and my professional life. I kind of mapped the role of the wife and mother onto my career, so I was taking care of Bill emotionally and these projects we worked on became my babies," she says. "The reason men can carry on with deceit for years is that they have experience separating work and home, but women don't. My instinct was to try to combine the two, and looking back, I think that's a large part of the reason I got into the relationship. I was sick of being tough and hard the way men are in their business dealings, and felt like this loving, maternal side of me had no outlet. The thing about being the boss's mistress is that you get to express both those sides in your professional life."

This "instinct" to combine professional and personal identities is by no means uncommon, and causes serious difficulties for many women who would never dream of sleeping with their bosses. Women who try to follow the prescriptions of the sexual script — be nice, modest, and cooperative — find that these instructions put them at a disadvantage in the working world. Many shy away from open competition or are derailed by its negative aspects: the criticism, the jealousy, the ill will. As we saw in the previous chapter, Nadine tried to defuse competition with her colleagues the same way she always had with her friends — through self-deprecation and one-downmanship — and wound up undermining herself professionally.

Other women downgrade their own ambitions for the same reasons that Nadine tried to personalize her professional relationships: they fear being disliked, they feel uncomfortable openly competing, and they worry that their success will engender hostility. "A lot of my women friends have eased themselves down to a lower professional level by taking jobs in other companies that are really a step backward in terms of their overall careers," says Margaret, the management consultant. "Some of them want to have kids and can't do it without scaling back, so it's depressing but understandable. But some of them just find the competitive atmosphere too toxic. If you're ambitious, you have to be able to take criticism and not view it as a personal attack. Women don't have much experience not taking things personally, and we don't have enough role models for doing it. What worries me is that there never *will* be any role models if talented women get scared and back off. Most of the ones I know who are backing off aren't doing it because their goals have changed. They're doing it because they can't separate their professional and personal identities, so they have a difficult time in a really competitive atmosphere."

Once Elaine began the affair, her professional and personal identities seemed to merge, and the competitiveness in her office seemed to vanish. She was blissfully unaware that her co-workers were gossiping disapprovingly, merely playing along with the pretense that her relationship with Bill was strictly professional.

If the man in such an affair is in a powerful position, his underlings certainly will not let on that they know what he's up to, and he becomes a human shield for the woman, as well. No matter what colleagues are saying behind her back, they are far more likely to be pleasant and deferential to her face; no one wants to risk offending him, so courtesy is extended to her. Similarly, no one will go to her to complain about his dumb decisions or the infuriating way he drones on and on, in love with the sound of his own voice. She has broken rank and she has his ear, thus she can be a helpful ally or dangerous enemy in her own right. Usually, she is entirely unaware that anyone is making these kinds of calculations to court her good opinion. All the woman may notice is that, at least on the surface, the atmosphere in the office has become cozy, friendly, and even domestic.

She can deny that competition exists, even as she is gaining a significant competitive advantage. She can become a player, without ever having to act like one. Elaine was privy to pillow talk that helped put her on the fast track; she also had the benefit of Bill's personal attention, advice, and guidance. She was able to perform at a higher level as a result, and he was in a position to ensure that her good work was recognized.

Furthermore, although their relationship did not begin with quid pro quo offers, as it happened, she *did* get promotions after they began having sex. While it may be tempting to view this as a straight exchange of professional perks in return for sexual services — a kind of retroactive form of harassment in which she received promotions for having sex, which also served as inducements to continue the affair — there was no coercion involved in their relationship.

Beyond that first ill-advised kiss, Bill did not abuse his power, and in fact, Elaine does not believe that his initial advance was motivated by anything more sinister than sexual attraction. At any rate, she had options: forget the kiss altogether, or lodge a sexual harassment complaint as per their company policy. She was in no way intimidated out of laying charges, and did not fear that doing so would harm her career. Nor did Bill attempt to silence her, pressure her into bed, or even so much as hint that she would receive professional rewards if she had sex with him.

As far as Elaine was concerned, Bill's kiss did not create a hostile climate but an exciting one, and he did not take advantage of his position of relative power. Rather, his power is precisely what attracted her. He made the initial advance, but she was the one who actively chose to escalate to a full-fledged, sexual affair. Her reasons — she was interested in him and deeply flattered by his interest in her, and she was bored, lonely, and in the market for romance — had nothing to do with coercion and everything to do with self-interest. They were, in short, not dissimilar from the reasons that anyone chooses to begin a sexual relationship.

For his part, Bill, like many people in positions of authority, chose to promote someone he liked and trusted. After their affair began, he was well-placed to assess Elaine's professional potential; he knew she'd be able to perform competently at a higher level, and he knew they would work well together. It's no surprise when men promote their golf buddies or when women hire other women because they like them more than equally qualified applicants, but when sexual attraction is thrown into the mix, decisions about advancement seem to take on a more menacing complexion: *abuse of power*. These accusations are almost always hurled only at men, partly because more men than women are in positions of power, but also because men are generally presumed to lead with their crotches while women are rarely suspected of such base motives.

In the sexual script, men are predators and women are defenseless prey, but real life is far more complex — and in real-life relationships, power shifts back and forth between partners all the time. Elaine felt sexually powerful, which she was, and professionally powerful, which she became, partly because Bill helped her. She did not view herself as being below Bill but beside him, a partner and an equal who understood his work and shared his interest in it. She joined the ad agency fully expecting that one day she herself might be a vice-president; she didn't need his help to reach the top, but it did accelerate her ascent.

Although we tend to think that a younger woman seeks an older man as a kind of father figure, Elaine was in the process of becoming her *father*, not, as she'd feared, her mother. By the time she began the affair with Bill, she had more in common with her father than with her mother, and she did not need or want to be Daddy's little girl. Yet, although she had achieved her goal of surpassing her mother, Elaine did not, in the end, entirely reject her values; she too chose a relationship in which she was expected to put her own goals on hold and take care of another person emotionally. It may not have been what she imagined in university when she talked about having it all, but in a very real sense, she did have it all, or at least, she was having it both ways. She had a brilliant career, a serious relationship, and she had broken the rules while still appearing to follow the prescriptions — empathize, nurture — of the sexual script.

Bill himself was in the midst of a full-blown mid-life crisis. He looked back over his shoulder and saw a column of hungry, younger people and he looked ahead and saw closed doors in the president's suite. Professionally, he felt trapped. He didn't view Elaine as a daughter figure, but as an ally. He was not attracted solely by her youth, but by the fact that she had a similar educational background, similar aspirations, and a good head for the business of advertising. Her status was important to him, not least because it legitimated his extramarital dalliance; his wife didn't understand the life he led, but

Elaine certainly did. She was his equal, intellectually, and they shared the same world. And, once she'd been promoted a few times, she was in a position where she could defend him, provide backup, and side with him in meetings. Their titles were not equal, but in fact, they functioned as partners: each looked out for the other, and their complementary strengths made them an unbeatable team.

Their rapport was genuine, as was their affection for each other, but each also viewed the other as a trophy. This is true in many relationships, but here, there was a professional as well as a personal aspect. To Elaine, Bill was proof of her own sexual magnetism and professional prowess; to him, she was proof that he wasn't over the hill sexually or washed-up professionally. He wanted to take on her youthful enthusiasm every bit as much as she wanted to take on his mature wisdom, and for the same professional reason: as a shield that would provide a competitive advantage and some protection from professional rivals.

Midway through their third year together, Elaine was no longer willing or able to conceal her anger about Bill's heel-dragging reluctance to leave his marriage and his insistence on knowing where she was at all times. They were having terrible fights. "I love you, that's why I want to know where you are," he shouted. It upset him that she didn't feel the same concern for him, didn't phone his office a dozen times a day when she was out of town.

"Why would I?" she replied. "I know where you are, you're in the office. What's the point of calling?"

"Don't you care about me?" he'd ask. "Don't you miss me? I can't stand being away from you."

"If you can't stand it, why haven't you moved out yet?" she lobbed right back. He started coming into her office (that came with the third promotion, a real office instead of a cubicle) to argue, so frequently that she began to get nervous about what it might look like to her co-workers, whether they could hear what was going on behind the closed door. She wasn't concerned about what might happen to him if people found out about them; she was worried about what might happen to her.

"I could see that people might say I'd traded firm breasts for seniority," she says. "I was worried that everything I'd achieved would be discounted, and I wouldn't be taken seriously any more."

When a shift at the top of the agency changed the constellation of power and everything was uncertain for a while, Bill's neediness increased to intolerable levels. They were fighting so much now that the tension was spilling over into the office; he'd started slamming doors and flying into a temper with employees again. She was too busy with her own work to have time to be maternal. "Get a grip," she said. "You're acting like a two-year-old."

Finally, she broke up with him. He cried and sent so many flowers that her apartment looked like a funeral home. She got lonely, she missed him, she felt that her life was empty of everything but pain, and she decided to take him back. But four months later, when he still hadn't left his wife, she broke up with him again. He said, "All right, if that's the way you want it." This time she was the one who cried, wept away an entire weekend. Even though she had initiated the split, the fact that he agreed with such seeming equanimity made her feel that she'd been dumped. Had he never intended to leave his wife? Had he been stringing her along the whole time?

Having to see each other in the office every day was a nightmare, and he cracked first, begging for another chance after only two weeks of strained smiles and trying to act normal in front of everyone else. He really was going to leave his wife, he declared, he meant it this time.

But Elaine was suddenly shying away from the responsibility of "wrecking so many other people's lives," as she put it. "I didn't want the guilt." His kids were pretty well all grown up, but still, it would turn their lives upside down. And his wife — well, Elaine had developed some empathy for her, now that she knew firsthand what it felt like to be separated from Bill. Nor did she entirely trust his account of the marriage. She knew how good he was at putting a certain gloss on events, and she'd learned that he saw the world pretty much as it was convenient for him to see it.

More than being concerned about having blood on her hands, however, Elaine was wondering if her own feelings were strong enough to justify the carnage. She was starting to think about things that had seemed irrelevant before, when her main goal had been having Bill all to herself. He was so emotionally demanding that she couldn't imagine having any energy left over for children, and besides, he was fifty-one — he'd be a senior citizen long before any child of theirs was old enough to drive.

Perhaps because he sensed her uncertainty, Bill finally did leave his wife, on Elaine's thirty-second birthday. One month later, Elaine implemented the second part of their plan: she left her job and moved to another advertising agency, into a parallel position at a slightly increased salary. Now they could finally stop living a lie and begin a normal life together.

And she tried, she really did, but fundamentally they were incompatible; they really *were* polar opposites in terms of personality, and didn't complement each other so much as grate on each other. She wanted to go out dancing, but he was an emotional wreck after separating from his wife and needed constant tending. It was awkward introducing him to her friends, and his friends — and children — had sided with his wife and wanted nothing to do with Elaine. Once they weren't working together any more, the spark between them seemed more intellectual than sexual. Maybe it had been so all along, Elaine thought.

If she'd still been in love with him the way she was at the beginning, perhaps none of this would have mattered. But he seemed smaller to her now than he had three short years before, when she was sitting at her desk reading reports about toilet paper. He was so clingy, so demanding, so needy, and she was tired of being the strong one all the time. Bill was not prepared to give her up without a fight, not after throwing away his marriage, and he begged, pleaded, and stormed. He phoned at two a.m., crying. Elaine said, "Go back to your wife — you can make it work." If she hadn't felt so guilty about his predicament, she would have said, "Go back to your wife — I don't have the energy any more to take care of both of us."

After all the tears and recriminations were over, she was left with some good memories and a tangible keepsake: a senior job at another ad agency. In just three years, she had more than doubled her salary, and leapfrogged over most of her co-workers into a powerful position at a new agency where no one knew or cared how she'd got there.

But she found the new job difficult, especially at first. "I went from being in a position where my boss trusted everything I said and wanted my opinion on everything to a position where my new boss's only concern is, 'Did you finish that memo?' All he cares about is whether or not I deliver on a particular task. I'm having to relearn how to be an employee," Elaine says. Even though she knew she was competent, and even though she believed she deserved every promotion that she had received from Bill, she was now aware that there had been some talk in their old office about how, exactly, she had reached the top echelons so quickly.

Looking back, she is beginning to question her own motives: "The main reason I stayed in the relationship with Bill so long was that I got addicted to the power. I forfeited the chance to work on a real future for myself that included a family, in return for a place at the table. I remember going to see a potential client about a deal that was worth millions. There were five of us from the agency and then some client people in the room, but everyone else just watched while Bill and I talked to the president of the company. I was only thirty-one, but I had access to a circle that wouldn't have been open to me otherwise, and it made me feel big and important. I *was* big and important. Now I'm struggling with the feeling that maybe I don't deserve the position I have at the new agency, maybe I did sleep my way to a job title that's a few notches higher than it should be. There's not a whole lot of morality in business — it's just about winning and the deal and making quota. Maybe I took that on, took on this very goal-oriented sexuality that was really only about self-interest."

In retrospect, she marvels at her own naivety: "I just didn't understand the difference between fooling around with a guy at a party and fooling around with the boss, because I'd never done anything that had consequences that couldn't be fixed the next day." Still, the consequences in her case seem to have been mostly positive. She had a serious relationship, she had companionship, and she enjoyed it while it lasted. As Elaine herself says, the cost-benefit ratio was always more favorable to her: "Bill was risking things he already had. I was risking not getting things that I *wanted* to have, like marriage and a family. That's a really big difference. I was speculating, and if it didn't pan out I could always move on. He was risking everything."

She still misses him, but she also regrets the lost time and worries that she may have jeopardized her own chances for what she now calls "a real future," which means a life like her mother's: a family, a house with a white picket fence. But whatever emotional losses she incurred, in professional terms, Elaine's gamble did pay off, handsomely.

Many women get ahead because they have sex appeal and/or good looks, and the same is true for men; a broad-shouldered, tall man with rugged appeal has an advantage in most professions over a jug-eared, pigeon-chested one. A large body of research demonstrates that conventionally attractive people get all kinds of perks in life: others judge them to be nicer and more intelligent than average-looking people, and they tend to get more attention from parents, to receive better grades in school, and to make faster professional progress as adults.[6]

Being female — particularly a young and attractive female — can be a significant asset in the office for the very same reasons that it can make one a target of harassment. Most women know this perfectly well, and some actively use their gender, looks, and/or youth as leverage in the workplace, playing on men's sexual interest in order to get what they want professionally. There's nothing inherently shameful about using one's physical charms to one's own advantage; there's no real qualitative difference between being attractive and having a pleasant phone voice or charming manner. Nor is there any real difference between trading on one's looks and trading on nepotism or school ties. It's understandable that people who want to get ahead use everything they have to do so; in business, the law of the jungle applies, as men comprehend so readily.

No one has to behave unprofessionally to express or capitalize on a sexual attraction. The curious thing about a current of sexual interest is both how intangible and how palpable it can be at the same time; not a single inappropriate word or action may betray it, but it is, nevertheless, there. A man does not need to grope or proposition a woman to signal his sexual attraction, and she need not perch on his knee, bat her eyelashes, lift her skirt, or even acknowledge his interest in order to profit from it. Particularly for young women in junior positions, low-level, unacted-upon attractions can be extremely beneficial: the powerful man pays attention to her and can give her opportunities that she might not otherwise have.

"Sexuality is a power tool for women," declares Laura, who is only thirty-four but already Bill's counterpart: a vice-president of a major advertising agency. Unlike Elaine, she has never had an office affair, but she readily confesses to using her sex appeal to get ahead: "I bluffed my way into advertising with no experience, and basically got my first job because the boss fancied me. He didn't do or say anything, it was just obvious. I wasn't the slightest bit interested in him, but the fact that he liked me meant that he went out of his way to help me. Advertising is administrative at the entry level, not strategic, and if you're bright and competent, you can fake it to a certain point. But I really had no clue when it came to things like writing a media plan, and wouldn't have even tried my hand at it if he hadn't been prepared to overlook my mistakes. He encouraged me and taught me how to do really advanced work, so by the time I got my next job, I was on my way. It makes me angry when any kind of flirtation is positioned as sexual harassment, because it makes women look so weak and spineless. If a man you work with is attracted to you, he's not abusing you or taking advantage of you — *you* can use *him*, get him in your corner professionally."

Laura did not play up to her first boss or lead with her pelvis or hint coyly that one day, if he played his cards right, she might be persuaded to have wild sex on top of the photocopier. She didn't have to; she merely made the most of every opportunity that his interest in her provided. "If he'd hit on me, I would've turned him down flat," she says. "But I don't think he was under any illusion that I was interested. He just liked having a twenty-two-year-old woman around, and it made him feel like a he-man to help me." His motives were, however, of no importance to her so long as he was acting in her best interests.

Now that Laura's the boss, she's still using men's attraction to her own advantage. "You can make some twenty-six-year-old smart-ass come to heel and do exactly what you want, and it's not even difficult. You don't have to get tarted up or vamp around the office — most men turn to jelly at the slightest sign of a woman's sexual confidence. I don't have a problem taking advantage of that, because there are real disadvantages to being a woman in an industry where you have to schmooze male clients. You have to walk a fine line so they don't get the wrong message or misinterpret the fact that you're asking them out to dinner. Sexuality is a liability sometimes, so when it's an asset, of course I'm going to use it."

It's important for women to acknowledge that female sexuality can be a source of power, even in the office. We need to remind ourselves of this fact because otherwise, we wind up connecting our sexuality only with weakness, and we learn to view it only as something that makes us vulnerable to exploitation. We learn to think that men are the only ones with sexual power, and as we shall see, this misperception winds up costing us dearly.

It is also important to acknowledge that women compete with each other professionally through sex. Clearly, the woman who merely capitalizes on a more powerful man's attraction and the woman who actually sleeps with him both gain a competitive advantage over other women. However unfair this is, it is unproductive to blame men or the patriarchy for it, because it denies that women are responsible for their own choices and accountable for their own behavior, and denies that women can be sexual and moral actors. But when we demonize such women, we reinforce the traditional belief that a sexual woman is a bad woman, which hurts all of us and only increases male power. It is a form of moral intimidation that keeps us working overtime to court our so-called sisters' approval — who may strike out anyway, regardless of what we do.

"Without a doubt, my looks have helped me professionally, but they've also hurt me," says Elizabeth, the strikingly beautiful woman who had such trouble with the popular girls in high school. "I know they've got me in the door in certain situations, but I also know that then I've had to work harder to prove that I'm capable, not just to other women but to men at my level. There's almost a hazing period where you have to prove you're more than a pretty face, and it never really ends. Every time you get a promotion, there are whispers: 'She must be sleeping with someone.'"

Rumors of sexual misconduct often plague successful women who have done nothing to deserve them. There is no male parallel — *he slept his way to the top* — and even if there were, the man who traded sexual favors for professional advancement would probably be applauded for his resourcefulness. Women suffer because of this double standard, but also use it to their own advantage. Gossip about women's supposed sexual improprieties is frequently started by other women, and this too is a form of competition that reinforces traditional and unequal sexual standards. The target feels besmirched and insulted; the rest of us get the message that if we succeed, other women will say nasty things about us and question our morality.

The woman who really is sleeping with the boss will be even more harshly punished by other women, if they get the chance. She may come in for passive-aggressive neglect by support staff — "The printer isn't working, so I can't finish your presentation" — as well as ostracism from women at her own level: "Sorry, we didn't know you'd want to come along for drinks." Higher up in the ranks, older women who fought in the front lines to overturn employers' perception that women are mere sexual playthings tend to take a dim view of women like Elaine, and there are enough of them in positions of power that they can stop an Other Woman in her professional tracks or make her work life miserable if they so choose. And if the affair ends, she finds herself in double jeopardy: she has aroused her co-workers' animosity and lost her protector.

Other Women rarely feel like winners in these competitions; some profit professionally as a result of their affairs, but almost all suffer emotionally. Although they may get ahead in the office, they usually wind up in a subordinate position in the relationship itself, sitting home alone on their birthdays, playing second fiddle to another woman while the man enjoys the best of both worlds. The fact that the Other Woman stands a very good chance of ending up a victim, however, has everything to do with her own choices, and her belief that she is an intimacy expert who can make any relationship work — which keeps her hanging on long after it has become clear that this particular relationship is no good for her.

It may seem odd that someone like Elaine, who has achieved goals that feminists could only dream of thirty years ago, would become involved in an affair that is the antithesis of everything feminism stands for. But one of the founding lies of sisterhood was that once women had power, they would not compete for men; in fact, competition for men was portrayed as the main obstacle to women's ability to get real power in the world. The reality, though, is that once women have power, they still want love, they still want to get ahead, and they still want things for themselves alone.

The truth of the matter is that some women have always been prepared to sell out their sisters, in a heartbeat, if there was something in it for them. Women don't do this because they aren't good feminists, or because they're evil people, or because they're powerless puppets when it comes to men. They do it because they are individuals with free will and strong desires. They are, in fact, sexual agents.

Chapter Four

Undercover Agents

Diane has short, jet-black hair, bright red lipstick, and a rack of earrings on her left ear. She is a college sophomore with a few philosophy courses under her belt, a closet full of thrift-shop dresses and men's blazers in a range of out-there hues, and a nineteen-year-old's firm conviction that she has it all figured out. If she were a boy, she would be called cocky, but she is a girl who has only recently started to refer to herself as a woman — the word still sticks in her mouth and comes out defiant — and beneath her hip costume and certainty is a hunger to be noticed. Her bright colors and big words ensure that she will be, although later, you cannot quite summon up the details of her pleasantly smudged face. Blue eyes — no, brown? Short? Or middling height? What you remember is her appetite for attention.

After freshman year, Diane didn't want to go back home to upstate New York, where she was the bright loner who wore weird clothes and lived on the wrong side of town. Instead, she stayed in Boston and got a job as a temp in a law firm — she needed to earn money, her scholarship didn't cover everything — which was fine for about a week, until the postcards from her friends began arriving, with their hectic messages about Amsterdam nightlife and misadventures in Rome.

In July, she'd bumped into Eric on the street, and they'd commiserated about being stuck in the city while everyone else was traipsing around with backpacks in foreign countries. Eric is preppy, pre-med, and clearly going places — not, in short, Diane's type. She tends toward clever cynics in Doc Martens, the kind of men who would be skeptical about Eric's chiseled blondness and rah-rah manner. But she was bored, she was single, and she found herself saying "sure" when he asked her out to dinner. "He's hardly electrifying, but he's not an axe-murderer, either," she explains.

They went out several times, unmemorable evenings that ended in tepid kisses and mild groping. Being pawed by a Big Man On Campus, even one who reminded her of a teddy bear, was not entirely unpleasant. In fact, she rather liked the way he stared at her mouth while they were talking, so obviously wanting to kiss her, and liked the fact that he was old enough not to need fake ID to buy beer.

Yet Diane had no romantic ambitions as far as Eric was concerned — she prided herself on staying a few steps ahead of the zeitgeist, and he was irredeemably conventional — so she wasn't even tempted when he tried, clumsily, to maneuver her into bed. Seeing him was primarily a diversion from the boredom of going into a stuffy law office every day and being ordered around by the career drones, and she didn't waste a moment worrying about the fact that he already had a girlfriend, Jane, who was off in Paris studying French. Eric was a summer amusement, that was all, and Diane was enjoying the novelty of toying with a man when she didn't really care whether he called again or not.

Nevertheless, this too was getting stale by the end of the summer. She was glad when registration finally rolled around and elated to be a sophomore, which meant a slightly larger dorm room and a more definite sense of belonging. Going to the first keg party before classes started was like rejoining the general population after a spell of solitary confinement, and she was so restless for a good time that she arrived unfashionably early, when the floor wasn't yet sticky with spilled beer and no one was locked in the bathroom, throwing up. It was still possible to navigate the room without having to shove, and although her own friends weren't there yet, Diane didn't feel out of place, not the way she had at the same time last year. In fact, she felt a rush of warmth toward people she hadn't thought about even once during the past few months, just glad to see their faces again.

Eric was already there, in his element, drinking with his buttoned-down friends. He gave her a dismissive wave and turned away, which surprised Diane, but then she noticed that Jane, the prodigal girl-friend, was by his side, kissing everyone on both cheeks and frothing over with French phrases. Well, well, Diane thought as she headed over, with nothing more than a little mischief on her mind, Barbie's back and Ken is nervous.

"Eric! How nice to see you again," she said, elaborately formal, and his cheeks bloomed with a sudden blush. Diane almost laughed out loud at the ease with which she'd thrown him off balance.

But Jane didn't even seem to notice. "You worked in a law firm? That's so great!" she trilled.

Diane suspected that Jane would act equally enthusiastic about summer jobs that involved flipping burgers and mopping floors. Jane's glee-club manner was smug and insincere, or at least that's how it seemed to Diane, who was suddenly not feeling well-disposed toward fine-boned blondes who had spent the summer flitting around Paris and were now effortlessly commanding admiration.

"That dress is so, umm, *you*!" Jane cried, so loudly that a few people turned to look, curious.

"I've had it for ages," Diane lied. She'd bought the dress specially for the party, but now felt like an overdressed ugly duckling compared to Jane, who was wearing a simple, pastel sheath that was cut modestly but left little to the imagination.

"Well, it really suits you," Jane announced in the tone of a staunch defender who doesn't care what anyone else says.

Diane felt that she had been insulted and that it was time to get her own back. "So," she said in her most innocent voice, "Eric tells me you were in Paris. How was that?"

The implication seemed to go right over Jane's head. She burbled on about France while Eric stared at his feet and hemmed and hawed like a cartoon character, making it plain that he had something to hide. Jane, however, didn't even appear to consider for a moment that Diane could be any cause for concern, and excused herself to skip across the room for an emotional reunion with another group of friends.

"Maybe you should just carry a sign saying 'I was a bad boy this summer,'" Diane murmured to Eric, who startled, his forehead creased with alarm, which made her smile. "Calm down," she said, "it'll be our little secret." He was the kind of guy who insists on buying a drink for the lady, so he handed Diane a beer and then pulled away a little from his frat-boy friends for some small talk of the so-what-courses-are-you-taking variety. Pretty soon, though, he was telling her a long, involved story about going sailing the week before, and then she was recounting the tale of her last day at work, when she'd finally blown up at the obnoxious lawyer she'd been telling Eric about during the summer, the one who'd treated her and the lifers on the support staff like his personal slaves.

The music was getting louder, more people were arriving, the party was taking on that wild, anything-could-happen feeling that Diane had been yearning for since June. She felt like the room wasn't big enough to contain her. "Come on, this is my favorite song," she said, grabbing Eric's hand and trying to pull him out to dance with her, even though she could tell he was one of those uptight guys who don't know what to do with their arms and shuffle around in little circles, hoping that no one is watching.

"I don't dance," Eric protested, which, after two beers, struck Diane as richly amusing. He was so stiff, so predictable!

"You give new meaning to the term white bread," she said, and riffed on that theme for a while. She was enjoying herself, not least because he seemed to find her exotic and supremely witty, and his friends, guys who were never interested in women with short hair and vintage clothing and lace-up boots, were really looking at her for the first time. The circle was expanding as other people drifted over to join them, and Diane was really on, tossing back beer and entertaining them by poking fun at Eric, who didn't mind a bit.

Across the room, Jane was also holding court, spraying smiles at a gaggle of admirers. Diane didn't get it, didn't get how a woman who appeared to have crawled out of a mold cast in the fifties could still attract men with such ease. And then, double-take — no, it couldn't be. But yes, Jonathan had joined the groupies bowing and scraping to Jane. Diane felt a flare of envy so visceral that she was aware of the searing sensation before her brain sorted it into words: *how unfair*. She'd had a crush on Jonathan — a hawk-nosed, slick-haired man she couldn't even look straight in the eye because she was afraid he'd see immediately just how hopelessly infatuated she was — ever since the first week of freshman year, but he'd never been more than polite to her. And now there he was, that paragon of coolness, basking in Jane's thousand-watt perkiness and — God! He was practically drooling!

Diane felt her face go hot, but she threw her head back, laughed uproariously, and generally tried to impersonate someone who was having the time of her life and couldn't care less about Jonathan. "All those old high school feelings of 'I'm not popular' and 'boys don't like me' just hit me like a cold breeze, and I started getting very, very flirtatious with Eric, much more flirtatious than I'd ever been," she says.

She touched his arm and nuzzled up against him and made it clear that she was prepared to do a whole lot more, which, she imagined, would seem tantalisingly risqué to a guy who was used to hanging around with uptight WASPs. She was right. Eric was increasingly flustered by her directness, which made her feel completely in control — until she noticed that Jane was tossing her hair infuriatingly and allowing herself to be persuaded to dance with Jonathan.

The fourth beer didn't take the edge off Diane's envy, but it did embolden her to do something about it. Where did Jane get off with her patronizing, Lady Bountiful routine, treating Diane like a charity case, when the fact of the matter was that her boyfriend had been panting after Diane all summer long? Who did Jane think she was, strutting around like she owned the world when anyone could see that she'd have to take her shirt off to count to two?

Well, Diane would show her. *She* could make Eric do whatever she wanted, and what she found herself wanting was to see just how far she could make him go. "I decided to go for it. In my own defence, I have to say I was pretty drunk by the time I started seriously coming on to him," Diane remembers. "I was trying to lure him back to my room, saying, 'Come on, it'll be fun.'"

He resisted, even though she said they'd only go for a minute, just long enough for her to pick up something she'd forgotten, but he had the irresolute air of a man who could be budged. She was brushing up against him, accidentally on purpose, remembering how, on one of their dates, he had stopped just short of begging her to go back to his place. "What's the matter?" she was now whispering in his ear. "No one needs to know."

Sensing that he was weakening, she delivered the coup de grace: "Eric, we really need to talk." Diane was so preoccupied with watching Jane that she hardly noticed when Eric leaned toward her and said, in his best jock-being-clever voice, "We *are* talking."

No, that wasn't what she meant, Diane said impatiently. He was starting to get on her nerves. "We need to talk about this summer," she said, implying that there were Emotional Issues to resolve. Her pained intonation was reflexive, really, one of those automatic responses she'd developed with uncommunicative boyfriends.

"It's the least you owe me," she finally said and stalked off in the direction of her room, so caught up in the drama she'd invented that she'd nearly convinced herself she had a right to be upset. Apparently she did convince Eric, who scuttled up the stairs after her, calling, "Hey, wait up," and worrying aloud that Jane might find out that they'd seen each other that summer.

Diane cut him off: "Don't worry. She's so busy talking about Gay Paree, she probably didn't even notice that we know each other."

She hadn't decorated her room yet and the place looked depressingly institutional, about as sexy as a prison cell, but she threw open the door with a triumphant flourish. "I was feeling a total sense of power, that I had him under my thumb and he preferred me to Jane," she recalls. "I'd lured him away from her in front of all those other people, and I felt good."

But she'd been so intently focused for the past hour on the goal of getting him to leave the party that she hadn't developed a plan for what to do if she succeeded. For a minute or so they just stood there awkwardly, the only sound the faint booming echo of the party down below, while Eric feigned a deep interest in her CD collection. They were losing momentum, and Diane was not so drunk that she couldn't hear the voice in her head, which was saying, *Let's get this over with.*

She wanted to get back the feeling she'd had a few minutes before, of being poised on a dangerous edge, so she said, "Jane doesn't have to know," in a low, throaty tone, and followed up with a kiss. She'd forgotten about that mashing, sloshing way he kissed, all eagerness and saliva.

"This isn't such a good idea," he started to say, but it sounded more like a question than a declaration, and then he wasn't saying anything because she'd pulled her dress over her head in one rapid, jerky movement and her arms were around him and they had fumbled onto the bed.

Diane was convinced that Jane was no match for her in the bedroom; women like Jane might have deeper cleavage and more pronounced cheekbones, but they were squeamish and girl-y when it came to sex, more than likely frigid. She expected Eric to be mesmerized by her erotic expertise, but after a few minutes, he was still distracted. "Look, I feel bad. Jane..." He trailed off.

"That didn't bother you this summer," Diane said, which came out sounding as piqued as she felt.

But the last thing she wanted was to scare him off or give him an excuse to leave; matters had gone too far for her to view his departure as anything but an affront. "It would be like he preferred the idea of Jane to the reality of me" is how Diane remembers her reasoning. "Here I am in the flesh right now and you'd still rather have her — that's how I would've read it if he'd walked out."

She knew she should be a little more indulgent and bolster his confidence, if only as a pre-emptive strike to protect her own self-respect, so, careful to soften her tone, she said it again: "Jane doesn't have to find out."

Eric, however, was still fretting. "He said that if we were going to start going out, he really should do the right thing and break up with Jane first. I was just saying, 'Don't worry about it, everything will be OK,'" Diane recalls. He really did like her, that much was clear, and she was not displeased by the prospect of Jane being dumped. But Diane wanted to foreclose any discussion about the future: "I didn't see any need to talk about it because I wasn't interested in going out with him."

Her objectives were far more immediate. "What I really wanted was for him to want me more than Jane," she says. "The goal was to get that feeling of being ravished, of having the guy want you so much that he throws caution to the winds and can't resist his desire."

But Eric was too uncomfortable, and at any rate, lacked sensual skills. Diane had never particularly enjoyed fooling around with him on their dates, and now found herself trying to pretend he was Jonathan. She has a fertile imagination, but even she could not sustain this fiction for more than a minute. Jonathan, after all, was the kind of man who would have known what he was doing. Eric clearly did not.

"From the way he went at it, it was pretty obvious that he didn't have a clue about how to please a woman," she says, with the brisk detachment of a theater critic. "Part of the problem was that he was not well-endowed, to put it diplomatically, and he was very embarrassed about that. Now, men can do glorious things to compensate, but he either didn't know how or was so self-conscious that it didn't occur to him. And it didn't help that both of us were drunk."

The sex was terrible: perfunctory, graceless, decidedly unecstatic. "The feeling I thought I would get never came," Diane says. "It's like people who try heroin, thinking about the great warm rush they're going to get when they stick the needle in, but they just wind up with a terrific headache, feeling really sick to their stomachs."

She was disappointed and a little revolted and already had a foretaste of the next morning's hangover when she reached over to turn on the light. "The look on his face was so horrible I don't think I'll ever forget it," Diane remembers. Apparently, Eric felt even worse than she did. "It was clear that he had done something he totally did not want to do. He was a decent enough guy that he felt responsible for people, and I worked that against him, going for the we-really-need-to-talk angle, which was bullshit. I think he sensed immediately afterwards how little he meant to me, that I was just using him to make myself feel good. I did it for the drama of leaving the party with fabulous Jane's boyfriend, but I had zero interest in him."

She wears a lot of rings, one on almost every finger, and she's playing with them now. It's a long while before she says anything else, and she doesn't look up when she does: "What happened next was so ugly that I don't want to say, so that I can seem nicer than I really am."

Then it comes out in a low, breathless torrent, how she and Eric were almost dressed again when there was a knock on the door and they both just froze — it was one of those cinematic moments when you know something really bad is about to happen — and Jane started calling through the door, "Eric? Eric? Are you in there?"

Diane was wondering how Jane knew where her room was, just the kind of irrelevant detail your mind latches onto in the midst of a crisis, and she and Eric were still paralyzed by alarm when Jane said, "I know you're in there and I'm not leaving until you come out." Her voice caught on the last word with the beginning of tears, and then she started crying, but they didn't move until, after an eternity of muffled sobbing during which neither of them could even look at the other, Jane went away.

There was no happy ending: Jane was devastated, she and Eric split up, and Diane could never speak to either of them again although she kept trying to think of something she could say that would make it all better. Even though months have passed, the hot, prickly sensation of shame still surges up, strong and sure, every time she thinks about that night.

According to the credo of sisterhood, women vie for male sexual attention because the patriarchy has decreed it will be so. The problem, apparently, is that women are trained to believe they are worthless without men, and then men are given all the power and resources, so women *must* compete for men in order to ensure their own survival. This cunning design has two sinister benefits: women will remain anxious to please men and do their bidding, and will be too divided among themselves to unite and demand change. Other variants on this theme of blaming the patriarchy for women's competition also bear more than a passing resemblance to conspiracy theories: women compete because they've been brainwashed by the beauty myth and need constant male affirmation of their attractiveness, or because they suffer from the epidemic of low self-esteem that afflicts women in a society run by men.

Surprisingly, given that sexuality is the most hotly debated issue in modern feminism, few feminists dispute the claim that women who compete through sex do so because they are oppressed in some way. The feminist analysis of female sexual agency centers on the pursuit of pleasure, but rarely, if ever, on the capacity to cause harm. Even those feminists who celebrate "bad girls" are referring to women who are "bad" only insofar as they flout the old double standard and assert their right to have sex on their own terms. There has been almost no discussion of whether women might not also be bad in the ways that men are said to be bad: aggressive, predatory, competitive, and powerful enough to hurt others through sex.

This glaring omission has had the effect of splitting off everything that is ugly and troubling about sex and, either directly or by implication, blaming men for it. It seems as though women have the capacity to be sexual actors, but never behave badly; furthermore, they can't harm men because men are too powerful and too invulnerable. The end result is to perpetuate oppositional thinking, wherein women's capacity as sexual actors is sharply circumscribed by their own moral superiority and by a conception of masculine sexuality that does not include passivity, and to maintain the myth of female innocence.

This myth is "absolutely infantilizing and embalming," writes Joan Cocks in *The Oppositional Imagination*. "It implies that women are not complex enough in desire, sophisticated enough in imagination, and dynamic enough in will to act in vicious as well as virtuous ways, out of passions, predilections, and motive forces that are not men's but their own."[1]

The idea that the patriarchy made Diane or Elaine do it is deeply insulting, not just to them, but to all women. The fiction of female moral superiority amounts to an insidious form of backlash that encourages women to believe they are powerless dupes who lack free will, the capacity to form intentions, and the ability to enact them. And because the collective goodness of women depends on the collective badness of men, this myth also encourages us to cultivate contempt for — and fear of — the "opposite," morally inferior sex.

Ironically, one of the aims of denying women's ability to act in vicious ways seems to be bullying us into a position where we will be so anxious to prove our moral superiority that we will not try to steal a sister's man — though why we should want men in the first place, given their depravity, is unclear. Pretending that women are only capable of sweetness and light is a way of keeping us chained to our saintly sisters, swearing fervent assent, and secretly feeling guilty, ashamed, and deeply unfeminine every time we feel a "masculine" impulse. Women who openly beg to differ can count on swift punishment: accusations of false consciousness and threats of being thrown to the dogs — men.

No matter how well-intentioned, any theory that rests on the notion that men are responsible for women's own feelings, choices, and behavior is bad news for women. It perpetuates gender stereotypes that are harmful to women and prevents us from believing we can take control of our own lives. Thus, it is unpleasant but necessary to acknowledge that women are quite capable of being truly bad, and sex is one of the most powerful weapons in our arsenal.

Now, there is also some validity to certain feminist insights into women's sexual competition. But while it is absolutely true that traditionally feminine women view others as rivals for male approval and protection, it is no longer true that all women need men to ensure their own economic survival. Women like Diane and Elaine can support themselves and fully expect to do so. Yet they continue to seek male sexual attention. Evidence of brainwashing and low self-esteem? Perhaps. It is indisputable that women are conditioned to take their measure through relationships — not least because cultural feminists themselves promote a cult of connection — and many women do care far too much about male approval. But it is also true that women are human beings, notably social creatures, and want men for their own self-interested reasons: companionship, entertainment, and sex.

Women are individuals with complex, often contradictory motivations. The claim that they are not sexual agents in competitions with other women, and that these contests are all about winning men, is an overgeneralization that amounts to a bizarre distortion of the facts. In reality, these competitions may have little to do with men and everything to do with one woman's desire for mastery over another.

When Jane was away and Diane had Eric all to herself, she didn't want him. "Being alone with him on a summer night while Jane was in France didn't do anything for me," Diane says. At the party and even later, back in her room, she still did not really want him.

What she wanted was to best Jane. "It was a conquest of her more than him," she says, "a way of proving that I was more powerful and more attractive. Competing in a sexual forum is one of the ways you assess your own value, and I wanted to prove that I was worth more than Jane. Eric was just the means for doing that, and it was very stupid and cruel, using him to try to hurt her."

Although by no means proud of using him, Diane feels no lasting remorse about Eric. "I remember thinking he was too innocent for the tawdriness of the situation, but he did have a choice and he had a greater responsibility to Jane than I did. Anyway, he was no saint, putting the moves on me while his girlfriend was away," she explains. "But Jane really was a victim because she had no choice. She's the one I feel guilty about, because I was trying to hurt her and I succeeded."

Jane was not caught in the crossfire of burning passion, endless love, or patriarchal imperatives. "She was the target all along. If she'd broken up with Eric before the party, I know for sure that I wouldn't have had sex with him," Diane admits. "It's hard to explain, because it was really nothing more than an intense feeling of jealousy."

It wasn't just that Jonathan liked Jane and ignored Diane. Everything about Jane — her clothes, her hair, her bounciness, her vacation in France, her saccharine sweetness — elicited Diane's disdain, but also aroused her envy. Jane was exactly where Diane wanted to be: center stage.

Envy is in some ways a healthy emotion, because it demonstrates that one wants to have more and be better. These aren't alien feelings that the patriarchy implants in women's souls; if anything, it is women's way of connecting with one another, emphasizing sameness and denying difference and bonding on the basis of weakness, which ensures that envy will thrive among women. We see a woman who seems to have more than we do, and we want what she has.

"Envy indicates our desire for sameness, *not* for differentiation. Unlike jealousy, which indicates we are perceiving a loss, envy implies desire — the desire for a connection we feel is disrupted by difference," writes Laura Tracy in *The Secret Between Us*, a study of women's competition. "We experience envy when we meet someone who is different from us and, we think, better than we are. We covet what that person possesses because her possessions, whether material, physical, or intellectual, disconnect her from us."[2]

But envy is one of those negative emotions to which women are supposed to be immune, so we have learned to express it covertly in our friendships: through concern, which is used to mask put-downs or to ensure that the friend who has what we want will still need us, and through passive-aggressive jockeying for position. If we feel we can't match the friend's accomplishments, we may compete downward for the title of most oppressed and the consolation prize that comes with it: reassurance that the woman who is worst off is also the most morally superior.

Sometimes we use these same covert strategies to express envy of women who are not our friends. But the fact that we don't have a bond to preserve with them also frees us to compete in other, equally indirect but more treacherous ways. The centrality of relationships in women's lives means that instead of bragging that we drive a faster car or got a bigger pay raise, as some men do, we are more likely to act out our envy by competing through third parties. We try to make sure that the people who are close to or who admire the woman we envy also think highly of us.

There is probably not a woman in the world who has not had this impulse, and most women have acted on it. In some small way on at least one occasion, many of us have used a man to make a point to another woman. Sometimes there's nothing sexual about this at all; we may use the man to show her that we're just as smart or good at our jobs or witty as she is.

But getting his sexual attention is usually the easiest and fastest route, although often, we couldn't care less about the man in question and will rebuff him firmly as soon as we've made our point. *I'll show her* is the object of the exercise, and a casual, flirtatious remark to a man — not necessarily her partner, any man who happens to be close by will do in a pinch — may be all that's required. *See?* we're saying to her. *I'm just as good as you are — maybe even better*.

The goal in this contest is *not* to win a man but to match or best a woman who's perceived as a rival. If the competition actually becomes sexual, however, it can turn into a blood-sport where the goal is to harm another woman. This seems to be what Diane intended, and she's still mystified by and ashamed of the strength of her feelings. "She hadn't done anything to me to justify how much I wanted to hurt her," Diane says. "It's not a nice thing to find out that you're capable of so much petty jealousy and anger, and capable of acting it out through sex."

The capacity to cause damage through sex is not a nice kind of power, and the prevailing script provides the perfect cover story for women: we are swept away by love or swept along by the force of male sexual desire, so when other women are hurt by our behavior, it's always an unfortunate accident, never our intention. This tidal wave theory of sexuality, in which women are compelled to have sex by forces of nature they are powerless to control — romantic love and/or the male sex drive — is seductive because it helps to maintain the myth of female moral superiority.

If women are not sexual actors in their own right, but instead are mowed down by men's overpowering sexual desire, they cannot really be blamed when other women get hurt by their behavior. Likewise, if women only have sex to express true love, they can't be held accountable when the expression of their deepest feelings winds up causing harm to other women; they have been transported by love, a mystical force that renders women unable to reason or make responsible choices.

The tidal wave theory gives women a first-line defense against guilt: *I wasn't in control, I'm not responsible, it's not my fault that she got hurt.* And if that fails, there is always the last-ditch plea bargain of the feminist fatale: *She'll be better off now, anyway. I'm setting her free, putting her on the path to independence, and one day she may thank me for it.*

This is one reason why Diane wanted to be ravished and swept along by Eric's passion: she could then deny responsibility, deny that her objective was to bring Jane down a peg, and avoid guilt. If only she could stage-manage Eric into ravishing her, she would have an airtight alibi: *I was just reacting and responding, swept along by his lust.*

I'm not a sexual agent but a sexual receiver. She could have the best of both worlds: bragging rights to the title of Most Irresistible, and a spot right beside Jane in the camp of passive victims, where women have no say over what happens to them and struggle through life at the mercy of oversexed men. Eric, however, did not comply. In fact, he bumbled through sex with a decided lack of zeal.

Paradoxically, Diane was taking an active role — both by seducing Eric and by competing with Jane — to try to achieve a passive goal: being chosen, being preferred, being found more attractive. She was breaking away from the role for women in the sexual script but aiming to affirm it; she took a very active approach to try to arrive at a passive destination, where she could avoid guilt and could convince herself that she had conformed to the script.

Traditionally, passivity has been the hallmark of femininity, and "female sexuality has been equated with the ability to attract," observes Laura Tracy. "Yet being sexual at all means being aware of and in control of desire. Right now, we're not even sure what a desiring woman looks like if she doesn't resemble a witch or a bitch."[3]

One of the reasons we're still not sure what a desiring woman looks like is that she is usually careful to appear in public with bits of seaweed in her hair and flecks of foam on her face, gasping for air and exclaiming over the size of the breaker that swept her off the shore. If this caught-in-a-tidal-wave costume slips off, as it often does when one woman is battling fiercely to win another's man, apologists rush in with blanket excuses to cover the exposed antagonist: *poor thing, she's so hungry for male approval, so low in self-esteem, so insecure.*

Although insecurity is frequently a factor when a woman seeks the sexual attention of a man who is already attached, very often it stems less from a pathetic need for male confirmation than from a much stronger feeling that another woman is better or has more than oneself. Some women cope with their feelings of envy by attempting to dispossess their rivals or dispose of them altogether, and taking their men is usually an excellent place to start, not least because afterwards they can talk about being swept away or swept along and plead innocence.

In reality, though, a sexual poacher is an active competitor whose aim is to beat another woman at her own game, and the man is not a prize — Diane, for example, had no desire to keep Eric — but a pawn. He functions simply as a mirror that she consults to answer the question, "Who is the fairest — or most successful, or perceptive, or intelligent, or entertaining, or best in bed — of them all?" The more estimable the female rival, the more reliable and believable the reflection provided by the male. But he does not have the power of judge and jury over her, and she often loses interest if he actually becomes available, because the challenge is gone and so is the point: proving that she is more powerful than her rival by snatching one of her most treasured belongings. Like Diane, she may not want to keep the man for herself — she just wants to prove to herself and the other woman that she can lure him away for an evening or two.

The man is being used, plain and simple, and like Eric, he may also wind up getting hurt. In the previous chapter, Bill was at the center of a triangle that included his wife and Elaine; Elaine took an active role in initiating their sexual relationship, but she did not set out to compete with Bill's wife, whom she didn't even know, much less envy. She did, however, wind up competing to provide the best, most nurturing relationship for Bill, who was in the pleasant position of being the focus of two women's attention. Eric's position, however, was entirely different. He was not center stage; the real drama was between Diane and Jane. The only reason Diane had any interest in him at all was because she viewed him as a way to prevail in an undeclared contest she had waged on a woman she envied.

Regardless of the Other Woman's motives, the man in a sexual triangle involving two women bears the sole responsibility for keeping any vows or promises he has made. But it's important to make a distinction between the man who inveigles a woman into a relationship by pretending he is single, thereby betraying not just one woman but two, and the man who is swept up in a contest between two women. It's ridiculously flattering to men to pretend that all Other Women are hoodwinked by treacherous rakes or so lovestruck that they can't help themselves — or that they are actually even attracted to the men in the first place.

Other Women like Elaine are primarily interested in the man himself; sexual poachers, however, have different motives. Anyone who has watched a sexual poacher in action knows that she targets not just men but other women. Many draw the line at flirting outrageously and draping themselves all over a man when his wife or girlfriend is near by. Others, like Diane, go further and move the contest into the bedroom, but are only trying the role on for an evening and promptly discard it because it makes them feel bad: too active, too destructive, too unfeminine. Some women, however, become serial poachers, interested only in men who are already attached — and interested in them only as long as they remain attached. They get hooked on the excitement and the thrill of conquest; dueling with another woman makes them feel alive, vital, and supremely powerful.

The career poacher doesn't always announce herself by wearing a slinky gown and a scheming pout à la Scarlett O'Hara, and it's more difficult to spot her in the fresh-faced woman wearing a headband and jeans. Most, however, share a few easily recognizable traits, starting with the coy flattery they exhibit with men, many of whose egos expand like balloons in response to the you're-so-big-and-important approach. They fail to notice that a sexual poacher says this to all the boys. She mocks men, playing them for fools, and dumps them as soon as she becomes bored.

Frequently, serial poachers court other women's friendship just as assiduously, with equal obsequiousness. There's a good reason: women tend to forgive, defend, and excuse women who seek connections with them, but are much more likely to attack those who hold themselves apart, even if their only crime is aloofness. But the average woman has a bloodhound's nose for a sycophant's hidden agenda, and at any rate, the professional poacher tries too hard. Invariably, then, she has few female friends. Often, she is the first to draw attention to this deficit, sighing, "I try so hard, and I don't understand why other women don't like me. I guess they're just jealous."

This points to her real motive, which is competition with other women. She rarely competes only through men, and may also compete over work, children, possessions, status, family background, and education. Men may be sexual beneficiaries of her rivalry — and may get burned by it, too, as Eric did — but they are certainly not the sole cause of it.

This is an old stereotype — the evil temptress — and feminists are right when they point out that we should be suspicious of it, because historically, all women who flouted the sexual double standard, even those who never poached on other women's territory, were called witches, sluts, and tramps. And it's also true that men invoke this stereotype to blame women for their own infidelities. "She made me do it," they say, and, "She threw herself at me" — tidal-wave defenses we are only supposed to accept from women.

But while it makes perfect sense to reject the label of temptress for every sexual woman and to reject the notion that all women compete through sex, it is absolute nonsense to pretend that some women do not behave this way some of the time. The problem with the stereotype is not that it's untrue, but that it misrepresents the woman's motives: the evil temptress is undiluted sex, and men are all she cares about. Really, other *women* may be all she cares about — men are just one way to match, best, or try to bring down those she views as rivals.

There is a vast difference between the high-flown public discourse on female innocence and what women themselves say in private, which is, "Look out, she's trouble." The woman on the street knows very well that she has something to fear from other women, and views a sexual poacher not as a dupe of the patriarchy but as an antagonist who uses sex as a weapon or a competitive test. In fact, many women believe that a skilful poacher is more powerful — and more culpable — than the men she bags.

Women expect men to behave badly in sex, and though we rail against them when they do, we are rarely surprised. Many women speak of men with disdain — *they think with their little heads, not their big ones* — and regard them as children who are incapable of controlling their sexual urges. Oddly, this view coexists with its opposite: men are lusty savages who master us with their desires and who terrorize us with them, too.

We expect better from other women. Even though women aren't the ones who make explicit promises to be faithful to us, they usually get the brunt of our fury when men stray. This is not because the patriarchy makes us so dependent on men that we are afraid to turn against them. It is because most women have a healthy respect for female sexual power, view men as perennial adolescents who cannot resist any temptation, and buy into the myth of female moral superiority.

Women who fail to live up to our expectations become targets of our undisguised loathing and most hostile forms of retaliatory aggression, and are staple villainesses in lowbrow romance novels, where they always come to a bad end. Likewise in Hollywood movies, where the sexual poacher is usually a single career woman in hot pursuit of a hapless, somewhat dog-eared man, who is rescued from her clutches by his nurturing wife, while the audience cheers and screams, "Kill the bitch!" Michael Douglas has made a career of being stalked by snarling, sexual huntresses: Glenn Close in *Fatal Attraction*, Sharon Stone in *Basic Instinct*, Demi Moore in *Disclosure*. All three films were attacked for their "misogynistic" portrayals of women, as though portrayals of bitchy, sexually powerful women are somehow intrinsically damaging to moviegoers, and as though the stock Hollywood female characters — simpering girlfriends who are mere appendages to the male leads — are not. Nevertheless, these movies did huge business at the box office and clearly struck a chord not just with men but with many women.

So did Margaret Atwood's upscale version of the same theme in her novel *The Robber Bride*, which showcases the magnificent destructive power of a classic sexual poacher. Atwood explained in a 1993 speech why she chose to write the novel: "I was sitting around one day thinking to myself, Where have all the Lady Macbeths gone? Gone to Ophelias, every one, leaving the devilish tour de force parts to be played by bass-baritones. Or, to put it another way: If all women are well-behaved by nature — or if we aren't allowed to say otherwise for fear of being accused of antifemaleism — then they are deprived of moral choice, and there isn't much left for them to do in books except run away a lot. Or, to put it another way: Equality means equally bad as well as equally good."[4]

Yet, when women are equally bad as men, they are punished far more harshly by other women. We condemn them for selling out their sisters or we pathologize them, calling them insecure zombies who have been brainwashed by the patriarchy. Either way, we are reaffirming the fable of female moral superiority: women aren't supposed to behave badly, and those who do are either aberrations or have been so severely traumatized by men that they cannot be held responsible for their own actions.

As we have seen, female innocence is belied by women's actual behavior in their relationships with one another and with men, but the expectation that we *should* be morally superior means we wind up silencing ourselves and staggering around under the weight of other people's emotional baggage, too. In sexual terms, this myth is in some ways even more damaging, because it requires us to deny the existence — and the collective complexity and individual intricacy — of our own sexual power.

Sex is the arena in which we feel most vulnerable both emotionally and physically, and it is also where women's behavior has historically been subject to the harshest and most restrictive social controls. As Germaine Greer argued in 1971, the freedom for women to discover and determine their own sexuality, which was for so long defined by men and viewed as the property of men, is essential to achieving social equality. "The chief instrument in the deflection and perversion of female energy is the denial of female sexuality for the substitution of femininity or sexlessness," she wrote in *The Female Eunuch*.[5]

Socially, women have made huge gains in terms of sexual equality in the past twenty-five years. We have new rights, new freedoms, new options, and no longer risk being ostracized, pilloried, or burned at the stake for having sex. However, many of us walk the walk but don't talk the talk of sexual subjects — even to ourselves. The reason is that the modern sexual script has not challenged traditional gender stereotypes about sexuality; rather, it has valorized the traditional feminine role.

Sometimes we play parts that we have been learning since childhood, but often we are improvising, trying to break out of constraining roles; at the same time, we attempt to appear to be staying in character and sticking to the fundamental plot outline, so that our actions meet the guidelines of social acceptability. "We expect our lives to follow certain scripts, and we make an effort to follow them, too," explain Judith Long Laws and Pepper Schwartz in *Sexual Scripts*. "We also try to make our experiences accord with these scripts, sometimes even reinterpreting reality so as to make it fit them better."[6]

In other words, even when we deviate from the sexual script, we usually refer to it to explain what we've done. The script is seductive because it tells us exactly where we stand and holds out the promise of resolving the messy complexities and ambiguities of real life. Many women aren't actually following this script, but are still using it to try to understand, interpret, and justify their own behavior. Instead of challenging its limitations, many of us pay lip service to the sexual script, and may not even see that there is a difference between our actual behavior and our perceptions of it.

Socially, women are freer than ever before, but psychologically, we remain trapped. We are terrified of being judged, and shy away from telling ourselves and telling one another the truth about our sexual selves because we don't want to be called sluts, prudes, whores, ice maidens, teases, deviants, or any of the other things we secretly fear we are.

Instead, we scramble to try to make our actions conform to the sexual script, which seems to let women have it all. We can assert sexual modesty — *I* certainly wasn't the instigator, *I* don't have those kinds of appetites — while boasting: he really wanted to, he couldn't help himself, he was so turned on by me that we wound up having sex. Every woman gets to be the star of her own drama, the irresistible erotic lure who drives men wild, but also gets to be the good girl, the one so well-bred that she never aches to be touched, never actively seeks sex, and never feels the surge of raw, carnal desire.

We should be challenging this script, not affirming it, and in order to do that, we need to be honest with ourselves about who we are and what we're actually doing and want to do sexually. Dishonesty is the last barrier to female sexual self-determination, but ironically, it is also one of the most difficult to surmount. The fear of judgment — especially judgment by other women — creates a vicious circle: we are afraid to tell the truth, but silence will not change the stereotypes. Honesty is the only way for women to reduce the likelihood of being judged.

In a way, therefore, I admire Diane. She was ruthlessly honest with herself about what she had done, thereby acknowledging the full possibilities of her sexual power. Because she can be honest, she recognizes that she has the most important kind of power of all: *the power to make sexual choices.* Moral superiority isn't something that women are born with — we have to choose it, and this requires that we admit that we *do* have the capacity to exercise free will when it comes to sex, and that sometimes we make mistakes for which we bear sole responsibility.

Until we acknowledge our own sexual agency, we will never truly be free and we will never own sex or define it for ourselves. We will continue to pay lip service to roles that we aren't even following, desperately trying to convince ourselves that we *aren't those kinds of girls,* even though, in fact, many of us *are.* We are in a terrible predicament when our bodies are freer than our minds, because many of us try to reconcile the split between the reality and the rhetoric by doing what the sexual script tells us we should have done in the first place: throwing our hearts into the breach. We try to convince ourselves we only have sex to express love, and wind up causing more damage to ourselves than men ever could.

I did not understand any of this when I was twenty-four years old. At the time I was in London, homesick and feeling guilty that I wasn't entirely enjoying living overseas, so I was relieved when an old friend came to visit but also felt it was necessary to prove to her that I was having the time of my life. So it was that on the first night of her visit, I dragged her to a black-tie party where I knew hardly anyone.

Within an hour I was standing alone at a window, watching her sail off in a cab with a handsome man, consumed by a potent mixture of jealousy, self-pity, and sanctimony. She had been in the country for less than twenty-four hours and had already abandoned me — and scandaled off with an attractive man. It didn't seem fair. When she returned to my flat the next day in the grip of a five-alarm pregnancy scare, however, my complex envy gave way to moral vanity. *I* would never get into such a mess, I thought, congratulating myself on my probity, although my virtue had been wholly untested the previous evening and I'd been rather upset about that at the time.

My friend was worried enough to want morning-after pills and lucky enough to find a sympathetic doctor who would prescribe them for a foreigner. But the remedy made her violently ill, so she lay in bed for two days, conquering nausea by telling herself that if she threw up the pills, she would most certainly need an abortion. I, meanwhile, fluffed her pillows and suggested, with what I imagined was tactful understatement, that perhaps this was all for the best, maybe she would be a little more responsible from now on.

I was careful to the point of paranoia about contraception and high-minded enough to believe that I could teach her a thing or two. My method was Socratic: once it became clear that the man didn't have a condom, I asked, why did she go ahead and have sex? She fought down queasiness long enough to reply that the combination of his charm, her own sense of anonymity, and the foreign setting had intoxicated her past the brink of common sense, so that at the crucial moment, she had thought, What the hell. She was well aware, she said, that she'd been irresponsible, but...

That "but" hung in the air, eloquently suggestive. At the time, it had seemed worth it, my friend seemed to say; she had been hell-bent on rapture, had found some, and could not dishonor her desire or her body's memory by pretending that her pleasure had been entirely worthless.

Her "but" and its implication of entitlement to purely physical pleasure — so greedy, so unabashed, so unfeminine — annoyed me, and I continued to press for a renunciation. Why did she have sex with a man who lived in *London*, of all places, a man she had only just met and would in all likelihood never see again?

She recognized this for the accusation it was and said, in the mildest tone possible, that I was hardly one to point fingers. "I was in love with every man I ever slept with!" I insisted, hotly denying that I had ever had casual — "meaningless" was the actual word I used — sex. She was either too ill or too magnanimous to rattle off a list of names and ask me whether it was really possible — although the list was not so very long — that I had loved every one. She spared me that embarrassment, and at any rate already knew the answer, knew it even before I did and long before I was prepared to admit it.

The truth of the matter is that I had a genius for convincing myself that I was in love after I had sex, and the main difference between us was that I would have slept with the man but tottered off the next day in the grip of an obsession for which no morning-after pill has yet been devised. Tossing and turning in a handsome man's bed all night long was all the proof I would have needed to believe that I was in love, and this "love" would only have deepened by the time I returned home to begin the vigil, waiting for the phone to ring.

Like my friend, I barreled into sex with no-strings bravado, especially if the man was reasonably attractive and noncommittal, in which case I saw him as an intriguing challenge. But my live-a-little attitude lasted only until daybreak, when it was replaced with Hallmark images of sunsets, secluded beaches, and eternal romance. I retroactively willed my heart to follow my body, and in the subsequent frenzy of insecurity — *why hasn't he phoned?* or, if he had phoned, *why isn't he madly in love with me?* — I forgot entirely the things I'd felt at the beginning of the encounter, which had nothing whatsoever to do with love.

In reality, I'd headed off to bed with a sense of high adventure. In the midst of a seduction, I had the thrilling conviction that I was inventing my own life and creating my own legend, and deluded myself into thinking I was liberated enough not to care what happened afterwards. Although hungry for admiration, I did not lack self-esteem; I had sex not because I wanted love but because I wanted power, and in the intensity of the sexual moment, believed that I had it.

Afterwards, however, when the narcotic effects of desire had subsided, there was the mundane reality of a stranger's morning breath. I couldn't face what my desires looked like in the light of day and did not want to take responsibility for the places they had led me, so the eagerness with which I'd embraced my sexual power the previous night could only be matched by the alacrity with which I sought to deny its existence in the morning.

I accomplished this feat by looking to the man, instead of to myself, to figure out what I was doing in bed with him. I wanted to believe that he had *caused* my desire, as though my desire was not something I owned and certainly not something for which I bore any responsibility.

Maintaining this fiction that he had created my desire — which was crucial not least because I was now concerned that he'd think less of me for hopping into bed with him so readily — meant that I had to endow him with mythic helpings of perception, intelligence, and character.

I rapidly grew enamored of this figment of my imagination and confused him with the flesh-and-blood version in the bed, and therefore was able to convince myself with relative ease that I was there because I was in love. Not only was I in love, but I was absolved of sin, guilt, or any blame for the fact that we had had sex. This paragon of perfection I'd created would surely know how I felt, see me for who I really was, and forgive my temporary fall from good-girl grace — which was, after all, not my fault but his.

The less I knew of the man, the easier it was to project all my fantasies, hopes and wishes onto him, and the more difficult it was to accept his refusal to likewise delude himself that what we had just shared was an expression of true love. I did not grasp that a man had a right to be alarmed if he went to sleep beside a woman who was talking and behaving like a free spirit, and awoke to find her prattling merrily about the future and clearing a space in his closet so she could install her own clothes. So, if he gently protested that he was not, in fact, in the market for a relationship, I was bewildered and saw it as an inexplicable about-face on his part.

After a few of these experiences, I began to believe — as did practically every woman I knew — that men were inscrutable sociopaths who feared strong, intelligent women. Many of us, however, were unwilling to give up while we still had some dignity to squander. Rather, convinced that these men secretly longed for us, we mounted campaigns to prove to them they had nothing to fear. Together, we'd rehearse what to say when we phoned them, how to convey a casual, couldn't-careless breeziness. *He's afraid of commitment*, we told each other and told ourselves, and came up with what seemed like a brilliant strategy: shanghai the man into a relationship by pretending that you yourself didn't want one. Of course, this particular piece of reverse psychology often backfired. Men took us at face value when we misrepresented ourselves as the kind of women who would make no claims on them, or alternatively, our intensity and mixed signals sent them running for cover.

Throughout my twenties, I went through periods of being thoroughly confused by men and feeling bitter toward the gender. What did men want, anyway? Not me, apparently. This was a dangerous frame of mind, because I did not swear off sex. Although I didn't pick up strangers in singles bars, I can't pretend that I had any deep knowledge of a few of the friends-of-friends with whom I had sex when I was in one of these moods. On more than one occasion I slept with a man chiefly because someone else had told me that he liked me, so he seemed like a sure thing. Even a gawky, rather homely man to whom I had previously been sexually indifferent seemed to develop pleasing qualities and erotic appeal as soon as I knew he had some interest in me, and the fact that he had noticed me at all made me think, Why wait?

Usually, though, I had so little respect for these men that I thought I was doing them a large favor by letting them have their way with me. I was after a quick ego fix, and nothing seems more promising in this regard than having sex with a man when you're convinced that you are the best thing that has ever happened to him. One of the more compelling aspects of this dream of omnipotence was my notion that the man would be forever grateful. It did not occur to me that perhaps he wouldn't recognize that I was doing him a favor and might in fact view the interaction in terms of equality.

If he assumed that I'd slept with him because I really liked him, I found myself silently fuming at his presumption — *me* like *him*? Wasn't it the other way around? — while simultaneously trying to convince myself that I had slept with him because I was in love. There were two feelings to reconcile, one true — *I never had much interest in this man and sleeping with him was probably a mistake* — and one false: *This is the man I once cared for deeply, twelve whole hours ago, which is why I went to bed with him. Sadly, the days of wine and roses are over.*

The only solution seemed to be screening my calls for months and slinking off in the other direction if I ran into him socially. I didn't want anyone else to find out that I'd had sex with him, because I'd feel compelled to provide a justification that was wounding to my own pride: No, really, it wasn't *sex*, it wasn't a *one-night stand* — we were *making love*.

I hurt some thoroughly decent men with these antics, and anyone who believes that all men are callous commitment-phobes should look up a few of the ones who had the misfortune to be on the receiving end of my "favors." In retrospect, I am amazed that I continued to believe I was a victim of cold-blooded men. I failed to make the connection: I wielded my power against men in exactly the same way that I accused men of using their power against me. On balance, I have to say I treated men worse than they treated me; there were some not-so-nice ones who hurt me badly, but I colluded in my own victimization by playing the game of convincing myself I was in love because I had had sex. I handed my heart over to them before they had even asked for it and long before they'd earned it, and then kept hanging on, no matter what they did, because I was "in love."

My relationships with men were not, however, always the stuff of bad farce. I did meet men, date them, decide I liked them, and then have sex with them, in that order, applauding myself for waiting. But "waiting" is generally understood as delaying sex until the third or fourth date, or at most, the third or fourth week. I still didn't know what the man would be like when he wasn't on his best behavior or what his values were or whether he'd be supportive of my career or any of the other things that were crucial to the success of the relationship.

The truth is that after a few dinners, a movie, and some witty repartee, sex is either recreation or an act of faith. Sometimes I was lucky and things worked out. Sometimes, however, I stayed in these relationships much longer than I should have precisely because I had created a compelling myth for myself about having been in love from the start, which was why I'd had sex.

Thus, I did get real power from sex, though the power to cause myself emotional pain and to hurt men was not what I had sought. I was unaware that being profligate with my heart to excuse the fact that I'd been profligate with my body made matters much worse. It took me years to figure out that sexual responsibility requires taking emotional as well as contraceptive precautions — and also requires treating men like human beings who have feelings. Because I couldn't be honest with myself about the shape of my own desires and the consequences of my own behavior, I ascribed more power to the men I had sex with than they ever had, and certainly far more than most of them wanted.

These tricks I played on myself sound laughable, and as a case study in self-deception, they are. But many women play similar tricks on themselves and it is of the utmost seriousness when the end result is a false feeling of powerlessness and a very real feeling of unhappiness. We perform this sleight-of-mind because in the prevailing sexual script there is nothing to suggest that women are motivated to have sex out of curiosity, or physical desire, or a craving for power, or because they want to be desired, or any of the other reasons apart from love that women actually do have sex. We learn that there is only one possible motivation for women: love.

According to this script, female sexuality is pale, gentle, reactive, and fundamentally romantic; women want candle-lit dinners and soul-baring disclosures, which redeem — but just barely — the vulgar physicality of sex. Male sexuality, however, is aggressive, genitally oriented, and essentially carnal: men will do almost anything to get off.

For women, in particular, this script is seductive because it seems to refute the old, blame-it-on-Eve view of women as the embodiment of sexual sin. Particularly in religious traditions, women *were* sex, which is why they had to be veiled or restricted from public life. The power of female sexuality was presumed to be so mighty that simply by walking down the street alone or revealing a well-turned ankle, a woman might tempt, corrupt, or provoke a man to sinful thoughts or deeds. Virtue was something women earned only by vigorously suppressing their sexuality: dressing and behaving modestly, viewing sex as a rather distasteful marital duty. Virtue was necessary to find a husband, and thus ensure one's own economic survival. Any open display of sexuality — and men were so vulnerable that women had to be extremely careful not to do anything that could be misinterpreted — made a woman suspect: hussy, harlot, whore.

Historically, being swept away by love was no excuse, unless the woman was married and the man doing the sweeping was her husband. Furthermore, as recently as twenty years ago there was almost no public recognition that women, either as individuals or as a group, can be oppressed through sex. Women were either good girls, free of dirty desires, or bad girls, who "wanted it" and wound up as social pariahs — or who "asked for it" by having the temerity to wear a short skirt or smile at a stranger or accept a man's offer of a ride home, and thus "deserved" everything they got. Madonnas or whores, either way, women were responsible for how men behaved toward them sexually.

Yet in the modern script, women aren't ever responsible for sex (unless they wind up pregnant and on welfare, in which case they are considered the sole authors of their fate by the very same people seeking to restrict sex education in the schools, shut down publicly funded birth control clinics, and roll back access to abortions). Largely because of increasing awareness of male sexual violence and economic exploitation of female sexuality, women are now assigned to a permanent moral high ground where female sexuality has only two meanings: love or subjugation. Women use sex to express love, but sex is also used against them, as a form of collective oppression and individual degradation. Even the traditional bad girls — the promiscuous ones who give it away, the prostitutes who sell it for a price — have been recast as misunderstood or misguided good girls with low self-esteem and histories of abuse, brainwashed by the beauty myth and desperate not for sex but for love.

The prevailing script sorts out roles very tidily by fusing sexuality with gender, as though one's biological sex dictated one's erotic desires, experiences, and interpretations. When sex is understood as a purely biological act, it makes good sense to talk about women (or men) as a group because we share certain anatomical similarities. But what we do, when, where, why, with whom, and how we feel about it before, during, and after — biology has very little to do with any of this, particularly not now, when effective birth control makes it possible to separate sex from reproduction.

It seems blindingly obvious, but in the public discourse about sex it is often ignored: women are different from one another, and so are men. Sex stubbornly resists easy categorization, because sexual motives, behavior, and responses are so strongly influenced by socialization, past experience, and deeply personal idiosyncracies, emotions, fantasies, desires, and sensations.

Even for an individual woman who has only one partner in her lifetime, sexuality is not a fixed trait like height or eye color. Sexual behavior is social behavior — it involves another person, even in fantasy — and thus it varies, because it is interactive and influenced by external factors like cultural ideals, the setting, the specific partner's behavior, and, of course, physical stimuli. In terms of its individual psychological and physiological dimensions, sexuality is not a trait but a *state* that varies depending on one's mood, appetite, health, feelings about one's body, and feelings toward the other person. Just as most of us exhibit a wide range of behavior throughout our lives — aggressive with the boss who steals credit, passive with the critical father — we also exhibit a range of sexual behaviors and experience a spectrum of sexual feelings and responses.

But given the doubt, guilt, fear, shame, anxiety, and high expectations attached to sex in our society, a script that tells us what sex is supposed to mean and how we should play our roles has mass appeal. Even people who scoff at astrology for dividing human beings into twelve types are avid consumers of bedtime stories about good girls and bad boys, loving saints and callous rakes, suffering martyrs and brutish villains. These caricatures provide a soothing antidote to the confusion of real life, where the meaning of sex is much more fluid, subjective, and frequently mystifying, and there's something in the script for both genders: men are reassured of their power, and women are reassured of their moral superiority.

Lacking any other reference points for understanding our own sexuality in all its complexity makes it extremely difficult for us to recognize and honor the possibilities of our sexual power. Instead, all too frequently, women turn that power against themselves, sometimes by literally handing it over to men.

Even as she heads off to bed with a man, a woman may find herself apologizing, blaming it on the wine or the weather, and saying, "I don't usually do this kind of thing." On one level, this is a pre-emptive strike: she is trying to protect herself from any judgment that the man might make, knowing perfectly well that if he's the kind to make judgments, they are unlikely to be in her favor. But if he believes that a woman who does what she is doing is a slut, he is also an arrant hypocrite — if she's easy, so is he. She should be putting her clothes back on immediately instead of inviting a ruling on her own virtue.

And frankly, any self-respecting man should be zipping his fly at this point, because he is more often than not dealing with a woman who doesn't want to be held accountable for what happens next. "I don't usually do this kind of thing" is generally the first not-so-subtle hint that afterwards a woman may be even more desperately seeking a justification to satisfy herself that she is *not that kind of girl*. As there is no better justification than love, she may very well attempt to affix herself to him with the tenacity of a leech and if that fails, resort to pleading, whatever-happened-to-us? phone calls. Alternatively, she may be so disgusted with herself that she will treat him like a pariah, strongarm him off the premises, and remember him thereafter as the man who defiled her.

Women have casual sex, or sex that seems to them in retrospect to have been premature, for all kinds of reasons: they believe that sex is a route to a relationship, they want to be the center of someone else's attention even just for one night, they want to experiment, they are lonely, they've decided to live a little, they want to get off. Afterwards, however, many of us seize on the idea of love because our notions about sexual liberation end with a close-up of a woman in the throes of pleasure, and do not include the scene of a woman with dark circles under her eyes and a stale, metallic taste in her mouth, clambering back into the crumpled outfit that had looked so alluring the night before. Some women find themselves in this situation and don't know what to make of it, so try to invest it with a meaning that will redeem its banality. Men may feel just as empty, but they don't need to pretend to themselves that the encounter was anything but physical, because they receive entirely different messages about sex: the more, the better; the greater the number of partners, the bigger the man.

Other women establish their alibi beforehand, explaining that the reason they slept with a man on the second date or didn't use birth control was that they were swept away by love. Although today women have the social freedom to have sex, few can give themselves psychological permission just to have fun or feed their egos or make the odd blunder. Ironically, the need to justify sex on the grounds of love can make sex seem much more important than it actually is and threatens to devalue love. If love is so easy to achieve that it can be felt for a man after one night, it's worth very little indeed. And if the proof of love is willingness to forgo contraception or otherwise forswear personal accountability, it should be something we avoid rather than seek.

Equating sex with love makes women feel less guilty about their own sexuality, but also makes them more likely to victimize themselves. The belief that sex *is* love often leads a woman to have sex when what she really wants is to be held, nurtured, and appreciated for who she really is — needs that casual sex won't satisfy. If what she wants is commitment, jumping into bed with a man very early on is a foolproof way to send the opposite message, because her actions suggest that for her, sex is a handshake, not an expression of love. A woman who cannot make her actions consistent with her beliefs, and who cannot even be honest with herself about what sex means to her, will never be able to communicate to any man what it is that she wants and needs and expects from him, either sexually or emotionally.

Until we are able to take responsibility for our own sexuality and our power to choose, we cannot admit that we have all kinds of psychological and physical reasons for wanting and having sex, and we continue to give other people the power to define who we are and how we should behave. This is the oldest kind of trap for women, and it's one we can escape only by being honest with ourselves and with each other.

But the modern sexual script keeps us strangers to ourselves. The reward is supposed to be a sisterly paradise where women are so morally superior that they never seek to hurt each other and never make mistakes, but this turns out to be a place where every woman does double duty, producing disinformation propaganda for herself and policing the borders of sexual correctness. Denying that women ever make mistakes or behave badly turns out to mean denying that we have any power to make choices at all; the end result is that we may become our own worst enemies in sex, talking ourselves into a kind of "love" that's self-destructive and into a misplaced fear of and contempt for men.

Women don't need a sexual script. What we need is a politics of error that takes account of our differences and explicitly recognizes that learning to use sexual power wisely is a process of trial and error. We need to feel that we are free to make mistakes, because we have unparalleled opportunities to make them: sexual roles and behavior have changed and continue to change, so much so that many of our most basic assumptions about gender differences have become anachronisms.

I n certain crucial respects, young women do not behave or even think about sex in the same way older women do. New norms of women's equality, the availability of reliable contraception and legal abortion, and the permissiveness ushered in by the sexual revolution — this combination has undermined many of the historical societal restrictions on women's sexual behavior. Women can now have sex without fear of pregnancy or of becoming social pariahs, virginity is no longer a prerequisite for marriage, and marriage is no longer the only route to economic security and social status. These are all dramatic changes, and they have occurred in the space of just thirty years.

As a result, gender differences in sexual behavior are fading among those born after 1960, largely because the sexual conduct and attitudes of young women have changed.[7] *The reality is that by a number of measures, young women today behave more like men of any age than like their mothers and older sisters.*

Consider the findings of a study published in the academic journal *Sex Roles* in 1993. Sociologist Ilsa Lottes of the University of Maryland studied more than four hundred heterosexual college students and reported, "There were no significant gender differences in age of first intercourse, frequency of intercourse, oral sex participation, prevalence of coitus, oral and anal sex, rating of how often their partner satisfied their sex needs and desires, and reactions to recent intercourse."[8]

Sexually speaking, male and female students are "remarkably similar," Lottes concluded. On average, the women in her study were twenty years old, happy with their sex lives, and experienced: one-quarter had had four or more sex partners, and another one-quarter had had seven or more.[9] Clearly, they have abandoned the "just say no" lines allotted to women in the sexual script. More than two-thirds said they had, on occasion, found themselves "alone, wanting or needing sex."[10] The idea of a woman wanting or needing sex, and moreover, wanting or needing it outside of the context of being groped by an ardent man, is completely incongruous with the prevailing script.

As Lottes explains, "women are beginning to assume roles once thought to be only appropriate for men." The vast majority of women in her study had asked men out on dates and paid the entire expenses; virtually all had split dating expenses with men. This is a remarkable change from just ten years ago, when researchers reported that only a minority of women were sharing date expenses, much less shouldering them entirely or asking men out.[11]

Women are also taking on traditional male roles and attitudes in the bedroom, and men want them to. When asked who should be the initiator in sexual relationships, three-quarters of both men and women gave the same answer: "men and women equally." Again, this is a significant change from earlier research, which found that men had a more egalitarian attitude than women did. For instance, in a similar study of university students published in 1985, 78 percent of men but only 59 percent of women believed that both genders should initiate sex equally; 41 percent of the women but only 18 percent of the men thought that men should be primarily responsible for initiating sex.[12]

The women in Lottes' study were not just talking about initiating sex in established relationships, but about making the first moves in new relationships. More than one-third had initiated sexual involvement with new partners; more than two-thirds of the men reported experiences in which women made the first sexual moves in a new relationship. This too is a major change: throughout the 1970s, researchers consistently reported that men almost always initiated sexual relationships.

There is, however, still one gender difference: "women's greater desire and need for emotion, affection, and commitment in their sexual relationships."[13] Along with many other researchers, Lottes found that a majority of women — 92 percent, in her study — believe that emotional involvement is necessary for intercourse most of the time or always. Surprisingly, two-thirds of the *men* agreed. In both cases, however, men and women are saying one thing and doing another: the majority admitted that they had, in fact, had sex *without* emotional involvement.

Lottes concluded, "[T]hese data taken together with other surveys... suggest that a majority of college women are sexually experienced and enjoy these experiences. Thus, with respect to many aspects of sexual behavior, gender differences are minimal and a convergence resulting primarily from the greater sexual experience of women has occurred."[14]

In recent years, many academic researchers have found substantial evidence of the erosion of the traditional double standard, but Lottes' study is unusually representative of a university population. Generally, psychologists and sociologists who study sex have difficulty obtaining groups of students who are demographically representative of the campus as a whole. They tend to survey those who are closest at hand: students majoring in the social sciences, who are more likely to be interested in and to have studied aspects of sex role socialization, and who may differ quite significantly from students majoring in, say, engineering. Furthermore, participants in academic sex surveys tend to be disproportionately white and female. Lottes' study, however, included students from thirty-one different majors, and they mirrored the racial demographics of the entire campus.

Nevertheless, college students are hardly representative of the general population; they tend to be young, to come from relatively high socioeconomic backgrounds, and to hold liberal, permissive beliefs. Furthermore, participants in university studies are almost never randomly selected. Rather, students usually volunteer to participate, and in return receive course credit.

So it might seem that these studies indicating a convergence in young people's sexual behavior and attitudes have little bearing on off-campus life. However, according to the most recent random sample sex survey of the American population, popularly known as the "Sex in America" study, that is not the case.

Formally called the National Health and Social Life Survey (NHSLS), the study is touted by its authors as "definitive" and the "most comprehensive" ever. Previous sex surveys like the Hite reports and those conducted by *Playboy* and *Redbook* were based on the responses of people who volunteered to be interviewed; people who choose to mail in surveys published in magazines are not necessarily representative of the general population either.

The NHSLS, however, was based on face-to-face interviews across the United States with 3,432 Americans aged 18 to 59. These respondents were selected at random and then approached by the researchers; about 80 percent agreed to participate. The more random the sample and the higher the response rate, the more representative and scientifically accurate a study is considered to be.

The NHSLS, then, was big news, and was widely reported as providing conclusive proof that the sexual revolution is over. As *Time* magazine summarized in its cover story on the NHSLS, "Over a lifetime, a typical man has six partners; a woman, two."[15] It appeared that Americans were having much less sex than anyone thought, that married people had the most satisfying sex lives, and that the roles of the sexual script had not been recast: women were still considerably more conservative than men.

The media paid no attention, however, to one of the survey's more striking findings: the large generation gap in women's sexual behavior. Relatively speaking, the conduct of men has changed only modestly over time. For women, however, the story is very different. The behavior of a young woman in the 1960s, at the height of the sexual revolution when the rallying cry was "Make love, not war," was quite unlike that of a young woman in the 1990s. Young women today are far more adventurous: those born after 1960 start having sex at a younger age and have many more premarital partners than any previous generation of American women.

The youngest women in the NHSLS, who were born between 1963 and 1974, are significantly different from their mothers and even their older sisters. They are almost twice as likely as women born just ten years earlier — and six times as likely as those born thirty years earlier — to have had multiple sex partners before the age of eighteen. Only a minority were virgins on their eighteenth birthday; 23 percent had already had one sex partner, 25 percent had had two to four, and 10 percent had had five or more.

Furthermore, the gender gap in terms of sexual experience, substantial for previous generations, was significantly smaller among the youngest group. Only 8 percent more men than women had multiple partners before they turned eighteen, and the difference was concentrated at the highest end of the scale, with more men than women reporting five or more partners.[16]

By the age of twenty, three-quarters of the youngest group of women had had multiple sex partners; one-third had had four or more. In short, most twenty-year-olds have already had at least as many sexual partners as *Time*'s "typical American woman" has in her *lifetime*.[17] In fact, in terms of the number of people they had sex with, the youngest women behaved more like the "typical man." Again, the only statistically significant difference between men and women born after 1960 was at the top end of the scale: roughly equal numbers had had between one and nine partners, but more men than women had had ten or more partners by the age of twenty.

Unfortunately, because of the way the NHSLS data are presented, it's impossible to tell how many sexual partners in total the youngest women have had since the age of twenty. But there are statistics on their sexual behavior in the twelve months prior to the survey, which provide solid evidence that unmarried women continue the pattern established in their teens. Sixty percent of those under the age of thirty were single when the survey was conducted; 25 percent of them reported having had two to four partners, and an additional 6 percent had had five partners or more, *in the previous twelve months*. Women in this age group who had been formerly married were even more likely to have had multiple partners in the previous year.[18]

Sex at an early age, numerous partners, asking and paying for dates, "wanting and needing" sex — clearly, young women are not following the traditional story lines. Although we tend to think of sexuality in terms of primal instincts and hard-wired reproductive drives, the changes in women's behavior make a very strong case for the theory that sexuality is in large part socially constructed. As sexologist Leonore Tiefer writes, "Human sexuality is not a biological given and cannot be explained in terms of reproductive biology or instinct. All human actions need a body, but only part of human sexuality has to do with actions and even that part only requires a body in the way that playing the piano does. What is done, when, where, by whom, with whom, with what, and why — these things have almost nothing to do with biology."[19]

They do, however, have a great deal to do with society. Sexual behavior is strongly influenced by social forces, mores, and definitions, which don't merely *restrict* us from doing what we would do naturally but actually *shape* our behavior, organize it, and define its meanings.

Not only are young women comparatively free of traditional restrictions, they have also received different messages about what sex is: "a central, if not *the* central, aspect of a relationship," in Tiefer's words.[20] A large body of research shows that young women (and men) expect to engage in sex in dating relationships, particularly "steady" relationships, which is certainly not an expectation their mothers had when they were the same age.[21] Moreover, there's a new emphasis on mutual pleasure, sex that satisfies both partners. Desire itself is now seen in terms of health: lacking it in sufficient proportions is classified as a dysfunction that requires therapeutic intervention by advice columnists, the medical establishment, and sex therapists.

These new ideas about sex and the removal of traditional restrictions on female behavior have had an enormous effect on women's behavior and beliefs. Yet we are still saddled with a script whose gender roles have not really changed at all.

Most young women, however, are not following it. And some are not even bothering to try to pretend that they are.

Sarah is twenty-four but she still has some of the coltish grace of adolescence, the improbably large eyes and sleek one-length-all-over brown hair and the lean legs of a trained ballet dancer. It's easy to picture her as she was at fourteen, on a full scholarship at a prestigious arts school far from home, flushed with the sweet arrogance of the baby of the family. She was going to be a star, just like her mama always said.

The ambience was heady, particularly for a girl from a small Southern town where everybody knew everybody else's business and if you were daring enough to sneak down to the quarry looking for trouble, your parents somehow heard about it within the hour. At the school, so long as you could dance until your calves knotted up and then keep on dancing through the pain, no one cared what else you got up to. "It was what college is like for most people, except I was so much younger," Sarah says. "It was probably not the healthiest atmosphere, living in a dorm with a bunch of sixteen- and seventeen-year-olds who were drinking and sleeping around and basically running wild."

For the most part, Sarah and her friends witnessed all this from an agonizing distance, tiptoeing around the dorm at night to listen outside the doors of the juniors and seniors — impossibly glamorous girls who said "fuck" and took the Pill and had actually been to New York City. Of course, the younger ones idolized them and longed, with all the wild, straining impatience of fourteen-year-olds, to imitate them.

Going home for the summer holidays was a culture shock. "Oh for God's sake, Mama," she said when her mother imposed a curfew. "I'm not a baby any more." Not that there was really anywhere to go in that pokey little town, mind you. The whole place seemed to shrink smaller and smaller each time she went back, so that Sarah felt like an Amazon scuffing up and down the streets, trying to hurry along the moment when she could leave again.

Finally — and it did seem like finally, after two years of watching other girls drink cheap jug wine and climb out the dorm windows looking for adventure — Sarah turned sixteen. She was restless, she was moody, she was sick of the endless, grueling labor of stoking her own ambition. Her Achilles tendons were too short and her breasts (the breasts she had once prayed for) were too large, at least by the exacting standards of ballet. Overcoming these physical limitations would have required a desire so fierce that just thinking about it made her tired. She didn't care if she never saw a pair of pointe shoes again. Life was passing her by.

As will happen to a sixteen-year-old girl with a woman's body and a hunger for experience and a firm conviction that she is special, she lost interest in boys her own age. Their fumbling attentions, perfectly satisfactory the year before, now evinced lavish disdain. *So* immature.

Sarah started washing her hair with eggs and painting her nails blood-red and climbing out the dorm windows herself with a pack of other girls. Shushing each other, they scaled down the side of the residence, too thrilled with their own daring to feel bad about the misery of the friends they'd left behind, the ones with braces or pimples or a flat-chested inability to pretend they were a day older than sixteen. Sarah and the others headed off to the local college bars with fake IDs they were never even asked to produce. There they ordered drinks with a suitably jaded air and set their sights on the big-game trophies: college men, so worldly and sophisticated.

After a few of these excursions, Sarah found herself a boyfriend and did not draw the line where she had previously drawn it, at everything-but. She went all the way with Mark, who was twenty-three — the number had such a weighty, pleasing ring that she found a way to work it into every conversation — but he didn't have to talk her into it. There was no talking her out of it. Yes, she had the usual fears — sex would hurt, she would be bad at it — and the physicality of the whole enterprise struck her as so preposterous that she could not imagine much ecstasy in it. But she was sixteen, an adult in her own mind and old enough to do whatever she wanted no matter what anyone else might think, so she got the Pill and hurled herself into sex as though it were a test of her courage.

After the first few times, she was surprised to find herself starting to enjoy the act itself. "Let's do it again," she'd prod Mark, wanting an instant replay of that moment when he flung his head back and groaned.

He was so old, so wise, so good-looking — she wanted to spend every moment with him. She stumbled dreamily through her dance classes, her stomach slopping around inside her when she thought about seeing him that night, and didn't care that she was falling behind. Ballet was so trivial compared to the wrenching violence of her own feelings.

When Mark announced after a few months that he was tired of dating a sixteen-year-old, she was dumbfounded. She had faith in the sheer force of her will and was used to getting her own way. "My mother instilled confidence in me, and going to the school gave me even more confidence. What I didn't have was an ability to accept failure," Sarah says. "When Mark didn't fall madly in love with me, it really threw me for a loop. My reaction to failure was to quit — if I couldn't have exactly what I wanted and if I couldn't be the best at something, I just gave up."

Quitting, in this instance, meant giving up on the whole idea of love. What was the point, if loving meant letting someone get close enough to hurt you that much? She felt she had been robbed — that's the only way to put it — and set about getting her own back, by proving to Mark that he had been a fool to break up with her and by proving to herself that she was no failure.

"I'd finally realized that I could *make* guys notice me, *make* them trail around after me, *make* them come to my room at night. It was like, Gee, these guys are so dumb!" Sarah says. "I slept with a very long string of older guys from my school and the college on the first day I met them. At first, I was a textbook case of equating love with sex, but when they didn't fall in love with me on the spot, my attitude was, 'To hell with you, I never want to see you again.' I was completely screwed up, drinking a lot, and after a while it just turned into a big power trip. I went a little bit crazy, drawing guys in and basically using them."

There was no double standard: promiscuity was a badge of honor for both genders. The coolest thing of all was to sleep with a guy and then brush past him the next day, acting as though nothing had happened. For Sarah, this was not much of a stretch: "Even while I was having a one-night stand, I was already targeting who the next person would be. I just wanted to get as many guys as possible."

She didn't want to open her heart to a man again. Once had been enough. Casual sex seemed to be a way to demonstrate her maturity and to gain power over men without risking anything emotionally. Everyone else at the school appeared to be doing the same thing: drinking and sleeping around and not caring much about anyone else. "It's weird because this was the late eighties and dancers were dropping like flies, dying of AIDS, but none of us connected that to our own behavior," she says. "We must have been the most deluded people on the planet."

What excited her was not sex so much as the idea of it. She enjoyed best the moments before any physical contact, sitting in her room babbling away and pretending not to notice that the guy could barely concentrate, his brain was so clouded with desire. The air was charged and she felt the thrill of complete mastery: *his fate is in my hands*.

"After the first kiss, I got very little out of it. But I felt like I had to go ahead and have sex, not because they pressured me but because I pressured myself," she says. What was the point of a seduction if you weren't prepared to follow through? Being a tease did not fit in with her new image of herself as an erotic champion.

About the sex itself, the best she can say, after lengthy consideration, is, "Well, it wasn't *horrible*. I never felt coerced into anything, but I didn't get a million orgasms, that's for sure. Basically I just faked it, pretending they were pleasing me and I was wildly turned on, when really, they weren't doing a thing for me."

She wasn't embarrassed to say what she wanted — she had done so with Mark — but it seemed to defeat the whole purpose of these conquests. Telling a man how to please her would be an admission of need, and besides, she didn't want to abandon herself to physical sensation, didn't want to lose control.

Watching a man give himself over to pleasure, while she simulated ardor and remained unmoved, seemed a form of radical sovereignty: "I certainly didn't feel used — I was using them, and felt completely superior. It was a power rush for me. I got off on the idea that they'd remember this night with me for the rest of their lives. And once it was over, I always kicked them out. I would go through the typically male thing: how soon would it be polite to ask them to leave? I never let any of them spend the night."

She relished replaying these exploits for her friends, dwelling on the men's buffoonery and ineptitude, how easy they'd been to fool and how surprised they'd been afterwards, when she displayed no interest in seeing them again. "When I think of locker room conversations, I think of men talking about how they scored and how great it was, and women talking about how disappointing it was and how the men didn't know what they were doing," Sarah says. "When I think of men talking about me the way that I talked about them, I want to crawl under a rock and die."

She left high school shorn of any desire to dance, and attended a small, parochial liberal arts college, where her behavior created

something of a scandal: she was considered a slut. "It surprised me
but I wasn't bothered by it, because most of the students led very
sheltered lives. My attitude was, 'Your mommy folds your underwear
for you, so why would I respect anything you say?' Since I was un-
apologetic and I wasn't a complete monster, they decided after a
while that I wasn't a slut, exactly. No, I was exotic and racy," she says.
"It was the kind of place where you could seriously imagine that they
held a meeting to hash out what label they were going to put on me.
And then in my final year, I got involved in a gross, obsessive love
triangle that was like something out of *Cosmo*, so they decided that I
was a tragic heroine."

Sarah cannot easily come up with a label for herself because she
had so many different reasons for having sex. Sex was a way to have
an intense connection with a man while keeping him at a distance.
Sex made her feel desirable, attractive, and in control. Sometimes it
was just another weird thing that happened when she was blasted,
sometimes she felt like a conqueror, and sometimes she did it to stir
her own senses. Sex made her feel liberated, cool, sophisticated.

"Mostly, sex made me feel powerful," says Sarah, who's now
twenty-four and a newlywed. She's planning to start a family soon,
and reports, "It's a bit weird, thinking about sex in terms of love and
babies when it's meant so many other different things to me."

If you passed her on the street, you would note her lanky good
looks and physical grace, never dreaming that she has what she calls
"a shady past." Even she can't quite seem to reconcile the hyper-fem-
ininity of the ballerina with the wantonness of the bad girl she was,
and speaks of the things she did with a faint air of wonder.

But when I ask if she regrets any of it, she doesn't hesitate: "No. For
one thing, I didn't feel too young to get married because I wasn't worried that I'd missed out on anything. And my husband was just as wild,
so it creates a sort of equality, knowing that both of you are capable of
the same kinds of things. The bottom line is that if I hadn't slept
around, I'd always wonder what it would be like. On the other hand, I
certainly wouldn't recommend promiscuity, because I think you're
probably doing it for the wrong reasons, and I can't imagine why anyone would want to sleep with that many people. I didn't get much out

of it in terms of sexual enjoyment, and I do regret that and wish I'd had more pleasure. But I don't blame anyone but myself for having more sex — and more bad sex — than I wanted. I was young and dumb."

In the modern script, women do not have sexual power, not even the relatively joyless brand Sarah describes. Many feminists would diagnose her as suffering from false consciousness; a woman who gets off by turning men on has merely eroticized her own oppression. Many social scientists would say that Sarah's promiscuity was caused by low self-esteem; she must have been pathetically insecure. Pop psychologists who theorize that men are from one planet and women are from another would diagnose her as seriously deluded; she couldn't possibly get power out of promiscuity, since she was just giving men what they wanted. Conservatives would say that Sarah's behavior just goes to show how pornography and the sexual revolution have hurt women; infected by the virus of immorality, she degraded herself. Liberals would say that she's in denial; she was doubtless victimized — the men were older, did not use condoms, and surely exploited her sweet innocence.

It's certainly more dramatic to view Sarah as a poor, misguided girl who was looking for love, not sex. But this would require pretending that she was someone other than who she actually was: a strong-willed, adventurous adolescent who attended a school where promiscuity was cool and supervision was minimal. She believes she exercised power by seeking out men instead of waiting to be chosen, and then dumping them unceremoniously after they had fulfilled the purpose of feeding her ego. "I certainly didn't feel used — I was using them," she says.

Sarah set her own limits and defined her own sexuality, and, as is often the case, in doing so she made some mistakes. She exercised self-determination, and learned the hard way that she had the power to use sex in ways that did not serve her own interests. Although she derived little sensual pleasure from these encounters, she did savor one heady delight: "the idea that they'd remember this night with

me for the rest of their lives." In short, she enjoyed the image of herself as a sex object.

"Sex object" is now a loaded term that evokes images of a powerless woman, diminished by the male gaze. But this is a case where the
political has become far too personal, erasing crucial distinctions —
the context, the woman's own subjective interpretations, the complexity of power itself — and subtler nuances. These distinctions are
critically important. As most women know perfectly well, there is a
significant difference between the political condition of objectification and the personal experience of it at, say, a party.

"As a political condition, objectification is a frightful state in which
women are ridiculed as baubles, 'protected' as figurines, and not paid
good money," writes Marcia Pally in *Sex and Sensibility*. "In the realms
of art, games, and sex, objectification is one of life's charms. No one
gets dressed up on a Saturday night to be ignored. At times, one
wants to be appreciated for all one's aspects by those who know one
thoroughly. At times, one wants to be desired by total strangers, to
grab the attention of a room. One wants the buzz of lust."[22] As Pally
points out, it is vital to distinguish between the political realm and the
realm of playful flirtation, because the former determines whether
we'll be able to put food on the table while the latter is a place for fun,
fantasy, and games that can be played for free.

Women want to be respected as equals to men, both politically
and personally, but most of us also want to excite admiration and
command sexual attention. We want to arouse "the buzz of lust" not
because we have been brainwashed to believe that our role in life is
to be playthings for men, but because there is power in it for us. As
Sarah puts it, "You just stand back and watch guys jump through
hoops and feel like you rule the world." When a man is in your sexual thrall he is also to some extent at your mercy, and many women
find it distinctly pleasurable when men are at their beck and call,
bowing and scraping.

"The pretense that no one is an object in a 'feminist' or Christian
seduction lies to women about sex and does women and men little
good," Pally observes. "One person may be the subject one minute,
the other later on, but at any moment someone is the object or the

game cannot be played. It is not only fun to play the object, it is powerful, as men who want women to be good girls know."[23]

Power and play are the reasons that few women would willingly choose to inhabit a world where men never viewed them as sex objects, even though it would mean welcome freedom from wolf-whistling strangers. While no woman wants to be viewed as a sex object every minute of the day by every man she meets, it is certainly pleasant to be thought sexy or ravishing by a boyfriend or husband — and, occasionally, by men with whom one has no intention of having sex.

Sex appeal is not something that men bestow on women by paying attention to them; it is something that women own and that some women develop to the level of an art form. While it is true that clear skin and a curvaceous figure can heighten a woman's sex appeal, unlike beauty, it does not consist solely of one's ability to live up to rigid cultural standards of physical perfection. It is frequently the case that women who are widely considered beautiful are curiously unsexy, and that women who will never be mistaken for supermodels exude powerful sexual charisma.

In real life, there are many more brands of sex appeal than the pouting, heavily airbrushed caricatures featured in *Playboy* and *Vogue*. There's the wholesome, corn-fed variety, and the slightly mysterious sexiness of women who seem richly amused by some secret they are just on the verge of sharing. There's the vampy, in-your-face wallop packed by the woman who leads with her pelvis, the brisk, slightly dangerous allure of the woman who leads with her brain, and the porcelain hauteur of the woman who exudes indifference. Sexiness can be languid and willing, energetic and imperious, voluptuous and gregarious, angular and arch, earth-motherly or exotic — the common elements are self-confidence and a sense of entitlement to attention.

Because confidence is such a crucial part of sex appeal, it is often true that the sexiest women are not waif-like adolescents or nubile aerobics instructors but mature women with savoir faire and a certain knowing playfulness. Think of Jessica Lange, Tina Turner, Helen Mirren, Diahann Carroll — admittedly all performing artists, but also all women who aren't pretending they're twenty and whose appeal stems in large part from this self-assurance. But theirs are just the names everyone knows. The sexy women most of us know personally are rarely the prettiest or the youngest or the thinnest of our acquaintances; rather, they tend to be the ones most comfortable in their own skins.

Not infrequently, a woman who wears her sexuality confidently elicits blushing, stammering, and general foolishness from men, along with suspicion and hostility from other women, who are all too aware of the power of female sexuality. "Look at the way she flaunts herself," we may hiss, maintaining a vise-like grip on our boyfriends and husbands. If they are so unwise as to attempt to defuse the threat by defending such a woman — some bland remark about how nice or smart she is and besides, she's just standing there making polite conversation — our response is more than likely to drip with sarcasm: "Oh, I see. Short skirts run deep, is that what you're saying?" The extravagance of our condescension for the sex object is only exceeded by our desire to eclipse her.

If sex objects were powerless, no one would feel threatened. But the fact is that a woman who excites desire has considerable power: she commands attention, which she can parlay into other kinds of power, and she is in a position to pick and choose, sexually. Some women feel threatened because they see her as a rival, or simply because she makes them feel inadequate; some men feel threatened because she rejects them or otherwise makes them feel puny, or because they fear the strength of their own desire. Women who wear their sexuality with confidence are routinely called all sorts of bad names precisely because they are powerful, and because they awaken a feeling of vulnerability in both men and women.

As Sarah understood intuitively, the sex object can also be a sexual subject, agent of her own desire. Frequently, the woman who is viewed as a sex object is well aware of her power, and it gives her the authority to stop men in their tracks when they do something that displeases her. The fluidity of power, the way it shifts back and forth between partners, is part of the endless fascination of sex.

Aside from movie stars, the classic sex objects that some feminists (and some members of the Religious Right and the victims-of-society wing of the Left) want most to rescue from the horrors of objectification, are those who work in the sex industry: prostitutes, strippers, and porn stars. In response, some women in the sex trade have formed organizations like COYOTE (Call Off Your Old Tired Ethics) and spoken out publicly against their would-be rescuers, declaring that they are not powerless victims and do not need to be rescued, but could use some help getting legislative measures passed to protect those who want to work in the industry and to end discrimination in the criminal justice system.

At a feminist conference in 1987, Margo St. James, a San Francisco representative of COYOTE, announced, "I've always thought that whores were the only emancipated women. We are the only ones who have the absolute right to fuck as many men as men fuck women."[24]

Of course, many women who work in the sex trade have never felt the right to anything in their lives, least of all self-respect. But some are there because they want to be, and/or because they can earn ten times more money in a single night of stripping or working for an escort service than they could at a minimum wage job. We may protest an economy that rewards the woman who takes off her top more richly than the woman who teaches preschool, but this doesn't change the fact that the first woman is already stigmatized and doesn't appreciate being patronized, as well.

Some sex trade workers argue that those who want to save them are motivated not by altruism but by fear. "I think they're transferring their fears," Amber Cooke, a retired stripper, told an interviewer several years ago. "Most women in one way or another understand the power of their sexuality. But a lot of women are afraid of that power, of how to hold that power, of how to use that power. And when they are confronted with someone who's comfortable doing that, it shakes them up. It challenges them. It makes them question themselves. When that happens, you become threatened and defensive; you react on that basis. The woman who is happy with her sexuality, quite satisfied to embrace it, embark on it, dance with it, enjoy it, then becomes the feared person. I don't believe it's so much morals as it is fear."[25]

Object, subject — only if individual women define for themselves where the line between the two lies can they define their own sexual experiences instead of being defined by them. This is the power of self-determination, and while it can bring great satisfaction, it can also be a whole lot less than glamorous and gratifying. Frequently, it may simply consist of the ability to make your own mistakes, particularly if you are, in Sarah's words, "young and dumb." Sometimes, it may mean behaving in ways that hurt others, as Diane discovered, and make you feel bad about yourself.

It can be awfully tempting simply to follow the modern script and blame men for these mistakes, but the refusal to take responsibility ultimately requires women to repudiate hard-won freedoms. Needing to blame somebody else implies that one's errors are really terrible traumas, so shameful that they cannot even be acknowledged as one's own.

We need a politics of error to replace the myth of female moral superiority, which costs us nothing less than our power. Pretending that women have none only grants more to men — an arrangement that few men will be anxious to redress — and encourages us to live in fear of what awful thing they will do to us next. It's the comparative badness of men, after all, that makes women so good: individually blameless and collectively aggrieved.

And there is another cost: women are required to deny their own complexity as individuals, and to deny the complexity of sex itself, which does not have a single, fixed psychological meaning, not even for a woman who has only one partner in her lifetime. Sex can be motivated by excitement or boredom, physical need or affection, desire or duty, loneliness or complacency. It can be a bid for power or an egalitarian exchange, a purely mechanical release of tension or a highly emotional fusion, a way to wear oneself out for sleep or a way to revitalize oneself. Sex can be granted as a reward or inducement, an altruistic offering or a favor. It can also be an act of selfishness, insecurity, or narcissism. Sex can express almost anything and mean almost anything, not just to men, but to women, too.

Paradoxically, while the gender gap in sexual behavior is actually narrowing among young people, there is increasing insistence that young women and men are further apart on the sexual spectrum than ever before. A new ending has been tacked on to the sexual script: men still pursue, women still resist — but men go ahead and do what they want anyway. Men are cast as hormone-addled aggressors who use any means necessary, including physical force, to get women into bed. Women have a cameo role as powerless, terrified sex objects, in constant danger of rape, coercion, and harassment.

Why, when gender differences are actually diminishing, have these old-fashioned notions that men lust and women love persisted? The answer is in part connected to the tumultuous history of modern feminism and the recent ascendance of one particular faction, with twin convictions: men and women are fundamentally different, and sexuality is the site of women's most severe oppression. But feminism is not and never has been monolithic, particularly on the question of sexuality.

In the late sixties and early seventies, sexual equality and freedom were major feminist goals; women's rights to sexual pleasure and to control of their own bodies were symbolic of their right to social equality. Therefore, it was important for women to rediscover their own sexuality, which was "thought of in terms of some type of inner essence available for self-expression, something separate from what you do when you have sex (usually seen in terms of an act with others)."[26]

Supported by Masters and Johnson's research proving that the clitoris is the central site of female sexual response, feminists focused on debunking Freudian theories that vaginal orgasms were "mature" and clitoral stimulation was selfish, deviant, and proof of stalled psychological development. Women were urged to take pride in their own bodies, to revolt against the idea that they were dirty "down there" and that sex itself was filthy, and to explore and act on their own desires. Feminists fought for reproductive rights while encouraging women to explore sexual pleasure, and for a brief time, vibrators, coloring books depicting women's genitalia, and feminist sex manuals attained the status of revolutionary tools that would help smash restrictive stereotypes and double standards.

Along with anger about the ways that women had been indoctrinated into sexual shame and self-denial, there was "a thrilling sense of new possibilities," writes Leonore Tiefer. "The emphasis on the clitoris as women's primary sexual organ was going to lead to massive sexual rechoreography and new status for the erotic potential of lesbianism. Masturbation for girls would become as expected and universal as for boys and lead to repertoires of sexual fantasy. Women would separate sexuality from reproduction as men did...consciousness-raising, education, female-centered health care, and so on would banish shame and passivity and women would discover or develop new sexual realities."[27]

This thrilling sense of new possibilities did not last long, however, because women soon discovered that having orgasms was not the same as having social power. Similarly, the "zipless fuck" promoted by novelist Erica Jong in *Fear of Flying* — sex for its own sake, disconnected from both love and reproduction — failed to provide deliverance. In fact, developing strong, loving relationships with men began to appear even more complicated when the traditional link between sex and commitment was broken. So, even as feminists were dismantling the old double standard, some began to wonder: why bother?

By the early seventies, many radical feminists were already declaring that the sexual revolution had been a colossal rip-off for women; men were the main beneficiaries, because they now had access to a larger pool of women whom they could sexually exploit and treat like dirt. Within a few short years, the early pro-sex strain in the modern women's movement, with its focus on physiological pleasure and its definition of sexuality as an internal essence to be awakened and expressed, was replaced by an increasingly critical analysis of heterosexual relationships.

As the political became personal, women were instructed to purge themselves of all forms of behavior that retained traces of the patriarchy. Sexuality came to be defined not as an instinctive drive but as a socially constructed set of preferences and behaviors that could be changed and adapted to suit one's politics. This redefinition stemmed in large part from tensions within mainstream feminism between lesbians and heterosexual women.

Some liberal feminists, who focused on legislative changes, feared that open tolerance of homosexuality would damage the movement's credibility; others denounced lesbians for playing butch, "male" roles, and questioned their devotion to the cause. "[T]he homophobia, and, to a lesser extent, the anti-sex attitudes within certain elements of the movement precluded lesbian feminists from promoting lesbianism as a sexual rather than a political choice," writes Alice Echols in her classic essay on changes in feminist sexual politics, "Taming of the Id." Instead, lesbian feminists achieved recognition and acceptance by "locating the discourse within the already established framework...that feminism is conditional upon separation from men."[28]

Lesbianism was championed in ideological terms: the purest form of feminism, the cleanest break from the patriarchy. Seemingly overnight, heterosexual women were put on the defensive: how could they change the world when they were sleeping with the enemy? Lesbians were the true sisters, the ones who lived out their politics in the bedroom, the upholders of the faith.

Initially, lesbian sex was described primarily in terms of its praiseworthy differences from heterosexual sex. "Women-loving-women meant gentler, non-possessive, non-competitive, non-violent, nurturing and egalitarian relationships," notes Lynne Segal in *Straight Sex*. She adds that this oppositional, prescriptive framework left even less room to discuss "the realities of heterosexual desire, now defined as 'male identified,'" and therefore bad.[29]

From the beginning, however, some lesbians and radical feminists vigorously rejected this framework as highly prescriptive and limiting, and argued that it did not describe their own desires, behavior, and relationships. Meanwhile, many heterosexual women were grumbling under their breath but holding their tongues, silenced by fear of being branded anti-feminist or homophobic, and by a combination of guilt about their "reactionary" heterosexuality and concern that they might in fact be suffering from false consciousness.

Perhaps more would have found their voices and started talking about the positive aspects of their sexual relationships with men were it not for mounting awareness of male violence. In 1975, Susan Brownmiller's enormously influential book *Against Our Will* became a bestseller. Its central thesis was that throughout history, "rape has played a critical function. It is nothing more or less than a conscious process of intimidation by which *all men* keep *all women* in a state of fear." Brownmiller argued that rape is a form of social control that men are uniquely equipped to exercise: "Man's discovery that his genitalia could serve as a weapon to generate fear must rank as one of the most important discoveries of prehistoric times, along with the use of fire, and the first crude stone axe."[30]

Furthermore, she argued, "The case against pornography [is] central to the fight against rape." Brownmiller contended that pornography teaches men to think of themselves as superior to women, and coaches them to become sexual predators. Therefore, she wrote, "Once we accept as basic truth that rape is not a crime of irrational, impulsive, uncontrollable lust, but is a deliberate, hostile, violent act of degradation and possession on the part of a would-be conqueror, designed to intimidate and inspire fear, we must look toward those elements in our culture that promote and propagandize these attitudes, which offer men...the ideology and psychologic encouragement to commit their acts of aggression."[31]

Consequently, many feminists began to concentrate on articulating a politics of male violence. Sexual danger, not sexual pleasure, became the most pressing issue on the feminist agenda, and pornography became a sort of shorthand for women's oppression. Pornography, according to some feminists, *creates* sexual danger, by portraying women as sexual commodities and by promoting violence: "pornography is the theory, rape is the practice" became their rallying cry.

"Visibility created new consciousness, but also new fear — and new forms of old sexual terrors: sexual harassment was suddenly *everywhere*; rape was an *epidemic*; pornography was a violent polemic against women. It was almost as if, by naming the sexual crimes, by ending female denial, we frightened ourselves more than anyone else," observes historian Ann Snitow. "Pornography became the symbol of female defeat: Look, they hate us, we could say, pointing to a picture."[32]

As a result of these theories about violence, the seeming intractibility of oppression, and the politicization of lesbian sexuality, radical feminism underwent changes so substantial that it emerged in the mid-seventies as an almost entirely new entity: cultural feminism. Cultural feminists believe that men and women are essentially, innately different, and always will be. Some believe that biology is destiny: as a function of the ability to give birth, women are naturally nurturant and empathic. Others believe that socialization plays a larger role in the development of these "womanly" qualities. All agree that women are superior to men in important respects: nonaggressive, more sensitive, and more loving.

As Alice Echols points out, cultural feminists adapted some of the ideas of lesbian separatism to make them palatable to a wider audience: segregation not from men but from "male values," and "bonding" with other women rather than bedding them. Not surprisingly, given their views on gender differences, cultural feminists see male and female sexuality as polar opposites. To them, "Male sexuality is driven, irresponsible, genitally oriented, and potentially lethal. Female sexuality is muted, diffuse, interpersonally-oriented, and benign. Men crave power and orgasm, while women seek reciprocity and intimacy," she explains.[33]

Throughout the eighties, the debate over pornography splintered feminism into warring factions. Many liberal and socialist feminists argued strenuously that a single-issue focus on pornography could not address persistent social inequalities that had nothing to do with sex or violence and everything to do with the traditional division of labor within families, differential socialization for boys and girls, and unequal opportunities at school and at work.

Many black feminists declared their unwillingness to denounce their black brothers, particularly not when their white "sisters" continued to marginalize them while paying lip service to equality. Furthermore, they pointed out that black men had, in Angela Davis's words, been "maimed and murdered because of racist manipulation of the rape charge."[34] The fear that a white woman might be raped by a black man had mobilized lynch mobs only a few years before; white men, on the other hand, actually did rape black women and no one gave a damn.

Broadly speaking, four feminist camps emerged promoting different positions on pornography. Some feminists, most notably Catherine MacKinnon and Andrea Dworkin, contended that pornography causes male violence, and that sex is the primary sphere of women's subordination. Others agreed that porn was distasteful, but deserved free speech protections; if the State was entrusted to crack down on sexually explicit materials, feminist works would be the first to go. A third group argued that the vast majority of pornography was not violent, and that legions of scientists had been unable to establish that there was any direct causal link between porn and male violence — in fact, some believed pornography might serve as a safety valve. A fourth group argued that porn was a potential force for good, so long as women began to take control of the means of production to create their own erotica, focusing on female-centered fantasy, desire, and pleasure.

Nevertheless, MacKinnon and Dworkin's argument is frequently misrepresented in the media as "the" feminist viewpoint on sex. This is not terribly surprising, because they affirm traditional gender stereotypes: women are weak and defenseless, men are powerful and aggressive. The right wing has enthusiastically endorsed their denunciation of pornography as intrinsically harmful to women — yet continues to seek to limit reproductive choice and reject women's demands for improved access to child care, employment protections, and increased funding for shelters and rape crisis programs.

During the pornography debates, many women who disagreed with MacKinnon and Dworkin were effectively silenced by charges that they didn't care about women and didn't care about rape. Consequently, female sexuality is now discussed primarily in terms of victimization and exploitation. Currently, lesbian feminists — not all, but some — are the most consistent and fearless challengers of this trend; some champion practices such as S&M, long considered sexually incorrect, as liberating for women, and openly protest the traditional equation of gender with sexuality.

Nevertheless, there has been very little exploration of the dimensions of female sexual agency outside the context of increasing pleasure and increasing sexual options. This is understandable, given that feminists who discuss the possibilities of female agency have had little enough time to develop a politics of pleasure, and have had to do so amidst charges that such a project is frivolous when there are bodies in the street.

But it's crucial that we begin focusing on creating a politics of error, because there is currently a sharp divide between public discourse and private reality, which does not just complicate our relationships with men and with other women. It is also creating a new set of sexual double standards.

Chapter Five

Double Talk

The beginning is familiar: They're both a little drunk. It's a big wedding in a big hall, one of those raucous, formal events that go by in a blur and come back as poorly spliced memories: a twice-divorced cousin crying at the bar, the bride in the bathroom dabbing at the spot of red wine on her dress, a rumpled usher dancing by himself to Motown.

Sam and Robin are familiar strangers, which is to say they are both friends of the happy couple and know each other's résumés. You can tell he's drunk because when the waiter puts a plate of chicken in front of him, he says, "I don't recall ringing for the stewardess." You can tell she's drunk because she starts to giggle in that spluttering way that gets more uncontrollable the harder she tries to stop.

They have noticed each other before, more than once, and others have noticed them weighing the option. They have more than a little in common and, as the groom will whisper to Sam later, it is no accident that they have been seated together — marooned, in fact — at a table of older relatives who don't appear to be on speaking terms. As the evening goes on, Sam and Robin stop trying to bridge the silence at the table with polite conversation. The focus of their attention becomes so narrow that from across the room they look like conspirators, heads close together, oblivious to the speeches, the toasts, the tossed bouquet.

It would be hard to say which of them seems more interested, because they are both so animated, so obviously ready for something more than just another disjointed evening in their twenties. When the older relatives leave early, he takes her hand and they drift out to the dance floor.

She says, "I hope you're not holding my hand because you think I can't walk a straight line."

"You know that's not why," he says, then insists on slow dancing to everything, even the fast songs.

"Every good wedding needs a scandal," she says, then has to scream it again, right in his ear. The music is that loud. It's one of those evenings when no one is thinking much about later, about the evidence of excess in someone else's wedding album.

Well after midnight, the reception ends and the lights are turned on full. By this point, Sam and Robin are clear-headed enough to feel self-conscious about remaining entangled on the dance floor but still drunk enough to think that the only thing wrong with this picture is that everyone else can see it.

Sam murmurs, "We should go somewhere." The suggestion hangs in the air like a question mark until Robin says, "To talk." They nod, they get their coats, they take a cab to Robin's place, splitting the fare. The roommate is asleep upstairs, so they head to the living room, where there's a television sitting on top of an old milk carton, a collection of unmatched chairs covered with stacks of old newspapers, and a green sofa that smells vaguely of wet dog. Robin apologizes for the mess and gestures toward the couch, saying, "It's the most comfortable place," but in fact it's lumpy, and too small. For both of them to fit on it, they have to press close together, and pretty soon their arms are wound around each other's bodies like streamers.

This is not an ideal arrangement, Sam notes after half an hour. What about upstairs, the bedroom?

"No, let's talk" is what Robin says.

"We could do that upstairs," Sam responds.

But the roommate is also upstairs, trying to sleep. "If we made any noise..." Robin trails off and they look at each other for a moment then. What they see is this: her pink linen dress crumpled up mid-thigh, his white shirt unbuttoned, their lips moist from contact. But they do not talk. What happens instead is that she lifts her mouth up to his.

By the time the question of relocating is raised again, it's two a.m. "Why not?" Sam asks.

"The reason," Robin says, staring at the empty wine glasses on the beat-up coffee table, looking for the right phrase, "is that we'll feel close in the morning without even knowing if we get along."

"But how is what we're doing right now any different?" Sam asks.

"What we're doing right now doesn't commit us to anything" is the gist of the answer, although it doesn't come out quite so fluently. Robin doesn't usually drink much, and is beginning to remember why.

Sam reels out a clothesline of objections, beginning with "But a commitment is what I *want*" and ending with the observation that it's far too late to go home. It's a faintly ridiculous moment, as they debate the taxonomy of intimacy half-clothed, their feet dangling off the end of the couch. Both of them are enunciating very distinctly, overcompensating for those last few glasses. The earnest, sophomoric quality of the situation makes them feel closer, punchy with late-night humor. But they are, after all, twenty-eight: old enough to know how disappointment feels, and also old enough to know that bad things don't usually start out feeling this right. It's not just the alcohol or the late hour; there's a current of electricity between them. Her smooth thighs, his broad shoulders, the unzipped dress and the shirt on the floor — all this brings them back to the urgency of the moment. "You have to know" — Sam's hand is sliding down, down, under the elastic of the underwear — "how much I like you. Remember that Christmas party, last year? I was so glad tonight when you said you were single again."

They're whispering now, suddenly more aware of the roommate upstairs. "Look," Robin breathes, "I don't want to do this. I mean, I do, but not now. We haven't even been on a date yet."

What difference, Sam wonders aloud, would a dinner and movie make? How could that formality make their attraction any more legitimate?

And so it goes, the rhetoric, the semantics, the increasing entanglement of their bodies. The tempo becomes predictable: resistance countered with compliment, protest of uncertainty met with declaration of honorable intent. Robin does not push Sam away, or get up, or convey anything short of enjoyment. But still, Robin says no, no, no, you may touch here but not there, you may do this but not that. We can go this far, but not that far. Not yet — not tonight.

"Why should we wait when we've known each other so long?" Sam asks, and then, annoyed, "I never would've guessed you were this uptight about sex." It is annoying to be questioned when you are right, to be distrusted when the current between the two of you is what you should trust, when you have been twisting and turning in each other's arms for hours, until the numbers on the digital clock read 3:07.

I don't think so, I'm not sure, we should wait — all these words begin to sound insubstantial at 3:07, when items of clothing are strewn across the floor and arousal insists on a different conclusion.

And they are unevenly matched: it's Robin's brain against both of their bodies. When someone is telling you what you want to believe, when the sweaty fact of your own desire is undeniable, when there's the promise of something that might be so much better than a recriminatory scene — how do you say no? Instead, Robin says, in a tone that communicates something less than enthusiasm, "I'm worried about AIDS, I guess. If — "

"I have a condom," Sam interrupts. Out comes the condom, maybe a little too readily, as though this moment were a foregone conclusion for at least one of them from the minute they found their seats at the reception.

Sam's hands are all over the place now, complaints about the sofa forgotten in the rush of sexual zeal. Now they can stop talking, stop playing these games, and do what they've both been wanting to do all evening. It will be worth the wait. So when Robin's hand moves down to anchor the underwear that is being tugged off, Sam doesn't stop. Why doesn't Robin say something, do something, get up at least? Maybe Robin is thinking about it, but then Sam says — and this might make just about anyone pause for a moment — "What is this, performance anxiety?"

And during that pause, the underwear comes off. "You know we both want it. Relax," Sam instructs. But Robin is crunched up on the sofa, clearly still uncertain, not saying anything at all. Which is when Sam snaps — and this is what clinches the matter — "What are you afraid of? Stop being such a prude!"

And so they have sex. Was it good? Was it bad? Those are the questions you would ask in the 1970s.

In the 1990s, it seems, there's only one question: Was it date rape?

Yes, say the trained volunteers on the rape crisis hotline, and the brochures in doctors' offices and university counseling centers agree: No is not an invitation to a protest campaign. No is not the starting gun for the race to yes. No does not mean "Go ahead, try to change my mind." No Means No.

Rape is an abhorrent violation of body, mind, and spirit. This is true no matter who the rapist is. But it is equally clear that force and consent are more ambiguous when they do not involve a knife-wielding maniac in a dark alley. What is force? Is it beating a woman, or continuing to fondle her after she says no? And what is a threat of force? Telling her she'll be beaten, or threatening to break up with her if she doesn't put out? How many drinks must a woman have consumed before she is considered unfit to give consent?

These questions are pressing because how they are answered influences the way we view *all* sexual situations. Rape is one extreme on the sexual spectrum; if it is broadly defined, then the spectrum itself changes.

So what, exactly, is date rape? Even researchers who have spent years studying this question do not agree; their definitions and interpretations vary greatly. But their studies have been highly publicized and the figures have entered public consciousness: one in four women — or, depending on the study, one in three, or one in two — will be victims of rape or attempted rape. The figures are so shockingly high that the discrepancies hardly seem to matter. Apparently, the average woman is more likely to be raped than to be left-handed.

Some critics, most notably Katie Roiphe, Neil Gilbert, and Camille Paglia, have questioned the prevalence of date rape and dismissed the oft-quoted one-in-four figure as mere "hype." They have picked apart specific, well-known studies and attacked the methodology and conclusions of academic researchers; they charge that the researchers are sloppy scientists with an ideological axe to grind. In return, their own arguments have been scrutinized for errors and their analyses have been severely criticized; they have been branded rape-deniers and victim-blamers. Already, this debate seems stale and most people have chosen a camp — why reopen it?

The reason is simple: *both sides have, in crucial respects, missed the real story*. According to a large and growing body of research that has been virtually ignored outside academic circles, many of their preconceptions about date rape are false, because they are based on erroneous assumptions about gender differences in sexual behavior. By wrangling over the validity of one set of statistics, date rape researchers and their critics are playing a numbers game that attracts a great deal of media attention but does not address what is really going on between women and men today.

As with the sexual harassment debate, both sides in the date rape controversy make competing claims about women but share the same underlying assumptions of the sexual script: men pursue sex, women set limits. The focus is male sexuality and where the debaters disagree is on the question of how women should *react*. Date rape researchers and activists say women are powerless victims of unstoppable sexual aggressors, whereas their critics say women are big girls now who can and often do use their power to set firm sexual limits and to repel men who try to cross them. In different ways, then, both groups have affirmed the gender roles of the sexual script: both describe a female sexuality that is essentially defensive and reactive, and a male sexuality that is essentially aggressive and active.

Any exploration of the reality, however, must be prefaced by an examination of the studies that have been the source of so much controversy. From the outset, it's important to understand the context in which the research has been conducted. First, virtually all studies on sexual coercion have been conducted on university campuses, partly because women between the ages of sixteen and twenty-four are, according to police statistics, at much higher risk of rape than other women, and partly because college women are ready subjects for academic researchers. Also, the prevalence of sexual violence is of particular concern to universities because of possible negative consequences for the institutions themselves, in terms of reputation and potential lawsuits. But these campus surveys suffer from the same limitations as studies on more positive aspects of sexual behavior: their samples are not randomly selected, so are weighted heavily toward white, middle-class students majoring in the social sciences.

Second, most studies are not directly comparable, because researchers' questions, definitions, and interpretations vary greatly. Scales to assess victims' reactions and perpetrators' motives differ from one survey to the next; in some, subjects decide whether they have raped or been raped, but in others, researchers decide. Researchers do not ask men, point-blank, "Have you ever raped a woman?" Nor do they ask women bluntly, "Have you ever been raped?" Instead, because they assume that neither men nor women may recognize their own experiences as constituting rape, researchers' questionnaires usually ask about past experiences of "unwanted sexual activity." As we shall see, the results obtained using this approach frequently tell us a great deal about how researchers themselves see the world and rather less about the actual experiences and subjective interpretations of university students.

The source of the oft-cited one-in-four figure is a 1985 survey of 3,187 female college students conducted by psychologist Mary Koss for *Ms.* magazine. She reported that 15 percent of them had been raped, and 12 percent had experienced attempted rape; 84 percent knew their attackers, and 57 percent of the assaults occurred on dates.[1] One of the strengths of the study is that U.S. colleges were randomly selected for participation, as were the classes of students at colleges that agreed to participate, thus increasing the likelihood that the results are representative of university populations.

However, this survey has become a lightning rod in the date rape debate, primarily because the decision to classify students' experiences as rape or attempted rape was made by Mary Koss rather than by the women themselves. The women were given a questionnaire that included ten questions about sexual violation, followed by several more questions about the context of the event and their reactions to it. Those who said they had intercourse when they didn't want to because they were threatened or physically forced were classified as rape victims. So were the women who responded affirmatively when asked, "Have you ever had sexual intercourse when you didn't want to because a man gave you alcohol or drugs?"

Skeptics and even some of Koss's staunchest supporters take issue with this question because it presumes that getting drunk is something men force women to do in order to rape them, and because it makes no distinction between sex that is nonconsensual at the time and sex that is in some way consensual but later, in the sober light of morning, regretted.[2] Nor does the question distinguish between women who communicated a lack of consent and women who did not — a crucial distinction, since the absence of consent is the legal test of rape in many jurisdictions. If women who checked the Yes box for that question — "Have you ever had sexual intercourse when you didn't want to because a man gave you alcohol or drugs?" — are omitted from the tabulation of sexual assault victims, the one-in-four figure becomes *one in nine* — a number that is, of course, hardly cause for celebration.[3]

But the controversy does not end there, because three-quarters of the students Koss later classified as victims did not label their own experiences as rape or attempted rape.[4] In fact, half of those Koss said were "raped" explained their own experience as "miscommunication," and 42 percent said that they had subsequently voluntarily had sex with the men she called "rapists."[5]

Koss argues that these women's experiences met the legal definition of rape. It does not seem inconceivable, since the term "date rape" is of such recent coinage, that many women surveyed in 1985 would not call it "rape" if they were forced to have sex while on a date.[6] After all, the public perception of rape as a crime perpetrated by strangers in dark alleys has begun to change only in the last fifteen years, primarily as a result of studies such as hers.

Critics contend that the women themselves are the best judges of what actually happened to them. If a woman doesn't call it rape, these critics say, neither should anyone else. Indeed, isn't feminist methodology explicitly committed to honoring women's own interpretations of their experiences, and making room in the social sciences for women's own voices? If Koss's results are recalculated, leaving out the responses of the students who said they had sex because they were drunk or high as well as those of the students who did not call their experiences rape, the figure for rape and attempted rape among her respondents drops to somewhere between *one in twenty and one in thirty-three.*[7]

It is troubling that Koss's survey — the landmark study on date rape — is open to so many different interpretations, and that on closer inspection, its findings become less clear rather than more so. It is disturbing that the statistics can be so readily cast in such different lights, depending on one's point of view. The problem is that the questions she asked have different meanings to different people, and thus it's possible to draw a number of different conclusions about the answers she received from the subjects in her study.

The Koss survey is by no means unique in this respect. This is the central problem of all academic research on sexual coercion: researchers try to ask questions that cover as broad a range of experiences as possible, but the questions are worded so vaguely that they are open to multiple interpretations. Even the most "scientific" research, then, can produce results that are by no means authoritative.

Consider, for instance, the more recent "Sex in America" study (the National Health and Social Life Survey introduced in the previous chapter). The authors deliberately avoided asking women about rape; rather, they chose to ask about "forced sexual experiences." Now, the NHSLS has an even better claim to being representative than the Koss survey, because its random sample was not limited to university students, but included women aged eighteen to fifty-nine. According to the NHSLS, 22 percent of the women surveyed — by implication, 22 percent of *all* American women — reported that they had at some point in their lives been "forced to do something sexual that they did not want to do by a man."[8]

"Force" is not defined, however, so it's impossible to tell whether the women were physically forced, threatened, verbally coerced, or simply felt they could not say no. Most important, it's also impossible to tell whether they communicated their reluctance in any way.

Nor is there any way to tell what, exactly, they felt forced to do. During a ninety-minute face-to-face interview with a female researcher, women were asked, "After puberty...did a male force you to do anything sexually that you did not want to do?"[9] The authors of the NHSLS report that "about fifteen percent" of the women answered yes to this question.[10] Those who did were then given a list of choices to describe what happened: kissing, touching the genitals, oral sex, vaginal intercourse, and/or anal intercourse. Uncharacteristically, although the survey presents detailed breakdowns of the frequency with which Americans perform various *unforced* sexual acts, no data whatsoever were published on which specific acts the women said they felt forced to perform. The authors don't tell us how the women actually answered.

There is, of course, a big difference in most women's minds — and in the eyes of the law — between feeling forced to kiss a man and feeling forced to have anal sex. But there is no way to tell from the NHSLS what proportion of the 15 percent of women who told researchers they had been forced to do something sexual actually indicated an act that would meet the legal definition of rape, nor whether their perception of force would in fact meet the legal criteria, nor whether they indicated a lack of consent — all critically important distinctions.

There is also a big difference in most women's minds between feeling pressured into trying a new sexual act with a steady partner, and being forced to have intercourse with a stranger. Again, the NHSLS collapses this distinction, though the authors do report that 54 percent of the women who said they were forced to do something sexual identified the man who forced them as their husband or someone they were in love with; an additional 22 percent said the man was someone they knew well, 19 percent said the man was an acquaintance, and 4 percent said he was a stranger.

Many rape researchers would see this as evidence that men tend to sexually assault women they know. However, many of the women themselves might have had something different in mind when they answered the question about forced sex. A woman might have said yes, thinking about the time that her boyfriend whimpered about "blue balls" and begged and carried on as though the world would come to an end if they didn't have sex, and finally, she just got sick of it and went ahead and had intercourse. Alternatively, a woman might have said that yes, she was forced, referring to a husband who had repeatedly stated a desire to perform oral sex on her, and eventually, though he never beat her or threatened her with reprisals, she felt she had to let him do it even though she herself felt squeamish about it.

In both situations, the women felt forced all right, but many of us would agree that there's a difference between these examples and those in which, say, a boyfriend or stranger looms over a woman, pinning her down with his body, and forcibly penetrates her. Not dissimilarly, many of us would agree that there is a difference between feeling forced to donate money to buy a gift for a co-worker and feeling forced to hand over one's wallet to a gun-brandishing ex-con. My intention is not to make light of the issue of forced sex, which is a serious and reprehensible crime whether committed by a husband or a stranger, but to point out that "force" has multiple subjective meanings and that the NHSLS questions are open to many different interpretations, as are its results.

Near the end of the face-to-face interview, women who participated in the NHSLS were also given a written questionnaire about forced sex to fill out and return sealed to the interviewer, on the grounds that they might feel more comfortable writing something down on paper than saying it to another person. However, there was a crucial — and astonishing — mistake in the wording on the questionnaire. The word "sexual" was omitted, so that the question read, "Have you ever been forced by a man to do something that you did not want to do?"[11] And this time, women were not asked to indicate which specific activities they'd felt forced into, so it wasn't even clear whether the context was sexual.

Some women might have written yes, meaning, "I've felt forced to do the dishes." Others might have been thinking about things like feeling forced to wear sexy lingerie, talk dirty, watch erotic videos, or terminate a pregnancy, since immediately prior to filling out the questionnaire, they were verbally questioned on their attitudes toward both pornography and abortion.[12]

At any rate, many more women — "over twenty percent" — responded affirmatively to the question as it was printed on the questionnaire. Although the NHSLS authors do concede that the written responses are "somewhat suspect" because the question was misworded, their overall figure — 22 percent of women have been forced to do something sexually — is based on "the union" of the verbal responses and the written ones. They did not average out the difference between "about 15 percent" and "more than 20 percent"; apparently, "union" means accepting the higher figure.[13]

Given the conflation of responses to two different questions, the lack of a definition of force, the absence of any information on whether the women communicated their lack of consent, and the absence of any distinction between acts as different as kissing and anal sex, the 22 percent figure tells us very little about women's actual experiences of sexual aggression. Like the Koss study, the NHSLS raises more questions than it answers.

Other studies, with smaller, university samples that were not randomly selected, compound the confusion about forced sex. Like the NHSLS authors, most researchers prefer broad descriptions — "sexual coercion," "unwanted sex" — precisely because they cover a wider spectrum of experiences. As the authors of a 1986 campus survey explain, "We argue that sexual assault need not involve penetration or threat or use of physical force, and that it can best be conceptualized as a continuum of various forms of unwanted sexual contact (i.e., unwanted grabbing or fondling through forceful, violent penetration)."[14]

In these all-inclusive terms, sexual assault is happening all over the place, according to a blizzard of studies of college students' experiences. Researchers report that large numbers of women students — from 50 to 96 percent — have experienced "sexual assault," ranging from unwanted kissing to fondling to intercourse.[15]

But unless one equates a kiss with violent penetration, it is virtually impossible to generalize about rape rates from these studies. Many of the leading researchers, however, do not seem to view this as a problem, because they believe that rape is the end point on a continuum of sexually coercive behavior. Some of their studies explicitly support expanded definitions of force that go far beyond physical violence or threats of it to include verbal coercion of the "please, please, please" variety. Men who use words to get the chance to cop a feel and men who use their fists to force a woman into intercourse are presumed to be acting on the same impulse for the same reasons; the effect on women of both these approaches is also presumed to be the same. These ivory tower assumptions do not square with the way most of us think about these matters in our everyday lives, and one thing is very clear: a study that tells us that 96 percent of women have been sexually coerced is *not* telling us that they have been raped — or even that they have been forced.

As psychologist Mary E. Craig explains in an exhaustive review of dozens of academic studies, researchers' definitions of sexual assault "vary from use of force or threat of force, to use of manipulative tactics such as falsely professing love, threatening to leave the woman stranded or attempting to intoxicate the woman... This lack of consistency limits the comparability of studies, and makes replication of results difficult."[16] She concludes, "It is difficult to estimate the true prevalence rate of coercive sexual behavior, as these rates are dependent on the definitions and measures used."[17]

Most activists and many feminists believe that these definitional problems are quite easily resolved if the woman's consent, not the man's force, is the only measure used to distinguish sex from rape. This is, of course, implicit in the dictum "No Means No." According to this slogan, even if no physical threat is implied or inferred, the violation of "No" with words of flattery, false promises, or threats to a woman's reputation is *still* a sexual violation. Most researchers draw a very clear line between verbal and physical coercion, but their statistics are often quoted in brochures and pamphlets that do not make the same distinction, where women are cautioned to think of words as weapons and warned that date rapists may conquer them with language: "Prove that you love me," "It's not fair to get me excited then not finish," "If you don't I will leave you," "It's not like you're a virgin," "Everyone else is doing it," "What — aren't you a woman?"

There is, apparently, no substantive difference between intercourse with a man who applies psychological pressure and intercourse with a man who applies physical pressure; the end result is the same.

Cock-tease, prude, ice maiden — this, it seems, is the date rapist's arsenal, and women are informed that they will likely suffer long-term emotional trauma if they fall prey to these tactics.[18]

And yet, despite the barrage of statistics and the re-education efforts, many people apparently still have difficulty grasping the intricacies of the No Means No mantra. Robin's story is one that date-rape authorities tell us is replayed again and again, like a broken record, always catching on the same phrase: Was I raped?

According to these authorities, the answer is yes; even if you weren't physically hurt or threatened, you were coerced. The lack of certainty does not suggest to them that the distinction between rape and sex has become dangerously unclear. Rather, they believe, it proves just how bad things really are: men are so brutish that many women can't tell whether they've just had a routine sexual encounter or whether they have in fact been sexually assaulted. Apparently, women are so oppressed and so unsure of themselves that they have to ask: Was I raped? So the counselors and activists reply patiently, with the same answer: No means no. You said no, or at the very least, you didn't say yes. You were raped.

Sam, then, the aggressor in this situation, is a rapist? Robin did, after all, say no repeatedly, but Sam just kept going, tugging off underwear and issuing orders: "You know we both want it. Relax!" and "Stop being such a prude!" According to the brochures, educational videos, and instructional seminars, Sam is a classic date rapist.

This would surprise her. Sam is not, as you may have assumed, a man. Sam is a woman, so is unaccustomed to thinking of herself in terms of aggression. After all, she could not physically overpower Robin even if she wanted to. Robin is a man, fully seven inches taller and almost ninety pounds heavier than she is. Lead on, provoke, seduce, yes, fair enough — but *rape*?

No, say the activists, of course not! Rape is, in their lexicon, an invasion, both in literal and figurative terms, for which women lack the crucial artillery. It is an act whose motive is both political — maintenance

of the patriarchy — and personal: controlling and overpowering another human being. Women are, according to this analysis, far too
powerless to commit rape. Moreover, they lack penises and, because
they are innately nonviolent and nurturing, also lack the motive.

According to the sexual script, women are more interested in love
than sex; no woman, apparently, has strong enough sexual desires to
pressure a man — most don't even have strong enough desires to make
more than a halfhearted attempt at sex under the best of circumstances. Men, on the other hand, want sex all the time, and according
to activists, many researchers, and many feminists, men have a vested
interest in perpetuating the patriarchy through a reign of terror.
Clearly, they are far too powerful to be coerced by a mere woman.

The modern sexual script insists that only women are objectified
and only men are aggressive about sex. Mary Koss explains why she
only asked *women* about their experiences of sexual coercion: "Virtually 100 percent of reported rapes involve female victims."[19] This reasoning is curious, given that the whole purpose of her project was to
uncover cases of unreported rape, and her findings demonstrated that
the vast majority of victims never report the crime. And the statement
is false: there is ample documentation of man-on-man rape, particularly in prisons, and of sexual abuse of boys by both men and women.

Koss goes on to assert that, "Under a sex neutral definition of rape, a
woman could rape a man but this would involve acts such as a group of
women forcibly holding a man down while they use carrots to penetrate
him anally." A woman cannot in her view rape a man via intercourse
"because it doesn't involve penetration of the victim by the offender.
Such an act would be penetration of the offender by the victim!"[20]

By this definition, then, women are always victims — even if they
are pressuring men into bed. Men, because they possess penises, are
always offenders — even if they are having unwanted heterosexual intercourse. Sex, it follows, can only be nonconsensual for one gender.

The large numbers of college women who tell researchers they
have had unwanted sex seem, if one ignores the women's own interpretations and the serious definitional problems that plague the research, to validate this analysis. See, many researchers and activists
say, even the most privileged women in society, those with university

educations and a passport to the upper income bracket, are not truly equal. They, too, are profoundly vulnerable.

But those researchers who have bothered to ask men about their experiences have made a curious discovery: large numbers of men, too, have sex when they don't want to. In a 1988 study of 993 college students, 63 percent of men versus 46 percent of women reported that they had had unwanted intercourse. More men than women cited gender role concerns — fears of appearing unmasculine, impotent, or homosexual — along with inexperience and peer pressure as reasons why they had had sex when they didn't want to. Clearly, the notion that real men want sex all the time and know how to get it creates internal pressure to prove one's manhood, and there are also external pressures from peers to seize every sexual opportunity and make the most of it.

However, although men cited internal and social factors more frequently than women, these were not the main reasons men had unwanted sex. Enticement — the other person just kept going, "trying to turn you on by touching you" — was cited by 57 percent of men as opposed to 39 percent of women. Some women are not, apparently, primly waiting for men to take the initiative, nor are they easily deterred by a man's reluctance. Men were also more likely than women to have unwanted sex because they were intoxicated, were more likely to regret it, and reported slightly more verbal and physical coercion from their partners than women did.[21]

This study was not conducted by a misogynist fringe lunatic but by Dr. Charlene Muehlenhard, a University of Kansas psychologist who is one of the most influential and respected sex researchers in North America. Her feminist credentials are impeccable; she has written at length about the social forces — traditional gender roles, economic and social inequality — that pressure women into unwanted sex, arguing that "for women to be truly free and autonomous, we must be free from all forms of coercion."[22]

In another campus survey of 796 students that she co-authored in 1988, 84 percent of women and 74 percent of men said they had experienced pressure to have sex when they didn't want to. Women, however, were significantly more successful in resisting: 39 percent had actually had unwanted intercourse, compared to 49 percent of the men.

This time, Muehlenhard and co-author Patricia Long wanted to know more about the types of pressure students experienced, and why, exactly, they had not wanted to have sex. Their findings merit close attention, because they directly contradict some treasured notions about gender roles and help to explain why so many young women *and* men are having unwanted sex.

More than 90 percent of both men and women who had engaged in unwanted sex said they had been pressured by their partners; 35 percent of the men and 11 percent of the women also felt pressure from their own friends to have sex. Roughly half of the men and women said they had wanted to have sex with that person, just not at that particular time or in that place. Fifteen percent of the men and 39 percent of the women had not wanted to have sex at all; 40 percent of the men and 12 percent of the women had wanted sex, but not with that person.

The number one reason that students who had unwanted sex did not, in fact, want to: it was "against their values." Since the majority of men *and* women were not averse to sex per se (rather, the timing was bad or the other person left something to be desired), "against their values" implies that they didn't feel that they cared enough for the other person. That 71 percent of men listed this as a reason for not wanting sex suggests that, contrary to popular opinion, all men are not automatons enslaved by their libidos. And there's more evidence: 45 percent also said they didn't want sex because it was too soon in the relationship, and 40 percent were averse because they were involved with someone else.[23]

Even men in steady relationships sometimes resist having sex with their partners, a piece of common wisdom that received scientific credence in a 1992 study in which college men and women filled out questionnaires and recorded aspects of their current sexual behavior over a two-week period. Ongoing, diary-like studies like this one are valuable because they do not rely on participants' perhaps faulty memories of things that have happened in the distant past, nor do they rely on retrospective judgments about what the experiences meant. In my opinion, these are the kinds of studies that tell us the most about sexual behavior, because they provide detailed information not only about outcomes, but about how people make sexual *choices* and about how their behavior varies over time.

The majority of women reported that they had initiated sexual activity, ranging from kissing to intercourse, with a dating partner on at least one occasion during the two-week period of the study. Although men were more likely than women to initiate, men and women were *equally* likely to reject a dating partner's sexual initiation.

"Aspects of the traditional script, such as women's role of restrictor and the depiction of men's preoccupation with sex, do not appear to characterize these dating relationships," observed the authors, psychologists Lucia O'Sullivan and E. Sandra Byers. They concluded that "men's and women's roles in sexual interactions appear to be converging in both dating and long-term relationships."[24]

According to the No Means No dictum, when a man behaves as Sam did, he's a rapist. Is Sam, then, also a rapist? This is not a hypothetical question. Sam and Robin are not their real names, and a few details that might identify them have been changed to protect their privacy, but what happened between them is very real. As we shall see, their story is not at all uncommon, according to a large body of research conducted by some of the most respected researchers in the field of coercive sexuality and published in premier academic journals.

"I don't think of myself as sexually aggressive," Samantha says, genuinely puzzled. She considers herself somewhat shy, in fact, and when she's not sleeping alone, disrobes in utter darkness so that no man will see her body in the same unforgiving light that she does when she stands in front of the mirror after a shower.

Her self-perception seems skewed; her behavior with Robin was anything but reticent, and her looks hardly merit insecurity. She is the kind of woman that men call cute: pug nose, high-maintenance brown hair that curls and waves and gets in her eyes when she talks, toothpaste ad smile. And she has the kind of figure that many women covet: a compact size eight.

She tries to resolve this paradox, saying, "I just thought Robin was being kind of childish, playing games. It was a battle of wits as much as anything, and in those terms, I *am* confident. I'm not afraid of a challenge. I knew that if I could present a good enough reason or get him to the point of no return sexually, I would win."

I would win. So many of the phrases used to discuss sex and romance are borrowed from the lexicon of gamesmanship: catching a man, cheating, knowing the score, and winning him back.

But what are the rules? For many of those born after 1960, the script their parents learned — all boys try, but good girls wait until the wedding night — seems as quaint as a Victorian comedy of manners. By the time Sam came of age, the Pill was widely available, abortions were legalized, and social mores had changed dramatically, particularly regarding premarital sex. Whereas in 1969, more than two-thirds of Americans believed that premarital sex was wrong, by 1983, the same number believed that it was either "not wrong at all" or "wrong only sometimes." By the late 1980s and early 1990s, even many of those who disapproved of premarital sex were not practicing what they preached; among unmarried people, one-third who said premarital sex is "always wrong" had in fact had a sex partner in the past year, and more than two-thirds of those who said "almost always wrong" were also having sex.[25]

Not only have attitudes about premarital sex changed, but so have attitudes about marriage. Girls are now counseled to delay marriage and encouraged to pursue careers; waiting until the wedding night is a different proposition altogether if you expect to get married in your late twenties or early thirties.

From the lofty vantage point of the 1970s and early 1980s, when Sam was a teenager, chastity appeared to be a step backward, a flight from modernity, and, for women, a betrayal of hard-won liberation from double standards. Sex had come to symbolize personal freedom, but ironically, many adolescents were having sex to conform: everyone else was doing it. Abstention, with its overtones of repression, was suspect. Sex was cool.

When Sam came of age there seemed to be no hard-and-fast rules, except those governing the etiquette of responsibility. Men were responsible for pleasure, both their own and their partners'. As always, men had to be endlessly eager and ready to demonstrate their prowess, but now had the added burdens of providing satisfaction every time and discussing their feelings afterwards. Women didn't have those concerns, at least; women are talkers almost by definition, and those who weren't sure what it meant for a woman to be good in bed did know that showing up was a large part of it. Women were responsible for avoiding pregnancy and, if they failed, for dealing with the unpleasant consequences.

Consequences were not, however, foremost in Sam's mind when she was sixteen. She remembers talking about girls who had done it, were doing it, as though they were an elevated species. In the early 1980s, in her high school at least, sex was what made girls into women.

Sex was not about the classes they sat through in ninth grade, those musty films on human anatomy and dry lectures on contraceptive methods. The decision to separate boys from girls for these lessons was the subject of great speculation; what, exactly, was the football coach telling the boys during those hours? In the girls' class, the gym teacher sat at the front of the room, clutching at the whistle around her neck while grimly pointing to diagrams and charts. She was too embarrassed to use certain words and once, floundering, said, "Girls, on your first night of love —" but could get no further, unable to make herself heard above the braying teenage hysteria. Already, many girls in the room knew firsthand that love did not factor into most first-night equations.

No, Sam thought, sex was not about biology or love. It was about the lip-glossed creatures who floated down the hall, having those whispered discussions in the bathroom that broke off abruptly whenever one of the uninitiated came in. In previous years, a few of these girls had been the objects of her pity or scorn, because they came from the part of town where a high school diploma signified the end, not the beginning, of further education. But sexual experience leveled these class distinctions, at least at first; all those who had it seemed to exist on the same plane, somewhere above girls like Sam.

Sex was something she wanted to have so she could be like them, so that when she wore a short skirt and heels she did not stumble down the hall feeling like a cross-dresser. The boy, his character, and whether she even really liked him didn't matter all that much because sex seemed, ultimately, to be less about connection than self-transformation. What it implied was not love but maturity. Sexual experience was certification of one's own coolness. Consequently, Sam didn't think about keeping or losing her virginity but about getting rid of it.

There were others who felt this need even more keenly, she says, remembering a bash one Friday night in grade eleven, at one of the sprawling suburban houses — the parents, of course, were away — that backed onto a ravine. Large quantities of vodka were being consumed, but they were for the most part good kids, smart enough to know that trashing the place would not be wise. Still, it was no one's idea of a tea party. The boys began throwing each other in the pool, then pushing a few shrieking girls in, and pretty soon others were jumping in voluntarily, shedding their clothes in trails across the lawn.

Sam watched all this from the sidelines, too self-conscious to join them. Hovering uncertainly on the patio, hoping she wouldn't be thrown in the pool yet feeling sorry for herself because no one even tried, she saw her friend Deborah emerge from the ravine and scramble back over the fence into the yard, Rob trailing behind. She'd *done it*, Deborah whispered to Sam, just took Rob's hand and led him into the woods behind the house. He was older, eighteen maybe, no one special, no one you'd want to date, but not an embarrassment, either. He was reasonably tall and pleasant enough, in a hopeful, puppyish fashion. Apparently Deborah was tired of waiting and had reached the point of thinking, He'll do. The look on her face now, as she began unbuttoning her shirt and heading toward the pool, was calm, bored even. *It's that easy*. Sam was amazed.

Maneuvering a boy into sex had seemed impossible to her — how did you even show him that it was all right to kiss you, that it was what you wanted? For years, she'd been trolling the sidewalk in front of various boys' houses, trying to look as though she just happened to be passing by and praying that the object of her attention would bound out of his front door to sweep her up in his arms. But the most she ever got was a distracted "Hey, what are you doing here?" She thought she'd die a virgin, probably, and used to flop down on her bed and stare balefully at her Bruce Springsteen posters for hours, wondering how those other girls did it, what magic words they used.

When she was seventeen, she figured it out: patient waiting and silent longing didn't work. Boys had to be prodded into making the first move. You had to pick one guy, someone not so good-looking or so popular that he was unattainable, and flirt relentlessly. There was no secret code to learn; it was simply a matter of making your own willingness unmistakably obvious.

This discovery was more exciting than the first time itself, which left her unmoved. "Mostly," she says, "I was just relieved to get it over with." Her first lover — "though calling him a 'lover' is quite a stretch," she laughs — was a fellow counselor at summer camp, a moody boy whose silences had intrigued her. Sam didn't tell him she was a virgin, hadn't wanted him to know, and the event was so hurried and excruciatingly awkward that she was glad it had occurred on the last night of camp, because she would be spared the embarrassment of ever seeing him again.

Afterwards, she began to pay attention to subtleties that had previously not concerned her. The absence of rules, she noticed, did not mean that sex carried no penalties. Girls who mistook sex for love were devastated when the ending was not happy. If you thought sex implied commitment, but in fact did not get so much as a phone call the next day, it was difficult to avoid concluding that your mother was right: boys don't respect you if you give them what they want.

How could sex mean liberation and love at the same time? It was liberating only if you didn't expect it to lead to anything. This is what Sam — insisting on "Samantha" now, which sounded more grown up — began to think when she got to college, a good college in the East that wasn't quite Ivy League but seemed rarefied enough after the midwestern suburbs. It was the kind of place where students wore black turtlenecks, frequented poetry readings at coffee houses, and spoke of Wall Street with profuse disdain. Sex was mandatory and the permutations seemed limitless, at least until her junior year, when AIDS was suddenly in the headlines (but only as something that happened to certain kinds of men).

There was no stigma attached to sleeping with guys you barely knew and cared about even less — unless it became a habit, in which case the nicknames were not kind. "The Gobbler" is what one unfortunate woman was called, and another, whose backup vocals were legendary in dorms across the campus, was dubbed "The Screamer." There were no analogues for men, not even for the one who spread herpes through a whole clique of English majors. Male promiscuity was viewed in more generic, even complimentary, terms: rakes, studs, swashbucklers.

Perhaps the double standard had not been entirely erased, Samantha began to think, maybe it was just fainter and thus more difficult to negotiate. Her own double standards, however, were even more confusing. "Sex was such an available commodity that in order to show a man that you wanted and expected something more, you withheld it for a while," she says. "The amount of time wasn't set in stone, unfortunately, but you didn't want to give him the idea that sex was so unimportant to you that it didn't mean anything when you did it with him. It was ridiculous, since we were all sleeping around so much that we could hardly pretend that sex was meaningful to any of us."

In the absence of rules, she had to devise some of her own: experiment *but only with men you don't care about*, be adventurous *but be cautious if you want something to last more than one night*, be spontaneous *but be calculating*. Sex was supposed to *mean* something to women, Sam thought: an expression of egalitarian freedom or of emotional commitment, which appeared to be an either/or proposition. Negotiating between these two poles required rules, particularly for a woman who wanted to feel in control at all times.

"If you just wanted to have some fun or if the guy was crazy about you, it didn't matter how soon you slept with him," Samantha explains. "Either you didn't want a relationship or you knew that he wanted one more than you did, so you had the upper hand. But if you cared more than he did, then it seemed like he had the upper hand, and the only way to balance things out was through sex."

Really, she recalls, there were two kinds of sex. There were the purely athletic, sometimes ill-advised encounters with near strangers, which could be exhilarating precisely because there was so little posturing, so little room for disappointment — you'd see the guy in the cafeteria and remember, that's all. Then there was the sex that came burdened with emotional expectations, where the act was meant to express something more than raw desire and to confer obligations.

Consequently, Samantha says, "I had a split personality about sex. When I was unattached I felt powerful, because I could pick and choose. We were all constantly congratulating ourselves on how liberated we were. But when I was really *interested* in a man, I'd get quite preachy and go on and on about what a serious commitment sex was and basically do a high-minded princess routine. Often it worked, so in one sense I felt in control because I got the man. But that feeling was always temporary because I also felt very insecure. The whole point of attaching all this value to sex was to ensure that the other person didn't screw around."

A relationship induced a form of instant amnesia that canceled memories of her own conquests and replaced them with nagging worries: Am I attractive enough, desirable enough, exciting enough to hold his interest? These anxieties crowded into bed with her, where, ironically, the sex was often more mechanical than it had been in the beds of strangers. If, sometimes, making love was less exciting, less theatrical than sex-as-sport — well, there were other compensations. You always had a date, so were spared the endless, convoluted men-are-such-pigs-and-I-wish-I-had-a-boyfriend bull sessions. You were superior, in a way.

Sometimes, with the boyfriend — the names changed, but the sensation did not — she felt completely detached, as though she were watching the event from the ceiling, coaching: *moan a little now, he'll like that.* Worst were the times she found herself thinking about the excitement in those strangers' beds while the boyfriend was working away industriously on her body. *Stop comparing!* she willed herself. *This is the good sex, the sex that equals love.* But afterwards, if he did murmur about love, she occasionally found herself restless and irritable. What she wanted to hear was that she had the best body on campus.

Many researchers rail against the inequities of the traditional sexual double standard yet embrace it in their own studies, asking men only about their role as *perpetrators* of unwanted sex. There's an explicit assumption behind this research: if a man does it, he's a rapist, but if a woman does it... Well, good girls *don't*.

By their own reports, however, many young women do. In a 1994 poll of 1,000 American women aged eighteen to twenty-five, 29.3 percent answered yes when asked, "Have you ever pressured a man into having sex?"[26] The poll was conducted by BKG Youth, a leading research firm that specializes in studying the attitudes of young people, and its findings are hardly unique. In a 1994 *Details* magazine survey, 56 percent of women agreed with the statement "It is acceptable to coerce someone into sex by any means possible," and 18 percent reported that they themselves had done so.[27]

Now, polls do not provide detailed analyses of respondents' attitudes and behavior, and magazine surveys are considered unreliable and unscientific, because respondents are self-selected and the samples are therefore not random. But those academic researchers who have looked into the matter have come up with similar figures. For instance, 19 percent of the female undergraduates in a 1988 study conducted by clinical psychologist Mary Craig admitted that they had coerced men into having intercourse. Compared to the other women in her study, those who were coercive had less traditional beliefs about gender roles, and reported being aroused by feeling powerful and in control of their sexual relationships.[28]

Similarly, in a 1989 study of female college students conducted by Dr. Peter Anderson, 50 percent said they had used some form of coercion to try to bring about sexual activity ranging from kissing to intercourse. The women's tactics sound strikingly "masculine": saying things they did not mean, continually arguing to wear down their partner's resistance, questioning their partner's sexuality, and threatening to end the relationship if they didn't get sex then and there. Moreover, the majority cited what is considered a typically male justification for this behavior: sexual arousal.[29]

Verbal pressure by women is not a rare phenomenon, according to numerous studies.[30] To take just one example, in a 1994 survey co-authored by Cindy Struckman-Johnson, a University of South Dakota psychologist who is a leading researcher of men's experiences of sexual coercion, 30 percent of 204 college men reported that they had experienced coercive sexual contact from a woman at least once since the age of sixteen. The vast majority of the incidents involved verbal pressure of some kind: men reported that women used "constant pressure," along with "nagging" and "pleading," to get sex. "Several said that the woman made them 'feel guilty' about either not wanting sex or [not] finding her desirable," Struckman-Johnson reports.[31]

Many people assume that men have control over their erections and thus it would be anatomically impossible for a woman to have intercourse with an unwilling man. But as any teenage boy knows, erections can be entirely involuntary and all too uncontrollable. Since 1948, when the original Kinsey report on men was published, it has been established that men can function sexually in almost any emotional state, including anger and terror.[32] More recently, men who have been raped by other men report that even though they feared for their lives, they were capable of performing sexually when their attackers manually or orally stimulated them.

Sexual readiness is a physiological phenomenon, and does not necessarily indicate psychological arousal. The same is true for women, who sometimes lubricate when they are raped, although they derive no pleasure whatsoever from sexual violation.[33] An erection is not always an indication that a man wants sex — upon waking, for instance, an erection usually signals not desire but a full bladder — and it is quite possible, as both women *and* men tell researchers, to pressure a man into unwanted intercourse.

Women now have a license to initiate sex, and they are by all accounts doing so. But, largely because the sexual script encourages them to believe that men are only after one thing, it does not seem to occur to women that some men may in fact not want to have sex with them, or that their own behavior is coercive.

Evidence that women sometimes misread men's signals is provided by a 1993 study conducted by psychologists Lucia O'Sullivan and E. Sandra Byers, who asked 201 men and women aged eighteen to twenty-nine whether they had experienced "disagreements in which a woman attempted to influence a reluctant man to engage in sex" within the past year. Significantly, more men than women said yes: 64 percent compared to 49 percent, which suggests that women are unaware of the extent to which they attempt to influence partners to have sex.[34]

Most women responded to a male partner's reluctance using a range of tactics: touching, flattering, and pouting or sulking were cited by a majority of respondents. About one-third tried to convince the men by talking about their "real feelings" toward them, or asking "Don't you find me attractive?" or simply taking off their own clothes to indicate their readiness and expectations. About one-quarter tried to sway an unwilling man by telling him how enjoyable sex would be, or by claiming that they were too aroused to stop.[35]

Again, men reported that women used more influence strategies, particularly more negative ones, than the women themselves thought they had used. And while two-thirds of the men said the reason for their reluctance was that it was too early in the relationship for sex or that the relationship itself was "inappropriate," most women thought the problem was situational, that it was simply a matter of wrong time, wrong place. The authors concluded, "As do men, women need to be sensitized to the impact of their behavior on their dating partners," adding that the emergence of female high-pressure tactics is "not a particularly positive aspect of the new sexual script."[36]

What is remarkable about all this is how stereotypically masculine these women's perceptions and actions seem, and how "feminine" the men's perceptions of the situation appear. Collectively, these studies provide evidence of a striking change in gender roles: some women now pursue sex with a zeal that their mothers once considered unique to men. As discussed in the previous chapter, there is a considerable generation gap among women in terms of other, less negative aspects of sexual behavior, too.

Apparently, this generation gap extends even to the realm of fantasy. According to Nancy Friday, young women's sexual fantasies are so different from their mothers' that they are "a new race." Friday is no academic researcher; she invites people to send her written versions of their sexual fantasies and then publishes the ones she receives, along with her own commentary. Obviously, her method is not scientific, but it does have the merit of revealing, in far greater detail than surveys and polls can, how large numbers of people think about sex. Her 1991 collection of women's fantasies, appropriately entitled *Women On Top*, maps the coordinates of the sexual generation gap: whereas their mothers daydreamed about being ravished by uncontrollable men, at least in part because they were not supposed to want sex themselves, many women in their twenties fantasize about ravishing, controlling, restraining, and even forcing, raping, and torturing men.

Young women are not, however, merely fantasizing. Like men, some of them act on their aggressive impulses. "[A] pool of women now exists with personality traits and attitudes that predispose them to be sexually coercive: they have a high need for sexual contact; enjoy the feelings of power and control; view men as sexual adversaries; or assume men are 'ever ready' and mutually interested in sex," writes Dr. Struckman-Johnson. "These women are likely to misread or ignore men's signals of sexual intent in dating encounters and consequently coerce them into unwanted sexual activity."[37]

In other words, many young women *want it*, and will do whatever is necessary to try to get it. It is, however, crucial to stress that women are far more likely to experience physical coercion than men are. Date rape, by which I mean unwanted sex with a man who is not a stranger and who uses physical coercion, physical violence, or threats to cause harm in order to get his way, is a very real problem. Like all forms of rape, it is a serious, violent crime that often causes severe, long-lasting trauma.

But the fact of the matter is that most women who are classified by researchers as victims of sexual assault have *not* experienced physical coercion. Like men, they tend to have unwanted sex because they are verbally and psychologically pressured into it. The media stereotype of the rampaging frat boy, using his strength and size to subdue a young woman, is simply not borne out by the research.

In most studies, women report very low levels of threat and almost no physical violence whatsoever.[38] For instance, in 1987, Charlene Muehlenhard and Melaney Linton conducted a study that closely replicated Mary Koss's findings: 14.7 percent of 341 women students "reported being involved in sexual intercourse against the woman's will, that is, rape." But when asked whether the man had used physical violence, such as slapping or hitting them, or threatening them with a weapon, *all* of the women classified as rape victims said no. However, 5 percent did report that the man had made threats, although the nature of those threats is unspecified, and 14 percent said that the man had "used physical coercion, such as holding her down."

Naturally, we wonder: how, then, did the rest of the men get their way? The number one modus operandi, cited by 55 percent of the women: *he just did it*, even after she indicated either verbally or in some other way that she did not want sex. As the authors conclude, "The nonviolent nature of these SA [sexual assault] attempts suggests that women might be able to avoid SA."[39]

Other features of these episodes suggest the same thing. Many of the women indicated they had been drinking; numerous studies show that after consuming alcohol, women tend to be less clear in communicating a lack of consent.[40] Both men *and* women reported "that the man had often felt led on during SA dates," which indicates that there was considerable miscommunication.[41] It is quite possible that in some of these instances, the women had simply failed to communicate that they did not want to have sex.

Clearly, holding someone down and/or issuing threats is forceful. Since the man virtually always has an advantage in terms of physical size and strength, he does not actually have to harm a woman to get his way. Threatening to do so, using intimidating body language, or simply using his weight to pin her down, is enough to ensure compliance. If these are the measures used to define rape, then 3 percent, rather than 14.7 percent, of the women in Muehlenhard and Linton's study were raped.

The difference between unwanted sex and unavoidable sex is significant: in the latter cases, there are elements of physical coercion, physical violence, or threats to cause physical harm. Unavoidable sex, regardless of how well one knows the aggressor, is rape. Many young women understand this distinction and make it themselves. For instance, in a 1988 study co-authored by Dr. Muehlenhard, 39 percent of the women said they had had *unwanted* sex, but only 3 percent deemed it *unavoidable*. In their written descriptions of the incidents in question, the 3 percent who deemed sex unavoidable clearly described acts of physical force and threats to cause physical harm that would meet even the narrowest definition of rape.[42]

Men's reports about their own behavior also suggest that physical violence is rarely a feature of sexual assaults, and that unwanted sex is not necessarily unavoidable. Men freely admit that they don't always stop when they encounter reluctance. Depending on the study, between 7 and 56 percent of college men say they have tried to just keep going when women say no, continuing to try to *turn them on and talk them into* more sexual activity, from kissing to fondling to intercourse.[43]

Nevertheless, there are also significant definitional problems with the research on men's self-reports of verbal coercion, as psychologists Ronald Ross and Elizabeth Allgeier point out in an important new study. The most common method of identifying sexually coercive men is through anonymous written surveys using a questionnaire that Mary Koss helped devise, which includes questions like "Have you ever had a woman misinterpret the level of sexual intimacy you desired?" and "Have you ever had intercourse with a woman because she felt pressured by your continual arguments?" Men who respond affirmatively are usually categorized by researchers as verbally coercive.[44] But Ross and Allgeier, who is a past president of the Society for the Scientific Study of Sex and the editor of *The Journal of Sex Research*, had a novel idea: get men to fill out the questionnaire, and then, in an open-ended interview, ask them individually, "What did you think the item was asking you when you were responding to it?"[45]

The items on the questionnaire are not, apparently, interpreted the same way by all men; in fact, there were as many as six different interpretations of any one question. For instance, consider what the men made of the question "Have you ever had a woman misinterpret the level of sexual intimacy you desired?" — researchers typically view this query as a roundabout way of discovering whether men have been in a position where they've coerced a woman. Consistent with other studies, 43 percent of the men in Ross and Allgeier's study said yes.[46] Afterwards, however, one-quarter of all the men said they thought the question was asking whether a woman had ever *overestimated* the level of their interest. "I thought it was asking whether I had been with a woman who thought I really wanted to go all the way when I really just wanted to kiss and touch," explained one man.

This wasn't the only alternative interpretation. Another 20 percent interpreted the question to mean, "Has a woman ever overestimated *or* underestimated your desire?" Some men thought the question was asking about general miscommunication over what each partner wanted sexually; others who ticked the Yes box did so because they had had sex with women who assumed that the act implied love, when in fact for the men, the act was purely physical. Some men simply thought the question was asking whether they had ever been turned down by a woman.[47]

As Drs. Ross and Allgeier point out, if men are interpreting the items on the questionnaire so differently, the "pencil/paper measures" of men's sexual coercion may be presenting a very skewed picture of what is really going on. And, they suggest, the same may be true for women — perhaps when women answer yes to a question on a survey about whether or not they have been coerced, the question may mean something entirely different to them than it does to the researcher.

At any rate, contrary to feminist expectations, men who are classified as "sexually coercive" do not score highly on the scales that have been devised to measure arousal to the prospect of dominating and humiliating women. For instance, in a 1989 study co-authored by Dr. Craig, *none* of the men she labeled coercive "reported arousal to the hatred and humiliation aspects of rape, or demonstrated a belief that relationships between men and women are adversarial by nature." Instead, they said they had verbally coerced women because they were "horny."[48]

Most men do not say, "Have sex with me or I will hurt you," and those who do are rapists. Rather, verbal coercion tends to consist of false statements — "But I really love you" — and threats are far more likely to be psychological, such as, "If you don't, I'll leave you."[49] College men who freely admit they are verbally and even physically

coercive say, again and again, that what they are after is *sex*. They do
not set out to degrade women, and they are, for the most part, nonviolent. This, Craig contends, "indicates that sexual coercion may be
a separate phenomenon from rape, and that the men who coerce
may be fundamentally different from criminal rapists."[50]

That there is a fundamental difference between coercion and
criminal rape should be patently obvious since women, too, freely
admit that they do it. *In fact, accepting the current definitions of and theories about sexual coercion requires that we also accept that there is an un-
acknowledged epidemic in North American society of truly staggering
proportions: not just women, but large numbers of men, too, are victims of
sexual violence.*

To most of us, this is an absurd proposition. We do not consider it
rape when a woman uses verbal coercion and psychological manipulation, or continues to fondle a reluctant partner who is not running
screaming in the opposite direction. Nor should we. The problem is
not that large numbers of men, too, are being date raped, but that the
definition of date rape has become so elastic that it now includes
episodes that have nothing to do with aggression, force, or even lack of
consent. By these lights, women look just as prone to coerce as men do,
which tells us, first, something is very wrong with the definition, and
second, women are not exactly the powerless victims they are made out
to be in both the modern sexual script and much academic research.

We urgently need to clarify the distinction between rape and sex
by taking a long hard look at what is really going on between men
and women, which requires that we abandon some cherished notions
about male sexual aggression and female moral superiority. Already,
there is plenty of research to indicate that many of the episodes classified by academics as sexual aggression or coercion are a far cry
from the media stereotype of date rape.

Not only is there generally a lack of physical violence or threats of
it, but the research shows that disagreement situations arise most commonly in established relationships. In the media, the date rapist is generally portrayed in Jekyll and Hyde terms: one minute he's a clean-cut
young man, asking an ingenue out for dinner, and the next minute he's
forcing himself on this woman he barely knows. In fact, in many of the

incidents classified by researchers as sexual aggression, the partners have been dating for some time and are unlikely to be people who have never had any sexual contact at all. Instead, as Dr. Craig summarizes in her review, "It is not until the couple has attained some level of erotic intimacy that sexual aggression is likely to occur."[51]

But "sexual aggression," as many researchers define it, is most likely to consist of verbal coercion, not physical force or threats of it. The woman may be saying, "Not now, I don't feel like it," and the man may be saying, "Come on, we haven't had sex for a week." Usually, these disagreements do not come entirely out of the blue; in most studies, they are preceded by some form of consensual sexual activity.

Whether many of these disagreements in fact constitute sexual aggression seems doubtful. Consider the findings of a 1988 study conducted by Dr. Byers and Kim Lewis. In their study, male and female undergraduates kept records of their dating behavior over a four-week period; each week, they filled out detailed questionnaires about their dates, and then submitted them anonymously.

The participants in this study reported that about three-quarters of their dates involved some form of sexual activity, ranging from kissing to intercourse. Disagreements in which the man wanted to go further than the woman did occurred during only 7 percent of all the dates.

In response to unwanted advances, 42 percent of women reported that they had said no, while 36 percent said no but implied that the advances might be accepted at some other time or place. Many of the women blocked the advance by moving the man's hand, or moving away from him altogether. None of the women reported getting up or slapping the man, and none reported that they got angry or asked him to leave.[52]

What most of the men did when faced with a woman's relatively demure indication of non-consent was to stop, immediately and unquestioningly, "many also apologizing." A minority of the men stopped but asked why, or attempted to convince the woman, or expressed displeasure. And an even smaller minority — about 16 percent — continued the advances; in response, women tended to reiterate their refusal more definitely.[53]

"[T]he present data indicate that coercive disagreements are not a 'regular' component of sexual dating interactions," Byers and Lewis concluded, adding that, "Even among the minority of dates that resulted in a disagreement about sexual activity, use of coercive strategies by men was the exception rather than the rule. Thus, these data do not support the stereotyped view that when disagreements about the desired level of sexual activity do arise, normative behavior for men is to use any strategy to 'convince' the woman to engage in the disputed behavior. Rather, it is more typical of men to accept the woman's decision."[54]

In Byers and Lewis's study, what the female and male participants describe is not frightening at all, and should be familiar to anyone who has ever had a sexual relationship. Steady partners rarely share exactly the same appetites for sex; sometimes one is not in the mood to do more than fool around, sometimes the timing is bad, or a guest is expected at any moment, or contraception is not available.

And these are precisely the kind of situations the study participants described, "not instances in which the man was trying to extend sexual boundaries," Byers and Lewis report. "Instead they represent different desires for sexual activities previously engaged in with a partner with whom they were romantically interested. *This type of communication would normally be expected in most dating relationships and would also be essential for maintaining a good relationship*" (emphasis added).[55]

One of the biggest problems with research on "unwanted sexual activity," now the preferred term because it is so inclusive, is that many researchers falsely assume that all unwanted sex is in fact nonconsensual and coerced. Again, there is a sharp dichotomy between public prescriptions and private reality, where many people freely consent to unwanted sex.

"Many of us have sex when we're feeling less than libidinous and often we do not regret it in the morning," according to the author of a March 1995 *Glamour* article entitled "Seven reasons to make love tonight — even if you don't feel sexy." There's testimony from women who have sex because their partners are anxious and can't sleep, or to make up after a fight, or because it's a special occasion, or because "having sex with your partner now means a payback later." As one of the women explains, "Relationships are an elaborate series of tradeoffs... I know he has a higher sex drive than I do, so it's not some dreadful thing to have sex when he wants to. He's a good lover: He puts himself inside my head during love-making and he pays a lot of attention to my pleasure."[56]

Yet, in most academic studies, these women's lack of consent and their partners' coercion would be assumed. Most sex surveys don't include open-ended essay questions, and there's no space to write, "Well, it was unwanted but it was also consensual and he didn't even know that I wasn't really in the mood. See, it was our second anniversary, and I wanted to make it a night to remember, so..." Instead, the women in the *Glamour* article would check off Yes to questions about having had unwanted sex, indicating that this was not the first time it had happened in their lives, and yet another study reporting shockingly high rates of nonconsensual sex would make headlines.

Many researchers "have made the incorrect assumption that participation in unwanted sexual activity is always nonconsensual," writes Dr. Lucia O'Sullivan. This assumption, she believes, has created "undoubtedly exaggerated" estimates of the risk of rape.[57] Dr. O'Sullivan came to this conclusion in 1994, after conducting a study in which 160 college students monitored their dating behavior over a two-week period, turning in detailed questionnaires at the end of each week. "Engaging in unwanted consensual sexual activity," she reports, "was generally not a novel behavior *for either the men or the women*" (emphasis added).[58]

The students in her study estimated that on average they had participated willingly in some form of unwanted sexual activity twelve times in their lives; there were no gender differences. During the two-week period of the study, however, nearly twice as many women as men — 50 percent versus 26 percent — reported engaging in unwanted but consensual sexual activities, ranging from hugging to fondling to oral sex to intercourse. Men's and women's descriptions of their experiences were "remarkably similar": they were romantically interested in their partners, wanted to please them, and "for the most part, these interactions were positive experiences."[59]

Most of the students had unwanted sex to satisfy their partners' needs or to promote intimacy and avoid tension, clear indications that "this behavior serves a bonding function."[60] And about two-thirds of those who had unwanted sex believed their own partners had done the same thing on numerous occasions, which suggests that they share a contract to try to please each other sexually even when their own sexual desire is at a low ebb. Certainly, having unwanted sex does not appear to harm their relationships. Most of the students were very or extremely romantically interested in their partners, and most reported that their romantic feelings did not change or actually increased subsequent to having unwanted but consensual sex. Two-thirds even said that engaging in the undesired sexual activity itself was pleasant; 85 percent said that being with their partners was pleasant.[61]

There were also some negative outcomes, however: about one-third of both women and men reported feeling emotional discomfort. And one-fifth, primarily women, reported a subsequent slight decrease in romantic interest toward their partner, but this was "related to the extent to which a respondent enjoyed time spent with his or her partner rather than the extent to which he or she enjoyed engaging in the unwanted sexual activity."[62]

Dr. O'Sullivan notes that if she had not asked the students whether they had freely consented to having unwanted sex, she could have reached the erroneous conclusion that one-third of them had been sexually coerced by their dating partners. "Social scientists need to recognize men's and women's contribution to their own participation in unwanted sexual interactions," she cautions. "Researchers in the past have concluded that experiences of unwanted sexual activity are characterized by the infliction of coercive tactics...while neglecting the decision-making process involved in freely consenting to engage in unwanted sexual activity."[63]

Just as Yes seems frequently not to correspond to actual sexual desire, No frequently does not correspond to an absence of sexual desire. No does not, in fact, always mean no, according to numerous studies conducted by different researchers: one-third of college women consistently report that they have, on occasion, said no even though they "had every intention to and were willing to engage in sexual intercourse."[64] Women say no when they mean yes for a variety of reasons: game-playing, concern that they will be perceived as just being interested in sex, and to slow sex down.[65] Tellingly, the tidal wave mentality, which dictates that women can never say yes to sex but must instead be swept away by love or swept along by the male sex drive, is also what leads some women to say no when they mean quite the opposite — which is, of course, just the excuse that rapists have claimed for years.[66]

Interestingly, however, what happens in the vast majority of cases is that when men hear no — even a no that means yes — they stop. Sex tends to occur only when the woman explicitly indicates that although she said no, what she really meant was yes.[67] Apparently, token resistance isn't really a holdover of old-fashioned feminine coyness, since equivalent numbers of college men also say no when they mean yes, for similar reasons.[68] In fact, according to Drs. O'Sullivan and Allgeier, "Token resistance appears to be a common dating behavior employed by both men and women in generally pleasant, nonadversarial interactions."[69]

Miscommunication of desire is, it seems, a universal phenomenon. But it's crucial that young women communicate clearly when they absolutely do not want to have sex, and studies show that women are least likely to do so when they are sexually aroused or have been drinking.[70] This is critically important to any discussion of sexual coercion, because most events classified by researchers as coercion are preceded by some degree of consensual activity, so women are likely to be aroused, and frequently they have been drinking.[71]

The best way to get a man to stop before he even starts is to be very direct right from the outset: I am not having intercourse with you tonight.[72] And the most effective response if he does try to go even a step beyond your stated sexual boundaries, but is *not* being physically violent, is to stop all sexual activity immediately and state clearly and unmistakably your lack of consent. If he persists, the best course of action is to get as far away from him as possible, all the while loudly and clearly stating No, and yelling for help if he appears undeterred.[73] If he won't take no for an answer, and resorts to physical violence or intimidation, let there be no mistake: he is a rapist, and the woman now needs all the courage and help she can get to press charges and ensure that he receives the maximum penalty.

Unwanted sex, even nonconsensual unwanted sex, is different from unavoidable sex, which is rape. It is an obscene trivialization of the severe trauma of sexual violation to lump the two experiences together, as though intercourse obtained through physical violence or threats were not really very different from intercourse obtained through persuasion and sweet nothings that turn out to be exactly that.

Fortunately, none of this research and none of these numbers support the public perceptions about the prevalence of date rape. What they do suggest is that sexual situations are often highly ambiguous and what both people want is frequently unclear. Many women have unwanted sex, for a variety of reasons. Cajoling, pleading, and false promises from men are sometimes the cause; peer pressure, internal pressure to prove one's femininity or sexual adequacy, a desire to please one's partner, and simply choosing to take the path of least resistance can also be causes. And the same is true for men.

Yet, although young women have been raised in a completely different political climate from their forebears and have been encouraged to claim "ownership" of their sexuality as a birthright, sex is still widely perceived in the time-honored way: as something men do to women. The common language used to discuss sexuality in the public arena — the media, mainstream academia, politics — is predicated on women's passivity and oppression. Sex is supposedly something only men are driven to pursue.

Like the textbook French taught in high school, this language is dated and often sounds stilted outside the classroom. Sexual politics are not fixed and unchanging, yet in the public discourse, they are often discussed as though they were.

Consequently, a bizarre paradox has developed: some young women who behave sexually as subjects, agents of their own desire, talk about themselves as objects. Fluent in the idiom of male oppression, they have trouble constructing a sentence in which they are not sexually victimized, objectified, or dissatisfied. And so, even as they rewrite the sexual script, they tell themselves they are merely acting out traditional, passive roles.

hat night with Robin, Samantha felt "this incredible sense of power," she remembers. It was the same thing she used to feel in college, when she was on the prowl with her friends: in control of her destiny, in charge of her desire. Flushed with the thrill of the chase, they crowded into the bathroom at parties, elbowing each other for mirror space, rating the bodies and sex appeal of the men outside the door.

The ecstatic moment when you knew you wouldn't be sleeping alone that night made up for the hangover the next day.

At the reception with Robin, she first felt it on the dance floor, her brain flooded with certainty, her body with anticipation: *I won't be sleeping alone tonight.* There had been a dry spell of almost eight months, during which she'd begun to wonder, half seriously, if she would ever have sex again. With her single friends, she discussed the difficulties of finding a man if you had any standards and how big the bed felt on restless Saturday nights.

Samantha had had enough bad relationships to know that she was better off alone right now, but still, she missed the rush and release of sex. Her sudden conviction on the dance floor — *he wants me* — gave her the heady, almost forgotten sensation of sexual power. And the condom in her purse seemed like proof of her authority: she was mature enough to be sensible, confident enough to be prepared for any outcome. What happened later on the couch was foreplay, she thought, a better-than-average opening act for the main attraction. It didn't occur to her that he might have other ideas.

Feeling powerful, free, in charge — all this aroused her almost as much as rolling around on the couch with Robin did. And at first, his reluctance only intensified her sense of sexual invincibility. If she weren't so irresistible, he wouldn't have to work so hard to keep from jumping into bed with her immediately. "The less willing he was, the more relentlessly I pushed," she says. The truth of the matter is that after a while, she was almost offended: she knew she was looking especially good that night; didn't he recognize how lucky he was to be with her? What was wrong with him?

And then, when he didn't give in, she began to wonder if maybe she wasn't so alluring after all. Did he find her breasts too small? Her touch too awkward? These were the questions she had always asked herself in relationships when she was worried about keeping a man's interest, not on the first night, and they made her frantic. She had been admiring herself throughout the evening, but now began to race through a bodily inventory: How do I smell? Are my thighs too big? Is my stomach bloated? Looking at the two mental pictures of herself, the one before they got to Robin's and the one after he said he didn't want to have sex with her, she wasn't sure which one to believe.

If he doesn't want to have sex, there must be something wrong with me. She took solace in his erection — seemingly undeniable proof of his attraction to her — but the words coming out of his mouth seemed to say something different: You don't turn me on. What else could "I think we should wait" mean?

She didn't feel very liberated or very much in charge any more. The more they talked, the more she felt control of the situation slipping away and the more it seemed that if she left it up to Robin, his decision would be nothing less than a verdict on her desirability. To him, she may have appeared unshakably determined as the evening wore on, but quite the opposite was true. "Why should we wait?" she asked, telling him how right they were for each other, while silently questioning first his normality and then her own sex appeal. "You know we both want it," she declared unequivocally, yet was smarting from the sense that she was being rejected, propelled not by lust but a hunger for reassurance.

All men want sex, after all. And if this one didn't, it must be her fault.

Before the resurgence of feminism as a social and political movement, scientific knowledge about rape was based almost exclusively on psychological studies of convicted, incarcerated rapists, who represented a minuscule — and unusually violent — proportion of men charged with the crime.[74] The theoretical underpinnings for these case studies came first from Freud, then other psychologists and sexologists, who proposed variations on the theme of mental illness: perhaps rapists were products of domineering mothers and weak fathers, or suffering from castration anxiety or feelings of sexual inferiority, or maybe they were frustrated homosexuals.[75] Sociobiologists focused on hormonal theories and studied brain function, seeking an evolutionary basis for rape; a few psychologists studied women who had been raped, trying to detect ways in which they had "precipitated" sexual assaults.[76]

Rape, the theorists had decided, is what some men with poor impulse control did when they wanted sex; whether his superego was underdeveloped or his hormonal secretions were overdeveloped, the rapist was a sexual deviant, experts tended to agree, more in need of psychiatric therapy than jail time.

The popular perception was that women were almost always to blame for their own victimization. There were only a few exceptions: married women, in which case rape was viewed as an infringement of a husband's property rights, and white women who accused black men, in which case rape was viewed as a threat to racial purity.

Most rape victims, however, were not viewed as blameless, and many were not even believed. If a woman had a "history," or was given to wearing tight clothes and venturing out alone, or cared so little about her reputation that she would flirt with a man or let him drive her home — well, what did she expect? And who could blame the man? Rape was viewed as something that happened primarily to bad girls, who had only themselves to blame if men got the wrong impression about their willingness to have sex. They must have been "asking for it" in some way.

Feminism revolutionized public perceptions about rape and changed, utterly, the way it was conceptualized and measured by social scientists. The opening salvo was Kate Millett's 1970 bestseller *Sexual Politics*, which provided a theoretical and cultural framework for deconstructing gender relations and reconfiguring rape in terms of power, not sex. "In rape," Millett wrote, "the emotions of aggression, hatred, contempt, and the desire to break or violate personality, take a form consummately appropriate to sexual politics."[77]

In the subsequent quarter-century, feminist researchers have corrected a monumental imbalance by focusing on the victims' experiences rather than the perpetrators', thus dispelling the myth that rape is only committed by strangers in dark alleys. Their research has proved that women are also raped by boyfriends, husbands, casual acquaintances, and close relatives, and that regardless of who the man is, it is still rape, it is still extremely traumatic, and it is still a crime. Activists have fought for and won substantial changes in the criminal justice system: men accused of rape are now more likely to be charged by the police and brought to trial, marital rape is a punishable crime, and women are more likely to be willing to testify against their attackers because information that was once considered "evidence" — past sexual history, for instance — is now much less likely to be admissible.

Most importantly, feminism has succeeded in reshaping the old, victim-blaming perception: she asked for it by wearing that skirt/going to that bar/smiling that way. Twenty years ago, the idea that no woman in any way asks for or deserves sexual violation was considered fairly radical; today, it is firmly established in the mainstream.

There are many feminist theories about rape, but two have been particularly influential. The first is that rape is an act of violence, not a sexual act. The second is that rape is sex as usual in North America; male sexuality is intrinsically violent. "Intercourse with men as we know them is increasingly impossible," as Andrea Dworkin puts it in *Woman Hating*. "It requires an aborting of creativity and strength, a refusal of responsibility and freedom: a bitter personal death. It means remaining the victim, forever annihilating all self-respect."[78] Fond of military metaphors, elsewhere she likens the penis to a "weapon," the act of intercourse to an "occupation," and argues that male sexuality is "the stuff of murder, not love." In fact, she believes, "under male domination, there is no phenomenological division between sex and violence."[79]

Interestingly, though this is clearly the more extreme of the two arguments, in some ways it has been more influential. Intellectually, many of us scoff: sex isn't rape! But emotionally, the argument has resonance, because many of us fear male violence and take precautions in our everyday lives to avoid it: taking cabs instead of the bus, avoiding underground parking garages. Understandably, after two decades of long-overdue consciousness-raising about rape, child abuse, and domestic violence, male aggression and male sexuality seem to be inextricably intertwined. Men are the predators, molesters, and batterers; women and children are the innocent victims. Every week, it seems, there is a new study documenting men's atrocities, or a new horrific instance of one man's violence makes headlines.

Regardless of the tenor of their own personal experiences with men, then, most women fear violence and believe that it is directly related to masculine physical characteristics: greater size, greater strength, and the all-mighty penis. We associate violence, and male sexuality, with testosterone; aggression and the male sex drive are often discussed as interchangeable concepts.

As Susan Faludi so convincingly argued in *Backlash*, many of us are strongly influenced by media reports that confirm traditional gender stereotypes. One of her examples was a widely reported — but entirely false — "discovery" by a team of academics from Harvard and Yale: single, college-educated women in their thirties "are more likely to be killed by a terrorist" than to marry.[80] Most journalists assumed this must be true, since it jibed with conventional wisdom that ambitious women are destined for empty, miserable lives, and did not bother to investigate the flawed study itself. Dozens of articles about the grim plight of single career women appeared, and before Faludi debunked the study, women all over North America were having panicky discussions about the supposed man shortage. Many of our ideas about what we can expect from the world are shaped by similar articles about studies and surveys that bear the heady perfume of science. *It must be true*, even the most skeptical among us think, *if all these experts keep telling me so.*

So we read about high rates of male physical and sexual violence, and this information inevitably influences the way we perceive the world. Not surprisingly, many people now believe that violence is intrinsically male, and that victimization is intrinsically female. The studies and articles confirm the most traditional gender division: men are aggressive, women are passive; men are violent, women are nurturing. The end result is that women feel morally superior but fear men more, which vastly increases men's power. "If women are weak and nonaggressive, they must depend on men for protection and fear harm from men against whom they cannot defend themselves," as psychologists Jacquelyn White and Robin Kowalski recently pointed out in the *Psychology of Women Quarterly*.[81]

But, as they argue, it is a myth that women are nonaggressive. It may be painful to discover that women are not as pure as we thought, but it also gives us power — and hope, because it then becomes clear that men are not genetically programmed to be violent.

Aggression can take many forms: physical or verbal, active or passive, direct or indirect. When psychologists speak of "aggression," they use the word differently than most of the rest of us do in everyday conversation. To them, it means the *intent* to cause harm, which women most certainly do display when they gossip viciously, poach on other women's sexual territory, and sabotage their friends with concern. Nevertheless, everyone "knows" physical aggression is a male prerogative. In the public discourse, female violence is almost always presumed to occur only in the context of self-defence. Even the most gratuitous acts are perceived as protective: Lorena Bobbitt chops her husbands penis off while he sleeps and convinces a jury that she acted in self-defence.

When a woman is violent, we look to the men in her life for explanations: what awful things did men do to her to make her act that way? The association between masculinity and violence runs so deep that many people automatically assume that even female violence is caused by men.

Women are, however, capable of *all* the forms of physical and sexual aggression that we have come to think of as uniquely male, and we can no more blame men for women's violence than we can blame women for men's. This is not to suggest that women are equally violent — they are not — or that male violence is not a pressing public issue. It most certainly is. But the capacity for aggression is *not* intrinsically male, and the widely held assumption that men are by nature aggressive while women are by nature passive and nurturing is simply not borne out by the facts.

In the modern sexual script, however, the personal has become so political that it requires denying women's capacity for wrongdoing in order to preserve their status as saintly victims. Currently, findings

on all types of female physical and sexual aggression are being suppressed; academics who do publish their research are subject to bitter attacks and outright vilification from some colleagues and
activists, and others note the hostile climate and carefully omit all
data on female perpetrators from their published reports.

By denying women's power to cause harm, however, the idea that
men are somehow genetically programmed to destroy gains momentum. This notion doesn't just train women to fear men as a group; it
also influences our perceptions of our own power in personal relationships with men. Women like Samantha are blind to their own
power, even as they are pressuring men sexually, because they think
of their own sexuality in terms of victimization and believe that men
are hard-wired for aggression. Because of these beliefs, they wind up
paying lip service to gender roles they aren't even following, and
continue to think of gender in traditional, binary terms: aggres-
sion/nurturing, villains/victims.

Although women are much less likely to be physically aggressive
toward strangers, there is substantial evidence of female physical aggression within intimate relationships. In the National Family Violence Surveys, random sample studies that were conducted in 1975,
1985, and 1992, more than 10,000 Americans were asked how often
in the past year they or other family members had responded to disagreements with physical violence. Murray A. Straus and Richard J.
Gelles, both highly respected social scientists who have been studying family relationships, gender, and power for twenty-five years, reported that "among violent couples, in about half of the cases both
partners were violent, in about one-quarter of the cases the husband
was the only partner who was violent, and in about one-quarter of
the cases the wife was the only one who was violent."[82]

According only to the *women's* self-reports of their own and their
partners' behavior, women were just as likely to assault their husbands as to be assaulted, and there were no gender differences in
either minor violence (e.g., pushing, slapping) or severe violence
(e.g., punching, hitting with an object).[83] Are women always acting
in self-defence? Apparently not, since women reported that they
struck the first blow in about half of the assaults, a finding that has

been replicated in numerous studies in both Canada and the U.S.[84] Of course, it is possible that many women hit first to ward off an attack; a woman who has been beaten by her husband on previous occasions might land the first blow as a pre-emptive strike. But even if in mutually violent couples the women are always acting in pre-emptive self-defence, the fact remains that in more than one-quarter of violent marriages, the woman is the *only* violent partner.

This seems to fly in the face of common sense and certainly presents a stark contrast to the sexual script's assumptions about women's "nature." However, as Dr. Straus points out, "even casual observation of the mass media suggests that just about every day, there are scenes depicting a man who makes an insulting or outrageous statement and an indignant woman who responds by 'slapping the cad,' thus presenting an implicit model of assault as a morally correct behavior to millions of women."[85] Not only is society tolerant of low-level violence from women, but men are instructed not to retaliate. A "real" man cannot be hurt by a woman, because she "hits like a girl" and he is supposed to "take it like a man."

Of course, the average man can cause considerably more physical harm with his fists than the average woman can, so, Dr. Straus cautions, "Although women may assault their partners at approximately the same rate as men assault theirs, because of the greater physical, financial, and emotional injury suffered, women are the predominant victims."[86] Recalculating the 1985 data to account for injuries does reveal a significant gender disparity: 3.7 per 1,000 assaults by husbands result in injury, compared to 0.6 per 1,000 assaults by wives.[87] Clearly, women are far more likely to be physically injured by men than vice versa.

Nevertheless, many researchers agree with Dr. Straus that physical assaults by wives are "a major social problem." First of all, women's violence increases the probability of retaliation by men; although men are not supposed to fight back, some do, and they can cause much more damage. Second, children who see their parents fighting physically learn that violence is acceptable; they are much more likely to become violent themselves, not just with siblings and in the schoolyard, but much later, with their own families.[88] Third, justifying women's aggression on the grounds that "he deserved it" or "it didn't really hurt" perpetuates the ideas that violence is acceptable and morally defensible — defenses that men can then invoke when they hit women because they're "nagging," or "overly emotional," or because "it was just a little slap."

Straus and Gelles's results have been replicated in more than thirty random sample studies of domestic violence, and researchers who study violence in dating relationships have turned up similar findings: women are just as likely to be physically aggressive as men are.[89] What is noteworthy about these findings is that women have the *capacity* for physical aggression. These statistics do not capture a truth that any woman who has ever engaged in a physical struggle with a man knows very well: regardless of an equal intent to cause harm, they are not equally matched. The average man can hit harder, kick harder, and has one ability that the average woman lacks altogether: he can restrain, pin down, and immobilize his partner. Unless she is armed, he is in a sense humoring and indulging her physical aggression, and *she knows it.*

Men who smack women around don't think that women are granting them some kind of indulgence. Men know that women cannot retaliate with equal force, and men know that they will have the upper hand in any physical struggle.

On paper, there are few gender differences in rates of domestic violence; in reality, in terms of both the physical assaults themselves and the resulting injuries, there are huge gender differences. Yet it is important to acknowledge that women have aggressive impulses and the capacity to act on them physically, because excepting instances of self-defence, violence is morally wrong, regardless of gender and regardless of whether it leaves a bruise. One of the reasons that the myth of female moral superiority flourishes is that there are double standards about what constitutes morality: when it comes to physical aggression, the standard is lowered for women, raised for men.

Furthermore, the notion that men inspire women's violence is refuted by the revelation that lesbians also batter each other, at rates that are estimated to approach those of heterosexual men and women. "Lesbians batter their lovers because violence is often an effective method to gain power and control over intimates," writes Barbara Hart in *Naming the Violence*, an anthology of essays about and testimonials from women who have been bitten, kicked, punched, thrown down flights of stairs, and assaulted with weapons, including guns, knives, whips, tire irons, and broken bottles, by their same-sex partners.[90]

The most disturbing evidence of female physical aggression does not concern other women or men, however, but children, who are more likely to be physically abused by their mothers than by their fathers. Mothers are the aggressors in 62 percent of the abuse cases that are reported to child protective services.[91]

Many cases are never reported to the authorities: an estimated 6.9 million American children are kicked and bitten, beaten up, hit with objects, burned or scalded, assaulted with weapons, and otherwise abused every year.[92] Doing something about this pressing problem requires acknowledging that maternal instincts do not guarantee children's physical safety.

While most women do not physically abuse their children, most mothers can readily understand aggressive impulses. Raising children is a difficult, frequently thankless and certainly socially underappreciated enterprise; women still have the primary responsibility for child care yet often lack adequate financial resources and social supports. Even the best-behaved children wilfully disobey on occasion, and understandably, most mothers sometimes feel trapped, isolated, and so frustrated that they want to walk out or lash out, although the vast majority never do so and never would.

It is dangerous to children to pretend that women don't have these impulses, and unfair to women. Myths about motherhood ensure that women will continue to shoulder a disproportionate burden of child care responsibilities, and guarantee that mothers will feel inadequate and guilty when they do feel fed up, overwhelmed, or angry. Furthermore, the notion that bringing up kids is something that all women are born knowing how to do directly contributes to some mothers' willingness to follow their instincts and haul off and hit a child to make him stop crying or to punish him for being bad or simply for making her life more difficult.

Although it is important to examine the causes of women's abuse of children — generally greater responsibility for child care, social isolation, economic inequality, and past victimization — these are explanations, not excuses. A child is no less damaged by physical abuse or neglect if the mother is the one doing the abusing or neglecting. And it may well be true in some instances that women lash out not because they feel socially powerless but because they believe they have a license for aggression in the domestic sphere. "The home is the realm where women are expected to hold and exercise authority, thus to the extent that power corrupts men, it may also corrupt women," suggest White and Kowalski.[93]

Women are also capable of sexual abuse of children, at rates that belie the popular perception that molestation is a crime only men commit. Men are, indisputably, responsible for the majority of child sexual abuse, but women too are perpetrators of this crime. According to the *lowest* estimate, women are the perpetrators in 14 percent of cases involving boys and 6 percent of cases involving girls.[94]

Many clinicians who specialize in treating incarcerated male sex offenders believe the figures may be much higher, because so many of the male rapists and pedophiles they treat were victims of child sexual abuse.[95] For instance, Dr. Nicholas Groth, a leading authority on male sex offenders, reports that 31 percent of the incarcerated offenders he studies were sexually abused as children; 41 percent of the abusers were female.[96] Similarly, a 1989 study of 170 male juvenile sex offenders found that 37 percent had been victims of sexual abuse; nearly one-third of their abusers were female.[97]

Some experts on sexual abuse contend that women are better able than men to mask sexually inappropriate behavior because they are primarily responsible for child care activities such as bathing and dressing. Moreover, women are rarely viewed with suspicion, since they are supposed to be nurturing and protective, not to mention sexually passive. "It is more likely that a woman's behavior will be seen as affectionate," writes Anne Banning, an Australian clinical psychiatrist, in a review of the literature on mother-child incest. "Society accepts mothers taking their sons to bed and may only question this in terms of over-dependency. It does not accord the same indulgence to fathers taking their daughters to bed."[98]

Although male perpetrators have been studied extensively, there are relatively few studies of female sex offenders, certainly many fewer than their rate of molestation merits. The existing research consists primarily of clinical studies based on relatively small samples of women who are in treatment programs. These studies are painful to read, not just because they describe the suffering of young children but because they debunk some treasured notions about women's sexual passivity, maternal instincts, and nonviolence.

In at least one significant respect, women who sexually abuse children are different from their male counterparts: they are far more likely to co-offend, that is, to act in concert with men.[99] But this does not mean that their role is passive and consists solely of permitting the sexual abuse to occur. Sometimes co-offenders actively procure children for men, sometimes they perform sexual acts with other adults in front of children, and sometimes they are very active participants in the abuse.

An extensive 1989 study of the clients in a Minneapolis female sex-offender program describes the behavior of several co-offenders in excruciating detail. "Kris," for instance, reports that her husband Tony suggested playing spin-the-bottle with their three young children. Their household was already physically violent in the extreme: Tony regularly beat Kris, who in turn beat the children. Initially, she was willing to play the sex "game" only because she was afraid that Tony would hit her if she refused.

Soon, the "game" included other relatives, both adults and children. In Kris's own words, "When the bottle would land on an adult, [the adult] would switch it to land on a kid, and we'd make them take off their clothes. The kids would start crying and we would try bribing them and then, if that didn't work, we'd spank them or beat them up a little bit. There was all kinds of sex acts performed...everything from touching to oral sex to intercourse."[100] Adults had sex with each other in front of the children, and with the children themselves.

"After a while it got to the point where I liked it," says Kris, who began playing spin-the-bottle when she was alone with her children. "Having sex with my sons was more enjoyable than having sex with my husband, because I had some control over what was going to happen instead of being ordered around and told what to do." Both independently and with other adults, she abused her children three times a week for two years.[101]

This is an extreme case, particularly for a co-offender. Many women who act wholly independently, with no coercion or assistance from men, are neither as violent nor as persistent as Kris. Those who independently molest girls, most often their daughters, are rarely lesbians; rather, they seem not to grasp that the girls are autonomous, separate individuals. Those who molest boys, however, frequently see themselves as benevolent teachers in sexual matters, or believe that they are in fact engaged in love affairs.[102]

The older woman who sexually "initiates" a boy is a staple of teen films, and is viewed socially not as a molester but as a philanthropist dispensing carnal wisdom. Legally, sex with a minor is statutory rape, but women who commit the crime are rarely prosecuted and even more rarely jailed. For instance, in 1994, a forty-two-year-old educational assistant went to trial in a small Oregon town for having sex with a fourteen-year-old male student. The case caused a local uproar, not least because the perpetrator was married to a district attorney and because four years earlier she had been caught sending steamy letters to another boy. Her sentence for having sex with her pupil? Thirty days under house arrest. As a local man commented to the Associated Press, a male school employee "would have been strung up" for committing the same crime.[103]

Mothers who abuse their sons seem to view them not in romantic terms but as temporary sexual partners, filling in for adult males when the women's relationships are in crisis or have ended. In a 1989 report on the victims of mother-son molestation, Oklahoma clinical psychiatrist Ronald S. Krug wrote, "The sexual abuse typically involved the mother satisfying her own emotional and physical needs for intimacy, security and perhaps power by actively seeking out the son, either on a nightly basis, or when she and her living partner were in conflict." He speculates that mother-son incest receives little attention because "males do not get pregnant, and the evidence of sexual abuse has not been present; a double standard in belief systems has existed in which fathers have the potential for evil and mothers are 'all good'; adult males have been too embarrassed to reveal their sexual activity with and arousal by their mothers; male children have been presumed to be unaffected by sexual abuse, and reports by sons have been ignored."[104]

Many of the mothers in Krug's study did not have intercourse with their sons, but rather engaged in indecent liberties: sleeping and showering with the boys, and mutual sexual touching. These activities are hardly benign, however, and boys who are molested in this way often suffer severe long-term effects, ranging from long-term sexual dysfunction to full-blown post-traumatic stress disorder.[105] Sometimes, boys who are sexually abused by women become profoundly disturbed, because they receive strong social messages that women are incapable of abuse and that boys are supposed to want sex, and because there are few support services for male victims.

Why do women commit these crimes against children? Clinical studies propose a fairly simple explanation: the vast majority who do so were victims of sexual abuse themselves. In a 1987 review of forty-four treatment programs, 93 percent of female sex offenders had been sexually abused.[106] Like male perpetrators, women who commit sexual offenses are often attempting to "resolve" the trauma they themselves experienced as children by re-enacting it. And like male perpetrators, some women deny that they have done anything wrong, or trivialize the consequences for the children, or blame their young victims for being "sexy" and "seductive," according to a 1994 study of incarcerated female sexual offenders conducted by Meg Kaplan, director of the New York State Psychiatric Institute's Sexual Behavior Clinic, and Dr. Arthur Green, a clinical psychiatrist.[107]

A number of recent, disturbing reports indicate that the transition from victim to perpetrator can occur at a very young age. A 1989 study by Toni Cavanagh Johnson, clinical director of a child sexual abuse program in Los Angeles, describes thirteen girls aged four to twelve, all of whom had been sexually abused and had gone on to molest even younger children. More than half the time, the girls molested siblings who had not been previously abused and were thus "objects of their jealousy and anger," Johnson writes. "The girls were generally not looking for orgasm or sexual pleasure. For the most part the girls were looking for a decrease in the feelings of anger, confusion, and anxiety." None of the girls had come into contact with the criminal justice system or had been court-ordered into treatment, because social services workers "tend to dismiss the sexual acting out behavior of girls." No one, Johnson concludes, took their behavior seriously.[108]

Further evidence of a double standard is provided by a 1988 study of twenty-eight girls aged ten to eighteen who were referred to the Juvenile Sexual Offender Program at the University of Washington. "Unlike the male offenders, none of the female subjects was referred for such 'hands-off' offenses as exhibitionism, peeping, or indecent phone calling," the authors reported. "The typical female adolescent sexual offender referred to our program was likely to have committed a serious offense (indecent liberties or rape) against a five-year-old child in a baby-sitting situation."[109] Most of the female perpetrators had been sexually or physically abused themselves; they tended to be younger than the boys referred to the program, they chose younger victims, and they were more than twice as likely to have raped their victims.

The vast majority of children who are sexually abused do *not* go on to become perpetrators. Yet it is clear that many child molesters were victims themselves, and this pattern is even more evident for female offenders than for their male counterparts. It also seems to be a recent development, linked to changes in gender roles and sexual mores. As Anne Banning observes, "Women are now struggling to be acknowledged and seek power to forge their own destinies. Could it be that in this struggle, those women for whom power is very important but who feel insecure, inadequate, and disempowered, may be predisposed to sexually abuse children if other predisposing factors also exist?"[110] This seems quite plausible as an explanation not just for many female sex offenders, but also for many male pedophiles.

Women are also capable of violently raping adult men, though it should be stressed that this crime is *extremely* rare. Nevertheless, it can occur, according to a 1982 case study bearing the prestigious imprimaturs of the Yale University School of Medicine and the Masters and Johnson Institute. Philip Sarrel and William Masters described eleven men they had actually treated, like a twenty-seven-year-old, 178-pound truck driver who picked up a woman in a bar and went with her to a motel, where he promptly passed out. When he woke up, he was blindfolded, gagged, and tied spread-eagled to the bed. Four women were in the room at that point, and he was instructed to "have sex with all of them." When, after two rapid-fire performances, he was unable to achieve erection, a knife was held to his scrotum and he was threatened with castration. The women took turns stimulating and mounting him, berating his inability to perform to specification, for twenty-four hours. They then took him to an isolated spot and pushed him from their car, still tied up and blindfolded.

He did not report the gang-rape to the police or anyone else, fearing that they would consider him "less than a man." He was thereafter sexually incapacitated and when he married, some months later, did not tell his wife why he was unable to get an erection. The truth emerged in therapy, a full year into their unconsummated marriage, when he was diagnosed as suffering from post-rape trauma syndrome.[111]

This case sounds improbable because we understand male sexuality in terms of aggression and female sexuality in terms of passivity. We have difficulty seeing men as sexual victims of women, even when the context is extremely violent. In one 1988 study, college students were presented with several hypothetical vignettes describing the violent gang-rape of a hitchhiker, conducted at gunpoint. The scenarios were worded identically, but in some cases, the victim was female and the attackers were male; in others, the genders were reversed. When the victim was male, he was considered far more likely to have encouraged or initiated the episode and to have enjoyed it, especially by male students; female attackers were also assumed to derive more sexual pleasure from raping. One student captured the overall male reaction when he scribbled in the margin of his survey, "Some guys have all the luck!"[112]

Female violence is present in only a tiny minority of all sexual encounters. Nevertheless, it is important to acknowledge that violence is not something that is programmed into male genes, and aggression is not uniquely male. Misperceptions about the connection between male sexuality and aggression pervade the public discourse on sexuality, and while they do not influence most women to behave pathologically, they do effect how we perceive power and morality in sexual situations.

Samantha was not violent and did not commit any crime; verbal coercion, whether perpetrated by men or women, should not be confused with sexual assault. But it is important to understand that commonly held misperceptions — only men are aggressive, female sexuality is essentially reactive — can blind women to their own coercive behavior. When they encounter reluctant men, women may actually believe that they themselves are powerless, as Samantha did, and may not perceive themselves as stage-managing reluctant men into sex. Rather, they think they are merely prompting men who have missed their cue in the sexual script: *all men want sex all the time*.

Feminist research and theories have, indisputably, provided valuable insights into the connection between rape and gender relations, sexual violence and equality, and the effects of rape on women. But any ideology that converts a personal experience into a political event is by its very nature limited and extremely rigid. And at least in terms of what researchers call sexual coercion and date rape, feminist ideology is not only limited in terms of its explanatory powers, it is dangerously misleading. While many feminists stress the similarity between the boy next door and the convicted rapist, emphasizing that both are motivated by a desire to control women and both are conditioned to act aggressively on that desire, there are, in fact, considerable differences, as we have seen. Furthermore, there is little place in the dominant feminist framework for female aggression and female sexual agency, and little analysis that helps women understand their own sexuality outside the context of personal victimization and social oppression. In fact, the feminist discourse on heterosexuality does not really pay much attention to women at all. Rather, most feminists concentrate on *male* sexuality, and they have portrayed it as uniquely violent, aggressive, and predatory.

Just as they have expanded the definition of pornography to include virtually any sexually explicit materials, Dworkin, MacKinnon *et al.* have expanded the definition of rape while exaggerating its occurrence. And they have won many new supporters by tossing around horrifying numbers: one in three girls is sexually abused, one in two women is raped. Rape is the trump card of the anti-pornography movement, the proof that the other side is wrong. It's crucial to remember, however, that they make little distinction between heterosexual sex and rape. Of course, if you view all heterosexual intercourse as implicitly coercive and the act of penetration as inherently violent, then the modern script they have helped to write makes perfect sense.

It should be good news that the reality falls far short of the threat portrayed in the modern script, but many feminists of all stripes greet this assertion as a heresy, as though *all* rape were being denied. The notion that women and particularly young women are in terrible, constant danger is tantamount to an article of religious faith in some camps, and thus any debate quickly veers away from the territory of facts to that of emotions. It is hardly surprising that a discussion of rape elicits strong emotions, since the act is such an obscene violation and such a potent symbol of women's very real vulnerability. And feminists who fought so hard to dispel victim-blaming quite understandably fear its return.

But there is a difference between blaming the victim and questioning what, exactly, constitutes victimization. And there is a difference between sympathizing with and defending women who are sexually victimized and encouraging all women to feel more fearful of victimization than in fact they should.

The fear of rape has restricted women's lives throughout history, as Susan Brownmiller argued so eloquently. She contended that this fear is one of the primary ways that the patriarchy controls women and keeps them dependent on men, because only a husband or father provides any kind of protection against the perception that one is fair game. It stands to reason, then, that fearing rape more and from more men — not just strangers in dark alleys but the boy next door — will further restrict women's lives. And Take Back the Night protests will not make a whit of difference if, in fact, most women are not attacked by strangers they encounter on a darkened street but by the very men they are dating.

For women, then, one cost of the myth of our essential innocence is that we must live in terror of men's power. It's the comparative badness of men, after all, that makes women so good: individually blameless and collectively aggrieved. The end result is that women feel morally superior but fear men more, which vastly increases men's power. The less women fear, the more free we are, and the truth is that the large body of research on sexual coercion does not support the inflated rhetoric of the modern sexual script. Acknowledging this in no way denies the existence of rape, which is, lamentably, all too real.

The alternative is, in fact, the real denial: clinging to moth-eaten notions about essential gender differences in sexuality, when the reality is that those differences are diminishing. The modern script that contains these old-fashioned ideas does not help us see who young women are sexually and in fact denies that substantial changes in behavior and attitudes have even occurred. It does not encourage women to continue to fight for ownership of their sexuality and self-determination, and actually encourages them to see themselves as far more helpless and powerless than they really are.

And this is the real danger: women are being coached to misperceive their own sexual "nature" and experiences, which has implications for virtually every aspect of their lives. We rely on a reductive sexual vocabulary in which males are active and females are passive, hardly aware that it prevents us from discussing what is really going on between women and men. At the same time that the definition of coercion is being broadened to include a multitude of nuances, definitions of gender roles are being narrowed: men are cast as sexual predators, women as prey.

In short, there's a vast and alarming difference between the rhetoric about sexual behavior and the reality. This gap — between actual conduct and common interpretations of it — is widening. And the result is that after three decades of feminism, women are becoming less rather than more able to understand their sexuality, and less rather than more able to eradicate gender role stereotypes and double standards. In fact, new ones are developing.

It's hard to understand why a woman would pressure a man into sex because it's hard to imagine a woman who would want it that much or a man who would want so much to avoid it. Samantha, too, has trouble with these ideas.

"I was feeling romantic," she says, though it seems that what she really means is that she felt like having sex. "But I *want* a relationship," she tried to convince Robin, and she even believed it herself.

The truth, in light of her actual behavior, seems harsher: she wanted to sleep with him first and consider any future they might have later. It never occurred to her that a man might worry about consequences, might connect sex with emotions, might have a different agenda for the evening than she did.

And she still does not believe that Robin's unwillingness had anything to do with him. "My own sexual attractiveness was on the line," she says. She had something to prove, and the way Samantha sees it, there was only one person under pressure that evening: herself.

Sexual politics have changed dramatically in the past three decades. Feminism helped to shape the generations born after 1960, and we — both men and women — are in some respects profoundly different from our parents. Products of a social revolution we did not engineer or even directly participate in, we grew up in an era when birth control was readily available, abortions were legal, homosexuals were coming out of the closet, and sexual mores were undergoing enormous change. It is inconceivable that our attitudes and behavior would not be affected by these transformations.

Young women, in particular, have had many more opportunities than any previous generation of women, as well as a deeply ingrained sense of entitlement to equality in the workplace, the home, and the bedroom. While it is true that sometimes we are frustrated or disappointed in one or all of those places, our expectations, unlike our mothers', have *always* been high.

Feminism and the sexual revolution freed young women to become sexual subjects, rather than mere objects, yet the language of sexuality has not caught up with us. Nor have we invented one of our own. In interviews with young women across North America, I was struck by the doubletalk about sex: again and again, women described their own coercive behavior but did not acknowledge its true nature. Men, they believed, had cornered the market on unacceptable sexual conduct, and the date rape statistics were often held up as unassailable proof that all men want sex all the time and will do just about anything to get it.

The reason we have to challenge the modern script is not that it ignores the victimization of men, but that we are paying lip service to essential sexual natures that do not actually exist. As we have seen, trying to follow the prescriptions set out for women in the sexual script is a losing proposition even for women who have never been sexually coerced or coercive. It makes us feel guilty about our own dark side, and it makes us feel terrified of men's dark side. Furthermore, if the goal is sexual equality, insisting on the demonization of male sexuality and the idealization of female sexuality is not progress. It is a call to arms in a phony gender war.

Verbal coercion is truly an equal-opportunity behavior, because it does not seem to depend on size, strength, or even the intent to cause bodily harm. Nonviolent coercion depends on psychological force; the ability to apply psychological pressure is unconnected to the amount of testosterone in one's bloodstream.

Yet, when women do it, it is called seduction. When men do it, it is called coercion. Women who are sexually manipulated are victims, but men...well, men in those instances are lucky. *They got some.* No one cares much whether they wanted any.

Chapter Six

Good Girls, Bad Boys, and Other Demons

E mma has poker-straight black hair, a small, pretty face that ta-pers off into a sharp, jutting chin, and a habit of chopping at the air with her hands when she wants to make a point. She is nineteen, a top student at a top university, an assured young woman whose dorm room is plastered with mementos of overseas trips and posters from art exhibitions. Friends are dropping by and the phone rings constantly, but Emma does not lose her train of thought. She has told her story many times, and has acquired the deliberate diction of an educator, repeating some of the key phrases several times to make sure they register.

"I am speaking out about what happened to me because I want to prevent it from happening to other young women," she begins, sitting cross-legged on her bed and leaning over to speak directly into my tape recorder to be sure that not a single word is missed. "The most profound effect that being raped had on me was to strengthen my belief in feminism. I basically discovered feminism as a result of this experience, and I feel a personal sense of commitment to the cause and to helping other women."

The man who raped her is, Emma says, the prototypical acquaintance rapist. That is, he doesn't look like a monster. "Dan is very good-looking and very intense. Magnetic, really," she explains, then sketches his profile with broad, sure strokes: black leather jacket, moody silences, a slightly raffish, tough exterior that seems to conceal more tender, sensitive depths. He is, in short, the kind of man you notice when you are nineteen years old, the kind of man you think about precisely because he does not seem to care what anyone thinks.

Emma got to know him when they were writing term papers for the same course, and the friendship developed rapidly: on Monday they barely knew each other, but by Friday, they'd developed habits and routines. She saved him a seat in the cafeteria at lunch; he dropped by her room in the evening to commiserate about the difficulty of the assignment. Somehow they'd start talking about other things, like their childhoods and Emma's recent breakup with her high school boyfriend, and wind up having all-night marathon discussions about the meaning of life.

All of this meant that Emma wasn't getting much work done on the essay, but she didn't care. She had the breathless sense of being seized by life, the feeling that absolutely anything was possible. Everyone seemed to be watching her as she walked across campus with Dan, laughing and tossing her hair from side to side. She liked the picture of herself with this aloof, sought-after man, but she was also wary. Dan had a reputation as a "heartbreaker," a bit of a ladies' man, "so I played it cool," she says. She didn't want to seem too eager, and she didn't quite trust her own ability to hold his attention. Emma wanted to play her cards right.

They had known each other for less than two weeks when he knocked on her door one evening, long after midnight. She was putting her books away and getting ready for bed, but his attention was so thrillingly new and flattering that she did not send him away, as she would have had it been anyone else. Instead, she invited him in and they talked for a while. It was a little awkward, she was self-conscious about her ratty pair of sweatpants and wished that her hair wasn't pulled back in a straggly ponytail, and conversation was stilted. After about twenty minutes, she said that she needed to sleep. He should go.

Dan gave her a mournful look, and told her that she was the only person who truly understood him. His father, he confided, was a cold taskmaster who constantly berated him for his artistic leanings and was trying to force him to study business. Until he met Emma, Dan said, he had felt hopeless, but now... Well, he was glad about the term paper, difficult as it was to complete, because it meant that he'd got to know her. She was so different from all the other girls, so much more interesting and perceptive and warm.

The air in the room was still, and the moment had an urgent, timeless quality: Dan was declaring himself, and Emma could feel her own heart opening in return. *I can help him*, she found herself thinking, *He needs me*. She was the only woman who could penetrate his reserve. And apparently, he wanted a relationship with her just as much as she wanted one with him.

Today, however, Emma has a different take on the situation. "He reminded me a lot of my ex-boyfriend. They both had that arrogant, angry-young-man appeal," she says. "Dan knew I was coming out of that relationship and he took advantage of my vulnerability. He kept looking at me with those sad eyes, saying that he didn't want to go."

Halfway out the door, he turned and announced that he couldn't bear to part without a goodnight kiss. "Just a little one," he pleaded. Emma said no, at first, but he looked so forlorn, so genuinely sad, that she did give him a peck on the cheek. Besides, she explains, "I thought if I did, then he would go home."

Instead, he said, "Now I really can't leave," and kissed her on the lips. It was late, everyone else in the dorm was asleep, his mouth was on hers, her hand was on the doorknob.

"At that point," Emma says today, "he'd already defeated me. He'd kissed me when I didn't want him to, so I kissed him back. But that was supposed to be it."

It wasn't. Still in the doorway, he kissed her again. In a voice edged with anger, Emma describes the scene in minute detail: his white T-shirt, his scratchy three-day stubble and nicotine-stained thumb, the two of them somehow winding up on her bed, on top of the comforter covered with tiny blue and yellow flowers, pushing the stuffed animals onto the floor to make room. At first they're just kissing, and she's making it clear, she's sure, that she doesn't want to do anything more than that. But his hands are running up and down her body, his voice is whispering not to worry. "No. Not there," she says when his hand lingers on her breast. He says, "Why? What's stopping us? We should do what we feel like doing." He says she is beautiful, and he has been yearning for this moment ever since the first night they stayed up talking. She says they should just go to sleep now, she is tired. They could sleep like this, together in the same bed, without...you know. Without actually *sleeping* together. Then his hand is on her breast and he is whispering in her ear again, as though they have not been through this before.

"He'd touch me and I'd say 'No,' and then he'd say, 'Why not? Why can't I touch you there?' It just went on and on like that, it was all a grand seduction to him. Every time I said no, he said that we shouldn't hold back."

There's a bitter, incredulous tone in her voice now, and she is looking down at her bed as though she still can't believe what happened on it. "He laid siege to all my emotional defenses and broke them down, one by one," she says. *You're the only person who understands me.* "He beat down my will," she explains. *You're so beautiful, so perceptive.* "It got to the point," Emma says, "where I was thinking, 'Maybe he means it.'" *Maybe he's in love with me.*

Dan "was very flirtatious. He was so persuasive that after a while," Emma says, "I gave in totally." She was confused and disoriented at the time, but now, three months later in the afternoon sunlight, she has figured out exactly what was happening: "He had an agenda. He'd decided that I was a challenge he was going to take on and conquer."

Then, suddenly, Emma is talking about the complaint she filed with the university, her meeting with the dean — but wait. She said that she "gave in" to persuasion, convinced that his compliments were sincere and that he wanted to have a relationship with her.

"Giving in is not consent, it's a survival strategy," she explains patiently. "What he did was like emotional warfare. I trusted him and sympathized with him because he'd had a really rough childhood, and he just used all that against me. I didn't want to sleep with him and I told him so. I said no. He coerced me, and that is rape."

Emma does not describe feeling threatened or being frightened, either before sex or after it, when they slept side by side until the morning, pressed together in her narrow, standard-issue dorm bed. Instead, she describes feeling exploited and being discarded, starting the very next day at lunch.

"He wasn't especially polite to me. In fact he started flirting with someone else. I was appalled," she recalls. "I was really anxious to see what was going to become of this."

All that week, Dan avoided her. No more romantic declarations, no more soulful discussions lasting until sunrise. Emma was weeping alone in her room, feeling that some corner of her soul had been cheapened, and then, "I suddenly thought, 'Wait a minute. Why am I blaming myself for what *he* did?'" She called the university's peer counseling hotline, poured out her story and its consequences, and asked, "Do you think I was raped?" Yes, the counselor told her, that was rape. She had said no, but he'd kept going. She mustn't blame herself.

Emma felt as though a huge weight had been lifted from her shoulders. Tentatively at first, she told a few close friends what had happened, and then, buoyed by their supportive wrath, she decided to "stop being a victim. I needed to take control of the experience by standing up for my rights." She did so by reporting the incident to the university authorities, and insisting that they provide more funding for the hotline, whose counselors were helping her get over the experience.

"Not that I am over it, because I don't think you ever get over the violation," she adds. "But I see myself as a survivor now, instead of a victim. And so I need to keep speaking out about what happened to me, educating other people and trying to change the climate here so that this does not happen to more women."

At first, Dan was unpleasant, screaming at her in front of her dorm the day after he was summoned to the dean's office. "He talked his way out of being expelled," Emma reports, "mostly because his parents are rich and they've donated a lot of money to the university. But everyone is watching him now. So many people know what he did that he won't get away with it again. It's incredible, the support I've gotten from other students and from the administration. A lot of people thought it was brave that I came forward. I don't think of it in terms of courage, really. I had no choice but to speak out."

Dan doesn't bother her any more. In fact, he hurries away in the other direction whenever he sees her. "He got what he wanted from me, so I'm not afraid of him. And I'm healing now," says Emma.

Her sense of injustice is real and raw. But it also appears to be related to the axioms she has learned, such as, "Giving in is not consent, it's a survival strategy." When Emma tells me that "No means no," her tone is unequivocal, definite, resolute — everything she was *not* when she was lying on her bed with Dan's arms wrapped around her. All the complications and hope and uncertainty of that evening are erased by these three words, which leave no room for ambiguity.

"That's blaming the victim," is what Emma says when I ask why, if she didn't even want to kiss Dan, she did kiss him back and let him come back into her room and joined him on the bed and quite willingly continued to fool around with him, never once trying to get up.

"But he wasn't hurting you," I say. "He wasn't threatening you. You weren't scared of him."

"No, but I should have been!" she exclaims. In her view, Dan is a master of what she calls "a form of mental attack," and is, therefore, "really dangerous."

Emma has acquired a small library of books and photocopied articles about date rape, and reading up on the topic seems to have inspired her to feel more devastated, more angry, and more depressed. She is entitled to her feelings, but without question, they would have been different had the evening with Dan been the first of many. "I made it clear that I was not into a one-night stand," she says, and her reason for giving in was that she was persuaded: *Maybe he really does want a relationship*. The next day, she was "really anxious to see what was going to become of this."

Would she have viewed it as rape if sleeping with him marked the beginning, not the end, of a romance? "No," she says. "But that's because I didn't know any better back then."

There is both genuine pain and defiance in her voice when she announces, "I never believed that one in four women are raped until it happened to me. I hate to think of myself as a statistic, it's like another form of depersonalization and degradation, but that's what I am."

Her experience is disturbing for a number of reasons, but the most important one is this: she would not consider herself a rape statistic had the outcome of her evening with Dan been different. If he had turned up at her door the next day bearing flowers, she would not have gone to the dean or filed a complaint or wound up sitting on her bed, talking into my tape recorder.

There is, however, no room in the new sexual script for grey areas and ambiguities. No means no, and anything that happens after that is rape.

Four of the women interviewed for this book described experiences that were, unambiguously, sexual assaults. Jessica recounted an episode with a male acquaintance at college, who lured her back to his room on the pretext of picking up a book, then pushed her down on his bed, held her there, and was in the process of tearing her clothes off when she managed to kick him, throw a glass at him, and get out the door. "It required a fair amount of violence on my part," she said, "but I wasn't afraid of him. It was more a deep sense of outrage, like, How *dare* you? I didn't feel traumatized by it. I just never wanted anything to do with him again."

Between the ages of eight and fourteen, Tonya's father sexually abused her several times a week. "I am still so deeply angry that I can't even afford to express it," she said, "because it might annihilate not just him but me. The most devastating aspect is that he told me I was special and that's why he was abusing me. He said I was his favorite — a few years ago, my sister told me he'd said the same thing when he was abusing her. I still feel huge guilt and shame about getting any physical enjoyment out of some of the things he did to me. My therapist says it's really common, feeling complicit because your body responded. Rationally, I know it's crazy, because I was a child and because he threatened me. He said, 'If you tell, they'll put you in a foster home and no one will love you any more.' But deep down, I still feel responsible and still feel that abuse is connected to love — those messages got implanted so deeply that I can't get rid of them. Years of therapy and I still haven't found a way."

Carol was chased around her apartment by a boozed-up, belligerent ex-boyfriend, who wanted to have sex again "for old times' sake"; she was able to summon the police before he achieved his goal. "I'm proud of the way I handled the situation," she said. "I knew he was serious, that he was going to go through with it and couldn't be talked out of it. Still, part of me was thinking, 'What a loser he is, so childish' — but the other part was thinking, 'Call 911.' Shortly after that, I swore off men altogether."

Jennifer was raped by a stranger who appeared in her bedroom at two a.m., having climbed through an unlocked bathroom window; he is still in jail, serving a twelve-year sentence. "It was very disorienting and scary at the time, and I remember just praying that my roommate would get home. I didn't think he was going to kill me, but I did think he was crazy and I had to keep him calm," she explained. "The cops caught him after he did the same thing to another woman about a mile away. The fact that he was nuts helped me recover faster. I still love men and I still love sex — he was just a psycho. In a weird way, I'm more confident now. I won't tolerate it for a minute if someone tries to take advantage of me, not just sexually but any way at all."

Each of these women had a complex, layered, highly individual response to her experience. All of them spoke of "knowing" that they were "supposed" to have a particular emotional reaction that they did not in fact have; all four, in one way or another, talked of struggling to define their experiences for themselves so that they would not be defined by them.

"Please don't call me a victim," as Jennifer put it. "I mean, I know I was a victim, but that isn't all I am or ever will be. Here's how I see it: That was one terrible event in a long life of events. I can't change the fact that it happened, but I have suffered enough for it, and I *refuse* to give that asshole the power to define my entire identity."

Jessica and Carol were lucky enough to manage to stop the men who were physically hurting and threatening them; in both cases, giving in really would have been a survival strategy. Tonya and Jennifer, for different reasons, had no choice but to give in; fighting back simply was not an option for either of them. Ideally, all of them would have pressed charges — as only Jennifer did, not coincidentally because she was raped by a stranger — because despite the differences in their experiences and reactions, they share one similarity: they are survivors of sexual assault.

It is an outrageous trivialization of what they endured to claim that Emma, too, was sexually assaulted by Dan. The difference between her experience and theirs is *not* that she engaged in some consensual sexual activity prior to intercourse. A woman has an absolute right to say No at any point in the proceedings, as well as a responsibility to ensure that she is communicating clearly, and any man who disregards her wishes and uses physical coercion, physical force, or threats of physical harm to force her to have sex is a rapist.

The difference is that Emma was not physically coerced, and by her own account, her "No" did not, in fact, mean No. She said no because Dan had a reputation as a "heartbreaker" and because she didn't want to seem easy, but he didn't need telepathic powers to figure out that what she really meant was "I'm not sure, maybe you could convince me." Her real meaning was obvious, since regardless of the words coming out of Emma's mouth, all her actions said Yes.

Emma freely admits that there was a contradiction between what she was saying and what she was doing, and explains it this way: she was "already defeated" when Dan kissed her in the doorway. Vanquished, she had no choice but to kiss him back and join him on the bed, where she continued to say No while behaving as though what she really meant was Yes. What else could she do? He'd already "beaten down" her will.

A more plausible explanation is that Emma returned Dan's kisses when they were standing in the doorway because she *wanted* to. She liked him and it felt good, good enough that she let him come back into her room, pushed all the stuffed animals off her bed, and kept on kissing him. But unless what they were doing was going to lead to everlasting love, it was vulgar and dirty as far as she was concerned. Tidal waves were necessary to justify having sex; she needed to be persuaded that they were going to *make love*, and Dan did not have to try very hard to convince her of something she wanted so much to believe. At the crucial moment, she was no longer saying no. She had already made the leap of faith: Maybe he means it, she decided, when he says he cares for me. Her No had become a conditional Yes: Yes, if sex leads to a relationship. Yes, if you'll still respect me in the morning.

Later, when it became clear that a relationship would not be forthcoming, Emma felt shame. It was humiliating to be known so intimately by a man who ignored her and flirted with other women in the cafeteria, not least because sex, unmediated by love, was dirty. She felt that she'd been defiled and that she wasn't a good girl any more; good girls only have sex with boys who love them. But then, when she thought about it a little more, she seized on what seemed to her to be the only alternative explanation: Dan was a very bad boy, one who deserved to be punished. Now, she saw another, more destructive kind of tidal wave: she had been swept along by the aggressive, brute force of the male sex drive.

"No should've been the end of it, but he just kept going," Emma told me. "He got me so confused, just wore me down to the point where I was totally defenseless.

"He was, like, 'Why? Why shouldn't we? There's nothing stopping us.' I was thinking, 'Oh, he's really serious, he really likes me.'"

The hotline counselors, university administrators, and fellow students who listened to Emma tell this same story agreed that she was date raped. To them, it seemed an open and shut case: No Means No.

But intercourse obtained by sweet talk is *not* equivalent to intercourse obtained by physical harm or threats of it; telling a woman that she is attractive, intelligent, and interesting is not the same as telling her that if she doesn't put out, she'll be forcibly penetrated, beaten, or killed. Furthermore, a No that means "Convince me" is *not* equivalent to a No that means "Absolutely not," and a woman does bear some responsibility for making her actions consistent with her words.

Emma didn't have sex with Dan because she was frightened or physically threatened or had no choice in the matter. She had sex because she believed it would lead to a relationship — and, since she equates her own sexuality with love, she *had* to believe that. Love was the only possible justification for sex.

It's hard not to feel a little sorry for Emma. Many women can empathize with her sense of grievance, because many of us have felt deeply wronged when men falsely implied — or we ourselves mistakenly inferred — that sex would lead to commitment. She certainly has a right to feel ill-treated: Dan was dishonest and manipulative.

But these are moral issues, not legal ones, and hers is a case not of rape but of regret.

If we do not make these kinds of distinctions, then we must also accept that Robin, in the previous chapter, was raped — by Samantha. In certain key respects, the two incidents are similar. Like Emma, Robin repeatedly said no but continued to engage in sexual activity; like Emma, Robin's hesitance was based on uncertainty about the emotional outcome; like Emma, Robin was subject to a sustained but-why-not? offensive. Both Samantha and Dan viewed their partners as adversarial challenges, and both zeroed in on their partners' particular vulnerabilities: Samantha questioned Robin's masculinity and accused him of prudishness, while Dan flattered Emma and waxed poetic about her beauty, warmth, and sensitivity. Both were manipulative, and both of them believed, with some justification in Dan's case, that their partners were also playing mind-games and merely feigning reluctance. But sex was not unavoidable in either case; neither incident included physical threats, physical coercion, or violence.

If anything, Samantha was more coercive and Robin was more reluctant, but no hotline counselor or dean of students would take Robin seriously for even an instant if he claimed that he had been sexually assaulted. The only reason Emma's claim was taken seriously was that she is female, thus presumed to be sexually powerless and incapable of erotic agency. Underlying these presumptions is another, more menacing one: male sexuality is intrinsically aggressive and violent.

In Emma's case, these precepts are not just false but misleading. More generally, these myths coach *all of us* to think that women are more helpless and men are more powerful than they actually are, and thus they perpetuate sexual inequality. New double standards are being created — only women are allowed to say no, and only women are allowed to equate verbal coercion with rape — while, paradoxically, the old double standard is reinforced: good girls don't *want* to have sex.

Subscribing to these double standards is what got Emma in trouble in the first place. She had suspicions about Dan: he played the field, he was a ladies' man. But she didn't want to kick him out of her

room and wait until she was sure of the nature of his intentions toward her; she was enjoying fooling around with him, and she didn't
want to blow what could be the beginning of a serious relationship.
So she had to convince him that she was not like the rest of the girls
he had slept with. She was a good girl who had expectations. She hit
on what seemed at the time like a good compromise: saying no when
what she really meant was "convince me." If she could persuade Dan
that she was not a slut, he wouldn't write her off as a mere one-night
stand. He'd want to spend the rest of his life with her.

One-third of women consistently tell researchers that on at least
one occasion they have said No to sex when what they really meant
was Yes; "liberated" women are as likely to do this as are women who
accept traditional gender roles. "The women's own acceptance of the
double standard at the time of the incident was unrelated" to their
behavior, reports Dr. Charlene Muehlenhard, who has conducted
several studies on token resistance.[1] Rather, she explains, women said
No when they didn't mean it because they believed that men would
think less of them if they said Yes; they believed that their *partners*
bought into the traditional double standard, in which men who have
sex are studs but sexual women are sluts.

In reality, however, the traditional double standard is fading. The
vast majority of college students — again, the only subjects in most
studies of sexual attitudes — use a single standard to judge men's and
women's sexual behavior: they say that it's just as acceptable for a
woman to have intercourse with a date or with a casual partner as it is
for a man.[2] "Equally acceptable" does not, however, mean "preferable"
— for either gender. In many studies, "permissive" women are evalu-
ated slightly more favorably than "permissive" men, but *both* are judged
negatively relative to women and men who don't have casual sex.[3] "Sexual experience with few partners and experience within committed relationships appears to be the societally-condoned 'appropriate' sexual
arena for both men and women," Dr. Lucia O'Sullivan concludes.[4]

Nevertheless, explains Dr. Muehlenhard, "women believe that
men accept the double standard even more than men actually do."[5]
This helps to explain why a woman might offer token resistance: she
wants to have sex with a new partner, but worries that he'll think less

of her if she admits it. She *thinks* she faces what Muehlenhard calls a "difficult choice. She can acknowledge her desire and risk being labeled 'loose,' 'easy,' or worse, or she can refrain from acknowledging it, thus engaging in scripted refusal."[6]

Scripted refusals, however, perpetuate gender stereotypes that directly contribute to rape-supportive attitudes among men. A man who encounters token resistance is much more likely, the next time a woman tells him No, to believe that she's only saying it, doesn't really mean it, and actually wants sex.[7] If we are ever going to create a world in which No really does mean No, it is essential that young women like Emma learn how to say No and mean it — *and this requires learning how to say Yes, for whatever reasons and under whatever circumstances they desire.*

Women are not going to learn how to do this from the modern sexual script, which puts them in a double bind: female sexuality is still associated with love, but the new component of victimization has been added. Women still can't own their eroticism, but now have new fears — many of which are misplaced or exaggerated — about male aggression and male power.

This is a toxic combination for all women, but particularly for young, earnest ones with a profound sense of sexual shame and a highly developed sense of indignation. After having sex with Dan, Emma found herself alone on a campus where well-meaning anti-rape activists operate with missionary zeal. She had been half listening to their messages about male power and aggression; she was well aware of the one-in-four statistic, and certainly had heard that No means No. She seized on the victim mantle because it absolved her of shame and guilt: *It wasn't my fault.* Now, she wears it with pride. No one can think any less of her for having had sex with a guy who dumped her the next day. *I was date raped.*

Anyone who wants to stop sexual violence should be concerned about this. It does Emma no favor to encourage her to believe that the correct course of action when the boy does not call the next day is to run to the dean crying "Date rape!" The false pretense that she is so powerless that one kiss and a few compliments can "beat down" her will renders Emma ludicrously easy to "coerce" — and it also renders her less able to resist genuine sexual violence. It discourages her from viewing herself as a sexual subject who is capable of making choices — including ones that later look like mistakes — and bears some responsibility for her own decisions.

Crucial distinctions are erased and significantly different issues are confused when false professions of love are labeled sexual coercion, as though a sexual violation has occurred. When a man who says "I care about you" really means "I'll stick around long enough to have an orgasm," the issue is not sexual trauma but emotional fraud. "Hold on a minute," the woman thinks afterwards, "I didn't agree to a one-night stand, I agreed to a *relationship*. I didn't sign on for sex, I signed on for *love*." And if, in the heat of the moment, she murmured "I love you" or some other endearment that now makes her cringe every time she thinks about it, she feels exposed. It's mortifying that a man who has clearly demonstrated that he couldn't care less about her knows that she cared, and maybe even still cares, for him. It feels like he has something over her.

Translating what is in reality an emotional disappointment into the altogether different language of sexual violation ignores the woman's own willing suspension of disbelief. Yes, it is reprehensible when a man exaggerates his feelings to get a woman into bed, but the fact remains that almost always he's not the only one who's lying to her. She has deceived herself if she believed that a man could really feel deep and abiding affection after only a few shared hours, or that any man who truly cared for her would be unprepared to wait a few days or weeks or however long it took until she too was absolutely sure she wanted to have sex.

It is vitally important to distinguish between the power to *make sexual choices*, which women most assuredly do have when they are not in any physical danger, and the power to *decide how another person will behave afterwards*, which we do not have — no one, regardless of gender, has that power. Choices must not be confused with outcomes; when they are, the woman who has sex and doesn't like the outcome is recast as a pathetic victim, forever scarred by a bad evening and forever unable to control her own life. "It takes a woman who agreed to sex because she wanted to be nice or loving or because she worried she'd be thought a bitch if she didn't — and it bolsters the very 'femininity' that encouraged her uncomfortable agreement," as Marcia Pally points out in *Sex and Sensibility*.[8]

Equating compliments with coercion, and confusing a woman's power to make sexual choices with her power to make another person have an ongoing relationship with her, has the effect of training women to feel far weaker and more helpless than they actually are, and it trivializes the severity and indignity of rape. It would be much more helpful to women like Emma to hear that learning to make good decisions, ones you can live with in the morning, requires separating the sexual act itself from the desire for a relationship. Emma needs to learn how to say No, and to do that, she also needs to learn that she has a right to say Yes. As long as women cannot own their eroticism, some will continue to use token resistance, and some will remain easy targets for smooth talkers who wax poetic about love.

Without a language for their own desire, an awareness of their own sexual power, and an understanding that sexual rights entail responsibilities, too, women can become their own worst enemies in the sexual arena. Trying to follow the modern script by connecting their own sexuality only with love and subjugation requires denying their own power to choose and forfeiting their right to make choices based on sexual desire and arousal.

Ironically, women who view the world in oppositional terms — good girls versus bad boys — are much more likely to make sexual mistakes. They can't give themselves permission to have sex simply because they want to; sometimes, they have sex when they don't really want to, because they think it will lead to a long-term relationship. And sometimes, they justify their own erotic longings by saying, "It's not that I'm turned on — I'm in love with this man." Either way, if sex does not lead to an ongoing relationship, they feel exploited and ashamed. Like Emma, they may view their own errors of judgment as terrible traumas perpetrated by aggressive, exploitative men — even when, in fact, they themselves are the ones doing the "coercing."

Alison has a way of looking at a man as though he's the only person in the world. She doesn't telegraph adoration but intensity, as if there's a strong possibility that he may impart all the wisdom she will ever need to know and she can't afford to miss a word. Men respond by puffing up around her, which is useful professionally, since it off-sets the unsettling fact that she is the first twenty-nine-year-old de-partment manager in the history of her company.

She looks every inch the middle manager: an auburn bob that ends in a ruler-straight line, crisp navy jackets with gold buttons, and no-nonsense skirts that don't show much leg. You can imagine her emerging from an earthquake carrying a purse that matched her suit, highstepping around the rubble to give rescuers a firm handshake and clear directions to the epicenter of the disaster.

Alison has a condo, a car, and a mother who phones every Saturday night to see if she has a date, which is why Alison also has a phone that displays callers' numbers, and why, this particular evening, she is not answering. "Don't you want to get that?" Doug asks, on the third ring.

"It's just my office," she calls from the kitchen. "If they know they can get me on a weekend, it will turn into a habit." Then she quickly turns the volume on the answering machine off, so that her mother's voice, concerned and accusing, will not flood the house.

Alison bluffs well, which is also useful professionally, especially when clients need some hand-holding and a reassurance that their in-vestments are safe. It happens often these days; the market is volatile, but she has been lucky so far, coaxing investors to ride it out, never betraying a hint of her own panic.

Doug is more awkward. Tonight he's restless, picking things up, then putting them down again. He doesn't seem to know what to do with his hands. It's the third night in a row that he hasn't been home for dinner, he announces, the third night since — gosh, who knows how long. "Gosh" is something he actually says. He also calls women "ladies" and cabdrivers "sir," as in, "Well, sir, how much do I owe you?"

For Alison, the fact that he talks like a character in a 1950s sitcom is a plus. It makes him sound gentlemanly and sweet, not at all like the men in her office, who call their assistants "hot pieces of ass" when they think Alison can't hear.

Doug would never say anything so crude. It's relaxing listening to him talk, because there are no lines to read between, there's no agenda. Right now, he's figuring that it must be at least eight years, some time back when he was a student, since he's had dinner alone with a woman who wasn't his wife. Ex-wife, he corrects himself. The divorce was finalized two months ago.

"It's nice to have someone else do the cooking for a change," he says at the table, which is close enough to a compliment for Alison. He doesn't need to know what an effort she's made with the veal marsala and the spaghetti-strapped black dress. In fact, it's something of a tribute that he doesn't notice. Maybe he just thinks she lives like this all the time. Anyway, the lack of polish is part of his appeal. It makes him seem more trustworthy.

Conversation is never a problem, because they've known each other since grade school and can always dredge up old memories if nothing fresh comes to mind. Doug still looks the same, wide-eyed and sturdy and blond, which is why she recognized him immediately in the supermarket six weeks ago. He was wandering aimlessly from one aisle to the next like he couldn't quite remember why he was there, his cart full of sad bachelor foods: chicken pot pies, TV dinners, bags of chips.

"You look so different!" he'd said once he got over the coincidence of running into her again after so many years, then poured out everything — the divorce, the computer business, the antiseptic apartment that didn't feel anything like home — right there in the store. Later, over a drink, they'd reminisced about their old school, comparing notes on what their classmates were up to now, filling in the blanks of the past seventeen years.

Since then, they've talked on the phone enough times that Alison has started bringing work home from the office instead of staying late. She doesn't want to miss a call. Doug seems to need someone to talk to, and has stopped asking if she minds that he talks so much about his divorce. "You *should* talk about it," she has said, more than once, not just to be nice but because she is fascinated.

Talking to Doug is like talking to her women friends: they dissect each other's hearts. On a more practical level, it's helpful to know where things went wrong, what mistakes to avoid with him, because Alison is already daydreaming about being married to Doug. At work, she finds herself easily distracted by the big question: after the wedding, should they stay in the city, which makes sense career-wise, or move to the suburbs, which might be better for their kids? Two girls and a boy, she has decided — she'd always hated being the only girl in a family of boys.

Tonight, after dinner, she and Doug are sitting in the living room sipping the cognac she bought for the occasion when he starts to tell her about his last night with his wife. He'd insisted that they go to the cabin by the lake, hoping that being alone with her, sharing the bed in front of the fireplace, would change things. He didn't know what else to do. Lisa's coldness, when everything had seemed to be going along just fine, had taken him by surprise. Never very demonstrative, she'd stopped wanting to have sex at all.

In the first few months he'd asked again and again what he had done, just to tell him so he could change. He bought a book on how to make love to a woman, tried to get Lisa in the mood with candlelight and soft music, but nothing worked. He thought it was just a phase she was going through, that it was still possible to find a way to make things go back to normal. But then, that last night in bed at the cabin, he'd reached over to touch her and she had stiffened: "Please don't." When he questioned her, she started to cry and said, "I don't love you any more. I don't think I ever have."

Doug did not believe her at first: What about their honeymoon in St. Lucia, that night they'd danced on the beach? Or the surprise party he'd thrown for her last year, when he'd bought a plane ticket to fly her sister in? Surely, she'd loved him then? No, Lisa said, not the way he meant. She loved him the way she might love a dear, old friend; there had never been any passion on her part. *Never.* This beautiful blonde Doug had been so proud to call his wife was telling him that everything they'd shared had been an illusion, a mirage. A lie. He felt like someone in one of those South American countries — disappeared, that was the word, that was the euphemism the authorities in those places used when they wiped someone out. He'd been disappeared. Eight whole years, everything that had happened since the day he'd met Lisa in a political science class, had been completely erased.

The next day they packed wordlessly and drove back to the city. Doug moved out that afternoon, leaving her the house and everything in it. "I keep going over and over it, but I still don't understand..."

He trails off and looks at Alison, as though she might know the answer. He looks so hurt and so vulnerable that she moves closer, puts her arms around him, and then they are kissing, for several long minutes, until he pulls away.

"It's all right, you're going to get over this," she soothes, running her hand up and down his leg. "Lisa just didn't know how to appreciate you. I wouldn't dream of hurting you."

He has the look of a small animal trapped in the headlights, and if Alison weren't feeling so tender toward him, she might laugh out loud. She has a sudden flashback to fifth grade, his tow-headed shock when Mrs. Reid mistakenly accused him of stealing another boy's lunch money and made him stand in the corner for an entire morning. Now, Alison knows, what Doug wants is some reassurance that she will not reject him. Clearly his problem is not feeling sure of his own attractiveness, so she takes his hand, gently, pulls him to his feet and begins to lead him to her bedroom.

Outside the door, he blurts, "I'm not ready for a relationship." *What he really means is that he is afraid of opening his heart again.* Alison figures that she needs to say something to allay his fear, and what she chooses is, "We're not talking about a relationship, we're just two people enjoying each other." It sounds stupid, even to her, and it's a lie. The truth is that making love will bring them closer and that is what she wants, a shortcut to intimacy. Afterwards, they can begin the new life she has planned for them.

So she tugs him into the room and unbuttons his shirt, murmuring about how good-looking he is, silently making a note to herself that she needs to take him shopping. The plaid shirts and chinos don't do a thing for him.

"I don't think we should do anything that would, you know, harm our friendship," he says, looking off over her right shoulder. *Obviously, he's worried about failing in yet another bed. And after a sexless marriage to a cold, blonde princess, who can blame him?*

"Come here," she pats the bed. "We can just lie here together." Doug perches on the edge and opens his mouth to talk, but Alison doesn't give him a chance, doesn't want him to make this difficult when it can be so easy. Before he can say a word, she raises herself up on one elbow and kisses him, softly at first and then with more seriousness of purpose, pulling him down toward her.

She believes his little murmurs are appreciative. If he isn't responding as ardently as she'd hoped, well, she could teach him. She, after all, is the one with the confidence of experience. Ill-gained, most of it, with men she'd rather forget, men who left her feeling hollow when the phone didn't ring the next day. That was one reason she'd thrown herself into her career: at work, the more she gave, the more she got. With men, it seemed to be just the opposite. Her intensity seemed to attract them, then scare them off. This wouldn't happen with Doug, she was sure, they were already too close for that.

"I can't do this," he says.

She shushes him: "You don't have to do anything. Just lie back and enjoy it." Alison unzips his pants, feeling generous. She's learned what men like, and Doug is going to be the beneficiary. This thought is particularly arousing: she is going to be the best lover he has ever had. Lisa might be blonder and slimmer, but clearly, from everything Doug had said, she was a washout in the bedroom.

Only when Alison is astride him and sex is imminent does she listen to what he has been trying to tell her. "This isn't right," he says, softly pushing her away. "Alison —" he stops, doesn't finish the sentence. Something about the tone of his voice makes her feel foolish, and she quickly pulls the sheet up around her body, suddenly conscious again of its imperfections. Doug begins pulling on his clothes, mumbling thanks for the dinner and saying he will call.

He does not, and at first she feels numb, but after two days she is angry. He's just like all the rest, she thinks. He liked the chase, not the catch. He complained about his ex-wife's frigidity but was really only

interested in women who looked like her, women like the perfect, improbably proportioned models in fashion magazines. He'd misled her,
calling her all the time and acting so interested, leaning on her for advice, comfort, and home-cooked meals. After two weeks, Alison has
figured out what happened: she was used, pure and simple.

Why didn't Doug ever call again? It was the topic of spirited debate about a month later, when I first met Alison in Chicago,
with two of her close friends. "Men haven't mastered the telephone,"
one sighed. "It's the same old story: they say they'll call and you
never hear from them again."

"I think he got scared of his feelings," said the other. "Men are
afraid of intimacy."

Theories flew around the table: men get frightened when they
feel you understand them. Men are emotionally immature. Doug
might phone out of the blue one day wanting to pick up where
they'd left off — men do that. They're threatened by independent,
successful women. Doug was a jerk, forget about him. All three
agreed on one key issue: Alison should under no circumstances
phone him, since he was the one who owed her an apology, and anyway, men don't like it when you phone them.

These wakes for lost love usually have a comforting tempo that
moves from calming sympathy to staccato outbursts about men in
general to lively, even giddy denunciations of the man in question.
This night was no exception.

"It seemed like fate when we bumped into each other after so many
years. We spent a lot of time together, Doug was calling all the time
and acting really interested, and then he just dropped me, quite casually, as though I didn't mean *anything* to him," Alison said, early on. "I
let him into my life, and that is what I can't quite get over, that he basically betrayed my trust. Everything was going so well, and then —
nothing. Not even a phone call. Didn't he at least value me as a friend?"

Later, when the general inferiority of men had been established
and black humor was at its peak, Alison leaned forward and said, "At

least there's one silver lining — I'm pretty sure Doug is impotent."
Great interest all round the table: Why? How did she know?

"He didn't want to have sex," she announced. "We were fooling
around and then he got really weird and just refused to go through
with it. All he wanted to do was get out of there. The only thing I
can think is that he's got some sort of sexual problem."

This revelation provoked a new flurry of theories: Doug might be
gay, might have a Madonna/whore complex, might have a sexually
transmitted disease —

"No," Alison dismissed that one out of hand. "He kept going on
and on about AIDS, how the whole dating scene had changed while
he'd been married. He was a bit of a prude, actually. I mean, why the
hell was he over at my house at eleven on a Saturday night?"

As her story emerged, piece by piece, everyone saw the same pattern: Alison had been exploited by a man who dumped all his problems
on her then dropped her as soon as she'd worked her healing magic.
No one considered for an instant that perhaps Doug had a good reason for not calling her again. Nor was the possibility raised that he
might feel that she'd tried to take advantage of him when he was particularly vulnerable. His embarrassment in the bedroom suggested to
no one that perhaps he'd just wanted to renew their friendship and
wasn't interested in having sex with her — Alison's assumption that she
knew his mind better than he did went unquestioned. Besides, what
red-blooded man who hadn't had sex for months would pass up the
main chance?

"It's not your fault," Alison was assured repeatedly. The problem
was with Doug, who'd behaved just like a man.

Although her behavior was very different, Emma had very similar
conversations with her own friends after her night with Dan.
Emma was verbally "coerced," Alison was verbally "coercive," but
they had the same reaction when a hoped-for relationship failed to
materialize: they denied their own sexual agency and blamed the
men. Emma viewed men as terrifying brutes; Alison viewed them as

insensitive little boys. Both believed they were, by virtue of gender, morally superior. They were good girls, and shared the same assumption: sex is a shortcut to intimacy. Since they thought of sex as something they were "giving" a man in return for an emotional commitment, they saw themselves as victims when the man scampered off afterwards, never to be heard from again.

They learned the same sexual script and the same simple formula for parsing complex situations: powerless, loving woman vs. powerful, aggressive man. Many women reflexively refer to this formula to interpret their own wildly diverse experiences, and they are encouraged to do so by anti-rape activists and male chauvinists alike.

Consider the book Emma refers to as "my Bible": *I Never Called It Rape*, a popular paperback which presents the findings of the Mary Koss survey that claimed one in four female university students is the victim of rape or attempted rape. "Boys are taught through verbal and nonverbal cues to be self-centered and single-minded about sex, to view women as objects from whom sex is taken, not as equal partners with wishes and desires of their own," writes author Robin Warshaw. "They view their relationships with women as adversarial challenges and learn to use both their physical and social power to overcome these smaller, less important people."[9]

Women, Warshaw says, are the perfect victims for these self-centered, single-minded sex fiends, because women learn that they should trade sexual favors for economic protection, and "are thus taught *what is basically a good lesson — that sexuality should occur within the context of a loving relationship* — for a bad reason — that is, because as defenseless women they need men to support and protect them" (emphasis added).[10]

These value-laden assumptions do not, however, square with reality. Warshaw, along with many anti-pornography feminists, suggests that men rape because they learn rape is a respectable pastime and women like it. This doesn't make much sense. Sane rapists — which is to say, most rapists — know perfectly well that they're doing something wrong. Our society promotes sexism, but it does not condone rape; similarly, our society promotes racism, but police officers who hurl racial epithets at African-Americans know that on the witness stand, they had better lie about it if they don't want to risk severe censure.

Men who rape don't do it because they expect to be applauded. If they did, they would not so frequently blame women for "making" them commit rape, or for "bringing it on themselves." Moreover, men don't rape because they believe they are strong and powerful. The exact opposite is true: men rape because terrorizing a woman is the only way they can prove to themselves that they are not as puny, unmasculine, and powerless as they feel. Men who rape women do so to *get* feelings of power, not because they already believe they *are* powerful. They do not, as Warshaw suggests, fail to notice that women have feelings; women's terror is what turns them on and what makes them feel powerful.

In another important respect, Warshaw's analysis of social conditioning is off base. The truth of the matter is that while men do receive some messages that women are objects, they also have real-life experiences with women. At their mothers' knees, they learn that women are far more complicated and more powerful than mere "objects" could ever be. "Any rapist who says otherwise, who says he thought women were objects, is trying to get off the hook," Marcia Pally argues. "Ambivalence about arousal and the wish to punish arousing women swirl about in the unconscious minds of most men. Rapists and batterers perform that wish in life. They hurt women, then claim the women deserved it and made them do it. They rely on the equation between sexy women and 'bad' ones. Image blamers [who invoke pornography] assume the same."[11]

More generally, Warshaw's analysis of gender socialization ignores the massive cultural changes of the past thirty years, which have had a profound effect on women's and men's attitudes and behavior. As we've seen, young women's and men's sexual behavior is in fact increasingly similar, largely because conditions beyond the bedroom have changed: among other things, women no longer need men to support them.

Numerous studies of boys' and girls' attitudes and expectations clearly indicate that conditioning has changed a great deal in the past few decades. Today, adolescent boys consistently report lower educational aspirations and less ambitious career plans than girls do, and adolescent girls overwhelmingly report that they plan to work after marriage and after having children.[12] "In fact," the authors of one large-scale study report, "there is almost total rejection of the full-time homemaker role."[13] Neither girls nor boys expect that when they grow up, the men will be lording it over the women and the women will be scurrying around trying to find good providers to take care of them.

Nor do all young men dismiss women as "smaller, less important people," good for only one thing: sex. Warshaw's analysis seems to imply that men do not want relationships, they only want to score; men do not value intimacy, they only care about maintaining their social power. On a practical level, men's intimacy aspirations are quantifiable: today, a substantial majority of male college students rank being husbands and fathers as more important and more satisfying than having careers.[14] Furthermore, 96 percent say that in a couple, the man's and woman's jobs are equally important.[15]

Attitudes do not, however, necessarily determine behavior. For instance, as explained in previous chapters, large numbers of men and women say love is a prerequisite for sex, but many report that they themselves have sex without love. Some researchers believe behavior changes faster than attitudes; others argue that the reverse is true; still others suggest that attitudes reflect beliefs about what other people should do, and individuals tend to see themselves as exempt from the rules they prescribe for the rest of the world. Whatever the case, just because pollsters uncover mountains of evidence to suggest that men's attitudes are increasingly egalitarian, it doesn't mean the playing field between men and women is now entirely level. It is not, and it won't be so long as a man who "babysits" his own children once in a while is viewed as exceptional — and so long as the myth of female moral superiority, which proscribes so many forms of "masculine" behavior, flourishes.

Nevertheless, any discussion of sexual behavior must take into account the fact that times have changed and so have sexual politics. Analyzing international relations by pretending geopolitics have remained static since the 1960s would be absurd, and it would create a myriad misunderstandings; the same is true of sex, but many people fail to perceive this because they view sexuality as a force of nature that is unaffected by social changes.

Even those cultural feminist analyses that do take account of social changes tend to portray them only in terms of creating new risk factors for women. Ostensibly, men have always been conditioned to view women as mere sex objects, but in the past, or so goes the argument, men were somewhat restrained by the chains of chivalry. Today, however, women are expected to put out, so many men apparently just go ahead and do whatever they want, raping, coercing, and sexually terrorizing women with impunity. The subtext is clear: the sexual revolution has been good for men, enlarging the pool of available partners, but disastrous for women, particularly young single women playing the dating game, who are exposed and defenseless in a climate of sexual threat.

This point is hammered home in the news media and on talk shows, and has spawned a new genre of reality-based drama: woman-in-jeopardy movies, mini-series, and soap operas. This message, accompanied by equally strong messages equating female sexuality with love, keeps women locked in a psychological prison where they become their own jailers, terrified of men and equally terrified of their own erotic impulses, wants, and needs. Male sexuality is aggressive, female sexuality is passive, and female moral superiority is proved by our victimization. Men lust — and rape. Women love — and are raped. Men are bad boys, women are good girls.

This politics of terror is also peddled in various cheery disguises, all of which share one distinguishing feature: an insistence on oppositional gender roles, and an equation of sexuality with gender. Consider John Gray, Ph.D., who has become a publishing phenomenon by repackaging traditional gender stereotypes in a series of books claiming that men and women are from different planets. Like Deborah Tannen, author of *You Just Don't Understand*, Gray aims to improve "cross-cultural" communication between the sexes. He starts by explaining, in the bestselling *Mars and Venus in the Bedroom*, that "men hunger for great sex, women long for romance."[16] According to Gray, women want cut flowers and yearn for men to take responsibility for planning dates, driving, ordering for them in restaurants, and paying for things. To get men to do these things, he declares, women have to offer something in return: they must renounce their right to say no to sex.

On the basis of no evidence whatsoever, Gray claims that it takes thirty to forty minutes of foreplay for women to become sufficiently aroused to have the kind of full-blown, romantic sex they like. Frequently, he says, women just don't want to make that kind of time in their busy schedules, and besides, they are generally in the mood for sex only when romance is in the air — say, when a new shipment of cut flowers has arrived. So, "quite commonly a woman will unknowingly give...rejecting messages" like 'No, I don't want to have sex' and 'No. I feel ill.'[17]

Well, this is just about the worst thing a woman can do, no matter how "unknowingly," because the man will feel "hurt" and "may begin desiring other women who have not yet rejected him, or he may just lose interest."[18] The woman who wants to keep her man should, as Gray devotes a chapter to explaining, just let him go ahead and have "guilt-free quickies," in which the only object is male orgasm. Instead of saying no, women are instructed to say, "I'm not in the mood for sex, but we could have a quickie," or "Don't worry about me tonight. Just go for it," or "I've really got a bad headache... I could give you a hand job right now."[19]

Gray enthuses that "these new communication skills" are good for women because they are then relieved of the burden of faking orgasms — they can just "lie there like a dead log" and the men won't mind one bit.[20] In fact, men *like* it, not because it seems a whole lot like marital rape, but because they don't get all tuckered out treating women like equals who have a right to pleasure.

Women, however, are granted no reciprocal rights: "Once a man verbally says he doesn't want to have sex, to a certain extent it is written in stone. If she persists in her attempts to initiate sex, he feels controlled or pressured to perform."[21] In fact, Gray cautions, women should not initiate sex too directly or too often — this also puts undue pressure on men. Better, he opines, for women to send indirect hints, and he provides a helpful list of ways they can do so. Wearing black lace or garters is a clear signal that a woman wants "hot, lusty, and intense sex"; white silky satin means she wants "sensitive, gentle, and loving sex"; a short and loose nightgown with no panties generally means "she doesn't need a lot of foreplay" and doesn't care if she has an orgasm or not; black bra and black panties means that she wants to be "up on top," and so on.[22]

Anyone who finds all this preposterous, not to mention insulting to women, should remember that Deborah Tannen and Carol Gilligan start with the same basic assumptions about gender differences. Their arguments seem more palatable than Gray's only because they laud women's "ethic of care" instead of advocating guilt-free quickies. But these positions are not so very different, since the myth of female moral superiority *requires* male aggression, insensitivity, and selfishness.

Interestingly, John Gray and Robin Warshaw, who completely disagree about how men and women should behave, also share some fundamental beliefs: men lust, women love; men are powerful hormonal savages, women are not sexual agents. Gray concludes that women should not initiate sex and should not say no when men initiate; Warshaw concludes that men are intimacy-impaired powermongers who do not listen when women say no. Politically, Warshaw's argument is more acceptable, but fundamentally, both arguments lead to the same conclusion: they keep women weak, by reaffirming the connection between female sexuality and love, and between male sexuality and aggression. They lie to women about the complexity of sex, power, desire, and intimacy by reiterating the gender roles of the sexual script: men pursue and initiate, women act as gatekeepers and limit-setters.

In real life, as we have seen, women do pursue and initiate sex, with both steady partners and new ones. Furthermore, according to an extensive body of research, women play a large and active role in what we mistakenly conceptualize as *male* sexual initiation. In fact, the man who approaches a woman often does so because she has signaled to him that she is receptive; if he is responding to her cues, it would be more accurate to say that *she* is the real initiator.

Researchers who have studied hundreds of interactions between men and women in singles bars consistently report that women are more active than men in initiating potentially sexual relationships.[23]

Women control the course of an interaction with a male stranger through eye contact and by employing what are called "nonverbal solicitation behaviors": primping, smiling and laughing at a particular man, touching him briefly, asking him for help, caressing him, and so on. Collectively, the technical term for this is proceptivity, which means "any behavior pattern a woman employs to express interest to a man, to arouse him sexually, or to maintain her sociosexual interaction with him."[24] Naomi McCormick, who has studied proceptivity intensively, writes that her own findings "strongly contradicted conventional expectations for women to be the passive recipients of male sexual advances."[25]

Most of us have another word for proceptivity — flirting — but the researchers do have something important to add to our understanding of the phenomenon. They've discovered they can literally predict which women will be approached by men: not the prettiest ones, but those who display the most nonverbal solicitation behaviors. "There appeared to be little relationship between physical attractiveness [of women] and...frequency of approach [by men]. That is, unattractive high-displaying subjects had a higher approach rate than attractive low-displaying subjects," report Monica Moore and Diana Butler, concluding that "the power of female nonverbal displays has again been demonstrated."[26]

Although men may not be conscious of the fact that they are responding to women's signals, women themselves are very aware that they use specific gestures, movements, and actions to draw men to them, and can describe their nonverbal displays in minute detail. For instance, in a study conducted by David Weis and Timothy Perper, who is one of the leading experts on proceptivity, women were asked to write down all the things they would do if they liked a man and wanted to have sex — however they defined it for themselves, ranging from kissing to intercourse — with him. Most listed nonverbal solicitation behaviors, but more than half went on to volunteer "contingency strategies": things they would do if the man was "recalcitrant."

In short, the majority of women fully expected that they might have to escalate, since men might not get the hint or might not take the bait, and were prepared with backup plans: talking about their feelings, touching the men, directly asking them to have sex, and so on. Liberated women weren't the only ones who talked about taking the lead; women who were conservative and held traditional beliefs about gender roles were just as likely to describe highly proceptive behavior.

"Although popular and scholarly opinion may say that women behave hesitantly and reluctantly with men, the data obtained here flatly contradict the belief that women invariably defer to, or rely on, men to initiate sexual encounters," conclude Drs. Perper and Weis.[27] Their findings and those of other researchers suggest that we should begin "reconceptualizing male-female sexual relationships" so that we "see the beginning of a sexual interaction not in the man's first *overt* sexual act (e.g., he touches her breasts) but in the prior proceptive interaction... [T]he woman sees his action as a *response* to her behavior, not as self-initiated by him and him alone."[28] Like other researchers, they conclude, "women exercise considerable power in these interactions."[29]

Most women know perfectly well that they sometimes have to work extremely hard to get men to make the so-called first move. A man's "initiation" may, in fact, follow *dozens* of moves on a woman's part. She may have spent months plotting, flirting, and trying to nudge him into taking the lead, all the while attempting to convey the impression that she was not actively seeking his sexual attention. Thus did Samantha stake out the houses of boys she liked, and Alison set the scene for a seduction with a new dress, a nice dinner, and cognac.

Their mothers had a phrase for such proceptive behavior: chasing the man until he catches you. But when they were young, the object was to get the man to the altar. Pregnancy outside of marriage was, of course, a very real fear and a powerful negative incentive for premarital chastity; many women performed a complicated juggling act, giving the man enough sexual activity to keep him interested but "holding out" so that there would be a reason for him to make a commitment — and so that she could preserve her own good-girl reputation and avoid pregnancy.

Traditionally, then, women were taught to view their sexuality in instrumental terms: sex was a carrot to be dangled in front of men, a quid pro quo bargain for a wedding ring. Conversely, sex could also

be used as a stick. Some women got pregnant, accidentally-on-pur-
pose, and nice boys were expected to do the right thing and march
down the aisle for a shotgun wedding. Once married, women could
continue this pattern, granting sexual access as a reward for good behavior, and withholding sex as a punishment. Desire, with its shameful, bad-girl overtones, was almost entirely absent from the discourse
on female sexuality.

Desire is still largely absent from this discourse, although female
sexual behavior has changed dramatically. Some of the traditional
motivations are now expressed in novel ways: whereas in the past,
women typically withheld sex in the hopes of getting a commitment,
today, some women are *rushing* sex for the same reason. They aren't
waiting weeks, months, or years — they're having sex at the earliest
opportunity, because they view it as a shortcut to romantic intimacy.
Emma believed that if she had sex with Dan, he would love her forever; Alison believed the same thing about Doug, but her approach
was far more active. She thought sex was her trump card, and she
wanted to play it as quickly as possible, so she and Doug could embark on the future she had planned out for them.

For Alison and Emma, the association between female sexuality
and love remains unchanged, but the rules of the game have changed
dramatically. Women can have sex earlier without fear of pregnancy
or social ostracism, but men are under no societal obligation to come
through with a commitment afterwards — particularly not if they've
only known their partners for a matter of hours or days.

From Alison and Emma's vantage point, this looks like a lose-lose
deal. "It was easier for our mothers," Alison said glumly. "They had a
lot more power because they could draw the line." She views freedom as a burden, although she is self-supporting, has had a lively
erotic career, and, without access to abortion services, would have
"had to get married" when she became pregnant at nineteen.

Freedom *is* a burden for women who continue to locate their own
sexuality in the realm of romance, where oppositional thinking reigns
and where a woman's main goal in life is to get a man. Traditionally,
sex was a woman's most valuable bargaining chip for commitment,
but today, the currency has been devalued. Sex is no longer a rare

commodity provided only by a few bad girls, and sex is no guarantee of a phone call the next day, much less a wedding ring. Thus, even women like Alison, who behave as sexual subjects, may still feel a false sense of powerlessness when sex does not lead to love. And if the most sexually aggressive women can feel this way, a milder-mannered romantic like Emma is virtually guaranteed to feel like a victim.

For centuries now, romance has been pushed on women as the remedy for all that ails them. In the traditional romance script, the heroine was a long-suffering, patient character who waited for her knight in shining armor. As the curtain closed, he was on his knees, felled by his love for her, which redeemed her existence and gave her life meaning. Feminists have pointed out how dangerous romantic ideology is for women, and how self-defeating: you sink into his arms and end up with your arms in his sink.

But the romance script persists, albeit in an updated, rewritten form designed to appeal to the modern woman, who has a job and little interest in spending her days darning socks and waiting for her prince to show. Today, the heroine is no Sleeping Beauty who expects to be rescued and animated by a dashing prince. Instead, she is a good girl who tames a bad boy. In the new script, women are not damsels in distress, but emotional saviors who rescue insensitive men, teach them to care and share, and are rewarded with perfect intimacy.

This is a female version of the traditional male quest narrative; women are active and the adventure is psychological. Armed with the tools of intimacy expertise, the woman takes on a bad boy, conquers his fear of commitment, and then supervises his emotional development. The less promising the man, the bigger the challenge and the more rewarding the triumph. A skilled intimacy expert, apparently, can help even the most seemingly hard-hearted macho man get in touch with the girlfriend within.

Clearly, Emma bought into this script. Dan was a classic bad boy, and Emma believed she could help him; he was wounded by a dysfunctional family, but she could heal him with intimacy expertise. Less obviously, Alison also subscribed to this script; she thought she could liberate Doug and rebuild his self-esteem. But he had already mastered the art of self-disclosure, so her main job was to roughen some of his soft edges, by teaching him how to dress like a real man and take charge in the bedroom.

Both Emma and Alison saw sex as a way to jumpstart the plot. After sex, they could get to work on these men, whom they viewed as projects, not partners. Sex, then, was not just a way to get love. It was also an opening gambit for emotional control: *Now we'll start a long-term relationship, and I'll fix his life, mold his personality, and make him need me.* Sex was an indirect bid for power.

When this bid failed, Alison and Emma did what good girls are supposed to do in the nineties: they pointed the finger at bad boys. *I didn't want sex, I wanted a relationship. I was cruelly misused and mistreated.* They blamed men for not wanting relationships with strong, intelligent women, but ignored their own sexist stereotyping: they sought troubled men whom they could reform, redeem, coddle, and control.

Women who believe they are intimacy experts are desperate for romantic relationships but are seriously deluded about their own power. They think that through sheer force of will, they can forge relationships and make them work. They also have delusions about their sexual power: they think they don't have any, and reflexively label themselves victims when sex doesn't lead to endless love. Confusing sexual choices with emotional outcomes, they define self-determination only in terms of happy endings.

The cultural willingness to recognize women as sexual victims, coupled with a continued emphasis on the centrality of relationships and romance in women's lives, provides no way out of this rut. Highlighting victimization and intimacy expertise without underscoring the possibilities of female sexual agency is the real lose-lose proposition for women. Women who believe their lives are worthless without men, and who can't give themselves permission to feel stirred by their own arousal or breathless with desire, will never believe they are in control of their sexual lives because they will not be able to recognize or acknowledge when they are exercising their power to choose.

But whether or not women recognize it, they may still have considerable sexual power. They can and do prod men into making the so-called first moves, they can and do take charge of sexual situations as Alison did, and they can and do try to use sex instrumentally, as a way of getting what they want. Frequently, what they want is control: control over men, which is what the myth of women's intimacy expertise seems to promise.

Sex, then, can be a preliminary bid for power, which is a secret a woman can keep from herself if she doesn't get the relationship she wants. *If I had power, my story would have a happy ending.* She does not see that regardless of the outcome, she is a sexual subject who made choices and acted on them. She has more sexual power than she knows, but quite a bit less emotional power than she hoped.

We need to ask why so many women continue to attempt to get power over men, when doing so makes them feel powerless to control their own lives. We need to question the so-called happy endings we strive for, because as we shall see, having power over men, sexually or emotionally, does not make most women feel particularly happy.

Although Jessica is many other things, sexy is probably the first word you would choose to describe her. "Cute" is too bland to capture the slightly sullen tilt of her mouth and far too wholesome for her mannerisms: brushing hair out of her eyes or putting on her coat, she touches herself the way a lover would. But she's not kittenish or preening. There's something defiant about her sensuality, and she insists on her own raw absence of innocence.

"I didn't make a distinction between one-night stands and having sex because you care about someone," Jessica says, then begins counting them off on her fingers, all the men she slept with before that distinction seemed important. Twenty-one, twenty-two, something like that, she decides. Most were accumulated during a two-year streak of wildness that was — she wants to make this clear at the outset — an aberration for her.

It's hard to come up with a precise number, she'd have to think about it longer, because the men have blurred together in her memory. It's funny how time makes men recede into the background, even men whose hands have mapped every inch of her body. In a way, she was oblivious to many of them even at the time.

"I went through a phase where I saw sex as a way to test my own power," she says. When sex becomes a way to prove something to yourself, it can be the ultimate act of selfishness, Jessica thinks. She works in the film industry (in a job more clerical than glamorous) and has a habit of squinting off into the middle distance when she talks, as though straining to see her words take shape on an imaginary screen. What she sees now is herself six years ago, twenty-six years old and stunned by grief. How, with so much love between them, could Paul leave? Why, when they were so right for each other, did he blithely move from her bed to another woman's as though it hardly mattered where he had been sleeping for the past three years?

She and Paul had shared their lives in every respect, but no one seemed to honor her loss. Her friends told her to cheer up, get back out there and start dating; her mother observed that it wasn't as though she and Paul had been married, and her sister passed on dog-eared paperbacks about women who love too much and men who love too little. They all seemed to think that love was some kind of disease that could be cured through a twelve-step program, rather than a profound, transforming experience. Jessica paced the apartment she and Paul had shared, seeing loss in every object — *his favorite chair, the bowl he bought at the flea market* — and feeling "completely insane. He didn't validate the depth of my feelings, and neither did anyone else," she remembers. "Everyone was saying, 'Get over it! Go find someone new.'"

What did love mean, if it could be dislodged so quickly and forgotten so easily by everyone else? Sex, apparently, was not about love, or why would Paul have left? They had had good sex, great sex even, but it wasn't enough to hold him. They hadn't even been arguing. He just walked out the door, no warning whatsoever, to be with a woman she'd never even heard of.

Jessica started to think there must be something lacking in her, some deficiency apparent to everyone but herself. It was as though Paul had taken all her confidence along with him when he left. She stared into the mirror: Am I getting ugly? Is that it? She noticed the beginnings of tiny lines around her eyes, then that her mouth was pulled down at the corners, as though something mean was about

to come out of it. To hell with trying to look good for men, she
thought, and didn't bother with makeup for a while. She started
smoking again, subsisted on junk food, played the same Patsy Cline
tape over and over, and cried until jagged, choking noises came out
of her throat.

After a month of steeping in misery, Jessica felt the first revitaliz-
ing jolt of anger. How *dare* he? She looked in the mirror again, and
decided things weren't so bad after all. She had thick brown hair, an
intelligent face, and a near-perfect body. Hadn't men been throwing
themselves at her for years? She started thinking about all the unconsummated flirtations, all the offers not taken up during those
years with Paul, and how foolish her fidelity now seemed. The cold,
pure rapture of being wronged cleared her head. She was an attractive woman, damn it, and she was going to prove it.

"I set out to rebuild my ego," Jessica remembers. Her job as a film
researcher didn't pay well and wasn't doing much for her ego, nor was
it proving to be the stepping-stone to power she had hoped it would
be. She had to look elsewhere: "I went into this conquest mode of
having sex with anyone I'd ever been attracted to. For about a year
and a half, I was on a nonstop quest for sexual validation and power."

She picked up a stranger at a party where everyone wore black and
cultivated a look of hip boredom, had flings with casual acquaintances, and finally had sex with a man who had been in love with her
for years, which turned out rather badly. He left hurt, puzzled messages on her answering machine for weeks afterwards, wondering
why she hadn't called. All Jessica felt was embarrassed for him. She
believed she was seeing sex clearly for the first time: it was the ultimate proof of her power over men. She could make them need her,
yet remain above need herself. She felt invincible.

And then she decided she wanted Russell, who was not just a friend
but also the star of her social circle. He was smooth, clever, charming,
and always seemed to know the right thing to say. Come to think of it,
there had always been a spark between them — Paul, in fact, had
sulked about their flirtation. "Oh for God's sake," Jessica had said at
the time, rolling her eyes, "Russell and I have been friends for years."
But at the time, she was secretly pleased to be singled out by Russell

and even more pleased that Paul noticed, although it also made her a little edgy. After that, she felt compelled to entertain when she was around Russell, as though she were constantly auditioning for his approval.

Well, she'd learned in the meantime that she could have any man she wanted, and was long past worrying about rejection. Her policy of not caring about men had scoured her clean of weakness. Russell had made his interest plain, so now all she had to do was act on it. The fact that her ex-boyfriend had viewed him as a threat made Russell that much more attractive; the fact that he was involved with her friend Shelley was no real obstacle. Jessica had known Russell longer, and besides, Shelley had forgiven his other extracurricular affairs, which seemed to Jessica like the fragment of permission she needed.

"I asked Russell to come over and help me hook up my CD player, but I didn't need help," she says flatly, not bothering to pretend that any of this was unpremeditated. "I wanted to sleep with him."

It was hot, her apartment had no air conditioning, and when Russell arrived at four-thirty on a Saturday afternoon, she was wearing only a white T-shirt and underwear. "Sit down and talk to me," she called from the couch, patting the seat beside her. When he sat down, she stretched out like a cat, letting the T-shirt ride up, thrilling to the sight of her own lean body. She poured herself some vodka, mildly interested in what would happen before they went to bed, how they would wind up there. It never occurred to her that they would not.

She can't recall what Russell said to fill the silence, she was too busy watching herself to take much note, but she does remember offering him a drink. When he said he didn't want one, she put the empty glass in his hand, wrapping her fingers around his, and slowly filled it. He downed it in one gulp, then got up and walked over to inspect the CD player. "This looks easy," he said, with the false, booming cheer of a man trying to change the topic.

He was sweating slightly and studiously avoiding looking at her. Simply by lounging around in a white T-shirt, she had reduced suave, sophisticated Russell to fiddling nervously among the boxes and wires on the floor. "Have another drink," she insisted. "You need to loosen up."

The fan was blowing, it was hot, he was crouching awkwardly on the floor. She started rubbing his shoulders and he shrugged her off, trying to pretend that they were both just kidding around, nothing serious was going on.

The vodka was singing in her veins, but Jessica felt completely calm. She remembers that she saw herself as "an overwhelming sexual lure," which is not hard to imagine, given her toned body and the way she moves. "There was never any doubt in my mind that I could make him have sex with me."

She draped herself around him and traced little patterns on his thigh and kissed the back of his neck, all the while feeling like a cold, glamorous seductress in a forties movie. She told Russell that, knowing him as she did, she didn't believe he could be happy with just one woman for the rest of his life. She told him that he had always wanted this, they both had, and nothing was stopping them now. Russell's qualms amused her: "At one point he started pleading with me, saying, 'Shelley and I have got to a point in our relationship where we're closer. I don't think I could go home and lie to her.' I'm not saying anything at this point, I'm just presenting my body. My strategy is, Let him talk, don't take it seriously."

In trying to turn him on, Jessica was turning herself on. Her body seemed to her to be utterly compelling, a temptation no man could resist. In retrospect, however, she sees the situation differently. "Looking back, I think he was just bewildered and didn't know what to do. I think he cared for me and wanted to appease me and that's what stopped him from just walking out," she says now.

He didn't walk out, but he didn't hop into bed, either, so after a while, Jessica took a more direct approach: "I jumped him, there's no nicer way to say it, and started taunting him. I said, 'You're so square it drives me crazy. Why can't you just let go? Do you think I'm going to be stalking you tomorrow?'"

It was a moot point, since Russell couldn't get an erection. "I started questioning my own desirability, which just made me more aggressive," Jessica says. "I tried everything but he couldn't get an erection, which made me furious and made him feel terrible. He felt that he ought to want sex even though he didn't, and that made it worse — he actually started having performance anxiety over the fact that he didn't want to have sex with me! I was making sarcastic little remarks, partly because my own ego was on the line but partly because I was really angry. I turned the whole thing around on him, so he was the one who was failing me, he was the one in the wrong."

Somehow, after a sustained harangue, Russell was able to perform. "He kind of went through with it, but it was so clear from his body language that he didn't want to," Jessica says. "It just lasted a few minutes. I think he faked an orgasm, if men can do that, then got up and left."

Still, she had got what she wanted, and she was pleased with herself until she ran into Russell at a party the following week. "I tried to insinuate this conspiratorial thing between us, that we had this naughty secret, but he kept his distance. I don't think he'd ever wanted to go beyond flirting — probably the reason he felt comfortable flirting with me before was because he never intended to act on it," she says. "After I crossed that line, he was really uncomfortable around me. I suddenly realized that he felt used, and he was right to feel used." She had, after all, seen him merely as a memento, a way of humbling Paul and certifying her own desirability.

"At the time I thought he just couldn't help himself, he was just responding to my body. It's upsetting to think I was capable of that much self-deception," Jessica says, then offers a catalogue of explanations. "He did it because he cared about me as a friend and because he was manipulated into a position he couldn't get out of gracefully. Also, because I insulted him and pushed all his buttons. I was thrusting my sexuality on him because of my rage toward Paul, and then when he didn't respond the right way, I transferred all that rage onto him. And I think I was trying to punish Shelley, like she didn't deserve to have a relationship if love had failed for me."

Jessica regrets what she did, regrets that she cared so little about anyone else's feelings, regrets that she hurt Russell. "But," she adds, "it's important to say that men have done to me what I did to him. The problem is that we inherited all this sexual freedom before we were old enough or wise enough to cope with it, and there were no rules to hold anyone to."

She tells me then about the male acquaintance at college who would have raped her if she hadn't fought back, the incident mentioned earlier in this chapter. And she remembers waking up one night during a camping trip with a group of friends when she was twenty-seven and finding Peter, a man she was not particularly close to, lying on top of her and rooting around wordlessly in her sleeping bag as though he'd dropped his keys. They had sex, for no reason she can remember other than that she felt sorry for him. And there were other times, other men with whom sex was an acquiescence, a matter of, Oh all right, fine, might as well.

"I never felt powerless in those situations. They didn't scar me or intimidate me or weaken me. It was always, Well, this is part of the chaos of promiscuity that I'm going through," she says. "When sex is disconnected from commitment, it's not a big deal to sleep with someone you don't particularly like. There are no rules, so who cares? But then you wake up one day and think, What are my boundaries? Why am I having sex with everyone? What does sex mean, anyway? Sex can mean anything, which is why total freedom is a really, really bad idea if you're not mature enough or smart enough to come up with a few rules for yourself."

Diane, the woman who "borrowed" Jane's boyfriend for a night, spoke of feeling "a total sense of power, that I had him under my thumb and he preferred me to Jane." Sarah, the dancer who attended boarding school, talked about the "power trip" of realizing "I could *make* guys notice me, *make* them trail around after me, *make* them come to my room at night." Similarly, Samantha felt "this incredible sense of power" on the dance floor with Robin, when she became sure that they would be having sex later on. Alison described the power of believing she would be the best lover Doug had ever had, and Jessica spoke about the power of feeling like "an overwhelming sexual lure" who could "make Russell have sex."

For all of them, power meant the power to attract, which conforms to the traditionally passive, feminine sexual stereotype: being wanted, being desired. Yet, these women were all active seductresses who staged their erotic adventures with elaborate props and plots, and described them as "conquests."

Nevertheless, even as they were breaking away from the sexual script, they tried to get men to play their appointed role as lusty savages. Sarah got off on the idea that she was driving men wild with desire, much as Alison did with Doug. Diane, Samantha, and Jessica all attempted to maneuver men into taking over midway through their own carefully orchestrated seductions. As Diane put it, she wanted to "be ravished" and sought the experience "of having the guy want you so much that he throws caution to the winds and can't resist his desire." All were active agents with passive goals: they desired the state of being desired.

Notably absent from their description of power is any mention of their *own* sexual desire, arousal, or pleasure. In fact, all of them described sexual experiences that were distinctly unsatisfactory in terms of physical pleasure. They defined sexual control in terms of having control *over* men, rather than being in control of their own bodies and their own pleasure. When they spoke of pleasure at all, they meant psychological, not physical, enjoyment: the pleasure of feeling they were one up on their partners so long as the men appeared to desire them more than they themselves desired the men.

Being sexually desired made them feel dominant. Feeling that men needed and wanted them more than they needed and wanted men made these women feel superior. Paradoxically, they viewed being ravished — by definition, a submissive experience — as the most dominant state of all, proof positive of their relative power and control over men. When they encountered men who failed to comply, by taking charge of sex, they felt most powerless — yet behaved most powerfully, if power is understood as having another person do your bidding.

Some women, like Samantha and Jessica, become verbally coercive because they are sexually aroused and because they view a man's reluctance as an indication that they themselves are insufficiently attractive. Others, like Alison, are coercive because they believe they are intimacy experts who know what's best for men, and because they hope sex will cement a romantic relationship. Whatever the motivation, many coercive women fail to perceive that they are stage-managing reluctant men into sex. Rather, they think they are merely prompting men who have missed their cue in the sexual script: *all men want sex all the time.*

To women who define sex in terms of emotional outcomes and to women who view sex as a way to certify their own attractiveness, men appear to have a monopoly on sexual power. Men are the ones who can deliver what these women want: relationships, or proof of their own desirability.

But the irony amidst all these paradoxes is that many men do not feel nearly as powerful as women think they do. And in many respects, a great deal of the power men do have in sexual relationships comes from *women's* continued attempts to be good girls and intimacy experts.

Chapter Seven

Men Are from Venus, Women Are from Mars

Women are intimacy experts, men are autonomous achievers. Women are expressive, men are instrumental. Women crave romance, men crave sex. These are the old oppositional dualities we have learned, and they shape our perceptions of our own lives.

Researchers who have actually bothered to study men's and women's behavior, however, have different stories to tell. Apparently, *men* are the more romantic ones; they are more likely to say things like "we're perfect for each other," and they fall in love faster and fall out of love harder than women do.[1] This is not a new discovery: in 1970, researchers who interviewed 700 young lovers reported that 20 percent of the men but only 15 percent of the women fell in love before the fourth date, and by the twentieth date, only 30 percent of the men but fully 43 percent of the women were still unsure whether they were in love.[2]

Similarly, Harvard scientists who charted 231 Boston couples' romances for two years discovered that, typically, the women decided whether and when to break up, but the men usually hung on to the bitter end. Furthermore, "The men felt most depressed, most lonely, least happy, and least free after a breakup. They found it extremely hard to accept the fact that they were no longer loved; that the affair was over and there was nothing they could do about it. They were plagued with the hope that if only they said the right thing...did the right thing...things would be as they were. Women were far more re-signed and, thus, were better able to pick up the pieces of their lives and move on."[3]

In *A New Look at Love*, Elaine Hatfield and G. William Walster review these and many other studies, concluding, "Men tend to fall in love more quickly and cling to a faltering love more tenaciously than do women." This makes sense, they say, when you consider that, traditionally, "it is the man who has official initiation privileges: he calls, invites, pursues, proposes... Thus, it's not so surprising to find that the man feels free to plunge headlong after the woman he wants."[4] Women, on the other hand, had to keep their wits about them, because they were making an economic choice as well as a ro-mantic one: would the man be a good provider? Traditionally, then, women were far more likely than men to tell researchers they'd marry someone even if they weren't in love.[5]

Today, women's economic dependence on men has decreased dra-matically. Those of us who can support ourselves now have the free-dom to make different kinds of romantic choices, because men are not our meal tickets — sometimes, the reverse is true. Furthermore, we too can plunge headlong after the men we want, asking them out for dates and paying the expenses. As we saw in Chapter Four, many young women are starting to do so, and many young men tell re-searchers that they enjoy being on the receiving end. Like women, they are flattered to be pursued — so long as they like the woman who's doing the pursuing.[6]

Women are also far freer to leave faltering relationships. In most cases, women are the ones who actively seek divorce, even though they are more likely to suffer for it economically, particularly if they have children. After divorce, the average woman's standard of living tends to drop, while the average man's tends to rise. But there's a flip side: men are, by virtually every measure, worse off emotionally. They are more likely to become depressed, more likely to attempt suicide, and more likely to feel unhappy.[7] And, according to the largest American study on the long-term effects of divorce, men are also more likely to feel bad for years. Five years after terminating a marriage, two-thirds of women but only one-half of men say they are happier; at the ten-year mark, 80 percent of women but only 50 percent of men say divorce was the right decision.[8]

Men, in fact, may be the ones who love too much: their mental health seems to depend on their relationships with women. Single men are twice as likely as married men to commit suicide; single men suffer from twice as many mental health problems, ranging from depression to nervous breakdowns, as single women.[9]

Women exercise considerable emotional power over men, yet may not even be aware of it if they are playing the role of intimacy experts, busily attending to men's feelings and needs while denying their own. If the relationship ends, however, the man's emotional dependency is revealed; he has lost his tender nurturer, who was working overtime to keep the relationship running smoothly and forever begging to know what he was feeling and thinking. He was the center of her world, and now he feels lost without her.

As Francesca Cancian suggests in *Love in America*, "Perhaps men are more romantic because they are less responsible for 'working on' the emotional aspects of the relationship, and therefore see love as magically and perfectly present or absent. Women, in contrast, may assume that love varies and depends on their own efforts." When women take on sole responsibility for repairing any flaws in the fabric of intimacy, "men's dependency on women remains covert and repressed, while women's dependency on men is overt and exaggerated."[10]

Sometimes, men's dependency is blindingly obvious, as it was in Elaine's affair with her boss. Frequently, single women who become involved with married men get hooked on the power they believe they possess in these affairs. *He can't live without me, he tells me so every day. He needs me so much that he's taking huge risks and breaking his marriage vows to be with me. He's so vulnerable — he tells me everything.* His weakness becomes her source of strength, which is why, so often, Other Women begin affairs feeling confident that they can handle the situation. The man's dependency is so obvious. Surely, it can lead to only one conclusion: he will leave his wife. The Other Woman feels powerful until the day she notices she no longer has the power to control her own life and get what she wants.

Male dependency does not, it turns out, make intimacy experts feel particularly powerful. They have the relationship that is supposedly crucial to their self-worth, but it makes them feel overburdened and shortchanged. There is no blissful happy ending: there's just more work to maintain the relationship, regardless of the personal cost. This alone should prove that our so-called intimacy expertise is not very good for us: *we wind up viewing men as projects, not partners, and we obtain a brand of power that doesn't even make us feel powerful.* In practice, intimacy expertise frequently boils down to working overtime to obscure both your own power and your partner's dependency.

This arrangement suits John Gray, author of the *Mars and Venus* books, just fine. He would like to see every woman on the planet caught in a Venus flytrap, worrying constantly that her man will leave unless she flatters his ego, lays in a multihued supply of lingerie, and offers herself up on a nightly basis. In return, she will get a relationship with a grown-up who behaves like an infant and requires the same kind of unselfish, neverending care. Gray goes so far as to suggest that a woman should not be honest if she doesn't like a movie that a man suggested. "To support him at those vulnerable and embarrassing times, she needs to focus on the positive and look for something that was good," he instructs.[11] Apparently, the male ego is so fragile that it might be shattered if a woman expressed an opinion of her own.

Rampant male insecurity is, in fact, Gray's real theme, and it is why he pushes romance on women so relentlessly. If women crave romance, they will feel worthless without men; if women crave romance, they can be bought for the price of a dozen roses. Romance keeps women on their toes, anxious to please and not minding if the man doesn't do his fair share of housework. Rather, convinced that men are omnipotent sexual animals who must be appeased, women will live in fear that men may up and leave if they make a misstep. They will prance around in satin underwear, placating and cajoling, never asking: What's in it for me?

Women will be so focused on their own insecurities that they won't notice just how much men need them. Nor will they find out that men are not powerful creatures from a distant planet. They are, in fact, fallible mortals with flaws and frailties who silently question their power, sexual and otherwise, all the time.

Jim is thirty-one, a lawyer who carries a whiff of the courtroom with him into a restaurant, studying the menu as though looking for loopholes that could be of use when the bill arrives. He is tall and good-looking in the quiet way of a prosperous man with conservative tastes, a square jaw, and comb tracks in his slicked-back hair. Everything about his appearance suggests restraint, but after a few drinks it turns out that he is a talker who will speak quite freely under the cover of anonymity.

"Pressure to have sex, pressure to have had sex" is what Jim remembers most clearly about his teenage years. "But the first time I really had a chance, I froze. Didn't know what to do, how to convert the opportunity."

His first chance came at the end of his junior year of high school, with an angular senior whose name he still says with something that sounds like reverence: Claire. They hung out at the same coffee shop, where she wrote furiously in a notebook that she closed whenever anyone got too close, and sometimes they had strange, intense conversations about politics that made him realize how little he knew. He was drawn to her and confused by her, unmoored by her fierce intelligence and direct questions.

"Want to go to the prom?" she asked one day, out of the blue. He had thought of Claire as the sort of girl who might run off to join the rebel army in some impoverished country, not the sort who would be anxious to see the homecoming queen crowned. But Jim didn't hesitate. Yes, he said, yes.

"Good," she said and turned back to her notebook, dismissing him. He didn't know why she'd chosen him or what, if anything, it meant, but he felt lucky.

The night of the prom, he almost didn't recognize Claire. Her hair was pulled back to reveal the sharp, delicate planes of her face, and she was wearing a complicated black dress with a long, flapping sash. Amidst the effusion of round-cheeked girls in pink satin, she looked like a long-necked, exotic bird, poised for flight. He was suddenly shy, unable to meet her gaze or hold her close during the slow dances. She seemed almost too beautiful to touch.

"We've observed the ritual," Claire said after a few hours, surveying the mashing, grinding bodies on the dance floor. "Now we can go."

Jim wasn't sure what she meant, whether he had let her down in some way. He'd thought they were having a good time, but he followed her out to the woods, where it was so quiet and he was so aware of being alone with her that he couldn't think of a thing to say. Claire took her shoes off and walked over the pine needles in bare feet, holding her back perfectly straight, talking about what the world must have been like before the white settlers arrived, bearing disease and weapons of destruction. Little bits of her dress were fluttering in the air, her voice was eddying off into the breeze, she seemed to be rushing on ahead of him, beyond his grasp. Jim wanted to latch onto her and shout, "Take me with you." Instead, he walked mutely beside her, listening to her talk, feeling like an idiot.

When they reached the edge of a clearing she stopped and faced him. It was too dark to see her eyes and there seemed to be miles separating them, although they were so close he could feel her breath. They stood like that for a long moment, until he finally realized that she was waiting to be kissed, and then there was the relief and reassurance of knowing what was expected, lying on the damp grass.

"I was doing the usual thing," Jim says. "Secure first base and immediately try for second. Just get as far as you can before she stops you." There were little hooks down the back of her dress and he was fumbling at them, trying to be inconspicuous and deft, hoping to be able to undo a few before she called a halt to the proceedings. "Here," Claire said, reaching around her back to help, then easing herself out of the dress. Jim spread his jacket out on the ground so she could lie on it, and then he had his arms around a nearly naked girl, with no clear idea of what to do next.

"It's one thing to talk about sex and look at *Playboy*, and quite another to know what to do when there's a real live woman there with an expectant look on her face. I had an idea of the mechanics, but only in the vaguest way," Jim recalls. "And in my fantasies, the focus had always been touching the woman for my own sake, like a kid in a candy store. It suddenly occurred to me that it was key to know how to turn a woman on, and I didn't have a clue. Below the waist was pretty much foreign territory, and I didn't want to do anything wrong because then she wouldn't want to see me again. I'm thinking about all this, and meanwhile a voice in my head is yelling, 'Go for it!' My reaction was blind panic, and then meltdown — total equipment failure."

Jim tried to cover, murmured something about her curfew and how it was probably time to start heading home. Claire said, "I don't have a curfew." He lied about the condom that had been in his wallet for a long, hopeful year, said he didn't have any protection and didn't want to get her pregnant. "You're sweet," she said and kissed him. Then she whispered not to worry, she was on the Pill.

"It was the strangest thing. My brain went Yes! but my body wouldn't respond. It was very confusing. Up till then, I'd had the opposite problem, getting hard-ons for no reason. Here I finally had a good reason, and I was impotent," Jim remembers. "I didn't know anything about performance anxiety — the whole concept of performance was new to me — so I didn't know how to process it. It was like every doubt I'd ever had about not being man enough was being confirmed, and there was a sense of being utterly alone. Ten minutes before I'd been completely caught up in her, but now it was all about me. Self-loathing, fear, shame — you name it, I had it."

He couldn't say anything to Claire. He cared too much what she thought, and besides, he didn't want her to find out he was still a virgin. She was older, on the Pill and thus undoubtedly experienced, and would think he was immature. A wimp. A failure.

"Women should never overestimate a man's fear that he's being compared to other men and will be found wanting," Jim says now. "That's at the root of the double standard, this terror that a sexually experienced woman will know just how bad you are and leave you for someone better."

Claire was the arbiter of his manhood, or so it seemed at the time. "I didn't want her to touch me, which might have helped, because then she'd know for sure that there was nothing going on down there. So I was swatting her hands away and trying to will an erection into existence, but the more anxious I got the more impossible it was," Jim recalls. "The whole scenario was like something out of Dante. She's lying back waiting and my fate depends on this shriveled piece of flesh."

Finally, Jim gruffly announced that he had to get home. "She got dressed and stormed back to the car. In retrospect, it's obvious that she felt rejected and didn't know why I was acting so cold. I wasn't saying anything, because I was too embarrassed and I was positive she was disgusted with me," Jim says. "I was also paranoid that she was going to tell and everyone would know."

The thing is, Jim says, he really *liked* Claire. Maybe that was the problem, he thought afterwards. Maybe he'd liked her too much. "But I thought the damage was done and there was nothing I could do to fix the situation. I just assumed she'd laugh in my face if I asked her out," Jim says. "You know, I still regret blowing my chance to have a relationship with her. When I meet a woman who reminds me of her, even a little bit, I go weak in the knees. She became an unattainable ideal for me."

His night with Claire established a pattern in his love life. With every new woman, he asked himself the same questions. Will I stay hard? Can I perform? Can I satisfy her? All of them pointed to the same big question: Am I man enough?

"A lot of the time, I was head over heels in love and scared that the woman wouldn't like me back, but somehow, the anxiety focused on my penis. Until I was twenty-one, I used to measure myself with a ruler, praying I'd grow. But then it just got too depressing," he says. "I thought I was too small to perform well, so every time I slept with a new woman, it was a trial by fire. I'd just be trying to get through it and come out the other side unscathed."

This attitude was not conducive to wild abandon. Nor, says Jim, was the attitude of many of his partners. "At a certain point, they tended to lie back and wait to be pleased, so it felt like a command performance, a test. I'm talking about supposedly liberated women with strong personalities, but when they got into bed, the approach was, 'Well, I'm here, aren't I? You're the man, you're supposed to take care of everything.' Sometimes it was passivity, just shyness," Jim says. "But sometimes it bordered on arrogance, like they were waiting to be serviced.

"Finally, when I was twenty-nine, I met my current girlfriend, who took a more active approach and taught me what she liked. I didn't have to fumble around blindly, so that helped build my confidence. The other thing that really helped was telling her about the anxiety," he continues. "For me, it was a big dramatic confession, but she just said, 'Relax, you're average. Every guy thinks he's too small.' She showed me an article that said the average man's erect penis is about five and a quarter inches long. I didn't know whether to laugh or cry. I'd spent half my life worrying about something that wasn't even an issue. To me, it's hilarious to hear the penis called a weapon. Mine was the enemy, the thing that was undermining me and failing me at every turn."

But didn't it deliver some pleasure, at least? Jim has to think about it for a while. Finally he says, "I'm giving the wrong impression if it sounds like I never enjoyed sex. Sure I did. But it didn't live up to my expectations, because the dream is that you're always hard and can go for hours, and there's some equality to the exchange. On the first count, I never measured up, so that took the edge off my pleasure. And equality has been pretty elusive. There's this fiction that you're taking from the woman, that she's giving you something precious just by being there, but the reality is that as a man, you can feel like you're the one doing all the giving. Giving her pleasure, giving her a part of yourself, giving yourself over to being judged. I'm not saying sex is a chore and there's no joy in it, because there is, especially if you really care about the woman. If you're in love, even mediocre sex can be incredibly pleasurable because it's emotionally intense and it's about more than just friction. But being responsible for a woman's good time and also responsible for your own is not a fifty-fifty deal."

In his view, it's practically impossible to redress the imbalance because "there's this idea that putting any demands on a woman means you're a sexist pig. You can't ask for, say, oral sex, because that would be demeaning to her. Yet she's allowed to demand oral sex and if you don't hop to it, that also means you're a sexist pig. The relationship I'm in now is the first one where there's been anything approaching mutuality in the bedroom, but still..." he trails off. "See, the assumption is always that I want it more than she does, even if she's the one who's initiating, and that my pleasure is a given but hers is something I owe her. I'm supposed to be grateful that she's letting me have sex with her, and in return, do all the work. It seems like women have more power in sex, because the expectations of male performance are so high but there's no equivalent standard for women."

The insecurities Jim describes are remarkably common. Men, it appears, also have great difficulty living up to their end of the sexual script: ever ready, ever hard, ever capable of providing unlimited satisfaction. In our society, femininity is not defined through sex, but masculinity is; a boy becomes a man when he has intercourse, but his manliness is conditional. He is only as masculine as his last performance. Thus, an organ that measures three inches or less in its flaccid state — which is to say, the vast majority of the time — seems to bear the burden of proof of his manhood.

Paradoxically, however, "sex places manhood in jeopardy, with its masculine ideal of autonomous selfhood threatened by the self-abnegation, the self-obliteration, that sexual desire engenders," writes Lynne Segal in *Straight Sex*. "In sex, as distinct from in most other social contexts, men who desire women may face their greatest uncertainties, insecurities, dependence and deference toward them."[12]

Although the bedroom is supposed to be where men feel strongest and most powerful, because they have so much to prove and because the possibility of failure — erectile failure and the failure to satisfy women — is ever present, it is frequently where men feel most vulnerable. Furthermore, for men as for women, sex entails longing, need, loss of control, and the sense that boundaries between two people are, if only for an instant, permeable. "Sexual experiences are so tied in with the most keenly felt but peculiarly inexpressible hopes and deprivations, promising either the confirmation of, or threats to, our identities as worthwhile or lovable people, that they can scarcely avoid invoking insecurities and anxieties," writes Segal.[13]

Men's relative socioeconomic power does not, as some feminists would have us believe, necessarily translate directly into sexual omnipotence. Like women, men have sexual anxieties; unlike women,

men's anxieties center on potency, size, and sexual skill. Like women, men have feelings; unlike women, men receive little encouragement to express their emotions openly outside the bedroom. As Francesca Cancian notes, "Sexual intimacy is the only 'masculine' way of expressing love that is culturally recognized in our society."[14] For men who adhere to masculine stereotypes, then, sex takes on enormous emotional significance.

Men themselves, after a promise of confidentiality, willingly elaborate on the theme of sexual vulnerability. "There's nothing to hide behind, you're totally exposed," says Matt, a thirty-three-year-old investment analyst. "The woman has access to every fibre of your being at a point when all your defenses are down, and I think men compensate by acting like assholes afterward. You do it because you feel you've let your guard down too much. Sex is the one place where men are really allowed to express emotions, so we funnel them all into this one thing and then they get heightened by the physical sensations and the intimacy of the act. It can be uncomfortable — there's a tension between wanting to let go entirely and wanting to pull back into yourself and bar all the doors so no one else can get in. You can be overwhelmed by the strength of your own feelings."

Three years ago, Matt's fiancée left him for another man, and much like Jessica in the previous chapter, he embarked on a plan to try to heal himself through casual sex. Unlike her, however, he found that it intensified his pain. "I'd be in the middle of sex and all this hurt and anger and grief would come up out of nowhere and smack me so hard I couldn't breathe. The intensity was literally unbearable, I had to stop and say, 'Sorry, gotta go,' and get the hell out of there. If you went and asked those women, they'd probably say I was an insensitive jerk, but it's really the opposite. I couldn't separate off my emotions. In everyday life I could, but in sex, the floodgates came crashing down," he says. "I'd always been a serial monogamist and had the usual fantasies of just going out and sleeping with a million women, but in practice, I couldn't do it. All these feelings would come up and attach themselves to whatever woman I was with."

Most women know firsthand just how vulnerable and insecure men can be, and spend ridiculous amounts of time and energy flattering male egos and faking orgasms to reassure men of their virility. Yet what Lynne Segal calls "myths of penile prowess" persist, directly fueling female terror and male sexual anxiety. We see this anxiety most clearly in the compulsive philanderer, who needs to prove, over and over, just how much of a man he is, yet never manages to convince himself. We see it in the man who seeks a penile extension or implant, spending thousands of dollars and risking complete loss of sensation in return for an added inch of length or width.

Anxiety is also manifest in the most rank forms of sexism: the crude bravado, catcalls, and boorishness of men whose sense of their own masculinity is so tenuous that they adopt a public posture of unflagging machismo, repudiating all things "feminine." Jim's question — *Am I man enough?* — is one that some men attempt to answer by putting women down, which they would not need to do if they did not believe that women were powerful and if they did not view women's power as a direct threat to their own manhood.

To men, women can seem the more powerful sexual players, because in the sexual script, women are the ones who accept and reject male advances, the ones who test male potency, and the ones for whom men perform. But when the penis is coded at its most benign as actively thrusting and at its most malignant as an invasive weapon, it's difficult to perceive that men might feel, much less actually *be*, vulnerable in sex. Furthermore, it's virtually impossible to perceive women as anything but receptive, passive vessels. This framework blinds us to the multiple psychological and subjective meanings that individuals attach to their own sexual experiences, and prevents us from acknowledging either women's capacity to act as sexual agents or men's capacity for passivity.

Even sex experts like the authors of the NHSLS seem to accept unquestioningly some myths of penile prowess. They did not give men a questionnaire asking if they had ever been forced into sex by a woman, although, as you may recall, they asked women if they had been sexually forced by a man. The researchers did, however, ask both women and men whether, before puberty, they had ever been sexually touched by an older adolescent or an adult; 12 percent of the men and 17 percent of the women said yes.[15] Those who said yes were then asked to indicate their relationship to the perpetrator, using a list that included such possibilities as "father," "uncle," "mother's boy friend," "older brother," and "stepfather"; no female counterparts were listed, although, as it turned out, almost two-thirds of the males had been touched by older females.[16]

Furthermore, in their analysis of these results, the authors of the NHSLS deemed female participants who were touched before puberty "victims," but dismissed the males' experiences as "the behavior of sexually precocious boys" — even though 31 percent of them were six or younger at the time of the incident, and another 26 percent were between the ages of seven and ten![17] What's most astonishing about this girls-are-victims-but-boys-are-not argument is that the boys were far more likely than the girls to have had intercourse with older adolescents and adults: 42 percent as opposed to 14 percent.[18] Apparently, a pre-pubescent boy is in control of a heterosexual encounter with a much older person simply by virtue of the fact that he has a penis.

Such unwillingness to acknowledge the possibility of male sexual passivity is particularly curious given that passivity is, in fact, the most common element of male fantasies, according to men's own reports on their sexual daydreams and to research on male clients' requests of prostitutes.[19] Jim explains that his sexual fantasies typically involve "a woman taking charge from beginning to end. What's appealing about it is the idea of being wanted that much, but even more than that, being free of responsibility and pressure to perform. I guess it's wanting to be like some of the women I've been with, just lying back and not worrying about anything." Such fantasies probably also reflect his wish to have the physical experience of sex mirror his actual psychological experience of it.

This longing for sexual passivity, so inadmissible in a society where passivity is considered subordinate and effeminate, is nevertheless detectable in many quintessentially masculine forms of behavior. It helps to explain the appeal of lap dancing, in which a naked woman squirms around on the lap of a man who is not allowed to touch her, and to explain why some men in positions of considerable power and authority pay large amounts of money to be trussed up, spanked, and ordered around by dominatrixes. It also helps to explain why in so much pornography, violence against women is rare whereas scenes of men being enticed and seduced by ravenous or manipulative women are staple fare. What turns men on about these images is not simply the notion that women are ever willing, but the fantasy that women will take over and relieve them of sexual responsibility, guilt, and shame.

Regardless of their own behavior, many men often *feel* passive in sex, because, like Jim and Matt, bed is where they feel most defenseless emotionally and most prone to self-doubt. *Was it good for you? Did I do OK?* And, as we have seen, some men actually *are* passive in sex, manipulated into a position that seems active only because of the cultural meanings attached to the penis. Ironically, the myths of penile prowess that make us view men as invulnerable are precisely what make them vulnerable to psychological manipulation. Robin and Russell, for instance, could have prevailed in any physical struggle with Samantha and Jessica, but they could not resist the internal and external psychological pressure to act like "real men."

"It's pretty easy for a woman to play on your weaknesses and insecurities," explains Alan, a twenty-seven-year-old accountant. "She can put you in a position where you feel you have something to prove, and even if you don't want to, you wind up going ahead."

He's referring to a specific incident in his own recent past. "A few months ago, a buddy of mine set me up with a woman named Carol, who's a good friend of his wife. We went out a few times, but there was no spark. She was nice and cute and everything, just not my type. The last time we went out, we saw a movie and went back to her place for coffee. It was very casual, just hanging out," he says. "So it's the end of the evening, I'm getting ready to go, and she says, 'Do you want to spend the night?' I was surprised. There'd been no hint that we were heading in that direction at all. Under other circumstances I might have gone for it, but the mutual friend angle made it more complicated. There's a certain etiquette around one-night stands — it's awkward if you're going to see the person again socially. Plus it was a weeknight, I was tired. I just wasn't up for it."

He tried to turn Carol down courteously. "I said I wasn't looking for a relationship, which is the polite way of saying 'No thanks,' but she goes, 'That's cool, neither am I,' and starts taking her clothes off, very businesslike. Her attitude was, It's all decided, let's get started."

Alan didn't want to insult her, but he also didn't want to have sex with her. His attempts to handle the situation with delicacy and tact, however, backfired. "She's doing this striptease number, I'm making excuses, and then she says, 'What's the matter, don't you find me attractive?' That's rarely the issue, but women seem to think it is. The real issue was that I wanted a good night's sleep and I didn't want to get involved with her, so what was the point?" he says. "It was a no-win position, because I was saying, 'No, you're very attractive,' and she was saying, 'Then what's the problem?' It went like that for a few minutes and then she said, 'Oh I get it, you're gay.' I'm a tolerant guy and not a gay-basher, but to be honest, as soon as she said that, I felt like I had something to prove."

He protested that he was one hundred percent heterosexual, and she insinuated that he was protesting too much, a clear sign that he probably had latent homosexual urges. "Picture it: there's a half-naked woman pulling this Freudian trip on me, and in the back of my head I'm thinking, 'Uh oh, what if she goes and tells my buddy's wife that I'm gay?'" Alan says. "Rationally, I know my friend knows I'm straight, and I know it shouldn't matter anyway. But on another level, it's not rational. I felt like I had to convince this woman and there was only one way. It's stupid. You shouldn't have to prove what a man you are to anyone, but I felt like I had to."

So he headed off to the bedroom for a less than ecstatic experience. "I just went through the motions with an eye on the clock. The faster I got it over with, the sooner I could leave," he says. "I felt a little resentful, because I didn't want to be there, but there was an obligation to make sure she had a good time. If sex is mutual, you want to make the other person happy, but with her, it was just a duty. The whole thing was very mechanical and crass."

Alan, too, has fantasized about being the passive partner in sex, "but this was *not* what I imagined. For one thing, I had to perform. And in that fantasy, you *want* sex. Maybe you're not consenting at first, but you do want it, whereas in this situation, I didn't," he says. "I didn't enjoy it, but I wasn't really mad about it, either, not at first. What happened was that she phoned me the next week and I blew her off, and then a couple of weeks after that I found out through my friend that she was going around saying I was sexually conflicted. At that point, I did get pissed off. I couldn't win, no matter what I did. It shows you how counterproductive it is to think you have to rise to a challenge, so to speak. You just wind up feeling used."

Like women who believe in tidal waves, men who believe in penile prowess are susceptible to the manipulations of partners who know the right lines and cues. But whereas some women cannot give themselves permission to say yes, some men cannot give themselves permission to say no. And afterwards, men are supposed to be grateful: *well, at least I got some.*

Many, however, do not feel grateful, especially if they are manipulated by a woman who has the emotional upper hand. "It's hard to say no if you're crazy in love and she doesn't care as much about you," says Greg, a twenty-nine-year-old actor. "The person who cares most has the least power in a relationship. You can turn into a doormat, saying, 'I'll do whatever you want, just don't leave me.' That can carry over into sex, absolutely, so you wind up doing things you don't really want to do."

Such was the case with Angela, his girlfriend when he was twenty-five. "I was totally obsessed with her. Anything she wanted, I was there. It's funny to talk about those relationships when you're out of them, but when you're in them, you're really in them. The world stops and all you want to do is be with that person," he remembers. "Angela realized she had me on a string, and the less she wanted the relationship, the more she took advantage of me. Near the end, she was threatening to leave all the time, throwing that in my face on a daily basis and using it as leverage."

One example readily springs to mind. "We were in Central Park and she said, 'Drop your pants.' I was like, 'Excuse me?' She said, 'Do it. Fuck me right now.' I didn't want to because it was a public place, but she was adamant. There was a very apocalyptic feel to the situation, like the relationship hung in the balance, so at a certain point I said OK and dropped my pants," he remembers. "There was an S&M element to it where she was trying to increase the humiliation factor. 'Everyone can see you, they're all laughing at you, you're so pathetic.' I was young enough to think, 'Oh, I guess this is cool, she's being so forceful, whether I want it or not.' It takes men longer to realize that it's not cool when someone else is treating you badly."

In Greg's case, that realization took only a few days, because Angela dumped him anyway. "I didn't feel dirty or ashamed, but taken advantage of, yes. The episode in the park stands out in my mind because it was so uncomfortable and humiliating. I don't even think she wanted sex particularly, it was more a case of, How far can I push him? I felt used, foolish, sexually inadequate," he says. "But see, I think that's just what happens when you're young. You get in these twisted relationships where you're exploited because you'll do anything to keep the other person. I've been on the other end, where women were crawling after me and I was the one calling the shots, and I know there were times when they had sex to try to keep me. I don't think it has anything to do with gender. It really just boils down to who cares most. Sex is where the power dynamic gets played out because it's the main thing that makes the relationship different from all your other relationships."

Today, men receive conflicting messages about masculinity. They are told to be more sensitive, but they are also told they must be sexually ever ready. They are told they are incompetent in the area of intimacy, yet they are also widely ridiculed if they make any public remarks that sound even vaguely touchy-feely. Unlike women, who are instructed to behave the same way in the private and public spheres — nurturing, cooperative, empathic — men are instructed to conform to traditional masculine stereotypes in public but to emulate women's intimacy expertise in private. Many of those who try say they are, nevertheless, punished for their efforts.

"Women say they want good listeners and men who can talk about their feelings, but then they dump you because you're 'not a challenge,'" says Michael, twenty-seven, a graphic designer. "I've heard that from three women now. At first I thought it meant I didn't make enough money or wasn't ambitious enough, but that can't be right. I know guys who don't even have jobs but who have no problem finding a woman to sponge off — they treat women really badly, and a lot of women seem to want that. They get off on the melodrama. Women get bored if they know they can count on you, because it's not 'romantic,' there's no conflict. It drives me crazy when I hear women complaining that there are no nice single men, because I'm having the same problem: I can't find a nice single woman who's really serious about a relationship."

Many of the men I interviewed expressed similar sentiments. Women, they said, were only attracted to men who conformed to traditional masculine stereotypes: rugged, unfeeling, unemotional, powerful, aggressive. Women, they told me, were the ones with all the power in relationships, because they dictated the terms of intimacy.

"The problem is that a lot of women only want to talk about feelings, which really means, 'Let's talk about us,'" Jerome, a thirty-three-year-old engineer, suggests. "It's narcissistic in a way, and I just don't think it's useful or even healthy to analyze your relationship on a daily basis. With my last girlfriend, every time I tried to talk about something else she'd accuse me of trying to avoid having a conversation. Talking about Bosnia or whatever didn't count. There's something screwed up about the idea that talking about what's going on in the world is less worthwhile than analyzing the dynamic of your relationship for the hundredth time. As far as I'm concerned, the relationship is very shallow if all you're doing is navel-gazing. And I don't think it's fair that everything I want to do is wrong because I'm a man. That's not equality."

Jeff, a thirty-one-year-old journalist, agrees. "There's a prevailing sense that women have a monopoly on feeling bad, and then that's wielded as an ideological stick. Men are trying to regain a stake in the private realm. They don't want to repeat their fathers' mistakes, but it's very hard because of this idea that men are emotionally stunted and everything we do is wrong, or immature, or hurts somebody."

Among his friends, Jeff says, the women are equal to the men in terms of earning power and the ability to control dinner table conversation. "They're successful, funny, charismatic women, but they don't admit that they are these strong characters. If it's ever raised, which is rare, they immediately lapse into victim stereotyping," he observes. "Sex is really at the root of it — it tends to hang over and shadow a lot of other issues. Male sexuality is invoked to stand for other sorts of power that men are said to possess, and every argument seems to come down to, Men rape, therefore women are powerless."

But, Jeff says, he and many other men have not and never would commit rape: "One of the lessons we've absorbed is that you don't just monster a woman. You don't jump her. I'm so afraid of being thought sleazy or lecherous that I don't declare myself. I hang back, but a lot of women find that very annoying, too. They want men to conform to stereotypes, but only when it's convenient for them. So we're caught in this strange trap, where men are supposed to be powerful but they don't feel that they are, and women have all kinds of power they won't admit to having."

This is the trap of oppositional thinking, and it is most constraining for women, who are taught to fear men and to think of themselves as the done-to, rather than as moral and sexual actors. So long as myths of penile prowess persist, and so long as we continue to equate male domination with male sexuality, female sexual agency will seem like an illusory, far-off goal rather than a here-and-now reality. When sexual agency is defined not in terms of biology or positive outcomes but in terms of choice — as it is for men — then it becomes obvious that many women already possess it. Any woman who of her own accord says yes to sex is demonstrating agency; any woman who feels stirred by desire is at that moment a sexual subject. Sexual agency has nothing to do with morality and it is certainly no guarantee of happy endings; if it ensured good behavior and everlasting bliss, then men would have been perfect creatures for centuries now.

Sexual agency merely consists of the ability to make free choices, and many of us, women as well as men, make decisions that later look like mistakes, either to us or to other people. We embark on sex with high hopes that come to nought, we make decisions that seem sensible at the time but we later regret them, and we behave in ways that hurt ourselves and/or other people.

Yet there is a public unwillingness to admit that women have the capacity to make mistakes. Although men as well as women are influenced and constrained by social forces when it comes to sex, only men are held to a standard of individual accountability — as they should be — while extravagant conspiracy theories are invented to absolve women of any wrongdoing. Assumptions about female moral superiority pervade the public discourse, where unhappy women are never authors of their own fate. Rather, they are whipsawed by the patri-archy and mistreated by individual men.

Likewise, there is a public unwillingness to admit that women, too, feel the tug of desire. We are not supposed to lust or yearn, but we do, all of us, sometimes in strange places. Whatever the circum-stances, female desire should be applauded, because it marks us as full-fledged sexual agents. Being able to say "I want" is the proof of our ownership of sex.

"How many of you ladies want to see some naked men?" the DJ asks. The response is unequivocal: eighty-four heads turn to face the dance floor in the center of the room. Conversations are abandoned, cigarettes are lit, and as the music surges, the DJ begins calling out a string of announcements: "Congratulations going out tonight to Deanna, celebrating her divorce!" Deanna, a plump young woman with big hair, is surrounded by six women friends, all of whom begin applauding vigorously. "Go, girl!" a woman across the room yells, and Deanna beams, giggles, and hoists her drink in the air.

So this is what she's been missing: going out with the girls on a weeknight, out to where the suburbs trail off and the highway begins, ordering shooters while naked men grovel for tips. Here, there's no shame about those extra few pounds, no need to smile coyly or feign interest in the guy's opinions, no fear of rejection. Deanna looks happy, and when the DJ makes the next announcement — "Good luck to Sharon, who's getting married next week" — she brays, "Big mistake, Sharon. Take it from me!"

It's the kind of cheerfully seedy place, complete with disco ball, brass rails and frayed armchairs, that encourages rowdy goodwill. The club is in a suburb of Toronto, but it could be anywhere in North America, and the patrons, most of whom are in their twenties and thir-ties, could be any women. The audience contains a mix of skin colors and body shapes and tastes in clothes, but despite the variety there are none of the sad, lonely losers who hover at the edges of every strip club for men. In fact, some of the women are exceptionally attractive, all hair and teeth and legs. A few are regulars, and clearly enjoy the fact that the beefy waiters in threadbare tuxes know them by name.

The DJ finishes his announcements: Sue Ann's birthday, Marcella's new job. "And now," he says, "let's have a big hand for Christopher." He says something about posing for *Playgirl* and winning a body-building contest, but Christopher's accomplishments are all but drowned out by the collective roar of women eager for a good time. He prances out onto the stage to the tune of "Born to Be Wild," sporting shades, black pants with zippers all the way down both legs, and a fixed smile. You would think, given the commotion, that these women had not seen a man for years. And maybe it's true that no one has seen a man quite like Christopher, who is deeply tanned and has a complicated coiffure of streaked curls that remain firmly in place as he gyrates around the stage.

In short order his shirt is off and he's running his hands all over his chest, flexing his abs and preening for the crowd. Deliberately, in time to the music, he shimmies over to a table of secretaries and pre-sents his backside for their inspection. They whoop their approval.

But this is nothing compared to what happens during the next song, when he undoes the zippers on his pants and they crumple deli-cately to the floor, revealing a neon-green shred of underwear. May-hem ensues. His dancing now takes the minimalist form of thrusting his hips in slow, wide circles. The smile is gone from his face, his eyes are focused on nothing in particular, and he removes the underwear, gently hopping from one foot to the other. By law, male dancers are required to hold a towel in front of themselves if they are fully nude, but Christopher's is the size of a washcloth. Not nearly big enough, at any rate, to disguise what's behind it: a semi-erect penis, springing off to the left, which slaps around lazily during his slow-motion twirls and loops.

"*Oh my God*," the women gasp as one. Deanna scrabbles blindly through her purse for her wallet, not taking her eyes off this sight for even a second. Husband, the sour bickering of marriage, divorce — all that goes clear out of her head as Christopher waves the scrap of cloth, playing peek-a-boo with the crowd. She tucks a ten-dollar bill into her bra and marches up to the stage, while Christopher dances across to meet her. Amidst appreciative squealing and hollering, he lowers himself to his hands and knees and then kisses his way up her body, retrieving the bill with his teeth. She does not touch him, that's not permitted, but she is clearly tempted; in order to refrain, she holds her hands behind her back as though waiting to be handcuffed. Throughout, she does not take her eyes off his penis, and afterward, she returns to her table fanning her face like a vaudeville trouper. Another woman takes her place on stage, nervously shifting from one foot to the other while Christopher wriggles and shimmies for all he's worth, which in this case is a crumpled handful of small bills.

Some of the women going up to the stage are clearly acting on dares from their girlfriends; others display no hesitation or embarrassment whatsoever. One woman flings herself onto her back, and Christopher performs push-ups over her body, almost but not quite touching her, finally tugging the money from her waistband and pulling her to her feet. With another woman, he's even more explicit: he heaves her up onto the brass rail surrounding the stage and mimes jackhammer thrusting, while she throws her head back and howls at the ceiling.

Then his three songs are up and there's a graceless moment after the applause, as he scrambles around the stage like a janitor, collecting various items of clothing. He pulls his underwear back on and positions himself by the bar, scanning the crowd for outstretched arms holding bills, hoping to be called over for a table-dance, which is where the real money is. No luck. A black man with long cornrow braids has taken the stage and he's break-dancing, spinning around on the ground and scissoring his legs back and forth and up and down, so that his leopard-print G-string flashes by in a blur. Christopher is forgotten; Deanna doesn't even look his way. She's waving a bill in the air as though signaling from ship to shore, summoning the new man out of the spotlight and over to her table.

As the evening progresses, the crowd appraises the men more skeptically, less generous with applause and tips. The fifth dancer, a man with long, dark hair and improbably muscle-bound proportions, arouses almost no interest at all. He's no less attractive than the others, but he has a glazed, caught-in-the-headlights diffidence. He seems not to have figured out that what the women respond to and reward is a caricature of masculinity, free of complications and self-doubt. The pleasure for them is all in the power of bringing a strong man to his knees: a mere snap of the fingers and he scampers over, anxious to please.

The women talk among themselves, paying no attention as this man dances away, so obviously uncomfortable that it's hard not to feel embarrassed for him. Deanna takes this opportunity to go the rest room. The spectacle of a naked man bobbing around the stage to heavy metal music is faintly ludicrous if he can't pretend that he's enjoying himself and there's nothing he would rather do than satisfy her. She came here to indulge a fantasy of omnipotence, to allow herself to be convinced that these hardbodied men are readily available and eager to prostrate themselves, worship her body, and fulfil all her secret desires.

This guy is too self-conscious, too much in need of reassurance, too much like an ordinary man. Calling him over to the table would be an act of charity, and Deanna is not feeling particularly charitable this evening. "He reminds me of my ex," she says on her way to the bathroom. "And his butt jiggles."

Christopher, still in his underwear, is lounging in the hall. "Hey," he says as she sails past, thrusting his chest out hopefully and flashing a don't-you-want-me-baby smile. But Deanna doesn't stop, just carries on to the bathroom, rushing a bit now. In a minute the next act, promisingly titled "Burning Desire," will start, and she doesn't want to miss a moment.

Thirty years ago, the prospect of clean-cut young women exchanging money for the favors of male strippers was unimaginable. Even today, strip clubs for women may seem to be a lark, or an exercise in irony: so tacky, they're hip. But some women who go to strip clubs are there to lust, stare openly, fantasize, and buy a few minutes of undivided sexual attention. Some women entertain the notion that the stripper notices and likes them, genuinely enjoys dancing for them, and is not merely simulating interest in the hope of a bigger tip — precisely the fantasy that some men who go to topless bars entertain.

Outside a strip club, of course, men are not defined by their looks to the extent that women are, although it is increasingly true that men's bodies are used to sell products. Commercials showing men cleaning the toilet and doing the laundry contend with those depicting young men lounging around in their underwear and sinewy construction workers being ogled by businesswomen. The cultural stereotype of the masculine sex object is every bit as much a caricature as its feminine counterpart, and in some respects seems more difficult for ordinary men to emulate. Women can mask a variety of "imperfections" with makeup, cosmetic surgery, and undergarments with hydraulic properties, but without the right genes and a single-minded dedication to exercise, men cannot achieve the requisite muscle definition. And no amount of bodybuilding will turn a man who is short, bald, weak-jawed, pigeon-chested, or hair-matted into an idol.

The more social and economic power women have, the freer they are to appraise men, quite openly, on the basis of their looks and sex appeal, and the more exacting their standards become. This is not to say that women no longer worry about their own looks and are no longer portrayed as brainless sex bombs. But within a generation or two, there may be something approaching parity in terms of sexual objectification. Even today, male versions of the dumb blonde abound in sitcoms and movies, and they are every bit as adorably kittenish and hopelessly vapid as their female counterparts.

And even today, some women openly admire men's bodies, making no secret of the impurity of their thoughts and the shape of their desires. Women and couples comprise an increasing proportion of the audience for pornographic videos, and women are now producing pornography themselves, ranging from soft-core heterosexual romances to literary erotica to hard-core girls-just-want-to-have-fun videos to S&M lesbian magazines.

Contrary to popular opinion, numerous studies show that women are just as physiologically aroused by pornography as men are.[20] "As soon as you turn on an erotic film clip, you immediately see an increase in vaginal blood flow," reports Ellen T. M. Laan, a psychologist at the University of Amsterdam.[21] Furthermore, although physiological measures of female arousal do not vary between types of films, women report much higher subjective levels of arousal — "I liked that" — to pornography in which women are active sexual subjects rather than passive sexual objects.[22]

Anyone who perceives women's lust as a paler, gentler shadow of men's has not attended a male bikini contest or a shopping mall appearance by a male star of a daytime soap, where teenage girls and grandmothers alike scream "Take it off!" and "Look at those buns!" At these events, some women climb over barricades and tackle bodyguards to try to secure locks of hair from the object of their desire, or deliver up-close-and-personal propositions.

When women are not yelling "Pick me!" to a shirtless man with a washboard stomach, but are doing the picking and choosing themselves, they approach the task with equal enthusiasm, judging from the annual bachelor auction that raises funds for the Multiple Sclerosis Society of Canada. The auction is a decidedly upscale affair that attracts hundreds of well-heeled businesswomen and society ladies. Armed with a glossy brochure listing such particulars as the bachelors' height, eye color, age, and hobbies, the women appraise each tuxedoed man as he struts his stuff down the runway, then bid thousands of dollars to secure weeklong vacations with the men of their choice in places like Rio and Paris. Any bachelor who goes on the auction block entertaining notions about women's demure appetites is disabused the moment he starts down the runway, when — if he is attractive, and smart enough to grovel — the whistling and catcalls begin, amidst spirited bulletins from the bidders regarding how, exactly, they intend to get their money's worth.

The women are nothing if not discriminating, and their commitment to charity does not extend to bidding on men with stooped shoulders and spreading bottoms. A man's appearance and sex appeal determine his market value, and in 1994, a mere weekend in New York with a 6'3" bachelor who had impressive biceps and bedroom eyes touched off a bidding war that culminated north of $5,000. Weeklong vacations with chinless, plump bachelors fetched less than half that

price, even though the destinations were more exotic and the auction-
eer literally begged for higher bids. Those bachelors who commanded
only suppressed titters and bargain-basement prices scurried from the
stage dazed with embarrassment, having discovered at least one un-
hoped-for answer to Freud's question about what women want.

Bachelor auctions and women pornographers are hardly everyday
features on the sexual landscape, but the himbo, toy-boy, and male
pinup are not just fads. They are here to stay, along with male groom-
ing products, penile implants and the Hair Club for Men. Whether
thirty years from now a book will appear damning the male beauty
myth remains to be seen, but in the meantime, many women are enjoying the power of the female gaze and are having a good laugh about the
amount of time men now spend in front of the mirror in the morning.

Although any number of male stars from Clark Gable to the Beat-
les have evoked hormonal hysteria, women are now beginning to express the same kind of appreciation for well-built nobodies in strip
clubs and mere men on the street. Expressing random, purely sexual
desire for anonymous men is a dramatic change for women who have
been trained to blush at the mention of sex and to vent pent-up desires only on icons. It is powerful for women to own desire and to
feel lust, to view themselves as sexual actors instead of as the acted-
upon, and to view men as erotic enticements rather than mere meal
tickets. Women are stronger when they escape the trap of binary
thinking, where they must be good girls and where desire means
only desiring the state of being desired.

In relationships, too, owning desire is good for women — and
men. Women who view themselves solely as erotic lures for their
boyfriends and husbands often feel weak and anxious. *He doesn't want
to have sex — does that mean he's not attracted to me any more? Does it
mean he doesn't love me any more?* Women who own their sexual selves,
who feel a right to express and explore their desire for men (or for
women), feel much stronger. And they *are* stronger, because they are
fully embracing equality, and challenging destructive myths about penile prowess and female innocence.

Many, many men *want* women to embrace sexual equality; in relationships where women are sexual equals, there is much less performance

pressure on men, and women are much less likely to use sex coercively, as a reward or punishment. As we have seen, many young women now initiate sex, and most young men want them to do so. Men don't want women to initiate sex solely because they themselves want more sex. Rather, men want women to want them, and men do not want to feel that sexual pleasure is something for which they bear sole responsibility. Many men would also like to drop the macho costume, and would like the freedom to be themselves in sexual relationships: weak as well as strong, passive as well as aggressive, wanted as well as wanting.

Interestingly, some women are beginning to complain that men can't keep up with *their* desires, and some men are beginning to employ the traditional feminine tactic of withholding sex to get power in a relationship. "Feeling inadequate or threatened by perceived loss of control, some men withhold sex as a means of restoring the 'power balance,'" explains clinical psychologist and sex therapist Janet L. Wolfe. She adds, "while women see sex as a stress *reducer*, a means of connection and source of joy, too many men now view sex as still one *more* stressor, one more area in which they have to 'perform.'"[23]

As with sex, so with love and friendship: owning desire and articulating what we want, need, and expect makes women stronger and happier. This sounds obvious, but a lot of us aren't doing it. So many women are driven by fears of being disliked that they rarely ask themselves, "What am *I* getting out of this relationship? Do *I* like this person? Am *I* satisfied?" We assume a reactive rather than an active stance, and spend a great deal of time worrying about what other people think of us instead of whether other people are good to us — and good *for* us.

Lately it has become fashionable to blame men for this tendency: apparently women's problem is the beauty myth, or the patriarchal virus of low self-esteem, or the media backlash. But men aren't entirely responsible for all women's problems, least of all in the realm of intimacy, where women are supposed to reign supreme.

The truth is that the kind of intimacy women are expert at creating is not always good for us, and it certainly doesn't answer all our needs.

In fact, women who take their measure through relationships are doubly handicapped: they don't feel they have permission to express the less-than-superior feelings that close relationships sometimes evoke, and they live in terror of abandonment. Telling women that they have unique emotional gifts only compounds the problem, because then women have dangerous delusions of power: *I can fix other people, make them love me, and live happily ever after.* But other people are far more difficult to control than, say, one's own performance at the gym, in school, or on the job. Moreover, the kind of power that's available in these kinds of relationships makes women feel distinctly out of control, simultaneously vulnerable and overburdened.

"Before I met my husband, I had a series of relationships where my heart was ripped out and thrown against the wall," explains Catherine, a thirty-year-old full-time mother. "My problem was that I had a fatal attraction to maladjusted men. I was going to make the difference, and that's a very compelling idea, that you can be the source of happiness and the person who pulls their life together. You flatter yourself into thinking that you have the power to change another person. There's a kind of machismo about it: 'Yes, he's manic-depressive and has a drinking problem, but I can fix him.' A man who treats you well and behaves like a grown-up seems boring. Where's the challenge, the excitement? I see this with my single friends all the time. They say, 'Oh, he doesn't have an edge,' or, 'He's just so predictable.' They're not ready for a relationship with an equal, someone who's reliable and mature and doesn't need a psychological makeover."

Invariably, women seem to be the ones who wind up feeling diminished and frustrated when they treat men not as equals but as little boys who must be indulged and instructed. "For the first few years of my marriage, I acted like my mother," says Naomi, a thirty-four-year-old health care executive. "I had a death grip on the household and wouldn't let go. I'd say, 'Gee Mark, such and such needs doing,' and feel angry that I had to articulate it and angry that I had to stand over him and supervise him while he did it. Then I got a job where I'm on the road a few days a week, and he got very proficient at keeping things running and initiating everything himself. I can see now that one of the reasons he didn't do that before was that I wouldn't let him. I was always putting myself in charge and then resenting him for not taking charge but at the same time, not permitting him."

We say we want intimacy, but frequently we behave as though what we're really after is control. We try to control men so they won't leave; we try to control other women's opinions so they won't say mean things about us. But these are things we *can't* control (though we certainly can make ourselves miserable trying to do so), and even if we could, most of us would soon become deeply bored. How could we respect or remain interested in or truly be close to people who bent themselves so readily to our will? The truth of the matter is that difference keeps relationships, whether sexual or platonic, lively, challenging, and rewarding.

"My best friend, Nancy, is a lawyer, so she really knows how to argue," says Carrie, a twenty-nine-year-old grade school teacher. "We don't do that dance of accommodation. In fact, we argue all the time, mostly about politics. It can get very heated, but at the same time it's safe, because we're still friends at the end of it. We can be screaming at each other across the dinner table about welfare reform but it doesn't mean we don't like each other. I love being pushed by her intellectually — it saves me from complacency."

The experience of open contest in a friendship, Carrie says, has had positive effects elsewhere in her life. "I used to take it very personally if I had a disagreement with another teacher or with a parent. Criticism got under my skin to the point where I'd toss and turn at night, beating myself up over it," she says. "What I've learned from Nancy is that having a disagreement isn't the same as being disliked, the two things aren't necessarily connected. I think I'm more effective at dealing with conflicts at work now because my emotions are less involved, I don't get so prickly. The reality is that some people are going to dislike you, no matter what, so you might as well speak your mind."

Let's be honest: one of the main reasons women's voices sound "different" is that we so frequently censor, edit, and silence ourselves, especially with other women. If intimacy expertise means feeling that we don't have a right to speak our minds — and believing other women are too fragile to handle the truth, and men are so obtuse that they just don't understand — then it is cause for condemnation, not celebration.

Ironically, though we cling to power in the emotional sphere, we can't seem to disown it fast enough in the sexual sphere. Although most women are not following the modern script, many are paying lip service to it or are still using it to try to interpret their experiences. The woman who has sex with a man she barely knows, or who poaches on another woman's territory, or who cheats on her own partner, or who has an affair with the boss can always refer to the modern script to establish an alibi: "*He* was the one who started it. I was swept away."

When sexual relationships turn out disappointingly, however, many women struggle against the it's-not-your-fault mantra of the modern script. Our friends tend to scold us for this: "There was nothing you could have done. He's a jerk, that's all." Sometimes that's an accurate analysis of the situation. There are certainly plenty of exploitative men in the world, and some of them are such good actors that they can bamboozle even the most canny and self-aware woman.

But sometimes we continue to resist, saying, "It *was* my fault," and, "I should have known." This is more than just the standard pose of the martyr — it is the posture of a woman trying to preserve her self-respect. By blaming ourselves, we protest the notion that we are just helpless puppets who've been jerked around and we reject the deeply insulting image of ourselves as powerless dupes. That self-image is wounding to our pride, and provides little hope that we will ever be capable of controlling our own destinies. Thus, we do the wrong thing — blame ourselves — for all the right reasons.

The truth of the matter is that a lot of the time, it *was* our fault and we really *should* have known. But taking responsibility at the time, not blame afterward, is the only way we will ever be able to feel that we are in control of our own lives. Could have, should have, would have — self-blame is a rearguard action. It is too much, too late, and it frequently makes women feel even worse about whatever defeat they have suffered. Responsibility doesn't require self-flagellation; it requires recognizing when and where we have choices, and being accountable to ourselves for the ones we make.

Women love, men lust — clearly, the real story is much more complicated, and far more interesting. The truth is that women are capable of all kinds of emotions and behavior — and so are men. But

this simple fact is a hard sell, because the habit of oppositional thinking is continually reinforced in our culture. From greeting cards to
news stories, from sitcoms to self-help bestsellers, from academic
studies to common wisdom, we get variants of the same message:
women want relationships, men fear intimacy; women are nurturing,
men are aggressive.

The world would be a simpler place if men and women really
were from different planets, aliens to each other with different psy-
ches, different desires, and different cultures. There would be no
confusion about where we stood or what we could expect. Change
would be impossible, of course, and war between the sexes would be
inevitable, but at least we would know where the battle lines were
drawn and who our allies were.

Change, however, is what most women want. We want equal opportunities, we want to get along with men, and we want to feel that
we have some control over our own lives. Over the past thirty years,
we have struggled to achieve these things, and in so doing have become adept at recognizing, naming, and challenging sexism. We have
debunked old myths: a woman's place is in the kitchen, a woman isn't
capable of doing a man's job, a woman who has sex before marriage is
a slut. Yet in struggling for equality, we have embraced some new
myths: we are more-than-equal when it comes to caring, sharing, and
keeping the peace, and we are more spiritual than sexual in the boardroom, the bedroom, and every place in between.

But we collude in perpetuating our own powerlessness and unhappiness when we continue to believe that men and women are psychological opposites. We close our eyes to all the evidence of women's
and men's similarities, our best hope for getting the kinds of equal
relationships we say we want with men. Instead, we learn to fear
male power, when what we really need to understand is male vulnerability. And we are coached to think that our own strength resides in
moral superiority, which is in fact the source of our most debilitating
weakness: a belief that we must remain good girls, forever unequal
and only half human.

Conclusion

Self-determination is what women want, but the myth of female moral superiority tells us that women cannot be actors in their own right. Apparently, women are too pure to harbor negative feelings and too virtuous to make mistakes. Agency — having some control over one's own life — is confused with happy endings. When things turn out well, women are given full credit, but when something goes wrong, we are absolved of responsibility.

Women are in a curious position: we have more power than ever before, largely as a result of feminism, yet many women say they feel powerless, and some are now blaming feminism. But feminists aren't the problem any more than men are the problem. The real problem is that the script for women's lives has not caught up with reality: we still learn that our lives should revolve around relationships, we still learn that men are sex-crazed bad boys, and we still learn that we should behave like good girls with our friends, colleagues, and lovers. Although some feminists do promote these messages, directly or indirectly, most do not. At any rate, these are messages we get from numerous sources, including the mass media, academia, politicians, educators, and the entertainment industry.

Whatever other effects these messages have, they are disastrous for young girls. One of the main reasons that one million American teenage girls become pregnant every year is that they do not use contraception. Having birth control on hand indicates that they expect and want to have intercourse, and many of them believe it is more shameful and more harmful to admit to sexual desire than to become pregnant or expose themselves to sexually transmitted diseases. About half of all teenage girls who get pregnant give birth, and only 10 percent of them put their babies up for adoption; teen mothers and their children are the poorest and most disadvantaged group in American society.

One million teenage pregnancies annually is an alarming number in light of the fact that right-wing politicians are succeeding in rolling back abortion rights and are threatening to kick teen mothers off the welfare rolls. It is an astonishing number in light of the fact that teenage girls today have better access to contraception and sex education than ever before.

Consider, however, that these girls grow up with the modern script, in which sex means only love or subjugation for women. They turn on the TV and see images of women who have sex and get love, women whose sexuality is depicted as a way to snare men, and women who are sexual victims. They switch channels and see images of romance as the primary goal and greatest joy of life, and see also that sex is *the* symbol of romance. Every day they are getting the message that sex is either a shortcut to intimacy or shorthand for victimization, but they are not getting positive images of women desiring, women as subjects, women taking charge sexually. They have no realistic idea of what female sexual pleasure looks like, since in most Hollywood films there is zero foreplay and women are portrayed as ecstatic enthusiasts of intercourse. Most teenage girls do not have a clue of what it means to own sex.

Currently, girls are taught defensive sexuality: how to say No, how to use birth control, how to react to *boys* who want sex. But scary lectures about the plight of teen moms and the ravages of disease present sexual responsibility only as an unpleasant duty that females must shoulder to avoid dire consequences. Telling girls that sex may bring heartbreak or worse doesn't work when the other option seems to be eternal love; telling them that sex may make victims of them doesn't work when the other option seems to be that sex may make victors of them.

Another reason that scare tactics don't work is that girls have sexual feelings and unbridled curiosity. They need to be taught that the worst thing to do with their desire is to suppress it or feel guilty about it or seek to deny its existence by failing to take contraceptive precautions. More than anything, they need to be aware of the wide range of sexual choices they have, so they will learn to view their sexuality as more than a bargaining chip to get love and as more than a site of oppression. Perhaps the most unfair thing we do to girls in this culture is to tell them they are blameless innocents right up to the moment they get a positive pregnancy test, when we begin pointing fingers and blaming them for destroying the fibre of our society. Needless to say, many girls are thoroughly bewildered by these mixed messages.

Girls urgently need female role models who are powerful sexual subjects, and an expanded notion of responsibility that includes the responsibility to honor their own sexuality by making good choices and feeling an absolute entitlement to pleasure. Girls need the rest of us to start talking honestly about what sex really means to us; we need to show them, through example, that they can become sexual agents and that there is more power for them in their own desire than in men's desire for them. Girls need to get the message that they are entitled to pleasure and that they are unlikely to get it if they cannot communicate their desires and if they are having sex primarily because they fear being dumped.

Frankly, if girls were taught that the minimum requirement for getting into bed with someone was being able to articulate their own sexual desires, many of them would be waiting a whole lot longer to have sex. Even adults who are long past the acute self-consciousness of adolescence find it difficult to say "I want" or "Touch me here" or "This is how I like it." Furthermore, if girls were taught that the *minimum* measure of a good sexual relationship is that they themselves get physical enjoyment out of it, they would not consent to having sex when they're so terrified of being judged that they are willing to risk pregnancy or disease. In fact, if girls got stronger messages about the importance of their own sexual pleasure — say, that pleasure is something they have both a right to demand from their partners and a responsibility to ensure for themselves — fewer of them would be having sex at such young ages with boys who don't have the faintest idea of how to please them.

Girls need to learn sexual agency as well as self-defence. Let there be no mistake: this is not an argument for promiscuity but for sexual power. Girls need to know that men do not feel nearly as powerful and women are not nearly as powerless as the modern script says. If they believe they are powerless, they believe they have no choices; if they know they are powerful, they see not only that they have choices but also rights and responsibilities. The modern script is a fiasco for girls because it encourages them to forge an identity that revolves around powerlessness, when in fact they have unparalleled opportunities for real power.

Appealing to their desire for power is far more effective than appealing to them on the grounds that they have a responsibility to their bodies. After all, they do not view their bodies as sacred vessels; they torture their hair, experiment with drugs and alcohol, race around without helmets on bicycles and without seatbelts in cars, stay up late and subsist on candy bars, or starve themselves until they faint in history class. But girls do want power. We should be telling them that they already have it, but they forfeit it the instant they deny responsibility for their own choices and actions.

All women need to think about this. We need to abandon the politics of sexual terror, with its false oppositions, and develop a politics of error, in which we allow ourselves and other women to make mistakes. For women, progress requires dispensing with the notion that we are men's opposites — and one another's duplicates, psychologically and sexually. It is this pressure to tailor ourselves to limiting roles and to deny our differences that makes women the most effective police of the borders of sexual correctness and the most formidable wardens in the prison of female moral superiority. We need to learn to view our differences not as threats to our solidarity but as the best protection of our collective power to choose.

The modern script does not allow individual women to see themselves as they really are, and self-knowledge is the only way forward.

If we want self-determination, we have to challenge the idea that agency is only present in happy endings. We have to resist, strenuously, the temptation to flee from responsibility because equality does not look the way we thought it would and power is not as glamorous as we'd hoped. Most important, we must reject entirely the notion of our own essential innocence. It is, in the end, a lie that costs us nothing less than everything: our power to choose a new kind of future for ourselves, one in which we are more than victims and less than saints, fully human and the equals of any man.

Notes

Chapter One: Best of Friends

1. Seidman, 1991, p. 91.
2. Cancian, 1987, p. 15.
3. Ibid., p. 18.
4. Ibid., p. 23.
5. Ibid., p. 24.
6. Quoted in Segal, 1994, p. 46.
7. Chodorow, 1978, p. 167.
8. Ibid., p. 291.
9. Gilligan, 1982, p. 8.
10. Cited in Wood and Inman, 1993, p. 284.
11. See Tavris, 1992, pp. 79–90, and Sommers, 1994, pp. 152–54, for discussions of academic criticism of Gilligan's findings.
12. Tavris, 1992, p. 60.
13. Ibid., p. 87.
14. Quoted in Wood and Inman, 1993, p. 287. They review college textbooks and academic research, and find a consistent bias against the "masculine" style of intimacy.
15. Ibid., p. 281.
16. Scott Swain, "Covert Intimacy: Closeness in Men's Friendships," in Risman and Schwartz (eds.), 1989, pp. 71–86. Swain reports that the male subjects in his research expressed intimacy with close friends by doing favors, competing, joking, touching, telling one

another about achievements, and sharing activities. For reviews of research on intimacy in men's same-sex friendships, see Wood and Inman, 1993, pp. 289–92, and Duck and Wright, 1993, pp. 709–13.

17. Cancian, 1987, p. 74.
18. Ibid., p. 75.
19. Monsour, 1992, p. 280.
20. Ibid., p. 285.
21. Ibid., p. 286.
22. Ibid., pp. 293–94.
23. Wood, 1993, pp. 40–41.
24. Wood and Inman, 1993, p. 282: "As feminine criteria for closeness went unchallenged, women's friendships were regularly described [by researchers] as closer than men's, and women's verbal, emotional style was advanced as the model for intimacy."
25. Eichenbaum and Orbach, 1988, p. 89.
26. Ibid., p. 170.
27. DePaulo, Epstein, and Wyer, 1993, p. 143.
28. Tavris, 1992, p. 268.
29. DePaulo, Epstein, and Wyer, 1993.

Chapter Two: Lies of Sisterhood

1. Sommers, 1994, p. 17.
2. Susan Faludi, "I'm Not a Feminist, But I Play One on TV," *Ms.,* March/April 1995, p. 39.
3. Evelyn Fox Keller and Helene Moglen, "Competition: A Problem for Academic Women," in Miner and Longino (eds.), 1987, p. 34.
4. Florence L. Geis, "Self-Fulfilling Prophecies: A Social Psychological View of Gender," in Beall and Sternberg (eds.), 1993, p. 24. Geis reviews numerous studies showing that so-called gender differences actually reflect power differences; when women are assigned the dominant, more powerful role in experiments, they behave in what we think of as "masculine" ways.
5. For a review of academic studies, see Bernice Lott and Diane Maluso, "The Social Learning of Gender," in Beall and Sternberg (eds.), 1993. Also of interest is Wheelan and Verdi's finding that stereotypical gender differences in communication patterns disappear after the first thirty to sixty minutes of a group meeting; thereafter, there are no significant gender differences in terms of

men's and women's amount or style of verbal input. See Wheelan and Verdi, 1992.

6. This phrase was coined by Paula Ross, "Women, Oppression, Privilege, and Competition," in Miner and Longino (eds.), 1987. Ross argues that an "oppression derby," in which women compete downward for the title of worst off, perpetuates the status quo.

7. Lakoff, 1990, p. 205.

Chapter Three: Potent Pleasures

1. Jeffrey Rosen, "Cheap Speech," *The New Yorker*, August 7, 1995, pp. 76–77.

2. See Fekete, 1994, and Sommers, 1994, for in-depth discussions of high-profile sexual harassment charges in universities.

3. Richardson, 1985, p.58.

4. Ibid., p. 105.

5. Ibid., p. 98.

6. See Karen Dion and Ellen Berscheid, "What is Beautiful is Good," *Journal of Personality and Social Psychology*, *24* (1972), pp. 285–90. Also Robert Agnew, "The Effect of Appearance on Personality and Behavior," *Youth and Society*, *15* (1984), pp. 285–303.

Chapter Four: Undercover Agents

1. Cocks, 1989, p. 182.

2. Tracy, 1991, p. 14.

3. Ibid., pp. 123–24.

4. Quoted in Katherine Dunn, "Call of the Wild," *Vogue*, June 1995, p. 205.

5. Greer, 1971, p. 59.

6. Laws and Schwartz, 1977, p. 19.

7. For instance, Sherwin and Corbett, 1985, p. 259, reported on changes in sexual norms at a single university over a fifteen-year time period: "if a sexual revolution occurred on the campus, it was predominantly a female revolution." Between 1963 and 1978, the percentage of sexually experienced women increased 41 percent; the percentage of sexually experienced men increased only 6 percent. See also Ehrenreich, Hess, and Jacobs, 1986.

8. Lottes, 1993, p. 661.

9. Ibid., p. 655.
10. Ibid., p. 652.
11. According to 1979 data, 31 percent of self-identified feminist women and 60 percent of nonfeminist women had never shared date expenses. S.K. Korman, "Nontraditional Dating Behavior: Date-initiation and Date Expense-sharing among Feminists and Nonfeminists," *Family Relations, 32* (1983), pp. 575–81.
12. Janell Lucille Carroll, Kari Doray Volk, and Janet Shibley Hyde, "Differences Between Males and Females in Motives for Engaging in Sexual Intercourse," *Archives of Sexual Behavior, 14* (1985), pp. 135–36.
13. Lottes, 1993, p. 664.
14. Ibid., p. 662.
15. Philip Elmer-Dewitt, "Now for the Truth About Americans and Sex," *Time*, October 17, 1994, p. 48.
16. Laumann, Gagnon, Michael, and Michaels, 1994, pp. 204–205 and 328.
17. Ibid., pp. 197–98.
18. Ibid., pp. 189–90.
19. Tiefer, 1995, pp. 6–7.
20. Ibid., p. 11.
21. See McCabe and Collins, 1984, and Roche, 1986. For anecdotal accounts of teenage girls' sexual expectations, see Thompson, 1995.
22. Pally, 1994, p. 73.
23. Ibid., p. 74.
24. Margo St. James, "The Reclamation of Whores," in Bell (Ed.), 1987, p. 84.
25. Quoted in Bell (ed.), 1987, p. 196.
26. Segal, 1994, p. 34.
27. Tiefer, 1995, p. 115.
28. Alice Echols, "The Taming of the Id: Feminist Sexual Politics, 1968–83," in Vance (ed.), 1984, p. 55.
29. Segal, 1994, p. 52.
30. Brownmiller, 1975, p. 5.
31. Ibid., pp. 390–91.
32. Ann Snitow, "Retrenchment versus Transformation: The Politics of the Antipornography Movement," in Burstyn (ed.), 1985, p. 112.
33. Echols, op. cit., p. 59.
34. Quoted in Segal, 1994, p. 59.

Chapter Five: Double Talk

1. For an accessible summary of the study's findings, see Warshaw, 1988; this popular paperback is published by the *Ms.* Foundation, and has an afterword by Mary Koss. For a more detailed, academic discussion of the Koss study, see Koss, Gidycz, and Wisniewski, 1987, and Koss, 1988.

2. For example, see Muehlenhard, Sympson, Phelps, and Highby, in press, p. 6: "in some ways, Koss's definition may be too broad; for example, it might be interpreted to include the exchange of sex for drugs or regrets about behavior that was consensual at the time, both of which we see as problematic but not as rape."

3. Sommers, 1994, p. 213. Note that Koss herself calculated this "one in nine" figure when criticized for the wording of the question regarding drugs and alcohol.

4. Koss, 1988, p. 10.

5. Ibid., p. 15. See also Warshaw, 1988, p. 63.

6. The term "date rape" first appeared in the mainstream media in a *Ms.* article on Mary Koss's research findings, September 1982, p. 130.

7. Sommers, 1994, p. 215.

8. Michael, Gagnon, Laumann, and Kolata, 1994, p. 225.

9. Laumann, Gagnon, Michael, and Michaels, 1994, p. 654.

10. Ibid., note 8, p. 335.

11. Ibid., p. 334.

12. Ibid., pp. 667–68.

13. Ibid., note 8, p. 335.

14. Berger, Searles, Salem, and Pierce, 1986, p. 19.

15. For reviews of research on coercive sexuality, see Craig, 1990, and Muehlenhard, Powch, Phelps, and Giusti, 1992.

16. Craig, 1990, p. 403.

17. Ibid.

18. For instance, consider the widely circulated American College Health Association brochure, 1987, "Acquaintance rape: Is dating dangerous?" Acquaintance rape is defined as "forced, manipulated or coerced sexual intercourse by a friend or an acquaintance... A woman is forced to have sex through verbal coercion, threats, physical restraint and/or physical violence." Apparently, the after-effects are the same, regardless of the "assailant's" method: "She may feel ashamed, guilty, betrayed and frightened... The psychological effects can be devastating and can last for a considerable time."

19. Koss, "Afterword: The Methods Used in the *Ms.* Project on Campus Sexual Assault," in Warshaw, 1988, pp. 191.
20. Ibid., pp. 191–92.
21. Muehlenhard and Cook, 1988.
22. Charlene L. Muehlenhard and Jennifer L. Schrag, "Nonviolent Sexual Coercion," in Parrot and Bechhofer (eds.), 1991, p. 115.
23. Muehlenhard and Long, 1988.
24. O'Sullivan and Byers, 1992, p. 445.
25. For summary and analysis of polling data, see Tom Smith, "Attitudes toward Sexual Permissiveness: Trends, Correlates, and Behavioral Connections," in Rossi (ed.), 1994.
26. BKG Youth, Inc. poll, conducted for *Esquire* magazine. *Esquire*, February 1994, p. 67.
27. *Details*, May 1994, p. 109.
28. Cited in Struckman-Johnson, "Male Victims of Acquaintance Rape," in Parrot and Bechhofer (eds.), 1991, p. 207.
29. Anderson, 1989, pp. 60–61.
30. See Muehlenhard and Long, 1988; Poppen and Segal, 1988; Muehlenhard and Cook, 1988; Struckman-Johnson, 1988; Anderson, 1989; Struckman-Johnson, in Parrot and Bechhofer, 1991; O'Sullivan and Byers, 1993; Struckman-Johnson and Struckman-Johnson, 1994.
31. Struckman-Johnson and Struckman-Johnson, 1994, p. 101.
32. See also Sarrel and Masters, 1982, p. 118.
33. Ibid., p. 118. See also "Science is Finding Out What Women Really Want," *New York Times*, August 13, 1995, p. E7.
34. O'Sullivan and Byers, 1993, p. 275.
35. Ibid., p. 277.
36. Ibid., p. 281.
37. Struckman-Johnson, in Parrot and Bechhofer, 1991, p. 208.
38. For example, see Muehlenhard and Linton, 1987; Rapaport and Burkhart, 1984; Craig, Kalichman, and Follingstad, 1989; Mynatt and Allgeier, 1990. All report high rates of male verbal coercion but low rates of male physical violence. Warshaw, 1988, p. 49, classifies the average rate of violence as "moderate" in the cases Mary Koss classified as rape: "Only 9 percent of the women said their rapists hit them; 5 percent were threatened with weapons."
39. Muehlenhard and Linton, 1987, p. 193.
40. In Koss's survey, 55 percent of the women classified as victims of rape or attempted rape said they were intoxicated at the time. Warshaw, 1988, p. 49.

41. Muehlenhard and Linton, 1987, p. 194.
42. Muehlenhard and Long, 1988, pp. 2–3.
43. Craig, 1990, pp. 397–401.
44. Ross and Allgeier, 1995, pp. 4–9.
45. Ibid., p. 12.
46. A virtually identical figure — 42 percent — was obtained by Craig, Kalichman, and Follingstad, 1989.
47. Ross and Allgeier, 1995, pp. 17–19.
48. Craig, Kalichman, and Follingstad, 1989, p. 430–31.
49. Ibid. Also see Craig, 1990, for review of studies of sexually coercive males.
50. Ibid., p. 430.
51. Craig, 1990, p. 413.
52. Byers and Lewis, 1988, p. 23.
53. Ibid., p. 22.
54. Ibid., p. 25–26.
55. Ibid., p. 26.
56. Laurie Abraham, "Seven Reasons to Make Love Tonight — even if you don't feel sexy," *Glamour*, March, 1995, p. 259.
57. O'Sullivan, 1994, p. 67.
58. Ibid., p. 43. Shotland and Goodstein, 1992, report that college students perceive both men and women to be obligated by sexual precedence; students in their study believed that if a couple had had intercourse before, neither partner should turn down the other and refuse sex after foreplay. This helps to explain why in O'Sullivan's study, men and women reported that unwanted but consensual sex was a fairly routine activity in their committed relationships.
59. O'Sullivan, 1994, pp. 59 and 65.
60. Ibid., p. 63.
61. Ibid., pp. 65–66.
62. Ibid., p. 66.
63. Ibid., p. 67.
64. O'Sullivan and Allgeier, 1994; Muehlenhard and McCoy, 1991; and Muehlenhard and Hollabaugh, 1988.
65. See Muehlenhard and McCoy, 1991, for a full discussion of women's reasons for token resistance.
66. Muehlenhard and Hollabaugh, 1988, p. 878.
67. Muehlenhard and McCoy, 1991, p. 453. Also relevant is Byers and Lewis's finding that most men in sexual disagreement situations with steady dating partners stop when they hear no (see note 53).
68. O'Sullivan and Allgeier, 1994.

69. Ibid., p. 1052.
70. See Byers, 1988, and Muehlenhard and Linton, 1987.
71. Craig, 1990, pp. 412–13.
72. Muehlenhard, 1988, p. 102.
73. Ibid., pp. 103–104. Men who reported that they had engaged in sexual coercion in the past said they would be most likely to stop if the woman was physically or verbally forceful.
74. Herman, 1989.
75. Donat and D'Emilio, 1992, pp. 11–13.
76. Ibid. See also Muehlenhard, Harney, and Jones, 1992, 223–33.
77. Kate Millett, *Sexual Politics* (New York: Touchstone, 1969), p. 44.
78. Dworkin, 1974, p. 184.
79. Dworkin, 1988, p. 179.
80. Faludi, 1991, p. 100.
81. White and Kowalski, 1994, p. 492.
82. In the 1992 study, however, the rate of wives' assaults had increased, while husbands' assaults had decreased. See Straus, 1993, and Straus and Kantor, 1994.
83. Straus, 1993, pp. 68–69.
84. Ibid., pp. 74–75.
85. Ibid., p. 79.
86. Ibid., p. 80.
87. Jan Stets and Murray Straus, "Gender Differences in Reporting Marital Violence and Its Medical and Psychological Consequences," in Murray S. Straus and Richard J. Gelles (eds.), 1990.
88. Straus and Gelles, 1990.
89. For information on other studies of female physical aggression, see Straus, 1993, pp. 70–71, and White and Kowalski, 1994, pp. 493–96.
90. Barbara Hart, "Lesbian Battering: An Examination," in Lobel (ed.), 1986, p. 174.
91. Christine Wright and Jean-Pierre Leroux, "Children as Victims of Violent Crime," *Juristat Service Bulletin*, *11*, p. 12. Also see Straus and Gelles, 1990.
92. Straus and Gelles, 1990.
93. White and Kowalski, 1994, p. 495.
94. This estimate comes from the American Humane Association Study, 1981, discussed in Finkelhor and Russell, 1984. Finkelhor and Russell also analyzed the National Incidence Study of Child Abuse and Neglect, and, after reducing its figures to account for female co-offenders, calculated that 13 percent of girl victims and 24 percent of boy victims are sexually abused by women.

95. For instance, Ann Burgess and colleagues reported in 1987 that 56 percent of the male rapists they studied were sexually abused in their childhood; almost 40 percent of the abusers were female. Study cited in Johnson, 1989, p. 572.

96. Groth and Burgess, 1979.

97. Cited in Gonsiorek, Bera, and LeTourneau, 1994, p. 54.

98. Banning, 1989, p. 567.

99. Mathews, Matthews, and Speltz, 1989; Knopp and Lackey, 1987; Finkelhor and Russell, 1984.

100. Quoted in Mathews, Matthews, and Speltz, 1989, p. 56.

101. Ibid., pp. 56–57.

102. Ibid., pp. 32–39.

103. "Hello again, Mrs. Robinson," *The Toronto Sun*, July 15, 1994, p. 50.

104. Krug, 1989, pp. 112 and 117–18.

105. Ibid, p. 117. See also Masters, 1986; Johnson and Shrier, 1987; Dimock, 1988; Finkelhor, 1990; Gonsiorek, Bera, and LeTourneau, 1994, pp. 52–55.

106. Knopp and Lackey, 1987.

107. Green and Kaplan, 1994, p. 958.

108. Johnson, 1989, pp. 581–83.

109. Fehrenbach and Monastersky, 1988, p. 150. For a detailed case study of a girl's transition from victim to perpetrator, see Higgs, Canavan, and Meyer, 1992.

110. Banning, 1989, p. 568.

111. Sarrell and Masters, 1982. For a journalistic account of woman-on-man rape, see Anthony Delano, "The Case of the Manacled Mormon," *New West*, February 12, 1979, pp. 13–22. Delano recounts the headline-making case of Joy McKinney, an American beauty queen who stalked a Mormon missionary all the way from Utah to England, where she abducted him at gunpoint, kept him tied to a bed for four days, and repeatedly had sex with him against his will — and against his religion. McKinney became something of a folk hero in England, and fled the country, unimpeded, before she stood trial on charges of kidnapping and assault. She never served time for her crimes; when she returned to the U.S., she did the talk show circuit and continued to stalk the man for years.

112. Smith, Pine, and Hawley, 1988, p. 110. Students also tell researchers that it is inappropriate and unacceptable for a man to kiss a woman who denies him consent, but acceptable and even complimentary for a woman to kiss a man who denies her consent. See Margolin, 1990, and Semonsky and Rosenfeld, 1994.

Chapter Six: Good Girls, Bad Boys, and Other Demons

1. Muehlenhard and McCoy, 1991, p. 457.
2. Many researchers have found no differences in the standards of sexually acceptable behavior for men and women. See Sprecher, McKinney, Walsh, and Anderson, 1988; Sprecher, 1989; and Lottes, 1993.
3. Sprecher, McKinney, and Orbuch, 1991, surveyed more than 750 students from three universities and reported that students of both genders rated men and women with high levels of sexual experience as the least desirable friends and spouses.
4. O'Sullivan, 1992, p. 22.
5. Muehlenhard and McCoy, 1991, p. 458.
6. Ibid., p. 457.
7. Ibid., pp. 458–59.
8. Pally, 1994, 151–52.
9. Warshaw, p. 92.
10. Ibid., p. 54.
11. Pally, pp. 74–75.
12. See Sommers, 1994, chapters 6–7. Also see Katherine Dennehy and Jeylan T. Mortimer, "Work and Family Orientations of Contemporary Adolescent Boys and Girls," in Hood, (ed.), 1993.
13. Ibid., p. 95.
14. Beth Willinger, "College Men's Attitudes Toward Family and Work," in Hood (ed.), 1993, p. 122.
15. Ibid., p. 120.
16. John Gray, *Mars and Venus in the Bedroom: A Guide to Lasting Romance and Passion* (New York: HarperCollins, 1995), p. 179.
17. Ibid., pp. 84–85.
18. Ibid., p. 84.
19. Ibid., pp. 82–83.
20. Ibid., pp. 79–80.
21. Ibid., p. 105.
22. Ibid., pp. 106–107.
23. See Moore and Butler, 1989, for a review of the research on proceptivity.
24. Perper and Weis, 1987, p. 456.
25. McCormick and Jones, 1989, p. 279.
26. Moore and Butler, 1989, pp. 211 and 213.
27. Perper and Weis, 1987, p. 474.
28. Ibid., pp. 474–75.
29. Ibid., p. 478.

Chapter Seven: Men Are from Venus, Women Are from Mars

1. See Cancian, 1987, pp. 75–77.
2. E.J. Kanin, K.D. Davidson, and S.R. Scheck, "A research note on male-female differentials in the experience of heterosexual love," *The Journal of Sex Research*, 6, pp. 64–72.
3. Charles T. Hill, Zick Rubin, and Letitia Anna Peplau conducted the study; this quotation summarizing its findings is from Hatfield and Walster, 1985, p. 49.
4. Ibid., p. 50.
5. See Cancian, 1987, pp. 75–77.
6. "Both traditional and nontraditional men perceive women who ask for dates as kinder, warmer, more thoughtful, and less selfish than women who do not ask for dates, and they are just as willing to date women who ask for dates as they are to date women who do not ask," report Muehlenhard and Miller, 1988, p. 398.
7. Faludi, 1991, pp. 25–26.
8. Ibid., p. 26.
9. Ibid., p. 17.
10. Cancian, 1987, p. 77.
11. Gray, op. cit., p. 187.
12. Segal, 1994, p. 255.
13. Ibid., p. 223.
14. Cancian, 1987, p. 77.
15. Laumann, Gagnon, Michael, and Michaels, 1994, p. 340.
16. Ibid., p. 341–43.
17. Ibid., pp. 341–42.
18. Ibid., p. 341.
19. Segal, 1990, pp. 213–15. Also see Suraci, 1992.
20. William A. Fisher summarizes the research in "Gender, Gender-Role Identification, and Response to Erotica," in Allgeier and McCormick (eds.), 1988, pp. 261–84.
21. Quoted in Natalie Angier, "Science Is Finding Out What Women Really Want," *New York Times*, August 13, p. E7.
22. Laan, Everaerd, van Bellen, and Hanewald, 1994.
23. Janet Wolfe, *What to Do When He Has a Headache* (New York: Hyperion, 1992), pp. 5 and 7.

Bibliography

Aizenman, Marta, & Kelley, Georgette (1988). The incidence of violence and acquaintance rape in dating relationships among college men and women. *Journal of College Student Development, 29,* 305–11.

Allgeier, Elizabeth Rice, & McCormick, Naomi B. (eds.) (1983). *Changing boundaries: Gender roles and sexual behavior.* Palo Alto: Mayfield Publishing Company.

Anderson, Peter B. (1989). *Adversarial sexual beliefs and past experience of sexual abuse of college females as predictors of their sexual aggression toward adolescent and adult males.* Doctoral Dissertation, New York University.

Aries, Elizabeth (1987). Gender and communication. In Phillip Shaver and Clyde Hendrick (eds.), *Sex and Gender: 7.* Newbury Park, CA: Sage Publications.

Banning, Anne (1989). Mother-son incest: Confronting a prejudice. *Child Abuse and Neglect, 13,* 563–70.

Beall, Anne E., & Sternberg, Robert J. (eds.) (1993). *The psychology of gender.* New York: Guilford Press.

Bell, Laurie (ed.) (1987). *Good girls/Bad girls: Sex trade workers and feminists face to face.* Toronto: The Women's Press.

Berger, Ronald J.; Searles, Patricia; Salem, Richard G.; & Pierce, Beth Ann (1986). Sexual assault in a college community. *Sociological Focus, 19,*1–26.

Bjorkqvist, Kaj (1994). Sex differences in physical, verbal, and indirect aggression: A review of recent research. *Sex Roles, 30,* 177–88.

— and Niemela, Pirkko (eds.) (1992). *Of mice and women: Aspects of female aggression*. San Diego: Academic Press.

Bolton, Frank G.; Morris, Larry A.; & MacEachron, Ann E. (1989). *Males at risk: The other side of child sexual abuse*. Newbury Park, CA: Sage Publications.

Burbank, Victoria K. (1994). Cross-cultural perspectives on aggression in women and girls: An introduction. *Sex Roles, 30*, 169–76.

Burstyn, Varda (ed.) (1985). *Women against censorship*. Vancouver: Douglas & McIntyre.

Bry, Adelaide (1975). *The sexually aggressive woman*. New York: Peter H. Wyden.

Byers, E. Sandra (1988). Effects of sexual arousal on men's and women's behavior in sexual disagreement situations. *The Journal of Sex Research, 25*, 235–54.

— and Lewis, Kim (1988). Dating couples' disagreements over the desired level of sexual intimacy. *The Journal of Sex Research, 24*, 15–29.

Campbell, Anne (1993). *Men, women, and aggression*. New York: Basic Books.

Cancian, Francesca M. (1987). *Love in America: Gender and self-development*. Cambridge: Cambridge University Press.

Caplan, Paula J. (1993). *The myth of women's masochism* (2nd ed.). Toronto: University of Toronto Press.

Cassell, Carol (1984). *Swept away: Why women fear their own sexuality*. New York: Simon and Schuster.

Caulfield, Marie B., & Riggs, David S. (1992). The assessment of dating aggression: Empirical evaluation of the conflict tactics scale. *Journal of Interpersonal Violence, 7*, 549–58.

Chandler, Joan (1991). *Women without husbands: An exploration of the margins of marriage*. London: Macmillan Education.

Chodorow, Nancy (1978). *The reproduction of mothering*. Berkeley, CA: University of California Press.

Christopher, F. Scott, & Frandsen, Michela M. (1990). Strategies of influence in sex and dating. *Journal of Social and Personal Relationships, 7*, 89–105.

— ; Owens, Laura A.; & Stecker, Heidi L. (1993). An examination of single men's and women's sexual aggressiveness in dating relationships. *Journal of Social and Personal Relationships, 10*, 511–27.

Cocks, Joan (1989). *The oppositional imagination: Feminism, critique, and political theory*. London: Routledge.

Craig, Mary E. (1990). Coercive sexuality in dating relationships: A situational model. *Clinical Psychology Review*, 395–423.

— ; Kalichman, Seth C.; & Follingstad, Diane R. (1989). Verbal coercive sexual behavior among college students. *Archives of Sexual Behavior, 18,* 421–34.

DeMaris, Alfred (1990). Male versus female initiation of aggression: The case of courtship violence. In Emilio C. Viano (ed.), *Intimate violence: Interdisciplinary perspectives.* Washington, D.C.: Hemisphere Publishing Corporation.

DePaulo, Bella M.; Epstein, Jennifer A.; & Wyer, Melissa M. (1993). Sex differences in lying: How women and men deal with the dilemma of deceit. In Michael Lewis and Carolyn Saarni (eds.), *Lying and deception in everyday life.* New York: The Guilford Press.

DiBlasio, Frederick A., & Benda, Brent B. (1992). Gender differences in theories of adolescent sexual activity. *Sex Roles, 27,* 221–39.

Dimock, Peter T. (1988). Adult males sexually abused as children: Characteristics and implications for treatment. *Journal of Interpersonal Violence, 3,* 203–21.

Donat, Patricia L.N., & D'Emilio, John (1992). A feminist redefinition of rape and sexual assault: Historical foundations and change. *Journal of Social Issues, 48,* 9–22.

Duck, Steve, & Wright, Paul H. (1993). Reexamining gender differences in same-gender friendships: A close look at two kinds of data. *Sex Roles, 28,* 709–27.

Dworkin, Andrea (1974). *Woman hating.* New York: E.P. Dutton.

— (1988). *Letters from a war zone: Writings 1976–1987.* London: Secker and Warburg.

Ehrenreich, Barbara; Hess, Elizabeth; & Jacobs, Gloria (1986). *Re-making love: The feminization of sex.* Garden City, New York: Anchor Press.

Eichenbaum, Luise, & Orbach, Susie (1988). *Between women: Love, envy, and competition in women's friendships.* New York: Viking.

Elliot, Susan; Odynak, Dave; & Krahn, Harvey (1992). *A survey of unwanted sexual experiences among University of Alberta students.* Edmonton, Alberta: Population Research Laboratory, University of Alberta.

Elliott, Michele (ed.) (1993). *Female sexual abuse of children: The ultimate taboo.* London: Longman.

England, Eileen M. (1992). College student gender stereotypes: Expectations about the behavior of male subcategory members. *Sex Roles, 27,* 699–716.

Estrich, Susan (1987). *Real rape.* Cambridge, MA: Harvard University Press.

Faller, Kathleen Coulborn (1989). Characteristics of a clinical sample of sexually abused children: How boy and girl victims differ. *Child Abuse and Neglect, 13,* 281–91.

Faludi, Susan (1991). *Backlash: The undeclared war against American women.* New York: Anchor Books.

Fehrenbach, Peter A., & Monastersky, Caren (1988). Characteristics of female adolescent sexual offenders. *American Journal of Orthopsychiatry, 58,* 148–51.

Fekete, John (1994). *Moral panic: Biopolitics rising.* Montreal: Robert Davies Publishing.

Feminist Review (1987). *Sexuality: A reader.* London: Virago Press.

Ferguson, Ann; Philipson, Ilene; Diamond, Irene; Quinby, Lee; Vance, Carole S.; & Snitow, Ann Barr (1984). Forum: The feminist sexuality debates. *Signs: Journal of Women in Culture and Society, 10,* 106–35.

Finkelhor, David (1990). Early and long-term effects of child sexual abuse: An update. *Professional Psychology: Research and Practice, 21,* 325–30.

— , & Russell, Diana (1984). Women as perpetrators: Review of the evidence. In David Finkelhor (ed.), *Child sexual abuse: New theory and research.* New York: The Free Press.

Fischer, Agneta H. (1993). Sex differences in emotionality: Fact or stereotype? *Feminism & Psychology, 3,* 303–18.

Fox-Genovese, Elizabeth (1991). *Feminism without illusions: A critique of individualism.* Chapel Hill: University of North Carolina Press.

Friday, Nancy (1991). *Women on top: How real life has changed women's sexual fantasies.* New York: Pocket Books.

Fromuth, Mary Ellen, & Burkhart, Barry R. (1989). Long-term psychological correlates of childhood sexual abuse in two samples of college men. *Child Abuse and Neglect, 13,* 533–542.

Gagnon, John H. (1990). The explicit and implicit use of the scripting perspective in sex research. In J. Bancroft, C.M. Davis, & D. Weinstein (eds.), *Annual review of sex research, Vol. 1* (pp. 1–43). Mt. Vernon, Iowa: Society for the Scientific Study of Sex.

Gaylin, Willard (1992). *The male ego.* New York: Viking Penguin.

Giddens, Anthony (1992). *The transformation of intimacy: Sexuality, love and eroticism in modern societies.* Cambridge: Polity Press.

Gilbert, Neil (1992). Realities and mythologies of rape. *Society,* May/June 1995, 4–10.

Gilligan, Carol (1982). *In a different voice.* Cambridge, MA: Harvard University Press.

Gonsiorek, John C.; Bera, Walter H.; & LeTourneau, Donald (1994). *Male sexual abuse: A trilogy of intervention strategies.* Thousand Oaks, CA: Sage Publications.

Grant, Linda (1994). *Sexing the millenium: Women and the sexual revolution*. London: Grove Press.

Green, Arthur H., & Kaplan, Meg S. (1994). Psychiatric impairment and childhood victimization experiences in female child molesters. *Journal of the American Academy of Child and Adolescent Psychiatry, 33,* 954–61.

Greer, Germaine (1971). *The female eunuch*. New York: McGraw-Hill.

Groth, Nicholas, & Burgess, Ann W. (1979). Sexual trauma in the life histories of rapists and child molesters. *Victimology, 4,* 10–16.

Hatfield, Elaine, & Walster, G. William (1985). *A new look at love* (2nd ed.). Lanham, Maryland: University Press of America.

Herman, Dianne F. (1989). The rape culture. In Jo Freeman (ed.), *Women: A feminist perspective* (4th ed.). Mountain View, CA: Mayfield Publishing Company.

Heyn, Dalma (1992). *The erotic silence of the American wife*. New York: Signet.

Higgs, Deborah C.; Canavan, Margaret M.; & Meyer, Walter J. (1992). Moving from defense to offense: The development of an adolescent female sex offender. *The Journal of Sex Research, 29,* 131–39.

Hood, Jane C. (ed.) (1993). *Men, work, and family*. Newbury Park, CA: Sage Publications.

Hunter, Anne E. (ed.) (1991). *Genes and Gender VI: On peace, war and gender*. New York: The Feminist Press at the City University of New York.

Irvine, Janice M. (1990). *Disorders of desire: Sex and gender in modern American sexology*. Philadelphia: Temple University Press.

Jeffreys, Sheila (1990). *Anticlimax: A feminist perspective on the sexual revolution*. London: The Women's Press.

Jesser, Clinton (1978). Male responses to direct verbal sexual initiatives of females. *The Journal of Sex Research, 14,* 118–28.

Johnson, Robert L., & Shrier, Diane (1987). Past sexual victimization by females of male patients in an adolescent medicine clinic population. *American Journal of Psychiatry, 144,* 650–52.

Johnson, Toni Cavanagh (1989). Female child perpetrators: Children who molest other children. *Child Abuse and Neglect, 13,* 571–85.

Kanin, Eugene J. (1994). False rape allegations. *Archives of Sexual Behavior, 23,* 81–92.

Knopp, Fay Honey, & Lackey, Lois B. (1987). *Female sexual abusers: A summary of data from forty-four treatment providers*. Orwell, VT: Safer Society Press.

Koss, Mary P. (1985). The hidden rape victim: Personality, attitudinal, and situational characteristics. *Psychology of Women Quarterly, 9,* 193–12.

— ; Gidycz, Christine A.; Wisniewski, Nadine (1987). The scope of rape: Incidence and prevalence of sexual aggression and victimization in a national sample of higher education students. *Journal of Consulting and Clinical Psychology, 55,* 162–70.

— (1988). Hidden rape: Sexual aggression and victimization in a national sample of students in higher education. In Ann Wolbert Burgess (ed.), *Rape and sexual assault, Vol. II.* New York: Garland Publishing.

— and Dinero, Thomas E. (1988). Predictors of sexual aggression among a national sample of male college students. *Annals New York Academy of Sciences,* 133–47.

Krug, Ronald S. (1989). Adult male report of childhood sexual abuse by mothers: Case descriptions, motivations and long-term consequences. *Child Abuse and Neglect, 13,* 111–19.

Laan, Ellen; Everaerd, Walter; van Bellen, Gerdy; & Hanewald, Gerrit (1994). Women's sexual and emotional responses to male- and female-produced erotica. *Archives of Sexual Behavior, 23,* 153–69.

Lakoff, Robin T. (1990). *Talking power: The politics of language.* New York: Basic Books.

Laumann, Edward O.; Gagnon, John H.; Michael, Robert T.; & Michaels, Stuart (1994). *The social organization of sexuality: Sexual practices in the United States.* Chicago: University of Chicago Press.

Laws, Judith Long, & Schwartz, Pepper (1977). *Sexual scripts: The social construction of female sexuality.* Hinsdale, IL: The Dryden Press.

Lawson, Annette (1988). *Adultery: An analysis of love and betrayal.* New York: Basic Books.

Lepowsky, Maria (1994). Women, men, and aggression in an egalitarian society. *Sex Roles, 30,* 199–211.

Lobel, Kerry (ed.) (1986). *Naming the violence: Speaking out about lesbian battering.* Seattle: The Seal Press.

Lottes, Ilsa L. (1993). Nontraditional gender roles and the sexual experiences of heterosexual college students. *Sex Roles, 29,* 645–69.

Macklin, Eleanor D. (1983). Effect of changing sex roles on the intimate relationships of men and women. *Marriage and Family Review, 6,* pp. 97–113.

Margolin, Leslie (1990). Gender and the stolen kiss: The social support of male and female to violate a partner's sexual consent in a noncoercive situation. *Archives of Sexual Behavior, 19,* 281–91.

Marvasti, Jamshid (1986). Incestuous mothers. *American Journal of Forensix Psychiatry, VII,* 63–69.

Masters, William H. (1986). Sexual dysfunction as an aftermath of sexual assault of men by women. *Journal of Sex and Marital Therapy, 12,* 35–45.

Mathews, Ruth; Matthews, Jane Kinder; & Speltz, Kathleen (1989). *Female sexual offenders: An exploratory study*. Orwell, VT: The Safer Society Press.

McCabe, M.P., & Collins, J.K. (1984). Measurement of depth of desired and experienced sexual involvement at different stages of dating. *The Journal of Sex Research, 20,* 377–90.

McCarty, Loretta M. (1986). Mother-child incest: Characterisitics of the offender. *Child Welfare, LXV,* 447–58.

McCormick, Naomi B. (1987). Sexual scripts: social and therapeutic implications. *Sexual and Marital Therapy, 2,* 3–27.

—, & Jones, Andrew J. (1989). Gender differences in nonverbal flirtation. *Journal of Sex Education & Therapy, 15,* 271–82.

— (1995). *Sexual salvation: Affirming women's sexual rights and pleasures.* Westport, Connecticut: Praeger.

Metts, Sandra, & Fitzpatrick, Mary Anne (1992). Thinking about safer sex: The risky business of "know your partner" advice. In Timothy Edgar, Mary Anne Fitzpatrick, & Vicki S. Freimuth (eds.), *AIDS: A communication perspective*. Hillsdale, NJ: Lawrence Erlbaum Associates.

Michael, Robert T.; Gagnon, John H.; Laumann, Edward O.; & Kolata, Gina (1994). *Sex in America: A definitive survey*. Boston: Little, Brown & Company.

Miller, Jean Baker (1976). *Toward a new psychology of women*. Boston: Beacon Press.

Miner, Valerie, & Longino, Helen E. (eds.) (1987). *Competition: A feminist taboo?* New York: The Feminist Press.

Mitscherlich, Margarete (1987). *The peaceable sex: On aggression in women and men*. New York: Fromm International Publishing Corporation.

Monsour, Michael (1992). Meanings of intimacy in cross- and same-sex friendships. *Journal of Social and Personal Relationships, 9,* 277–95.

Moore, Monica M., & Butler, Diana L. (1989). Predictive aspects of nonverbal courtship behavior in women. *Semiotica, 76,* 205–15.

Morgan, Robin (ed.) (1970). *Sisterhood is powerful : an anthology of writings from the women's liberation movement*. New York: Random House.

Muehlenhard, Charlene L. (1988). "Nice women" don't say yes and "real men" don't say no: How miscommunication and the double standard can cause sexual problems. *Women and Therapy, 7,* 95–108.

—, & Linton, Melaney A. (1987). Date rape and sexual aggression in dating situations: Incidence and risk factors. *Journal of Counseling Psychology, 34,* 186–96.

—, & Cook, Stephen W. (1988). Men's self-reports of unwanted sexual activity. *The Journal of Sex Research, 24,* 58–72.

—, & Hollabaugh, Lisa C. (1988). Do women sometimes say no when they mean yes? The prevalence and correlates of women's token resistance to sex. *Journal of Personality and Social Psychology, 54,* 872–79.

—, & Long, Patricia J. (1988). Men's versus women's reports of pressure to engage in unwanted sexual intercourse. Paper presented at the Western Region meeting of the Society for the Scientific Study of Sex, Dallas, March, 1988.

—, & Miller, Eric N. (1988). Traditional and nontraditional men's responses to women's dating initiation. *Behavior Modification, 12,* 385–403.

—, & McCoy, Marcia L. (1991). Double standard/Double bind: The sexual double standard and women's communication about sex. *Psychology of Women Quarterly, 15,* 447–61.

—; Harney, Patricia A.; & Jones, Jayme M. (1992). "Victim-precipitated rape" to "date rape": How far have we come? *Annual Review of Sex Research, Vol. 3* (pp. 219–53). Mt. Vernon, Iowa: Society for the Scientific Study of Sex.

—; Powch, Irene G.; Phelps, Joi L.; & Giusti, Laura M. (1992). Definitions of rape: Scientific and political implications. *Journal of Social Issues, 48,* 23–44.

—; Sympson, Susie C.; Phelps, Joi L.; & Highby, Barrie J. Are rape statistics exaggerated? A response to criticism of contemporary rape research. In-press, *The Journal of Sex Research.*

Murphy, John (1988). Date abuse and forced intercourse among college students. In Gerald T. Hotaling; David Finkelhor; John T. Kirkpatrick; & Murray S. Straus (eds.), *Family abuse and its consequences: New directions in research.* Newbury Park, CA: Sage Publications.

Mynatt, Clifford R., & Allgeier, Elizabeth Rice (1990). Risk factors, self-attributions, and adjustment problems among victims of sexual coercion. *Journal of Applied Social Psychology, 20,* 130–53.

O'Sullivan, Lucia (1994). *Consenting to noncoercive sex: College students' experiences of unwanted consensual sexual interactions in committed dating relationships.* Doctoral Dissertation, Bowling Green State University.

—, & Byers, E. Sandra (1992). College students' incorporation of initiator and restrictor roles in sexual dating interactions. *The Journal of Sex Research, 29,* 435–46.

— (1992). Too little or too much? The effects of sexual experience on judgments of men's and women's personality characteristics and relationship desirability. In-press, *Sex Roles.*

—, & Byers, E. Sandra (1993). Eroding stereotypes: College women's attempts to influence reluctant male sexual partners. *The Journal of Sex Research, 30,* 270–82.

— , & Allgeier, Elizabeth Rice (1994). Disassembling a stereotype: Gender differences in the use of token resistance. *Journal of Applied Social Psychology, 24,* 1035–55.

— ; Lawrance, Kelli-an; & Byers, E. Sandra (1994). Discrepancies in desired level of sexual intimacy in long-term relationships. Paper presented at the annual meeting of the Canadian Sex Research Forum, Elora, September, 1994.

Pally, Marcia (1994). *Sex and sensibility: Reflections on forbidden mirrors and the will to censor.* Hopewell, New Jersey: The Ecco Press.

Parrot, Andrea, & Bechhofer, Laurie (eds.) (1991). *Acquaintance rape: The hidden crime.* New York: John Wiley and Sons.

Perper, Timothy, & Weis, David L. (1987). Proceptive and rejective strategies of U.S. and Canadian college women. *The Journal of Sex Research, 23,* 455–80.

Pirog-Good, Maureen A. (1990). Sexual abuse in dating relationships. In Emilio C. Viano (ed.), *Intimate violence: Interdisciplinary perspectives.* Washington, D.C.: Hemisphere Publishing Corporation.

Pollitt, Katha (1994). *Reasonable creatures: Essays on women and feminism.* New York: Alfred A. Knopf.

Poppen, Paul J., & Segal, Nina J. (1988). The influence of sex and sex role orientation on sexual coercion. *Sex Roles, 19,* 689–701.

Rapaport, K., & Burkhart, B.R. (1984). Personality and attitudinal characteristics of sexually coercive college males. *Journal of Abnormal Psychology, 93,* 216–21.

Richardson, Laurel (1985). *The new Other Woman: Contemporary single women in affairs with married men.* New York: The Free Press.

Riggs, David S.; O'Leary, K. Daniel; & Breslin, F. Curtis (1990). Multiple correlates of physical aggression in dating couples. *Journal of Interpersonal Violence, 5,* 61–73.

Risman, Barbara J., & Schwartz, Pepper (1989). *Gender in intimate relationships: A microstructural approach.* Belmont, CA: Wadsworth Publishing Company.

Roche, J.P. (1986). Premarital sex: Attitudes and behavior by dating stage. *Adolescence, 21,* 107–21.

Roiphe, Katie (1993). *The morning after: Sex, fear, and feminism on campus.* Boston: Little, Brown and Company.

Rose, Suzanna, & Frieze, Irene Hanson (1993). Young singles' contemporary dating scripts. *Sex Roles, 28,* 499–509.

Ross, Ronald R., & Allgeier, Elizabeth Rice (1995). Behind the pencil/paper measurement of sexual coercion: Interview-based clarification of men's interpretations of sexual experiences survey items. In-press study.

Rossi, Alice S. (ed.) (1994). *Sexuality across the life course*. Chicago: University of Chicago Press.

Rubin, Lillian B. (1985). *Just friends: The role of friendship in our lives*. New York: Harper & Row.

— (1990). *Erotic wars: What happened to the sexual revolution?* New York: Farrar, Straus & Giroux.

Sanderson, Christiane (1995). *Counselling adult survivors of child sexual abuse*. London: Jessica Kingsley Publishers.

Sapadin, Linda A. (1988). Friendship and gender: Perspectives of professional men and women. *Journal of Social and Personal Relationships*, 5, 387–403.

Sarrel, Philip M., & Masters, William H. (1982). Sexual molestation of men by women. *Archives of Sexual Behavior*, 11, 117–31.

Segal, Lynne (1990). *Slow motion: Changing masculinities, changing men*. London: Virago Press.

— (1994). *Straight sex: Rethinking the politics of pleasure*. Berkeley: University of California Press.

Seidman, Steven (1991). *Romantic longings: Love in America, 1830–1980*. New York: Routledge.

Semonsky, Michael R., & Rosenfeld, Lawrence B. (1994). Perceptions of sexual violations: Denying a kiss, stealing a kiss. *Sex Roles*, 30, 503–20.

Sherwin, Robert, & Corbett, Sherry (1985). Campus sexual norms and dating relationships: A trend analysis. *The Journal of Sex Research*, 21, 258–74.

Shotland, R. Lance, & Goodstein, Lynne (1992). Sexual precedence reduces the perceived legitimacy of sexual refusal: An examination of attributions concerning date rape and consensual sex. *Personality and Social Psychology Bulletin*, 18, 756–64.

Siegel, Judith M.; Golding, Jacqueline M.; Stein, Judith A.; Burnam, M. Audrey; & Sorenson, Susan B. (1990). Reactions to sexual assault: A community study. *Journal of Interpersonal Violence*, 5, 229–46.

Simon, William, & Gagnon, John H. (1987). A sexual scripts approach. In James H. Geer and William T. O'Donohue (eds.), *Theories of human sexuality*. New York: Plenum Press.

Smith, Ronald E.; Pine, Charles J.; & Hawley, Mark E. (1988). Social cognitions about adult male victims of female sexual assault. *The Journal of Sex Research*, 24, 101–12.

Sommers, Christina Hoff (1994). *Who stole feminism? How women have betrayed women*. New York: Simon & Schuster.

Sorenson, Susan B., & White, Jacquelyn W. (1992). Adult sexual assault: Overview of research. *Journal of Social Issues*, 48, 1–8.

Sprecher, S. (1989). Premarital sexual standards for different categories of individuals. *The Journal of Sex Research, 26,* 232–48.

— ; McKinney, K.; Walsh, R.; & Anderson, C. (1988). A revision of the Reiss premarital permissiveness scale. *Journal of Marriage and the Family, 50,* 821, 828.

— ; McKinney, K.; & Orbuch, T.L. (1991). The effect of current sexual behavior on friendship, dating, and marriage desirability. *The Journal of Sex Research, 28,* 387–408.

Steinmetz, Suzanne K., & Lucca, Joseph S. (1988). Husband battering. In Vincent B. Van Hasselt; Randall L. Morrison; Alan S. Bellack; & Michel Hersen (eds.), *Handbook of family violence.* New York: Plenum Press.

Straus, Murray A. (1993). Physical assaults by wives: A major social problem. In Richard J. Gelles & Donileen R. Loseke (eds.), *Current controversies on family violence.* Newbury Park, CA: Sage Publications.

— , & Gelles, Richard J. (eds.) (1990). *Physical violence in American families: Risk factors and adaptations to violence in 8,145 families.* New Brunswick, NJ: Transaction Publishers.

— , & Kantor, Glenda Kaufman (1994). Change in spouse assault rates from 1975 to 1992: A comparison of three national surveys in the United States. Paper presented at the World Congress of Sociology, Bielefeld, Germany, July 19, 1994.

Strossen, Nadine (1995). *Defending pornography: Free speech, sex, and the fight for women's rights.* New York: Scribner.

Struckman-Johnson, Cindy (1988). Forced sex on dates: It happens to men, too. *The Journal of Sex Research, 24,* 234–41.

— , & Struckman-Johnson, David (1994). Men pressured and forced into sexual experience. *Archives of Sexual Behavior, 23,* 93–114.

Suraci, Patrick (1992). *Male sexual armor: Erotic fantasies and sexual realities of the cop on the beat and the man in the street.* New York: Irvington Publishers.

Tannen, Deborah (1990). *You just don't understand: Women and men in conversation.* New York: Ballantine Books.

Tavris, Carol (1992). *The mismeasure of woman.* New York: Touchstone.

— , & Wade, Carole (1984). *The longest war: Sex differences in perspective* (2nd ed.). San Diego: Harcourt Brace Jovanovich.

Thompson, Edward H. (1991). The maleness of violence in dating relationships: An appraisal of stereotypes. *Sex Roles, 24,* 261–78.

Thompson, Sharon (1995). *Going all the way: Teenage girls' tales of sex, romance & pregnancy.* New York: Hill and Wang.

Tiefer, Leonore (1995). *Sex is not a natural act and other essays.* Boulder, Colorado: Westview Press.

Tisdale, Sallie (1994). *Talk dirty to me: An intimate philosophy of sex*. New York: Doubleday.

Tracy, Laura (1991). *The secret between us: Competition among women*. Boston: Little, Brown and Company.

Turk, Cindy L., & Muehlenhard, Charlene L. (1991). Force versus consent in definitions of rape. Paper presented at the Midcontinent Region meeting of the Society for the Scientific Study of Sex, Kansas City, June 1991.

Valverde, Mariana (1985). *Sex, power and pleasure*. Toronto: The Women's Press.

Vance, Carole S. (ed.) (1984). *Pleasure and danger: Exploring female sexuality*. Boston: Routledge and Kegan Paul.

Vines, Gail (1993). *Raging hormones: Do they rule our lives?* London: Virago Press.

Walsh, Anthony (1991). Self-esteem and sexual behavior: Exploring gender differences. *Sex Roles, 25*, 441–50.

Warshaw, Robin (1988). *I never called it rape*. New York: Harper & Row.

Waterman, Caroline K.; Dawson, Lori J.; & Bologna, Michael J. (1989). Sexual coercion in gay male and lesbian relationships: Predictors and implications for support services. *The Journal of Sex Research, 25*, 118–24.

Welldon, Estela V. (1988). *Mother, madonna, whore: The idealization and denigration of motherhood*. London: Free Association Books.

Wheelan, Susan A., & Verdi, Anthony F. (1992). Differences in male and female patterns of communication in groups: A methodological artifact? *Sex Roles, 227*, 1–15.

White, Jacquelyn W., & Kowalski, Robin M. (1994). Deconstructing the myth of the nonaggressive woman. *Psychology of Women Quarterly, 18*, 487–508.

Wood, Julia T. (1993). Engendered relations: Interaction, caring, power and responsibility in intimacy. In Steve Duck (ed.), *Social context and relationships*. Newbury Park, CA: Sage Publications.

— , & Inman, Christopher C. (1993). In a different mode: Recognizing masculine styles of communicating closeness. *Journal of Applied Communications Research, 21*, 279–95.

Zona, Michael A.; Sharma, Kaushal K.; & Lane, John (1993). A comparative study of erotomanic and obsessional subjects in a forensic sample. *Journal of Forensic Sciences, 38*, 894–903.

Acknowledgments

In many respects, books are collaborative ventures, and this one is no exception. *Lip Service* is based on interviews conducted between 1993 and 1995; the names and some identifying details of all interviewees have been changed to protect their privacy. First and foremost, I am indebted to these women and men, who spoke so candidly and eloquently about the most private aspects of their lives. Without their personal and intellectual contributions, this book could not have been written.

I'm grateful to all the researchers and writers whose work has informed my own, particularly those who shared in-press articles: Peter Anderson, E. Sandra Byers, Charlene Muehlenhard, Ronald Ross and Elizabeth Allgeier. Lucia O'Sullivan deserves special mention for her unstinting professional generosity and sound advice.

My agent Sarah Lazin provided expert counsel and wise guidance, and Kenneth Whyte of *Saturday Night* magazine gave me constant encouragement and the opportunity to try out some of these ideas in his pages. Jem Bates, Jill Lambert, Virginia Evans, and the production team at HarperCollins carried me over the finish line with good cheer.

It's a pleasure to thank my friends and family, who provided practical help, impractical amounts of affection, and a modicum of sanity to the proceedings: Helen Fillion, Judy Wade, David Dowden,

Karen Cossar, Janine Burger, Isabel Vincent, Ruth Martin, Irene Tuazon, Carolyn Livingston and Caspar Sinnige, and Rudy Falk and Lana Bryant. For advice, constructive criticism, and generally making themselves invaluable, heartfelt thanks go to Serena French, Jennifer Hollyer, Catherine Keri, Gillian Kerr, Ellen Ladowsky, Marie-Susanne Langille, and Michael Totzke. I am especially grateful to Paul Elie for his sharp suggestions, sharp editorial pencil, and careful readings of the manuscript in various stages of disarray.

I was very fortunate to work with two endlessly patient and gifted editors. Iris Tupholme got the ball rolling and paid numerous house calls to retrieve it, keeping me on track with common sense, tough questions, and, on one unforgettable occasion, white wine. Peternelle van Arsdale sustained me with unflagging enthusiasm, dry wit, perceptive insights, and meticulous editing.

Finally, I have an incalculable debt to those I rely on most. Patricia Pearson is my sounding board on all manner of things, and many of the ideas in this book were refined through conversations with her. Fiona Hart was there at every turn with comic relief, support, and excellent suggestions. Sarah Kramer, truly the best of friends, urged me on and picked me up every time I stumbled. Will Falk advised, dissented, inspired, and endured, all the while working a second shift at home and providing daily reminders that intimacy expertise does not depend on gender. Elinor Fillion played many roles: loving mother, long-suffering researcher, first reader, and staunch ally. Above all, she gave me the courage of my convictions, and this book is dedicated to her with profound gratitude.